THE COMPLETE WORKS OF
ALEXANDER PUSHKIN

VOLUME TWELVE

LETTERS: 1833 – 1837

TRANSLATED BY J. THOMAS SHAW

MILNER AND COMPANY LIMITED
2003

Milner and Company Limited
P.O. Box 18, Downham Market,
Norfolk PE38 0LT

First published by Milner and Company Limited 2001
Second reprinting 2003

©Milner and Company Limited.

All rights reserved. No part of this publication
may be reproduced, stored in a retrieval system, or
transmitted, in any form or by any means
without the prior permission in writing of
Milner and Company Limited.
Within the U.K., exceptions are allowed in
respect of any fair dealing for the purpose of
research or private study, or criticism or review,
as permitted under the Copyright, Designs and
Patents Act, 1988, or in the case of
reprographic reproduction in accordance with
the terms of the licences issued by the
Copyright Licensing Agency. Enquiries
concerning reproduction outside these terms
and in other countries should be sent to
Milner and Company Limited
at the address above.

British Library Cataloguing in Publication Data
Data available

Distributed outside the United Kingdom
and the Republic of Ireland by
Charles Schlacks, Jr., Publisher
P.O. Box 1256, Idyllwild, California 92549-1256, U.S.A.

ISBN Complete Works: 0 907681 06 9
ISBN Letters: 1833-1837: 0 907681 16 6

Typeset by Silverdart Ltd, Unit 211, Linton House, 164-180 Union Street,
London SE1 0LH

Printed in Great Britain by Antony Rowe Ltd.,
Chippenham, Wiltshire.

130 reprint

68604

THE COMPLETE WORKS OF
ALEXANDER PUSHKIN

LETTERS: 1833 – 1837

THE COMPLETE WORKS OF ALEXANDER PUSHKIN IN ENGLISH

1. Lyric Poems: 1813 – 1820
2. Lyric Poems: 1820 – 1826
3. Lyric Poems: 1826 – 1836
4. Eugene Onegin
5. The Bronze Horseman, and Other Narrative Verse
6. Boris Godunov, and Other Dramatic Works
7. The Captain's Daughter
8. The Tales of Belkin
9. The Queen of Spades, and Other Prose Fiction
10. Letters: 1815 – 1826
11. Letters: 1826 – 1833
12. Letters: 1833 – 1837
13. Critical and Autobiographical Prose
14. History of the Pugachev Rebellion
15. History of Peter the Great, and Other Historical Prose

THE EDITORIAL BOARD
OF THE COMPLETE WORKS OF
ALEXANDER PUSHKIN

Iain Sproat (U.K.), Chairman
Professor Leonid Arinshtein (Russia)
Professor John Bayley (U.K.)
Professor A.D.P. Briggs (U.K.)
Professor Anthony Cross (U.K.)
Professor Paul Debreczeny (U.S.A.)
Professor S.A. Fomichev (Russia)
Academician Dmitri Likhachev (Russia)
Professor J. Thomas Shaw (U.S.A.)
Professor Nikolai Skatov (Russia)
Professor William B. Todd (U.S.A.)
Professor Vadim Vatsuro (Russia)
Tatiana Wolff (U.K.)

GENERAL PREFACE

To Russians, Alexander Pushkin is the greatest of all Russian writers. In the English-speaking world, however, his genius has been too little recognised. Part of the reason for this lack of recognition is that much of what has been published of Pushkin's writing in English – and much of it, including some of his most important work, has never been published at all – has appeared in a haphazard way, with a "Selection" here, and a few translated poems in a general anthology there, all brought out under different imprints, over many years. Certainly, the complete works of Pushkin have never before been published in English. This edition, published on the 200th anniversary of his birth, remedies that long omission.

It is the main and fervent hope of the Editorial Board that the publishing of *The Complete Works of Alexander Pushkin* in English for the first time, will help to lead many new English-speaking, but non-Russian-speaking, intelligent, general readers to a knowledge and a love of Pushkin's writing; and to an understanding of why, in Russia itself, Pushkin is held as being so far above other great Russian writers, like Tolstoy, Dostoevsky, and Chekhov, who have traditionally been more highly regarded in the English-speaking world.

Thus, in undertaking this work, the Board has sought to give practical effect to Pushkin's own words that "translators are the post-horses of civilization."

As regards how the Editorial Board has gone about the work of fulfilling what might be called the missionary purpose of this edition – namely, to help bring a greater understanding of Pushkin to English-speaking readers – two separate but linked elements should be mentioned. First, that, too often in the past, the prose fiction of Pushkin has been undervalued. Second, that to most non-Russian-speaking readers, the genius of Pushkin in translation will be most readily and vividly evident through his prose, poetry notoriously losing more in translation than prose.

Notwithstanding the many qualifications and elaborations of those two statements that could, and, in other contexts, should be made, it is sufficient to say here that, in this edition, both matters have been served in a new way. On other publishing occasions, Pushkin's prose fiction – his one completed novel, a handful of uncompleted novels of greatly differing lengths, short stories, tales and fragments – has all been lumped together in one volume; or else a selection has been made. Of course, it is easy to understand, and indeed to sympathise with, and even, on balance, to approve the publishing circumstances which dictate such formats. Nonetheless, such formats can diminish, in some degree, the individual stature of each work. In this edition, therefore, *The Captain's Daughter* is published alone in one volume, this solitary setting helping to give appropriate prominence to the brilliance and importance of the work; *The Tales of Belkin*, and the associated work, *The History of the Village of Goryukhino*, are also published, for similar reasons, in a single volume; and likewise *The Queen of Spades, and Other Prose Fiction*.

The composition of this latter volume is, of course, not wholly satisfactory, in that it combines such disparate prose works as the masterpiece, *The Queen of Spades*, and another finished tale, *Kirdzhali*, together with the unfinished novels, *Dubrovsky*, and *The Moor of Peter the Great*, and other shorter, unfinished works. Nonetheless, publishing three separate volumes of prose fiction, as described above, seemed, on balance, the best format for presenting this work to English-speaking readers.

Another innovation of *The Complete Works of Alexander Pushkin in English*, the publishing of a prose translation of *Eugene Onegin* alongside a verse translation, owes its existence to a similar judgment about the importance of prose to English-speaking but non-Russian-speaking readers, in any attempt to understand, however partially, the genius of Pushkin. *Onegin* was, after all, called "A Novel in Verse" by Pushkin himself, so that a translation into prose, the usual form of novels, alongside one in verse, seemed to the Board, justified. For similar reasons, Turgenev, in an attempt to convey something of the greatness of *Onegin* to French readers, published his own translation of *Onegin* in French prose. More detailed arguments about translating *Onegin* into prose will be found in Professor John Bayley's introduction to that volume, and in the Note by the translator, Roger Clarke.

On the question of which translations to use throughout the Complete Works, the Editorial Board made their selection on the principle of which translations were, in the Board's balanced judgment, the best, regardless of when those translations were made, or whether they had been published previously or not. Thus, for example, in the case of Pushkin's lyrics, although the great majority of those published in this edition were specially commissioned by the Board – at one moment there were about a hundred translators around the world, working on new versions of the lyrics – other translations will be found in these pages which derive from earlier generations.

Of course, the principle of choosing "the best" translation, is one simpler to enunciate than to fulfil. In practice, this principle meant – to take again the example of the lyrics – choosing the translation which stuck both most closely and pleasingly to the spirit of Pushkin, and to his metre and rhyme scheme. Verses however fine, which, purporting to be translations of Pushkin, could be more accurately described as "verses based on an idea of A.S. Pushkin", were rejected.

In matters of translation, the Editorial Board was of the same mind as Andrew Marvell in his poem, written in 1651, *To His Worthy Friend, Dr. Witty*:

> "...So of Translators they are authors grown,
> For ill translators make the book their own.
> Others do strive with words and forced phrase
> To add such lustre, and so many rayes
> That but to make the vessel shining, they
> Much of the precious metal rub away.
> He is translation's thief that addeth more,
> As much as he that taketh from the store
> Of the first author. Here he maketh blots

That mends; and added beauties are but spots...
You have translation's statutes best fulfil'd
That handling neither sully nor would gild."

The Editorial Board acknowledges with gratitude the help and advice which it has received from many people and institutions. In particular, the Board gives thanks to the President of the Russian Cultural Foundation in Moscow, Mr. Nikita Mikhalkov, for his generosity in allowing the scholarly resources of the Foundation to be put so extensively, and over so long a period, at the disposal of the Board. One member of the Editorial Board, Professor Leonid Arinshtein, deserves special mention, praise and gratitude for all his great work, during ten years, in overseeing the research and scholarship of this edition of The Complete Works of Pushkin: it has been a unique and essential contribution, and one far beyond the call of duty. The Board wishes also to thank Mr. Paul Wolstencroft, and his colleagues, of the Barfield Group; Mr. Georgy Priakhin, General Director of Voskresenie Publishers in Moscow; successive members of the British Embassy in Moscow, and of the former Soviet Embassy, and subsequently the Russian Embassy, in London; Oxford University Press, Everyman's Library, and Stanford University Press, for their generosity in copyright matters; Dr. David Budgen for his valuable work in helping to get the translations under way; Mr. James Vyvyan; Mr. Ignat Avsey; Miss. Olga Ponomareva; and Mrs. Vera Arinshtein. The Board wishes particularly to acknowledge with gratitude the immense amount of work devoted to the Russian texts by Dr. Irina Yurieva. The Board is also extremely grateful for the valuable work on the collating of Pushkin translations, of Mrs. Dina Newman, Mrs. Chloe Belskaia, Miss Vladilena Koroleva, and Miss Arabella Saker. In the early years of the project, the Board was greatly encouraged by the enthusiastic support of Count Nicolas Sollohub, and Sir Isaiah Berlin. The Board also wishes to acknowledge with gratitude the encouragement of the two patrons, His Royal Highness Prince Michael of Kent, and Mrs. Raisa Gorbachev.

Sadly between the publication of the first five volumes of The Complete Works of Alexander Pushkin in English, and that of the second five, three persons who, from the early days, had been closely involved with the project, died: Mrs Gorbachev, Academician Likachev and Professor Vatsuro. Each of them, in their individual ways, had contributed importantly. The Editorial Board pays deep tribute to them. In recognition of their contributions, their names will continue to appear in each volume of The Complete Works.

Professor Nikolai Skatov, head of the Institute of Russian Literature of the Russian Academy of Sciences, joined the Editorial Board following the publication of the first five volumes.

IAIN SPROAT
Chairman of the Editorial Board

CHRONOLOGY OF PUSHKIN'S LIFE

1799: Alexander Sergeyevich Pushkin born in Moscow.

1801: Earthquake in Moscow: Pushkin's earliest memory.

1807: Wrote his first verses – in French.

1811: Enters the new lycée at Tsarskoye Selo, near St. Petersburg, a school founded by the Tsar to prepare the sons of noblemen for a career as Government ministers, or as diplomats.

1814: First publication, anonymously, of Pushkin's verses, in the St. Petersburg Magazine.

1815: Public success of his poem, *Reminiscences of Tsarskoye Selo*. The leading Russian poet of the day, Derzhavin, names Pushkin as his successor.

1817: Leaves the lycée. Takes up a post in the Ministry of Foreign Affairs. Begins work on his first narrative poem, *Ruslan and Ludmila*. Also writes ode, *Liberty*.

1818-19: Pushkin suffers three serious illnesses, brought about by his dissipated life-style. Frequents radical political circles. Liberal poems by Pushkin circulated in manuscript.

1820: Publishes *Ruslan and Ludmila*. Pushkin is exiled by the Tsar to south of Russia. Travels in Caucasus and Crimea. Studies English to read the poems of Byron in the original. Begins first "Byronic" poem, *The Captive of the Caucasus*.

1821: In exile in Kishinev, writes *The Robber Brothers*, and *The Gabrieliad*.

1822: Writes *The Fountain of Bakhchisaray*. Pushkin is acclaimed as "the Russian Byron". Tsar Alexander I is so moved by *The Captive of the Caucasus* that he contemplates a reconciliation with Pushkin.

1823: Pushkin's exile is transferred to Odessa. Under the influence of Byron's *Don Juan*, Pushkin begins writing *Eugene Onegin,* which he is to continue writing for the next eight years.

1824: *The Fountain of Bakhchisaray* is a great literary and financial success. Writes *The Gypsies*. Sentenced to exile in Mikhailovskoye, in the north of Russia, for the promotion of atheism. Writes *Memoirs*, which are later burned.

1825: Publication of the first chapter of *Eugene Onegin*. Writes *Boris Godunov*.

1826: The first collection of Pushkin's lyrics is published, and sold out in two months. The new Tsar, Nicholas I, frees Pushkin from exile. Writes *The Prophet*.

1827: First visit to St. Petersburg after six years of exile. Writes *The Moor of Peter the Great*, based upon his great-grandfather, Hannibal.

1828: The Church proceeds against Pushkin for his blasphemous poem *The Gabrieliad*. Tsar Nicholas I protects Pushkin. Writes *Poltava*.

1829: Travels through the Caucasus to Arzerum. Sees action in battle with the Russian Army, against the Turks.

1830: Becomes engaged to Natalya Goncharova. Stranded at Boldino by a cholera outbreak, Pushkin writes about 30 lyric poems, the *Little Tragedies*, *Tales of Belkin, The History of Goryukhino, The Little House in Kolomna,* and the last chapters of *Eugene Onegin*.

1831: Marries Natalya Goncharova. Writes the *Fairy Tales*. Tsar Nicholas I appoints him as historian of Peter the Great.

1832: Birth of his first child, Mary. Writes *Dubrovsky* and *Rusalka*.

1833: The first complete edition of *Eugene Onegin* is published. Birth of his eldest son, Alexander. Travels to Urals. Writes *History of Pugachev Rebellion, The Queen of Spades, The Bronze Horseman,* and *Andzhelo*.

1834: Pushkin leads an unhappy life in court circles at St. Petersburg, with mounting debts, and jealousy of his wife's admirers.

1835: Birth of his younger son, Gregory. Publication of selected works: narrative verse, and prose, in two volumes, and lyric poems in four volumes.

1836: Becomes editor of *Sovremennik* magazine. Death of his mother. Writes religious poems, and *The Captain's Daughter*. Birth of his last child, Natalya.

1837: Continues work on *The History of Peter the Great*. Shot in a duel, over insults to his wife's reputation, and dies two days later.

CONTENTS

THIRD VOLUME – LETTERS: 1833 – 1837 *(Vol. 12)*

General Preface to *The Complete Works*	vii
Chronology of Pushkin's Life	xii

*For the prefaces by J. Thomas Shaw to the Letters,
see Letters: 1815 – 1826 (Vol. 10)*

Part X.	Inspector General in the Pugachev Country July, 1833 – December, 1833	
	Letters 452-475	599
	Notes	623
Part XI.	Gray-Haired Kammerjunker – Petersburg December, 1833 – August, 1834	
	Letters 476-527	633
	Notes	678
Part XII.	Cares and Woes – Petersburg August, 1834 – December, 1835	
	Letters 528-587	693
	Notes	733
Part XIII.	*Contemporary* Journalist – Petersburg December, 1835 – October, 1836	
	Letters 588-646	747
	Notes	785
Part XIV.	Sole Defender of Honor – St Petersburg November, 1836 – January, 1837	
	Letters 647-674	803
	Notes	821
INDEX		831

All Notes are by J. Thomas Shaw

[452]
> To ALEXANDER KHRISTOFOROVICH BENKENDORF
> July 22, 1833. In Petersburg.
> (Rough draft; in French)

My General,

Circumstances oblige me to go and spend two or three months in the near future on my lands in Nizhny Novgorod—I should like to take advantage of this opportunity, and make a trip to Orenburg and Kazan,[1] which I am not yet familiar with. I beseech His Majesty to permit me to see the archives of these two provinces.

[453]
> To ALEXANDER NIKOLAEVICH MORDVINOV
> July 30, 1833. In Petersburg.
> (Second rough draft)

Dear Sir, Alexander Nikolaevich,

I hasten to respond with all sincerity to Your Excellency's questions.[1]

In the course of the past two years I have occupied myself with historical researches alone, and I have not written a single line that is purely literary.[2] I need to spend some two months in complete solitude, so as to rest from these most important labors and to finish a book[3] which I began long ago and which will provide me with money, which I am in need of. I myself am ashamed to spend time on vain occupations, but what is to be done? It is they alone that provide me with independence and with the means to live with my family in Petersburg, where my labors, thanks to the Sovereign, have a more important and useful purpose.

Except for my salary, which has been appointed for me by the generosity of His Majesty, I have no fixed income; whereas, life in the capital is expensive, and with the increase in my family, expenses increase, too.

Perhaps the Sovereign will wish to know precisely what kind of book I want to finish writing in the village; it is a novel, the greater part of the action of which takes place in Orenburg and Kazan, and that is why I should like to visit both these provinces.

With the most profound respect and complete devotion, I have the honor to be, Dear Sir,

Your Excellency's
Most humble servant,
Alexander Pushkin.

July 30.
Chernaya Rechka.

[454]

To Pavel Voinovich Nashchokin (?)
July, 1833(?). Petersburg.

I am sending you my ugly phiz.[1] Say, how much do you want for your carriage? There are buyers.

A.P.

[455]

To Natalia Nikolaevna Pushkina
August 20, 1833. From Torzhok to Petersburg.
Torzhok. Sunday.

Dear little wife, here is my detailed Odyssey for you. You remember that when I left you I set off into the very storm. My adventures began at the Troitsky Bridge. The Neva was so high that the bridge was reared up. A rope was stretched across, and the police were not letting carriages through. I very nearly turned back to Chernaya Rechka.[1] However, I crossed the Neva higher up, and I left Petersburg. The weather was terrible. The trees along the Tsarskoselsky Prospekt were just strewn all around; I counted some fifty of them. The wind was blowing the puddles violently. The swamps were stirred up into whitecaps. Fortunately the wind and the rain were beating at my back, and I most calmly kept my seat all this time. Did anything bad happen to you Petersburg inhabitants? You didn't have a new inundation,[2] did you? What if, in riding about, I missed this one, too? That would be vexing. The next day the weather cleared up. Sobolevsky and I went ten miles on foot, killing, along the roadside, snakes which had foolishly surrendered to rejoicing at the sunshine and had crawled out onto the sand. Yesterday we arrived safely at Torzhok, where Sobolevsky raged because the linen was dirty. Today we woke up at 8 o'clock, breakfasted well, and now I'm turning off to Yaropolets,³ and I'm leaving Sobolevsky alone with the Swiss cheese. There, my angel, is a detailed account of my journey. The coachmen are harnessing up six horses to the carriage, frightening me with the muddy side roads. If I don't drown in a puddle, like Anrep,⁴ I'll write you from Yaropolets. I shall hope for letters from you in Simbirsk. Write me about your mastitis and the rest. Don't spoil Masha, and take care of your own health; don't coquet on the 26th.⁵ But you'll say, there's nobody to do it with!⁶ But just the same, don't coquet. I greet Katerina Ivanovna [Zagryazhskaya] and kiss her hand with the tenderness of Ermolov. I give all of you a big kiss, and I bless you, Mashka, and Sashka.⁷

Greet Vyazemsky when you see him. Tell him that the storm prevented me from saying good-by to him and having a chat about the almanac.⁸ I'll see what I can get done about it on the road.

[456]
To Natalia Nikolaevna Pushkina
August 21, 1833. From Pavlovskoe to Petersburg.

You couldn't guess, my angel, where I'm writing you from: from Pavlovskoe, between Bernovo and Malinniki,¹ about the last of which I have probably told you a lot. Yesterday when I turned off onto the country road to Yaropolets, I discovered with pleasure that I would go past the estates of the Vulfs, and I decided to visit them. At 8 o'clock last evening I arrived at my good Pavel Ivanovich's, who was as glad to see me as if I were a member of the family. Here I found a great change. Five years ago Pavlovskoe, Malinniki, and Bernovo were full of uhlans and young ladies, but the uhlans have been transferred and the young ladies have become dispersed. Of my old girl friends I found only the white mare, on which I made a trip to Malinniki. But she no longer prances under me, no longer is spirited, either. And in Malinniki, instead of all the Annettes, Evpraxias, Sashas, Mashas, etc.,² there lives only Praskovia Alexandrovna's manager Reichman,³ who treated me to some schnapps. Veliasheva, whom I once lauded in verse, lives here in the neighborhood. But I'll not go to see her, for I know you wouldn't want me to. Here I am stuffing myself on jam, and I have lost three rubles in twenty-four rubbers of whist. You see that in all respects I am innocuous here. I am being asked about you a lot: whether you are just as pretty as they say and whether you are a *brunette* or a *blonde*, a *slender* or *plump* little thing. Tomorrow before dawn I'm setting off for Yaropolets, where I shall spend several hours and then set off for Moscow, where I suspect I shall have to stay three days or so. I forgot to tell you that in Yaropolets (my mistake, in Torzhok), the fat Mlle. Pozharskaya[4]—the same one who brews excellent kvas and fries excellent cutlets—as she was accompanying me to the doors of her inn, answered me in response to my compliments, "You ought to be ashamed to notice the beauties of others when you yourself have such a beauty that I, when I met her (?), gasped." And you should know that Mlle. Pozharskaya is the spit and image of Mme. George,[5] only a little older. You see, my little wife, that your fame has spread over all the provinces. Are you satisfied? Be healthy, all of you. Does Masha remember me? And she hasn't pulled some new pranks, has she?[6] Farewell, my plump little brunette (is that right?). I am behaving well, and there's nothing for you to pout at me about. This letter will reach you after your name day.[7] Have you looked in your mirror and assured yourself that nothing in the world can be compared with your face?[8] But I love your soul even more than your face. Farewell, my angel. I send you a big kiss.

[457]
To Natalia Nikolaevna Pushkina
August 26, 1833. From Moscow to Petersburg.
August 26. Moscow.

I wish you happiness on your angel's day,[1] my angel: I kiss you in the eyes, sight unseen. And I'm writing you the continuation of my adventures—from the attic of your Nikitskaya home,[2] where I arrived safely yesterday from Yaropolets. I arrived in Yaropolets late Wednesday. Natalia Ivanovna [Goncharova] couldn't have received me better. I found her well, though beside her was lying her walking cane, without which she can't get far. I spent Thursday at her house. We talked a lot about you, about Mashka, and about Katerina Ivanovna [Zagryazhskaya]. Your mother seems to be a little jealous of her on your account. However, although she complained about the past as usual, it was nevertheless with less bitterness. She very much wants you to spend next summer with her.³ She lives very isolated and quiet in her ruined palace and is cultivating vegetable gardens over your great-grandfather Doroshenko's⁴ ashes, to which I went to pay my respects. Semen Fedorovich,⁵ a great friend of mine, took me to the tomb and showed me the other sights of Yaropolets. I found an old library in the house, and Natalia Ivanovna permitted me to take out some books I need. I picked out a score and a half or so of them, and they will arrive together with jam and liqueurs. Thus my foray on Yaropolets has been by no means fruitless.

Now, little wife, listen to what's happening to Dmitry Nikolaevich [Goncharov]. Like a reigning prince, he fell in love with Countess Nadezhda Chernysheva⁶ *from her portrait*, after hearing that she is a plump, black-browed, and rosy-cheeked wench. Twice he made trips to Yaropolets in the hope of catching sight of her, and he actually did succeed in finding her in church. Then he up and went into a frenzy. He writes from the Zavod that he is head over heels in love with *la charmante et divine comtesse*, that he can't sleep at night, and that *son charmant image*, etc., and he asks that Natalia Ivanovna [Goncharova] without fail arrange a match for him with *la charmante et divine comtesse*; Natalia Ivanovna went to Kruglikova's⁷ and carried out the commission. They invited *la divine et charmante*, who flatly refused. Natalia Ivanovna is worried about what effect this news will produce. I'll bet he won't shoot himself. What do you think? And you should know that he started up this affair away back last winter and very much suspected *la divine et charmante comtesse* of a propensity for Muraviev (the saintly).⁸ For this reason he went once to ask him with all possible diplomatic subtlety, like Skotinin of his nephew: "Mitrofan, do you want to get married?"⁹ You see what a rogue he is! And he didn't tell us a thing. Muraviev answered him that he is more likely to become a monk, and your brother rejoiced and went and asked of the countess *son coeur et sa main*, assuring her by letter *qu'il n'est plus dans son assiette ordinaire*.¹⁰ I almost died laughing as I read his letter, and I regret that I didn't persuade him to let me have it for you.

I left Yaropolets at night and arrived in Moscow yesterday at noon. Your father¹¹ did not receive me. They say that he's quiet enough. Nashchokin told me that Yuriev's¹² money has been sent to you. Now I feel relieved. Sobolevsky is here *incognito* hiding from the moneylenders, like a real English *gentlemen* [sic],[13] and he is redeeming his promissory notes. On the road he behaved decently and fulfilled faithfully the conditions which I proposed, to wit: (1) to go halves in paying for the post horses, and not to shortchange his comrade. (2) Not to f——t, either openly or furtively, unless in sleep and at night, at that, and not after dinner. I shall stay in Moscow for some time; that is, two or three days. The calash needs some repairs. The country roads were nasty: six horses had difficulty in dragging me along. I shall be in Kazan about the third. From there I'm going to Simbirsk. Farewell; take care of yourself. I kiss all of you. Greet Katerina Ivanovna [Zagryazhskaya].

[458]
To Natalia Nikolaevna Pushkina
August 27, 1833. From Moscow to Petersburg.

Yesterday was your name day; today is your birthday. Many happy returns for you and for me, my angel. Yesterday I drank your health at [I. V.] Kireevsky's, together with Shevyrev and Sobolevsky; today I'll drink it at Sudienko's. I'm leaving day after tomorrow —my calash will not be ready before that. Yesterday when I arrived at home late I found on my table the calling card of Bulgakov,[1] the father of the beauties, and an invitation for an evening. It was his wife's name day, too. I didn't go, because I don't have ball dress, and so as not to have to shave off my mustache, which I'm letting grow out for the road. You see that it's hard to get to Moscow and not do a little dancing. However, Moscow is boring; Moscow is empty; Moscow is poor. There are even few cabs on its boring streets. On the Tverskoy Boulevard one comes across two or three beggar women in tatters, and some student in spectacles and a uniform cap, and Prince Shalikov. I was at Pogodin's, who they say is married to a beauty.[2] I didn't see her, and I cannot most humbly report to you with regard to her. I haven't seen Nashchokin the whole day. Chaadaev has become fleshier, handsomer, and healthier. Nikolay [N.] Raevsky is here. Neither he nor his brother[3] died—it was some Brigadier Raevsky[4] who died. Tell Vyazemsky that his namesake, Prince Peter Dolgorukov,[5] has died—after receiving a certain inheritance and not having time to squander it in the English Club, which local society laments. I haven't been in the club—very likely I have been expelled, for I have forgotten to renew my membership. I would have to pay a fine of three hundred rubles, and I'd be willing to sell the whole English Club for two hundred. [M. F.] Orlov, Bobrinsky,[6] and others of my old acquaintances are here. But I'm fed up with my old acquaintances—I'll not see anybody. An important piece of news: signs in French, which were destroyed by Rostopchin in the year you were born, have appeared again on the Kuznetsky Most.[7] I wandered along the bookshops as I usually do, but I found nothing worthwhile. The books which I took for the road have gotten beaten and rubbed to pieces in my trunk. I'm so angry today because of this that I wouldn't advise Mashka to get capricious or war with her nursemaid; I'd give her a thrashing. I kiss you. I greet Aunty.[8] I bless Mashka and Sashka.

[459]
To Natalia Nikolaevna Pushkina
September 2, 1833. From Nizhny Novgorod to Petersburg.
September 2. Nizhny Novgorod.

I didn't have time to write you before my departure from Moscow. Nashchokin saw me off with champagne, hot punch, and prayers. I had difficulty in getting the coachmaker to give me my carriage; I don't have much luck with coachmakers. The road is in good shape. But in the environs of Moscow no horses are to be had. Everywhere I had to wait several hours, and with difficulty I managed to drag to Nizhny today—that is, after five days and nights. I've had time only to go to the baths, and of the city I shall say only that *les rues sont larges et bien pavées, les maisons sont bien baties*.[1] I'm going to the Fair[2] which is displaying its last things, and tomorrow I'm setting out for Kazan.

My angel, I feel I have acted stupidly, in leaving you and beginning a nomadic life again. I can vividly imagine the 1st: Parasha, the cook, the cabby, the druggist, Mme. Sichler, etc., pester you for what is owed them. You don't have enough money. Smirdin makes excuses to you. You're worried, you're angry with me—and it serves me right. And this is still the good side of the picture—what if you have abscesses again, what if Mashka is sick? And other, unforeseen things that could happen ... Pugachev isn't worth it. The first thing you know I'll spit on him—and come to you. However, I shall go on to Simbirsk, and there I expect to find some letters from you. My angel, if you will be sensible—that is, well and calm—I'll bring you from the village some goods worth a hundred rubles, as the expression goes.³ What weather we are having! Hot days, light frosts in the morning—luxury! Is this the way it is where you are? Are you taking walks along Chernaya Rechka, or are you still shut in?⁴ In any case, take care of yourself. Tell Aunty that though I'm jealous of her over you, I ask in the name of Christ and God that she not abandon you and that she look after you. Farewell, children, until Kazan. I give all three of you an equally big kiss—you especially.

[460]
To Natalia Nikolaevna Pushkina
September 2, 1833. From Nizhny Novgorod to Petersburg.

September 2.

My angel, I wrote you today upon jumping out of the calash, and still stupid from the road. I didn't tell you anything, and I didn't report most humbly to you with regard to anything. Here's an accounting for you from Saint Natalia's day¹ itself. In the morning I went to [A. Y.] Bulgakov's to make my excuses and to thank him, and while doing that to persuade him to give me a certificate² for the station masters, who have very little esteem for me, notwithstanding that I write excellent rhymes. At his house I found his daughters and [N. V.] Vsevolozhsky *le cocu*,³ who is galloping from Kazan to all you people in Petersburg. They invited me to an evening at the Pashkovs'⁴ summer house; I didn't go, thus sparing my mustaches, which have only scarcely bristled out. I dined at the home of Sudienko, my friend, the comrade of my bachelor life. Now he's married, too, and he has two youngsters,⁵ and he has stopped playing cards. But he has an income of 125,000, and with us, my angel, that's yet to come. His wife is a quiet, shy un-beauty. We dined as a threesome, and without standing on ceremony I proposed the health of my name-day celebrator,⁶ and we all downed, without making a face, a goblet of champagne apiece. The evening, at Nashchokin's—and what an evening! Champagne, Lafite, hot pineapple punch—and all to your health, my beauty. The next day I ran across Nikolay [N.] Raevsky in a bookshop. *Sacré chien*, he said to me with tenderness, *pourquoi n'êtes-vous pas venu me voir?*—*Animal,* I answered him with feeling, *qu'avez-vous fait de mon manuscrit petit-Russien?*[7] After this we set off together as though nothing had happened, with him holding me by the collar in plain sight of everybody, to keep me from jumping out of the calash. We dined together, the two of us (my error: in a threesome with a bottle of Madeira). Then to vary my life, I spent another evening at Nashchokin's. The next day he gave me a farewell dinner with sterlets and hot punch, they put me in my calash, and I went forth onto the highway.

Oh, little wife, I'm afraid! Now I must make an important confession. Shall I say the little word to you? Will your little heart survive it? I have purposely stretched out my letter with telling about my Moscow dinners, so as to reach this fateful spot as late as possible. Well, so be it. Be informed that at the second station, where they wouldn't give me horses, I ran across a certain town governor's wife who was going with her aunt from Moscow to her husband and was being slighted at all the stations. She received me quite badly and, in a drawling sing-song, began to try to shame and persuade me: "Aren't you ashamed? Who ever heard of such a thing? Two teams of three horses have been standing in the stable since yesterday, and you won't give me either one of them." "Really?" I said, and went to take these teams for myself. The town governor's wife, seeing that I am not the station master, became very much embarrassed, began to beg my pardon, and she so touched me that I yielded to her one team, to which she had every right, and hired myself another—i.e., a third, and left. You will think that there's no harm done yet. Wait, little wife. That's not all yet. The town governor's wife and her aunt were so enraptured by my knightly deed that they decided not to leave me, but to travel under my protection, to which I magnanimously consented. In this way we almost reached Nizhny itself—they have lagged three or four stations behind—and now I'm free and alone. You will ask whether the governor's wife is pretty. That's the trouble, she was not pretty, my angel Tasha. That's just what I'm grieving about. Ugh! I'm through. Let me go, and have mercy on me.

Today I was at the governor's, General Buturlin's.[8] He and his wife received me very kindly and affably; he persuaded me to dine with him tomorrow. The Fair has closed down—I walked about the emptied shops. They made the impression on me of the departure after a ball, when the Goncharovs' carriage has already left.⁹ You see that notwithstanding the city governor's wife and her aunt I still love Natasha Goncharova, whom, sight unseen, I kiss just anywhere. *Addio mia bella, idol mio, mio bel tesoro, quando mai ti rivedro?* . . .¹⁰

[461]
To NATALIA NIKOLAEVNA PUSHKINA
September 8, 1833. From Kazan to Petersburg.

September 8. Kazan.

Hello, my angel. I've been in Kazan since the fifth, but till now I have not had the time to write you a word. Now I'm on the way to Simbirsk, where I hope to find a letter from you. Here I've been spending my time with old men, contemporaries of my hero;¹ I've gone all over the environs of the city, I've looked over the sites of the battles, I've been making inquiries, I have noted things down, and I'm very content that I have not visited this locale in vain. The weather is fine—but keep your fingers crossed. Before the rains, I hope to have toured every place I proposed to see and to be in the village² at the end of September. Are you well? Are all of you well? On the road I saw a little one-year-old girl who runs about on all fours like a kitten and already has two little teeth. Tell this to Mashka. Baratynsky is here. He's coming in to see me right now. Until Simbirsk. I'll tell you about Kazan in detail—now there's no time. I kiss you.

[462]
To ALEXANDRA ANDREEVNA FUCHS
September 8, 1833. In Kazan.

September 8, 1833.

Dear Madame, Alexandra Andreevna!¹ I am sending you my address, together with my cordial thanks, and I hope that your promise to come to Petersburg is not merely a civility. Receive, dear Madame, the expression of my deep gratitude for your affably receiving a traveler to whom his momentary stay in Kazan will long be memorable. With the most profound respect, I have the honor to be [. . . .]²

[463]
To Natalia Nikolaevna Pushkina
September 12, 1833. From Yazykovo to Petersburg.

> The Village Yazykovo, forty miles from
> Simbirsk. September 12.

I'm writing you from the village of the poet Yazykov, whom I've dropped in on, but have not found at home. Day before yesterday I arrived in Simbirsk, and from Zagryazhsky[1] I received the letter from you. It delighted me, my angel, but all the same I shall scold you a little. You have abscesses,[2] but you write me four whole pages. Aren't you ashamed of yourself! Why couldn't you have told me about yourself and the children in four lines? Well, so be it. God grant that you are well now. I'm glad that Sergey Nikolaevich [Goncharov] will be with you; he's very nice and won't bore you. There's nothing to tell you about Ivan Nikolaevich [Goncharov]. I hope that his wedding will be broken off. From everything it appears that all the family has taken advantage of his upset condition, in order to lure him into their toils. The authorities, if the matter ever gets to the authorities, will probable take this into consideration, too. It will be necessary to settle the business with money. If the girl is not with child, then there's no great harm done. I should think that there'll be no duel with the father or with the cobbler-uncle. If the house is suitable,[3] then there's nothing to do but take it —but stay there a while, at least. Your finances are worrying me a great deal; you have too little money. The first thing you know, you'll be making new debts without paying off the old. I'm traveling— with profit I think. But I'm not yet at my destination, and I haven't got anything written. I go to sleep and dream of arriving in Boldino and locking myself in there.

From Kazan I wrote you several lines[4]—I had no time. I was being dragged around the environs, the fields, the taverns, and I landed at an evening at the home of a *blue stockings*,[5] a forty-year-old, unendurable woman, with waxed teeth and dirty nails. She opened up her notebook and read me some two hundred verses,[6] as if there were nothing unusual in that. Baratynsky has written verses to her, and with astonishing shamelessness he praised her beauty and genius to the skies. I just expected that I would be compelled to write in her album—but God was merciful. However, she took my address and is threatening me with a correspondence and with coming to Petersburg, upon which I congratulate you. Her husband[7] is an intelligent and learned German, in love with her, and in amazement at her genius. However, he was very obliging to me, and I am glad that I made his acquaintance. Today I'm going to Simbirsk. I shall dine at the governor's, and by evening I'll set out for Orenburg, the final goal of my journey.

I found here Yazykov's older brother,[8] an exceptionally noteworthy person, and whom I'm ready to love as I love Pletnev or Nashchokin. I spent the evening with him, and I left him for you. But now I'm leaving you for him. Farewell, little angel wife. I kiss you and all the others—I bless the children with all my heart. Take care of yourself. I'm glad that you're not with child. I greet Katerina Ivanovna [Zagryazhskaya] and your brother Sergey [N. Goncharov].

Write me in Boldino.

[464]
To Natalia Nikolaevna Pushkina
September 14, 1833. From Simbirsk to Petersburg.
[September] 14. Simbirsk.

I'm in Simbirsk again. Night before last I left, setting out for Orenburg. I had barely gotten out onto the highway when a hare ran across in front of me.[1] The devil take it. I would have given a great deal to have hunted it down. At the third station when they began to harness up my horses for me I noticed that I had no coachmen—one was blind; the other was drunk and had hidden himself. After raising as much of a row as I could, I decided to return and to travel another road. On this road there are six horses at each station, and the post goes four times per week. They started back with me— I dropped off to sleep—I woke up in the morning—what did I see? I hadn't returned even three miles. A hill—the horses wouldn't pull up it—about twenty peasants around me. The devil knows how God helped—finally we climbed it, and I returned to Simbirsk. I would give a great deal to be a borzoi; I certainly would have hunted down that hare. Now I'm going by a different road.[2] Maybe it will be without adventures. I've kept on hoping that I would receive here, as consolation, at least some news of you. But no. How are you, my little wife? How are you and the children? I kiss and bless all of you. Write me often, and write all kinds of nonsense that has to do with you. I greet Aunty.

[465]
            To Natalia Nikolaevna Pushkina
    September 19, 1833. From Orenburg to Petersburg.
                       September 19. Orenburg.

I've been here since yesterday.[1] I reached here with difficulty. The road is most boring. The weather is cold. Tomorrow I'm going to see the Yaik Cossacks.[2] I'll spend some three days with them—and I'll set out for my village, by way of Saratov and Penza.

What is it, little wife? Do you miss me? I'm lonely for you. If I weren't ashamed to, I'd return straight to you, without having written a single line. But that's impossible, my angel. In for a penny, in for a pound—that is, I left to write: so write, then, novel after novel, long poem after long poem. And I just feel that the spell is coming over me—I'm composing, as it is, in the calash; what will it be like in bed?[3] One thing is greatly annoying me: my manservant.[4] Imagine the tone of a Moscow government office worker, stupid, talkative, drunk every other day, who eats my cold grouse for the road, drinks my Madeira, ruins my books, and at the stations calls me now a count and now a general. He simply infuriates me. What a fine fellow my Ippolit was![5] Apropos of the tribe of Ham,[6] how are you getting along with your household? I'm afraid you don't have enough servants. Shouldn't you hire somebody? I rely on the women, but how are you coping with the menservants? All this disturbs me—I'm as mistrustful as my father. I haven't said anything yet about the children. God grant health to them— and to you, little wife. Farewell, little wife. Don't you expect any letters from me until I get to the village. I kiss you and bless all of you.

How well I am behaving myself! How satisfied you would be with me! I'm not paying court to the young ladies, I'm not pinching the station masters' wives, I'm not coquetting with Kalmuck girls[7]— and a few days ago I refused a Bashkir girl, notwithstanding my curiosity, very forgivable in a traveler. Do you know, there is a proverb: in a foreign land, even an old woman is a gift of God. Look to it, little wife. Take example from me.

[466]
To Natalia Nikolaevna Pushkina
October 2, 1833. From Boldino to Petersburg.
October 2.

My darling, I've been in Boldino since yesterday—I thought I would find letters from you here, but I didn't find a single one. What's the matter with you? Are you well? Are the children well? My heart sinks when I think about what may be. As I was approaching Boldino, I had the gloomiest premonitions. So that when I found no news from you whatever, I almost rejoiced—I was so afraid of bad news. No, my darling, it's bad for a married man to travel. It's a different matter for a bachelor! He doesn't think of anything, no death saddens him. You should have received my last letter from Orenburg. From there I went to Uralsk. The local ataman[1] and the Cossacks received me famously, gave me two dinners, drank bottoms-up to my health, vied with each other in giving me all the information I wanted—and stuffed me on fresh caviar, prepared in my presence. As I was departing (on September 23) in the evening a rain came up, the first since I left. You should be told that this year there has been a general drought and that God obliged me alone by readying for me everywhere the finest kind of road. But on the return trip He sent me this rain, and in a half hour made the road impassable. And that's not all: there was a snowfall, and I broke in the winter road by going some thirty-five miles on a sleigh. As I was passing Yazykovo, I dropped in there. I found all three brothers.[2] I dined with them very merrily, spent the night, and set off for here. After entering the boundaries of Boldino, I met some priests, and I became as infuriated with them as at the Simbirsk hare.[3] All these encounters are not for nothing. Look out, little wife! The first thing you know, you'll get all spoiled in my absence, you'll forget me—you'll start really playing the coquette. My only hope is in God and Aunty. Maybe they will preserve you from the temptations of the social whirl. I have the honor to report to you that, as for me, I am as pure before you as a newborn babe. On the road I paid court only to old women of seventy and eighty—and I didn't even look at the very young, bepissed sixty-year-old ones. In the village of Berdy,[4] where Pugachev was encamped for six months, I had *une bonne fortune*—I found a seventy-five-year-old Cossack woman[5] who remembers that time as well as you and I remember 1830. I was in no hurry to get away from her, and I beg your pardon for not even thinking of you. Now I hope to bring a lot of things into order, get a lot written, and then come to you with the booty. The post arrives at Abramovo[6] on Sunday; I'm hoping for a letter—today is Monday, I'll be waiting for it a week. Farewell—I am leaving you for Pugachev.[7] Christ be with you, my children. I kiss you, little wife—be sensible and well.

[467]
To Natalia Nikolaevna Pushkina
October 8, 1833. From Boldino to Petersburg.

My angel, I have just now received two letters from you at once, the first ones since the Simbirsk ones. How they reached me, I don't understand: you write "to the Novgorod Province, to the village Abramovo, from there," etc. And not a single word about the district. Don't forget to add *in the Arzamas District*. If you don't, I wouldn't be surprised if there may be more than one village Abramovo in the Nizhny Novgorod Province, just as there may be more than one village Boldino. Two things are disturbing me; that I left you without money and perhaps with child, too. I can imagine your cares and vexation. Thank God you're well, that Mashka and Sashka are alive, and that you've rented a house, even though at a high price.[1] Don't scare me, little wife. Don't say that you have started really playing the coquette. I'll come to you without having succeeded in getting anything written—and without money our ship will go aground. You'd better leave me in peace, and I'll work and hurry. Here I've already been in Boldino a whole week. I'm bringing into order my notes about Pugachev, but for the time being verses are still dormant. If the Tsar will authorize the Notes[2] for me, we'll net some thirty thousands. We'll pay half our debts and start living in clover. Thank you very much for the news and for the gossip. If you see Zhukovsky, kiss him for me and congratulate him upon his return and upon his star; write me how his health is.[3] My cordial greeting to the Karamzins and Meshcherskys. Explain to Sofia

Nikolaevna [Karamzina] that if I didn't go to see them in Dorpat, it was solely because of not having the money for post horses for the 350 extra miles.[4] I didn't write them, because I kept on thinking I would get there. It's a pity that you haven't seen [Alexandra O.] Smirnova; she must be killingly funny after her trip to Germany;[5] [S. D.] Bezobrazov is acting sensibly in marrying Princess Khilkova.[6] He should have done it long ago. It's better to set up housekeeping for oneself than to dangle after others' wives all one's life and to claim others' verses as one's own. Don't coquette with Sobolevsky and don't be angry with Nashchokin; thank God he sent the 1500 rubles.[7] And have no regrets about the 180—just spit on it. Just what are those 50 rubles sent to you by my father? Aren't they the interest on the 550 he owes me?[8] I wouldn't be surprised! Here they're very strongly advising me to take over for myself the legacy of Vasily Lvovich [Pushkin];[9] and I'd like to, but for that, first, money, and, second, free time are necessary; and I don't have either. What do you think of Kraevskaya?[10] No wonder Otreshkov[11] has been dangling after her. I had no idea I would land in her memoirs and in that way attain immortality. Greet her for me, if you see her. And greet all my charmers: Khitrovo, first. How has she withstood my absence? I hope with the firmness worthy of the daughter of Prince Kutuzov. So the Ficquelmonts[12] have come? I rejoice for you; how successful will the balls turn out for you? Really, aren't you with child?[13] Why are you so touchy? Farewell, darling. I'm somehow not very well today. My little stomach aches, like [P. K.] Alexandrov's. I kiss and bless all of you. I greet and thank with all my heart Aunt Katerina Ivanovna [Zagryazhskaya] for her kind solicitude. Farewell.

October 8.

[468]
To Natalia Nikolaevna Pushkina
October 11, 1833. From Boldino to Petersburg.

My angel, one word: go see Pletnev and ask him to have all the ukases relating to Pugachev copied from *The Collected Laws*[1] (for the years 1774 and 1775 and 1773) *before my arrival*. Don't forget.

How are your finances? Are you with child? Don't expect me this month; expect me at the end of November. Don't hinder me, don't scare me, stay well, look after the children, don't coquette with the Tsar or with Princess Lyuba's fiancé.[2] I'm writing, I'm in the midst of bothers, I see nobody—and I shall bring you a world of all sorts of stuff.[3] I hope that Smirdin is punctual. In a few days I'll send him some verses.[4] Do you know what they're saying about me in the neighboring provinces? This is the way they describe my activities: when Pushkin writes verses—before him stands a quart of the *finest* liqueur—he gulps down a glass, a second, a third—and then he starts writing! That's fame. As for you, the fame of your beauty has reached our priest's wife, who assures me that you've got everything, not only face but figure. What more would you wish? Farewell. I kiss and bless all of you. I kiss Aunty's hand. Can Masha talk? Can she walk? What about some little teeth? I whistle along with Sasha. Farewell.

October 11.

[469]
To Natalia Nikolaevna Pushkina
October 21, 1833. From Boldino to Petersburg.

Today I received your letter of October 4, and I thank you heartily. Last Sunday I did not receive a letter from you, and I had the stupidity to pout at you. But yesterday such misery seized me that I can't remember such spleen coming over me before. I'm glad you're not with child and that nothing will prevent you from distinguishing yourself at the balls now going on. Apparently Ogarev[1] is very fond of the Pushkins; to hell with him. I don't prevent you from coquetting, but I demand of you coldness, propriety, dignity—still not to speak of the irreproachability of conduct which has to do, not with *tone*, but with what is really the most important of all. Why should you want, little wife, to vie with the Countess [Nadezhda Lvovna] Sollogub? You're a beauty, you're a real female woman—but she's a bag of bones. Why should you beat her out of her admirers? It's just as though Count Sheremetev[2] were to set about doing me out of my Kistenevo peasants. Who else besides Ogarev is paying court to you? Send me a list in alphabetical order. And write me, too, what places you go, and how the Karamzins, Meshcherskaya, and the Vyazemskys are. Tell Princess Vyazemskaya that she is wrong in being concerned about the portrait of Vigel, and that *on that side* my conduct is above any suspicion, but that out of esteem for her request I shall put his portrait *behind* all the others.³ Incidentally, she promised me her portrait, but up to now she has not kept her word. Reproach her for me. You probably have already seen Zhukovsky and Vielgorsky. How is Zhukovsky? They write me that he has become healthy and young again. Is it true? Just why did you want to marry him to Katerina Nikolaevna [Goncharova]? And what about Katerina Nikolaevna—will she come to see us or not? Just imagine, last Sunday instead of a letter from you I received a letter from Sobolevsky, who needs money for *pâtés de foie gras*, and who is undertaking an almanac⁴ to that end. You understand how his letter and requests for verses (what do I mean *requests*—commands, contracts for verses made to order) have angered me. And it's all your fault. Just how is my toothless *Puskina*? Oh, those teeth! And how is red-haired Sasha? And who'd he get red hair from?⁵ I hadn't expected that of him. Of myself I'll tell you that I am working in lazy, slip-shod manner. All these days my head has been aching, spleen has been gnawing on me. Now it's better. I've begun a lot, but I don't feel up to anything; God knows what's happening to me. I've become old and weak in mind.⁶ I'll come to rejuvenate myself with your youth, my angel. But don't expect me before the end of November; I don't want to come to you with empty hands—in for a penny, in for a pound. And don't you scold me. Thank for me my precious Katerina Ivanovna [Zagryazhskaya], who doesn't let you have your way in the loge. I kiss her little hands and ask her for God's sake not to leave you to the mercies of your adorers. I kiss and make the sign of the cross over Mashka, red-haired Sashka, and you. The Lord be with you. Farewell; I'm sleepy. October 21. Boldino.

[470] To Natalia Nikolaevna Pushkina
October 30, 1833. From Boldino to Petersburg.

Yesterday I received, my darling, two letters from you. Thanks. But I want to upbraid you a little. You seem to have overdone your coquetting. Look here: it's not for nothing that coquetting is out of fashion and is considered a sign of bad tone. There's little sense in it. You rejoice that male dogs are running after you like a little bitch, with their tails like a poker, and sniffing you in the a——; that's something to rejoice over! It's easy, not only for you, but even for Paraskovia Petrovna[1] to train the bachelor ne'er-do-wells to run after you. All you need is to trumpet it about, "I," quote, "am quite willing." Here is all the secret of coquetry. *Where there's a trough, there'll be swine.* Why should you receive men who are paying court to you? You don't know whom you may run into. Read A. Izmaylov's fable about Foma and Kuzma.[2] Foma stuffed Kuzma on caviar and herring. Kuzma began to ask for something to drink, but Foma wouldn't give him anything. So Kuzma gave Foma a thrashing, for being a rascal. From all this the poet adduces the following moral: "Beauties! Don't feed men on herring if you don't want to give them something to drink; otherwise you may bump up against a Kuzma." Do you see? I ask that none of these academic luncheons[3] be at my house. Now, my angel, I kiss you as if nothing were amiss, and I thank you for describing to me your dissipated life frankly and in detail. Have your fun, little wife, only don't overdo it, and don't forget me. I want to see you coiffured *à la Ninon*[4] so much that I don't know what to do; you must look marvellously sweet that way. Why hadn't you thought before of that old whore and borrowed her coiffure from her? Describe for me your appearing at balls, which, as you write, have probably already begun—and, my angel, please don't coquette. I'm not being jealous, and I know, too, that you won't cast prudence to the winds. But you know how I dislike everything that smacks of the Moscow young lady, all that is not *comme il faut*, all that is *vulgar*. . . .[5] If upon my return I find that your sweet, simple, aristocratic tone has changed, I'll divorce you, Christ be my witness, and out of misery I'll become a soldier. You ask how I am getting along and whether I have not gotten better looking. In the first place, I have grown a beard: *a mustache and beard are a fine fellow's boast—when I go out on the street they call me uncle.* (2) I wake up at 7 o'clock; I drink coffee, and I lie around until 3 o'clock. Not long ago I got into a writing vein and I have already written a world of stuff.[6] At 3 o'clock I mount my horse, at 5, I take a bath, and then I dine on potatoes and buckwheat porridge. I read until 9 o'clock. There's my day for you. And they are all just alike.

Ask Katerina Andreevna [Karamzina] not to be angry with me. You were bearing a child, I didn't have any extra money, I was hurrying off in a different direction—and I just couldn't make it to

Dorpat.[7] I greet her, [Ekaterina N.] Meshcherskaya, Sofia Nikolaevna [Karamzina], the Princess [Vera] and Princesses [Maria P. and Praskovia P.] Vyazemskaya. Tell [Idalia G.] Poletika that I'll come in person for her kiss, for, tell her, they won't accept them in the mail. And how is it that Katerina Ivanovna [Zagryazhskaya] let you have your own sweet way? Oh, Lord Jesus Christ! I kiss Masha and ask her to remember me. What kind of rash does Sasha have? Christ be with you. I bless and kiss all of you.

October 30.

[471]
To Vladimir Fedorovich Odoevsky
October 30, 1833. From Boldino to Petersburg.

I am at fault, Your Highness! Completely at fault. I arrived at the village and thought I would get into a writing vein. Nothing of the kind happened. Headaches, financial cares, laziness—the laziness of the rural nobility, of the landowner—have so overcome me that God forbid. Don't expect Belkin; all joking aside, apparently he is deceased; he will not be at the housewarming, either in Gomozeyko's living room or in Panko's garret.[1] He is apparently not worthy to be in their company. . . . And it would not be a bit bad to get into that cellar! Now I shall report to Your Highness that when I was in Simbirsk I saw the unassuming woman-recluse[2] about whom you and I talked before my departure. She's not bad looking. The governor seems to be protecting her much more zealously than his wife does.[3] That is all that I was able to observe. Her lawsuit seems to be over with.

You gladdened me with the news of Zhukovsky.[4] God grant that his present store of health will suffice him for five years or so; and then somehow may he get well.

I greet Gogol. How about his comedy?[5] It's got something.

All yours,
A. Pushkin.

October 30.
Boldino.

[472]
To Natalia Nikolaevna Pushkina
November 6, 1833. From Boldino to Petersburg.
November 6, 1833. Boldino.

My darling little wife, I don't remember very well what I wrote you by the last post. As I remember I was a little angry—and my letter may have been a little harsh. I shall repeat to you a little more gently that coquetry leads to nothing good, and although it has its delights, nothing so quickly deprives a young woman of that without which there is neither domestic well-being nor tranquillity in her relationships toward society: *respect*. There's nothing for you to rejoice over in your victories. Ninon [de Lenclos], the whore from whom you've borrowed your coiffure (N.B.: you must be very pretty in that coiffure; I was thinking about that tonight), used to say: *Il est écrit sur le coeur de tout homme*: "*A la plus facile*."[1] After that, take pride, if you will, in stealing men's hearts. Think this over well, and don't cause me needless worry. I'm leaving soon, but I shall stay in Moscow for some time on business.[2] Little wife, little wife! I'm traveling the highways, living three months in the remote steppe, stopping in nasty Moscow, which I hate—for what? For you, little wife. So that you may be tranquil and may sparkle with health, as is fitting at your years and with your beauty. But see that you take care of me, too. To the cares, inseparable from the life of a man, don't add family worries, jealousy, etc., etc.—not to speak of *cocuage*, about which I read a whole dissertation in Brantôme a few days ago.[3]

What is my brother doing? I don't advise him to go into the civil service, for which he's just as unfit as for the military. But at least he has a healthy a——, and he would nevertheless go farther in the saddle than in a chair in a government office.[4] It seems to me that we shan't get by without a European war. This Louis Philippe is like a cataract in my eye. The time will come for us to show him what's what—then Lev Sergeich will again go reap, as our assessor says, some laurels and myrtles. Meanwhile I advise him to twiddle his thumbs, a pleasant and healthful occupation. Here I was about to take the notion to take over Vasily Lvovich's legacy.[5] But the trusteeship has so plundered him that it's not even to be thought of, unless Benkendorf might intercede. I'll try it, when I arrive in Petersburg. A letter to my father is enclosed. He is probably already there. I shall bring you a lot of verses, but don't noise it about: if you do, the almanacsters will pester me to death. I kiss Mashka, Sashka, and you. I bless you, Sashka, and Mashka. I kiss Mashka—and so forth, up to seven times. I should like to be with you by Aunty's name day.[6] But God knows.

[473]
To PAVEL VOINOVICH NASHCHOKIN
November 24, 1833. From Petersburg to Moscow.

What about it, Pavel Voinovich, how are your domestic circumstances? Has it been decided?[1] I'm so eager to find out the dénouement that I don't know what to do; I left your novel at the most intriguing point. I don't dare hope—but one may hope. *Vous êtes éminemment un homme de passion*[2]—and in an impassioned state you are able to do what you would not even dare to think of in a state of sobriety; just as once when drunk you swam across a river, though you didn't know how to swim. The present affair is like that—take off your shirt, cross yourself, and splash off from the bank. We—Prince Fedor [F. Gagarin] and I—shall follow you in a boat, and somehow or other you'll scramble out onto the opposite side. Now I'll tell you about my journey.[3] I accomplished it successfully. Lelenka[4] did not bother me; he's very nice, i.e., silent. All our relationships were bounded by my pushing him away with my elbow when he would lean against my shoulder at night. I arrived with him well and unharmed. And since the river has not yet frozen hard and there are no bridges yet, I sent him off to Lev Sergeevich [Pushkin], by doing which I have probably done him a favor. When I was leaving Moscow my Gavrila was so drunk and he so enraged me that I ordered him to climb down from the coach box, and I left him on the highway, in tears and hysterics, but all that had no effect on me—I thought of you. . . . Just you order your Gavrila in a skirt and *kacavejka*[5] to climb down from the coach box—enough of this brawling. At home I found everything in order. My wife was at a ball; I went to get her—and I took her away to my place, like a uhlan taking off a young provincial lady from the name-day celebration of a town governor's wife.[6] My financial affairs have got all tangled up in my absence, but I am thinking of untangling them.[7]

I have seen my father. He is very glad of my proposal to take over Boldino.[8] He has no money. My brother's in evening dress and is very decorous. Sobelevsky has won his lawsuit,[9] and he's going to where you are. Write me, if you have time. Give the note to my manager.[10] My respects to Olga Andreevna.   November 24.

[474]
To Alexander Khristoforovich Benkendorf
December 6, 1833. In Petersburg.

Dear Sir, Count Alexander Khristoforovich,

I make bold to forward to Your Highness a poem which I should like to publish,[1] and on the occasion of this to request from you an authorization which is important to me. The bookseller Smirdin is publishing a journal,[2] in which he has asked me to participate. I can consent only in case he may undertake to present my compositions to the censorship and take the necessary steps with them, on a basis of equality with the other writers who are participating in his enterprise. But I did not wish to tell him anything definite without your knowledge.

Though I have attempted to utilize as infrequently as possible the permission, so precious to me, of burdening the attention of the Sovereign Emperor, I now nevertheless make bold to request the Highest's gracious permission for me to do so: I once thought of writing a historical novel relating to the times of Pugachev,[3] but after finding a multitude of materials, I abandoned that notion and wrote *The History of the Pugachev Affair*.[4] I make bold to request through Your Highness the permission to present it for His Highest's examination. I do not know whether it will be permissible for me to publish it, but I dare to hope that this historical fragment will be of interest to His Majesty, especially in connection with the military actions of that time, which are until now little known.[5]

With the most profound respect and complete devotion, I have the honor to be,
                Dear Sir,
                    Your Highness's
                        Most humble servant,
December 6, 1833.   Alexander Pushkin.
SPb.

[475]
To Pavel Voinovich Nashchokin
Between December 13 and 20, 1833.
From Petersburg to Moscow.

I have received two sad letters from you, dear Pavel Voinovich,[1] and I've been waiting for a third, while impatiently wanting to know what's happening to you, and what direction your affairs of house and heart are taking.[2] But you are probably too distraught, and I don't know what to hope for: has your fate changed, has it quieted down? Do write me about that, and in detail.

On your name day[3] my family (including Grigory Fedorovich)[4] drank your health and wished you all good luck. About Lelenka[5] I have no news. He is living at Eristov's, and I'm receiving letters addressed to him from Moscow. His insane father wrote me an insane letter, which I am already tardy in answering. He is worried about the calligraphic labors of his son, and about whether the boy isn't weeping and whether he isn't homesick for his family. Reassure the old man as best you can.

I don't know whether I'll be in Moscow in January. Uncle's heirs are making me foolish proposals—I have rejected the legacy.[6] I don't know whether they will enter into new negotiations. Here I've been having financial unpleasantnesses. I came to an agreement with Smirdin, but I was compelled to break the contract because the censorship did not pass *The Bronze Horseman*.[7] That's a real loss for me. If they won't pass *The History of Pugachev*, then I'll have to go to the village. All this is very unpleasant. I'm relying on getting your money for you, however; I'm thinking of proceeding in the spring to my complete works.[8]

All my folks are well—your godson [Alexander A. Pushkin] kisses you; he's a fine boy. I haven't talked yet with Pletnev about Pavel,[9] because there's no hurry. Farewell; I greet Prince [F. F.] Gagarin—and I wish happiness to you both.

A.P.

NOTES TO PART X

Letter 452
1. Pushkin wished to make the trip to Orenburg and Kazan in order to visit the scene of the Pugachev uprising, for historical researches on Pugachev and for his novel, *The Captain's Daughter*. The Pushkins' lands in the province of Nizhny Novgorod were the paternal estates of Boldino and Kistenevo. This letter also includes, in its final form, which has not survived, Pushkin's request for permission to go to Dorpat to visit Ekaterina Andreevna Karamzina, who was in deep mourning because of the death in 1833 of her fifteen-year-old son, Nikolay Nikolaevich Karamzin. Pushkin was at once given permission to go to Dorpat, but he was asked for more information regarding his reasons for wishing to make the trip to the Ural region. Pushkin's further explanations are given in Letter 453.

Letter 453
1. In the absence of Count Benkendorf, his assistant, Alexander Nikolaevich Mordvinov (1792-1869), handled Pushkin's request (Letter 452) for permission to visit the Ural region. Pushkin's letter is in response to Mordvinov's letter transmitting Nicholas I's inquiry as to why Pushkin wished "to interrupt his activities" and make a trip to Orenburg and Kazan. Pushkin received the desired permission to make the trip, and a four-month leave of absence.
2. Pushkin exaggerates. He had written his unfinished *Dubrovsky* and several shorter things, though, to be sure, his literary output had decreased greatly.
3. Pushkin's novel of the Pugachev uprising, *The Captain's Daughter*, the preface of which is dated August 5, 1833. However, upon his return from the Ural region, Pushkin did not complete the novel at once, but wrote his *History of Pugachev*, a work of historical research. He did not complete his *Captain's Daughter* until 1836.

Letter 454
1. Pushkin's self-deprecatory remark is in agreement with the recorded opinion of many of his contemporaries, who often alluded to his "African" features and appearance. When Pushkin married Mlle. Goncharova, there were comments about the wedding of "beauty and the beast."

Letter 455
1. Pushkin departed from Petersburg, together with his friend S. A. Sobolevsky, during a storm on August 17. He left his wife and children behind in a summer house in the suburb of Chernaya Rechka.
2. The allusion is to the Petersburg flood of November 7, 1824, which occurred while Pushkin was in exile in Mikhaylovskoe and which is mentioned in several letters. Pushkin described this flood in *The Bronze Horseman*, perhaps his poetic masterpiece, which he wrote while on this trip.
3. Yaropolets was the estate of Pushkin's mother-in-law, in the Volokolamsk District, in Moscow Province.
4. Roman Romanovich Anrep (d. 1830), an officer Pushkin met in the Caucasus in 1829. He died of exposure after wandering into a swamp in an attack of madness.
5. Mme. Pushkina's name day and the date of the annual ball commemorating the Battle of Borodino.

6. The allusion is undoubtedly to Nicholas I, who was abroad—for which reason the ball was postponed.

7. Sasha is the affectionate diminutive, and Sashka the rough-affectionate diminutive of the first name of Pushkin's son, Alexander Alexandrovich Pushkin.

8. Vyazemsky had proposed to Pushkin that together they publish another *Northern Flowers*. Nothing came of the idea.

Letter 456
1. Pavlovskoe was the estate of Pavel Ivanovich Vulf. It was near Ivan Ivanovich Vulf's estate of Bernovo and Praskovia Osipova's estate of Malinniki.

2. The "Annettes" included Anna Nikolaevna Vulf, Anna Ivanovna Vulf, and Anna Petrovna Kern. There was only one person present with each of the other names or diminutives mentioned: Evpraxia Nikolaevna Vrevskaya (nee Vulf), Alexandra Ivanovna Osipova, and Maria Ivanovna Osipova.

3. Karl Reichman (d. 1835), a German, manager of Osipova's estate, Malinniki. In 1834 Pushkin invited him to manage his paternal estate of Boldino, but Reichman declined.

4. Daria Evdokimovna Pozharskaya, proprietress of an inn in Torzhok.

5. She has been variously identified as the tragic actress Marguerite Joséphine Wemmer (1787-1867) and as the Pushkins' midwife.

6. Apparently Pushkin is asking whether his daughter has been ill again.

7. August 26.

8. Pushkin set to rhyme the story of Snow White, in his *Tale of the Dead Tsarevna and of the Seven Heroes*, before he returned home from this trip. It was written on November 4, 1833, at Boldino.

Letter 457
1. On her name day, Saturday, August 26.
2. The Goncharovs' Moscow house.
3. The invitation was accepted. Pushkin's wife and children spent the summer with her mother at Yaropolets in 1834.
4. Peter Dorofeevich Doroshenko (1627-1698), hetman of the Ukraine, Mme. Pushkina's great-great-great-grandfather, the ancestor to whom the estate Yaropolets was given.
5. Semen Fedorovich Dushin, manager of the estate Yaropolets.
6. Countess Nadezhda Grigorievna Chernysheva (1813-1853).
7. Countess Sofia Grigorievna Kruglikova, nee Chernysheva (1799-1847), sister of Nadezhda Grigorievna Chernysheva.
8. Andrey Nikolaevich Muraviev (1806-1874), writer on religious themes.
9. Pushkin's quotation is from Fonvizin's famous comedy *The Adolescent*, Act II, scene 4. Pushkin, in an epigram on Muraviev in 1827 had called him, instead of Apollo Belvedere, "Mitrofan Belvedere."
10. Pushkin is obviously giving direct quotations in all the French in this letter, including Dmitry Goncharov's offering of "his heart and hand," and his statement that "he is not his usual self."
11. Nikolay Afanasievich Goncharov, who was mad.
12. Vasily Gavrilovich Yuriev, an officer who lent money at interest.
13. Pushkin's English.

Letter 458
1. Alexander Yakovlevich Bulgakov (1781-1863), the Moscow Post Director, and

as such in charge both of the mail and of post horses. Pushkin had met him in 1826; their relationships were good, though not close, until Bulgakov intercepted one of Pushkin's letters to Pushkin's wife (Letter 488, q.v.). His wife was Natalia Vasilievna Bulgakova (1785-1841), and his daughters were Ekaterina Alexandrovna Bulgakova (b. 1811) and Olga Alexandrovna Dolgorukova, nee Bulgakova (1814-1865).

2. Pogodin married Elizaveta Vasilievna Vagner (1809-1844) on July 8, 1833.
3. Alexander Nikolaevich Raevsky.
4. Unknown. "Brigadier" was a rank between colonel and general.
5. Prince Peter Mikhaylovich Dolgorukov (1784-1833), had just died of the cholera.
6. Count Alexey Alexeevich Bobrinsky (1800-1868), grandson of Catherine the Great.
7. Count Fedor Vasilievich Rostopchin (1763-1826), the Commander-in-Chief in Moscow in 1812, the year Mme. Pushkina was born. He is presented at considerable length in Tolstoy's *War and Peace*. Kuznetsky Most (literally, Smith's Bridge) is a street in Moscow.
8. "Aunty" here and in subsequent letters is Katerina Ivanovna Zagryazhskaya, Mme. Pushkina's aunt.

Letter 459
1. "The streets are broad and well paved; the houses are well constructed." Pushkin seems to be quoting some book of travels.
2. The famous Nizhny Novgorod Fair, which opened on July 15 and closed on September 8—the most famous of all Russian fairs.
3. Pushkin is quoting from a song.
4. After giving birth to their son Alexander Alexandrovich Pushkin, on July 6.

Letter 460
1. August 26.
2. The excuses were for not attending a ball given by Bulgakov. Bulgakov, as Post Director, could give Pushkin a "certificate" so that he could more easily receive horses for traveling by post chaise.
3. "The cuckold."
4. Sergey Ivanovich Pashkov (1801-1883) and his wife, Nadezhda Sergeevna Pashkova (1811-1880).
5. In 1829 Sudienko married Nadezhda Mikhaylovna Miklashevskaya (d. 1876). The sons mentioned are Iosif Mikhaylovich Sudienko (1830-1892) and Alexander Mikhaylovich Sudienko (1832-1882).
6. Mme. Pushkina.
7. "You dirty dog, . . . why haven't you come to see me?"—"You beast, . . . what have you done with my Little Russian manuscript?" The manuscript is unknown.
8. Mikhail Petrovich Buturlin (1786-1860), military and civil governor of Nizhny Novgorod. His wife was Anna Petrovna Buturlina (1793-1861). Pushkin dined with them on September 2 and probably September 3. Buturlin suspected Pushkin of being an inspector general sent by Nicholas I, and Buturlin sent on a letter to Orenburg, where Pushkin's old friend, Count Vasily Alexeevich Perovsky, was the governor, warning of Pushkin's being en route, and telling of his suspicions as to the reason for Pushkin's trip. Pushkin gave the theme to Gogol, who used it in his *Inspector General*. It is ironic that whereas Pushkin was being taken for an inspector general by one official, actually the secret police sent out instructions that surveillance be maintained over him and

his conduct while he was in the Pugachev country. However, the order for this surveillance did not catch up with him while he was there.

9. That is, in 1830, before Pushkin's marriage.

10. "Farewell, my beauty, my idol, my beautiful treasure. When shall I see you again.?"

Letter 461
1. That is, of Pugachev.
2. Boldino.

Letter 462
1. Alexandra Andreevna Fuchs (d. 1853) kept a literary salon for twenty-five years. She herself wrote verses and ethnographical articles. She was the wife of Karl Fuchs (1776-1846), a German who became Professor and then Rector of the University of Kazan, and who was also noted as an amateur local historian and ethnographer. It is perhaps worthy of note that Pushkin's letter to her is in Russian, though his letters to women (except his wife) are predominantly in French.
2. This letter, like Pushkin's other letters to Mme. Fuchs, was published later by her, and without the complimentary close and signature. The original manuscript copies of these letters have not survived.

Letter 463
1. Alexander Mikhaylovich Zagryazhsky (1796-1878), governor of Simbirsk, and a relative of Mme. Pushkina.
2. From mastitis.
3. Apparently Mme. Pushkina and the children moved into this house in September. The rent was 4800 rubles per year, 96 percent of Pushkin's official salary. Their landlord was Alexander Karlovich Olivio.
4. Letter 461.
5. Pushkin's English. The reference is to Alexandra Andreevna Fuchs. Pushkin's description of her is obviously completely unjust. Mme. Pushkina's inclinations to be jealous are clear from several comments Pushkin makes in the letters written during this trip.
6. Poems addressed to her were by Khomyakov, Yazykov, Baratynsky, and Ivan Kireevsky, among others.
7. Karl Fuchs.
8. Peter Mikhaylovich Yazykov (1798-1851).

Letter 464
1. Pushkin was very superstitious. A hare crossing his path was the equivalent, among us, of a black cat.
2. There were three different routes which Pushkin could take. Pushkin left Simbirsk on September 12, and, the second time, on September 15.

Letter 465
1. Pushkin spent three days in Orenburg, the house guest of the Simbirsk governor, his old friend Vasily Alexeevich Perovsky. On the day Pushkin wrote this letter, he visited the town of Berdy, some five miles from Orenburg (see Letter 466).
2. Cossacks who lived along the Yaik (now Ural) River. They were in the town of Uralsk, where Pushkin spent three days.

3. Pushkin usually wrote mornings in bed, with his notebook propped up on his knees. For Pushkin's literary works written during this trip, see Letter 468, and note 3.

4. Gavrila. Some of these traits are depicted by Gogol for the servant in his *Inspector General*.

5. Pushkin's former servant.

6. That is, hinds, boors.

7. The allusion is to an event which happened to Pushkin in the Caucasus in 1829, and which he describes in his *Journey to Erzurum*. His attempts at "coquetting" with the Kalmuck girl were unsuccessful, but the occurrence led to his poem, "To a Kalmuck Girl" (1829).

Letter 466

1. Vasily Osipovich Pokatilov (d. 1838).

2. Pushkin spent the night of September 29 at Yazykovo, and left for Boldino the next day. The three Yazykov brothers were Peter Mikhaylovich Yazykov, the poet Nikolay Mikhaylovich Yazykov, and Alexander Mikhaylovich Yazykov (1799-1874).

3. See Letter 464. Priests were also "bad luck."

4. A settlement about five miles from Orenburg. Pushkin visited it on September 19.

5. Buntova (d. after 1848). When she was fourteen or fifteen, Pugachev saw her on the street and ordered that she be taken to a public bath for him. She gave Pushkin considerable information which he made use of in his works on the Pugachev uprising. Tolstoy presents as typical a hussar of Pushkin's generation similarly using a public bath for relations with a woman, in his *Two Hussars* (1856).

6. A post station eight miles from Boldino.

7. That is, to work on the Pugachev materials.

Letter 467

1. See Letter 463, and note 3.

2. Pushkin is thinking of the separate publication of the historical materials which he compiled and published in his *History of Pugachev*.

3. Zhukovsky had returned to Tsarskoe Selo in September, after spending the summer abroad for his health. Zhukovsky received the "star" of the order of St. Stanislav, on August 30, 1833.

4. For Pushkin's earlier intention to visit Mme. Karamzina in Dorpat, see Letter 452, note.

5. The Smirnovs spent the first ten months of 1833 in Germany.

6. Princess Lyubov Alexandrovna Khilkova (1811-1859). The marriage took place in November, 1833.

7. What money Pushkin means is not known.

8. Nothing is known of Pushkin's financial affairs with his father at the time.

9. Boldino had been jointly owned by Pushkin's father, S. L. Pushkin, and his uncle, V. L. Pushkin. His uncle's heirs wished Pushkin to buy their inherited share (see Letter 472).

10. Neither she nor her memoirs have been identified.

11. Probably N. I. Tarasenko-Otreshkov.

12. Count Karl Ludwig Ficquelmont, the Austrian ambassador, and his wife, Countess Daria Fedorovna Ficquelmont, daughter of Elizaveta Khitrovo.

13. She was not.

Letter 468

1. Pushkin had been given a copy of the *Complete Collected Laws* in February, 1832 (see Letter 425). Pushkin wished these materials for his *History of Pugachev*.

2. S. D. Bezobrazov, fiancé of Lybov (Lyuba) Alexandrovna Khilkova (see Letter 467).

3. During his stay at Boldino in October and early November, 1833, Pushkin had his last really productive short literary period, which can be compared in this respect, only with the autumn of 1830. During early autumn, 1833, Pushkin wrote, in addition to *The History of Pugachev, The Bronze Horseman, The Tale of the Fisherman and the Fish, The Tale of the Dead Tsarevna and the Seven Heroes*, and *Angelo* (an adaptation of Shakespeare's *Measure for Measure* into the form of a narrative poem), in addition to a number of shorter things (for some of which, see note 4).

4. Pushkin no doubt is referring to the works of his which appeared in 1834 in Smirdin's *Library for Reading*: the poems, "The Hussar," "Budrys and His Sons," "The Voevoda," *The Tale of the Dead Tsarevna and the Seven Heroes*, and the tale, "The Queen of Spades."

Letter 469

1. Nikolay Alexandrovich Ogarev (1811-1867). Apparently his attempts at paying court to Mme. Pushkina were described in a letter of hers.

2. Count Dmitry Nikolaevich Sheremetev (1803-1871) was an extremely wealthy landowner.

2. Mentioning Vigel, Pushkin again refers to his homosexual proclivities.

4. It did not appear.

5. Pushkin forgets that his brother Lev had red hair.

6. *Staram stala, i umom ploxam*. Pushkin is quoting an expression used by a Kazan Tatar about Catherine the Great's vicegerent in Kazan, Prince Platon Stepanovich Meshchersky (1713-1799).

Letter 470

1. Probably Praskovia Petrovna Vyazemskaya.

2. "The Forbidden Beer" (1829). Pushkin spells out Izmaylov's meaning.

3. Pushkin was dissatisfied with the luncheons at meetings of the Russian Academy; vodka was served there instead of wine.

4. See Letter 440, note 9. The illustration opposite page 525 shows a portrait of Mme. Pushkina, made much later, with this hairdress.

5. Pushkin uses the same expressions, in French and English, with regard to the heroine Tatiana, who lives up to these standards, in *Evgeny Onegin*, Chap. VIII, stanzas 14-15.

6. See Letter 468, and note 3.

7. For the projected trip to Dorpat, see Letter 452, note.

Letter 471

1. Pushkin's *Tales of Belkin* were attributed by him to his "deceased" friend Belkin. Pushkin further speaks of Gomozeyko, pseudonym of Odoevsky, and Panko, pseudonym of Gogol. Odoevsky had proposed that he, Gogol, and Pushkin publish an almanac in the "form of a three-story house," of which Odoevsky would take the living room, Gogol the attic, and Pushkin the basement. Pushkin declined, and the almanac did not materialize.

2. Unidentified.

3. The governor was Alexander Mikhaylovich Zagryazhsky. His wife was Karolina Osipovna Zagryazhskaya.

4. That his health was better. See Letter 467.

5. Gogol's *Vladimir, Third Class*.

Letter 472

1. "It is written on the heart of every man: *'to the easiest to get.'* "
2. Pushkin spent three days in Moscow, about the middle of November. He arrived in Petersburg before November 24.
3. Pushkin refers to *La Vie des dames galantes*, by Pierre de Bourdeille, Seigneur de Brantôme, sixteenth-century memoirist and historian. This book begins with a discussion of cuckoldry.
4. Lev Sergeevich Pushkin, who had served in the Russian army which put down the Polish Revolution, had retired from the military service, and was "twiddling his thumbs" in Petersburg.
5. See Letter 467, and note 9.
6. November 24. Pushkin was in Petersburg on that day and attended the name-day celebration of Ekaterina A. Karamzina.

Letter 473

1. Nashchokin was still in the midst of extreme domestic turmoil with his gypsy mistress, Olga Andreevna, because of his desire to leave her and marry Vera Alexandrovna Narskaya (d. 1900).
2. "You are to a high degree a man of passion."
3. From Moscow to Petersburg.
4. Unidentified. He is mentioned again in Letter 475. "Lelenka" is a diminutive of the name Alexey.
5. That is, Olga Andreevna.
6. Pushkin went to the place where the ball was being held, found and seated himself in his wife's carriage, and had a servant tell her to come home on very important business. When she climbed into the carriage, it was into his embraces. L. N. Tolstoy, twenty years later, presents a hussar and a provincial lady in such an adventure in his *Two Hussars*, as being typical of hussars in Pushkin's generation.
7. Pushkin had in mind selling the works he had written in the autumn of 1833 to Smirdin at a good price.
8. Pushkin took over the management of his father's estate Boldino in April, 1834.
9. Unknown.
10. M. I. Kalashnikov. The note undoubtedly had to do with the attempted remortgaging of Pushkin's Kistenevo serfs.

Letter 474

1. *The Bronze Horseman*. Nicholas I allowed the publication of only a fragment of it during Pushkin's lifetime.
2. *A Library for Reading*, which began to appear in 1834. Pushkin contributed to it until plans for his own journal, *The Contemporary*, began to crystallize, late in 1835. Smirdin offered Pushkin fifteen thousand rubles per annum to continue to collaborate with him, instead of publishing his own journal.
3. *The Captain's Daughter*.
4. *Istorija Pugačevščiny*. Pushkin actually entitled his work *The History of Pugachev*, but Nicholas I required him, before he would allow publication, to change the title to *The History of the Pugachev Revolt*.
5. Benkendorf transmitted to Pushkin the Tsar's permission for the poems Pushkin wished Smirdin to publish to be sent to the usual censorship, but the Tsar wished to see *The History of Pugachev*.

Letter 475
   1. This letter was never delivered. See Letter 286, and note.
   2. Nashchokin fled from his gypsy mistress Olga Andreevna in January or February, 1834, leaving her in possession of his Moscow house and considerable money. Shortly afterward, he married Vera Alexandrovna Narskaya.
   3. Rather, his birthday, December 8. Nashchokin celebrated his name day on the Day of Peter and Paul, June 29.
   4. A dwarf who was attached to the Goncharov family.
   5. See Letter 473, and note 4.
   6. V. L. Pushkin's heirs included his common-law wife, Anna Nikolaevna Vorozheykina, and his daughter by her, Margarita Vasilievna Bezobrazova, nee Vasilieva (1810-1889).
   7. See Letter 474.
   8. Pushkin's complete works were not published during his life.
   9. Nashchokin's son by Olga Andreevna.

PART XI

GRAY-HAIRED KAMMERJUNKER — PETERSBURG

December, 1833—August, 1834

Pushkin, 1836 or 1837. *Gravure by T. Wright.*

[476]
To Alexander Khristoforovich Benkendorf
Between February 7 and 10, 1834. In Petersburg.
(Second rough draft; in French)

In submitting to His Majesty the second volume of Pugachev, I take the liberty of speaking to Your Excellency about circumstances concerning me, and of having recourse to your customary kindness.

By permitting the publication of this work, His Majesty has assured my fortune. The sum which I shall be able to realize from it puts me in the position even to accept an inheritance which I have been forced to renounce for lack of some forty thousand rubles which I did not have. This work will procure them for me. If I can be the publisher of it myself—without having recourse to a bookseller—fifteen thousand would be enough for me.

I request two things: one, that I be permitted to publish my work at my own expense in the special printing house under M. [M. M.] Speransky's supervision, the only one where I am sure of not being tricked—the other request is to receive, as a two-year loan, fifteen thousand, a sum which will permit me to devote to the publishing all the time and care which I should.[1]

I have no right to the favor which I solicit, except the kindnesses which I have already received—and which give me the courage and the confidence to have recourse to you again.—I entrust my very humble request to Your Excellency's protection.

I am, Count,
Your Excellency's
Most humble [. . . .]

[477]
To Stepan Dmitrievich Nechaev
February 12, 1834. In Petersburg.

Dear Sir, Stepan Dmitrievich,[1]

I make bold to have recourse to Your High Excellency with a most humble request.

By the wish of the Sovereign Emperor, the archdeacon[2] of the

Court church at Tsarskoe Selo, on account of drunkenness, has been expelled from the Court department and has been transferred to that of the diocese. According to the order of the Synod, he must be sent back to his diocese. The archdeacon, a man no longer young, and with a family, requests, as a favor, that he be left in the local diocese. The sense of the Sovereign's command would be fulfilled just the same, for not a word was said in it to the effect that he be sent to his *own* diocese.

The archdeacon, I know not why, has addressed himself to me, supposing that my weak voice might be honored with your attention. In any case, I could not refuse to intercede for him, and I commend my client to your magnanimous protection.

With the most profound respect, I have the honor to be,
  Dear Sir,
    Your Excellency's
      Most humble servant,
        Alexander Pushkin.

February 12, 1834.

[478]
  To Alexander Khristoforovich Benkendorf
    February 26, 1834. In Petersburg.

Dear Sir, Alexander Khristoforovich,

Not having now the means, independently of the booksellers, to proceed to the publication of the work which I have written, I make bold to have recourse to Your Excellency with my request for the disbursement from the Treasury, in the form of a loan at the established interest rates, of twenty thousand rubles, the same to be repaid in full in two years, with payments to be made at whatever dates the authorities may choose to set.[1]

With the most profound respect, I have the honor to be,
  Dear Sir,
    Your Excellency's
      Most humble servant,
        Alexander Pushkin.

February 26, 1834.

[478a]
    To Countess Elizaveta Ksaverievna Vorontsova
       March 5, 1834. From Petersburg to Odessa.
                     (In French)
Dear Countess,
Here are several scenes of a tragedy which I had intended to write.[1] I desired to place at your feet something less imperfect; unfortunately, I have already made disposition of all my manuscripts, and I have preferred to be at fault toward the public, rather than not obey your commands.

May I dare, Madame, to speak to you of the moment of happiness which I experienced upon receiving your letter, at the mere idea that you have not completely forgotten the most devoted of your slaves?
              I am, with respect,
                Countess,
    March 5   Your most humble and most
     1834   obedient servant,
   Petersburg.   Alexander Pushkin.

[479]
           To Vladimir Fedorovich Odoevsky
              March 15 or 16, 1834. In Petersburg.
Are you going to the meeting at Grech's? If so, then let's go together. It is terrifying to go alone: they might beat us up.[1]

[480]
           To Vladimir Fedorovich Odoevsky
                 March 16, 1834. In Petersburg.
The point is the *Konversations-Lexikon*:[1] I sniffed it out. I agree with Your Highness that this evening has its loathsome and its interesting side. I shall go to Grech's, for I have received permission to do so from Pletnev, who is conscience incarnate. Let's go. What can we lose? After all, this will be a communal gathering of all the republic.[2] We'll watch and listen to everything—but we'll not join the gang of thieves.[3]
                                                        A.P.

[481]
To Pavel Voinovich Nashchokin
The middle of March, 1834. In Petersburg.

You can't imagine, dear friend, how I rejoiced at your letter. In the first place, I receive from you a whole notebook: proof that you have the time to spare, the paper to spare, the peace of mind, and the urge to chat with me. From your first lines I see that you are calm and happy. Every word destroys gossip, half of which I did not believe, but the other half of which disturbed me greatly. Sobolevsky and Lev Sergeevich were dining with me. When I read your letter first to myself and then in the hearing of your friends, we were all pleased; we all wished you happiness. Natalia Nikolaevna [Pushkina] is impatiently desirous of becoming acquainted with your Vera Alexandrovna,[1] and she asks you to make them friends sight unseen. She sincerely loves you and congratulates you. . . . But first let's talk business, i.e., about money. When you sent me off from Moscow, you remember that we thought that you could get along without money from me; for that reason I have not made my arrangements. I had in my hands, and quite recently, a good round sum, but it has melted away, and I shan't have any money before October. But I'll provide you with your three thousand in a short time, in instalments which I shall set, taking my circumstances into consideration. Here they have been saying that you lost *on credit* all that you were due to receive from your brother.[2] You can't imagine how that has disturbed me, but now I am relying on the change in your life. You no longer need the shocks of *quinze el va* and *plié*[3] in order to dispel your domestic woes. They say that unhappiness is a good school: perhaps. But happiness is the best university. It provides the finishing touches for the education of a soul capable of the good and the beautiful, such as yours is, my friend; such as mine is, as you know. Of course, we're even, if you are obligated to me for your marriage—and I hope that Vera Alexandrovna will love me, just as Natalia Nikolaevna loves you. Just imagine, my wife came very near to dying a few days ago. The present winter has been horribly abundant in balls. In Carnival there was dancing even twice a day. Finally came the last Sunday before Lent. I think: "The balls are over with, thank God!" My wife was in the palace. Suddenly I saw that she was becoming ill—I took her away, and after we got home she had a miscarriage.⁴ Now she's (keep our fingers crossed) well, thank God, and in a few days she's going to the Kaluga village to her sisters', who are suffering terribly from the caprices of my mother-in-law.⁵ I had already taken over your debt to Vyazemsky before I received your letter. Andrey Petrovich [Esaulov] is in a terrible state. He has been dying of hunger and going out of his mind. Sobolevsky and I have been helping him parsimoniously with money, but generously with counsels. Now I'm thinking of sending him off to the regiment as a bandmaster. He's an artist in soul and in habits, i.e., nonchalant, indecisive, lazy, proud, and flighty. He prefers independence to everything else. But a beggar is yet more independent than a day laborer. I'm holding up to him as examples the German geniuses who have overcome so much woe, to win fame and a crust of bread. How much do you owe him? Do you want me to pay him for you? My circumstances have become still more difficult, and here's the occasion for it: A few days ago my father sent for me. I arrived. I found him in tears, my mother in bed—all the house in horrible agitation. "What's going on?"—"They're levying a distress on the estate."—"You must hurry up and pay the debt."—"The debt is already paid. And here's the letter of the manager."⁶—"Then what's the trouble?"—"There's nothing to live on until October."—"Go to the village."—"There's nothing to do it on." What's to be done? I'll have to take the estate in hand and set support money for my father. New debts, new bothers. But I must do it: I should like to set at ease my father's old age and arrange the affairs of my brother Lev, who in his way is just such another artist as Andrey Petrovich [Esaulov], with the difference that he has no knowledge of any art. My sister Olga Sergeevna has had a miscarriage and is with child again. This is all simply marvellous.

Here are some other pieces of news for you: I've been a Kammerjunker⁷ since the month of January. *The Bronze Horseman* was not passed. Losses and unpleasantnesses! On the other hand, *Pugachev* has been passed, and I am publishing it at the Sovereign's expense. This has quite solaced me; all the more that, of course, in making me a Kammerjunker the Sovereign was thinking of my rank rather than of my years—and he surely didn't intend to humiliate me. As soon as I get my affairs arranged, I'll get busy on yours. Farewell; expect some money.

[482]
To Mikhail Petrovich Pogodin
About (not later than) April 7, 1834.
From Petersburg to Moscow.

I rejoice at the opportunity to have a frank talk with you. The Society of Lovers[1] has treated me in such a way that I absolutely cannot have anything to do with it. It elected me a member along with Bulgarin, at the very time when he was unanimously blackballed in the English Club (N.B.: in the Petersburg one) as a spy, a turncoat, and a slanderer, at the very time when I was compelled in answer to his vilifications to publish the article on Vidocq;[2] I had to prove to the public, which was rightly astonished at my long-suffering, that I have the full right to disdain Bulgarin's opinion and not to demand satisfaction from a notorious scoundrel prating of honor and morality. And then what happens? At the same time I read in Shalikov's gazette: "*Alexander Sergeevich and Faddey Venediktovich, these two coryphaei of our literature*, have been awarded, etc."[3] No matter what you say, it's a slap in the face. I believe that the Society, in this case, behaved like Famusov, without having any intention of insulting me:

I'm glad to have just anybody, you know.[4]

But it was my duty to return at once the certificate of membership which was sent to me. I did not do so, because at that time I did not feel like being bothered with membership certificates—but I simply cannot have anything to do with the Society of Lovers.

You ask me about *The Bronze Horseman*, about *Pugachev*, and about *Peter*. The first will not be published. *Pugachev* will come out by fall. I am approaching *Peter*[5] with fear and trembling, as you are the chair of history.[6] Altogether, I am writing a lot for myself, but I am publishing against my will and solely for money. Why should one want to appear before the public, which does not understand one, so that four fools may berate one just short of obscenity in their journals for the next six months? The time was when literature was a noble, aristocratic field of endeavor. Now it is a flea market. So be it.

[483]
To Grigory Alexandrovich Stroganov
About (not earlier than) April 11, 1834.
In Petersburg.
(In French)

I am very sorrowfully paying the penalty for the vain fancies of my youth. Lelewel's[1] accolade seems harsher than exile to Siberia; I thank you,[2] however, for having been so kind as to transmit to me the article in question:[3] it will serve me as the text for a sermon.

Please, Count, tell your wife[4] that I am at her feet, and accept the assurance of my high esteem.

Alexander Pushkin.

[484]
To Iosif Matveevich Penkovsky
April 13, 1834. From Petersburg to Boldino.

Father has seen fit to put at my complete disposal the management of his estate; accordingly, confirming the power of attorney which he has given you, I hereby notify you that you are to refer directly to me with regard to all business having to do with Boldino. Send me without delay an accounting of the money which has been delivered by you to my father from the time you took over the management, and also which you have received on loan and in payment of indebtedness, and next how much unsold grain remains, how much uncollected quitrent, and how much (if any) arrears. You are to proceed also with the chattel inventory of Boldino, so that the same will be ready by the month of September.[1]

April 13.
A. Pushkin.

[485]
To Ivan Ivanovich Lazhechnikov
The first half of April, 1834. From Petersburg to Tver.
(Rough draft)

With keenest gratitude I received your letter of March 30, and the manuscript about Pugachev.[1] The manuscript was already known to me; it was written by the academician Rychkov, who was in Orenburg at the time of the siege. In your copy I found several interesting additional points which I shall make use of without fail.

In passing several times through Tver, I have always wished for an opportunity to present myself to you and to thank you, in the first place, for that true pleasure which you provided me in your first novel,[2] and, in the second place, for the consideration with which you have honored me.

With impatience I await your new novel, an excellent fragment of which I have read in Maximovich's almanac.[3] Will it come out soon? And how are you thinking of publishing it? For God's sake, not in parts. These instalments are hard on the patience of the numerous people who read and esteem you.

With the most profound, etc.

[486]
To Natalia Nikolaevna Pushkina
April 17, 1834. From Petersburg to Moscow.

April 17.

How are you, little wife? How's your trip?[1] And how are Sashka and Mashka? Christ be with you! Be hale and hearty, and hurry up and get to Moscow. I am expecting a letter from you from Novgorod, but meanwhile here is an accounting of my bachelor mode of life. Day before yesterday I returned from Tsarskoe Selo at five o'clock in the afternoon and found on my table two cards, one to a ball on April 29, and an invitation to appear the following day at Litta's; I guessed that he was intending to give me a dressing down for not having been at mass. And indeed that same evening I found out from Zhukovsky, who dropped in on me, that the Sovereign has been displeased at the absence of many Chamberlains and Kammerjunkers, and that he commanded that we be informed of it. In the palace Litta harangued us with great heat, saying: *Il y a cependant pour les Messieurs de la Cour des règles fixes.* To which Naryshkin observed to him, *Vous vous trompez: c'est pour les demoiselles d'honneur.*[2] I made my excuses in writing. They say that we are going to march in pairs, like Institute girls. Just imagine that I, with my gray beard, would have to strut alongside Bezobrazov[3] or Remer[4]—nothing would induce me to do it! *J'aime mieux avoir le fouet devant tout le monde*, as M. Jourdain says.[5] This morning I was sitting in my study, reading Grimm⁶ and waiting for you, my angel, to ring,⁷ when Sobolevsky came to see me with the question of where we were going to dine. Then I remembered that I had wanted to fast and prepare for the mass, but I nevertheless had already broken the fast. Nothing could be done about it; we decided to dine at Dumé's, and meanwhile we began to bring the library into order. Your aunt came to ask about you, and learning that I was in my dressing gown and for that reason would not come out to her, she herself came in to me —I fulfilled your commission, we talked, grieved, and worried about you a little, and we decided to reiterate our requests and demands—that you take care of yourself and remember our exhortations. Then I went to Dumé's, where my appearing produced general merriment: "Bachelor, bachelor Pushkin!" They began to ply me with champagne and punch and to ask whether I wouldn't go to Sofia Ostafievna's.⁸ All that embarrassed me so that I don't intend to go to Dumé's any more, and I'm dining at home today, having ordered Stepan⁹ to bring cold fish-and-vegetable soup and *beafsteaks*.¹⁰ I spent yesterday evening at home; today I woke up at seven o'clock, and I began writing this detailed report to you. I'm sending you your mother's letter, which arrived day before yesterday. I'll write her. Meanwhile I send you a hug and a kiss, and I bless all three of you.

[487]
   To Natalia Nikolaevna Pushkina
   April 19, 1834. From Petersburg to Moscow.
 My darling, I am sending you two letters which I unsealed out of curiosity and stinginess (so as to pay less postage for weight), and also a prescription for some drops. As a favor to me, don't forget to reread Spassky's¹ instructions and to follow them. By now, little wife, you ought to be near Moscow. The farther you go, the better you feel; but, as for me! . . . Your sisters are expecting you. I can imagine everybody's joy. See to it that you don't act like a little girl. Don't forget that you already have two children, and that you have lost a third by miscarriage. Take care of yourself. Be careful. Dance in moderation. Don't overdo your fun. And, most important, hurry up and get to the village. I kiss you affectionately and bless all of you. How is Mashka? I'll bet she's really glad that she can rampage to her

heart's content! Now here's an accounting of my behavior for you. I stay at home, I dine at home, I don't see anybody, and I receive only Sobolevsky. Day before yesterday I played a fine trick on Lev Sergeevich. Sobolevsky, as if with nothing special in mind, asked him to dine at my house. Lev Sergeevich showed up. I made my excuses to him, as to a gourmet, that, not expecting him, I had ordered myself only cold fish-and-vegetable soup and *beafsteaks*.[2] Lev Sergeevich is content with that. We sit down at the table. Fine fish-and-vegetable soup is served. Lev Sergeevich gulps down two plates. He sops up the sturgeon. And then he asks for wine. He is answered that there is no wine.—"What do you mean, there's not any?"—"Alexander Sergeevich has ordered that it not be put on the table." And I state that I've been on a diet since Natalia Nikolaevna's departure—and drink water. You should have seen the despair and the sardonic laughter of Lev Sergeich, who probably won't come to dine with me again. During all this time Sobolevsky kept on adding water, now in a tumbler, now in a wineglass, now in a long goblet—and he plied Lev Sergeich with it, who kept standing on ceremony and refusing. Here's an example for you of my innocent doings. I am impatiently awaiting your letter from Novgorod, and I'll take it immediately to Katerina Ivanovna [Zagryazhskaya]. For the present—farewell, my angel. I kiss and bless all of you. Yesterday we had our first thunder—thank God, spring is over.

April 19.

[488]
To Natalia Nikolaevna Pushkina
April 20 and 22, 1834. From Petersburg to Moscow.

Friday.

My little angel wife! I have just now received your letter from Bronnitsy—and I thank you with all my heart. I shall impatiently await news from Torzhok. I hope you will get over your tiredness from the journey all right, and that in Moscow you will be healthy, merry, and beautiful. I sent your letter to Aunty, instead of taking it to her myself, because I am reporting myself as being ill, and I am afraid I might meet the Tsar. I am spending all these holidays at home. I have no intention of going to see the Heir, with congratulations and greetings; his reign is yet to come, and I probably shall not live to see it. I have seen three tsars: the first ordered my little cap to be taken off me, and gave my nurse a scolding on my account; the second was not gracious to me; although the third has saddled me with being a Kammerpage close upon my old age,[1] I have no desire for him to be replaced by a fourth.[2] Better let well enough alone. We shall see just how our Sashka will get along with his namesake born to the purple: I didn't get along with mine.[3] God grant that he not follow in my footsteps and write verses and quarrel with tsars! Then he wouldn't outshine his father in verses, but neither would he fight windmills. But now enough of nonsense; let's talk about business: Please take care of yourself, especially at first. I dislike Easter Week in Moscow. Don't heed your sisters and gad about having a good time from morning till night. Don't dance at a ball until matins. Be moderate in having your fun; go to bed early.—Don't let your father get at the children. He could frighten them and goodness knows what else.[4] Take better care of yourself during your periods. While in the village, don't read the nasty books in your grandfather's library; don't soil your imagination, little wife. I permit you to coquette to your heart's content. Don't ride horses that are too spirited (on which point I humbly beseech Dmitry Nikolaevich). In addition, I ask you not to spoil either Mashka or Sashka, and if you should not be satisfied with your German woman or wet nurse, I ask you to get rid of her immediately, without any scruples, and without standing on ceremony.

Sunday. Christ is risen, my dear little wife. I am lonesome, my angel. I am lonesome with you away. I can't get your letter out of my head. You seemed to me to have gotten too tired. You will arrive in Moscow. You will rejoice your sisters. Your nerves will be taut. You will think that you are completely well. You will stand up all night at the Easter service. And next you'll be lying all stretched out in hysterics and fever. That's what is alarming me, my angel. So much that my head is going round and round, and I can't get it off my mind. Will I be able to wait it out until you have dashed off to the village? The Grand Duke has recently taken the oath of fealty. I was not at the ceremony, because I am reporting myself ill, and I really am not very well. Kochubey[5] was made a chancellor. There is a multitude of gracious acts: six Ladies in Waiting, your friend Natalia Obolenskaya[6] among others, but still not our Mashenka Vyazemskaya.⁷ It's a pity and a vexation. The Heir was very touched; the Sovereign, too. In general, they say, all this produced a powerful effect. On the one hand I very much regret that I did not see the historical scene and that when I get old I shall not be able to speak of it as a witness. Another piece of news: Merder[8] has died. It is still a secret from the Grand Duke, and it will poison his youthful joy. Arakcheev has died, too. I am the only one in all Russia who regrets it[9]—I had not succeeded in arranging to see and have a long talk with him. Aunty has given me a chocolate billiard table—it is charming. She sends you lots of kisses and has a fit of the spleen on your account. Farewell, all my folks. Christ has risen; Christ be with you.[10]

[489]
To Natalia Nikolaevna Pushkina
April 24, 1834. From Petersburg to Moscow.

Tuesday. I thank you, my angel, for your letter from near Torzhok. You are sensible, you are well—you are feeding the children porridge —you're near Moscow. All that made me very glad and calmed me; otherwise I wouldn't be myself. We are having a noisy, stormy Easter Week. Yesterday I was at [Ekaterina Andreevna] Karamzina's, and Timiryazeva[1] and I quarreled. Today I'm going to Aunty's with your letter. Tomorrow I'll write you a lot. For the present I kiss you and bless all of you.

[490]
To Natalia Nikolaevna Pushkina
April 28, 1834. From Petersburg to Moscow.

Well, little wife! At long last we have received a letter from you. As I count it, you were to have arrived in Moscow on Maundy Thursday (and thus it happened), and for nine whole days there was no news from you. Aunty got very scared. I was more calm, knowing that you had dragged up to Torzhok all right, and supposing that the bothers of the arrival and the joys of seeing everybody would keep you from thinking about letters during your first days there. However, I had begun to feel bad, too. Thank God that you have arrived, that you and Masha are well, that Sashka is better. Probably he has recovered completely. Isn't he sick on account of his wet nurse? Order her to be examined, and wean him. It's time. Give my regards to your sisters. Ask them from me not to spoil Mashka—i.e., not to heed her tears and cries. Otherwise I won't have any peace on account of her. Take care of yourself, and, as a favor to me, don't catch cold. What's to be done with your mother? If she herself does not want to come to see you, go see her for a week or two, though that means extra expenses and extra bothers. I'm horribly afraid of family scenes for you. May the Lord remind you of King David and all his meekness!—Please do not enter into close relationships with your father, and don't show the children to him. He can't be depended on in his condition. If you don't watch out, he might bite off Mashka's little nose.[1] Now here's my most humble report. I spent Easter Week decorously at home; the only thing I did was to go yesterday (Friday) to [Ekaterina Andreevna] Karamzina's and [Alexandra Osipovna] Smirnova's. I didn't put in an appearance at the park where the swings are; tomorrow there'll be a ball,[2] at which I won't appear either. This ball is turning everybody's head, and it has become the subject of all the talk of the town. There will be eighteen hundred guests. It has been calculated that, assuming a minute per carriage, it would take ten hours for everybody to drive up. But the carriages will arrive three at a time, and consequently the time will be cut to a third. Yesterday all the city, except me, went to see the hall. Sobolevsky is here, but he borrowed fifty rubles from me, and since then he hasn't been back. Lev Sergeevich is moving today from [V. V.] Engelgardt's to our parents'. I have the honor to observe to you that your cabman asked, not for Rhine wine, but Rhenish (i.e., every white, dry, grape wine is called Rhenish). Your observation about the education of the Russian people is very just, though, and it does you honor and gives me pleasure. *Dis-moi ce que tu bois, je te dirai qui tu es.*[3] Do you drink camomile tea or *eau d'orange*? Aunty dropped in on me day before yesterday to find out about your health, and she coquetted with me from her carriage. Today I'll take your letter to her. Farewell, my angel. I kiss you, and I bless all of you. I send my regards to your sisters. . . . Oh, I'd like to let slip *une bonne plaisanterie*, but I'm afraid of you. *Addio*.

Saturday.

[491]
> To Natalia Nikolaevna Pushkina
> April 30, 1834. From Petersburg to Moscow.
>
> St. Thomas' Monday.

Yesterday the nobility ball finally was held.[1] The carriages began to drive up at six o'clock. I went out strolling around the city, and I passed by [D. L.] Naryshkin's house. A multitude of people was thronging. The police were clamoring at them. An illumination was being prepared. Without waiting until twilight, I went to the English Club, where a fantastic thing happened to me. In the club I was robbed of 350 rubles,[2] robbed not as at *tintere*, not at whist, but as people are robbed on the city squares. What do you think of our club? We've outdone even the Moscow [English Club]! You think I've been angry; not in the slightest. I'm cross at Petersburg, and I rejoice at its every loathsomeness. Returning home, I received your letter, my dear angel. Thank God you're well, the children are well, you're a good little girl, you leave the ball before the mazurka, and you're not gadding about the parishes. One thing's bad; you couldn't refrain from going to Princess Golitsyna's ball.[3] And going there is just what I asked you not to do. I don't want my wife to go where the hostess permits herself discourtesy and disrespect. You're no Mlle. Sontag,[4] who is invited to a party and then not even looked at. Moscow ladies are not my idea of a good example. Let them gad about in the anterooms of people who don't even look at them. Good enough for them. Little wife, little wife! If you don't heed me in such a trifle, then how am I to keep from thinking. . . . But God save you. You say: "I didn't go to see her; she herself came up to me." That's just what's bad. You could and should have paid her a visit, because she has a position of high honor at court and you're the wife of a Chamber Page;[5] that's an obligation of service. But there was no need for you to go to a ball at her house. I swear it vexes me—I don't even want to continue my letter.

[492]
> To Natalia Nikolaevna Pushkina
> April 30, 1834. From Petersburg to Moscow.

My dear wife, my little angel wife—I've already written you today, but somehow my letter got off on the wrong foot. I began with *Te*

Deum, but I shifted over to *De Profundis*. I began with tendernesses, and I ended with a slap in the face. Pardon me, little wife. Forgive us our debts, as we forgive our debtors. I forgive you for the ball at Golitsyna's,[1] and I'll talk to you about yesterday's ball, which all the city is talking about, and which they say was very successful. Nothing more magnificent was ever seen. It was not too crowded and there were plenty of ices; so that it would have been very good for me. But I was among the common people, and the whole city passed in front of me in carriages (except the poet Kukolnik,[2] who passed in some old *fourgon* with some sort of tattered boy footman on the box—which was a true, poetic manifestation). I'll check about the gowns and let you know. I wrote you that some money was stolen from me in the club. Don't believe it. That's low slander. The money has been found and brought to me.[3] You are wrong in thinking that I'm in Sobolevsky's clutches and that he is soiling your furniture. I don't see him at all, and I've made friends again with Sofia Karamzina. She's at a wedding today, Bakunina's.[4] There's another fine wedding: Vorontsov is getting married—to K. A. Naryshkin's daughter,[5] who has not yet had her coming-out. Now, of wealthy eligibles, only Novomlensky[6] remains, for Sorokhtin, you say, has died. Whom will he choose? Alexandra Nikolaevna [Goncharova] or Katerina Nikolaevna [Goncharova]? What do you think? You'll probably get this letter only in Yaropolets. I've already written to Natalia Ivanovna [Goncharova]. Kiss her little hands for me, and tell her a lot of tender things. Farewell, wife. I kiss and bless you, and all of you.

A.P.

[493]
To Dmitry Nikolaevich Bantysh-Kamensky
May 1, 1834. From Petersburg to Moscow.
Dear Sir, Dmitry Nikolaevich,

Permit me to express to you my most profound gratitude for the letter, a precious token of your favor, and for the photograph of the seal of the Pretender, which I immediately sent off to be engraved.[1] I have his portrait, and it, too, is being engraved. With impatience I shall await the biography of Pugachev, which you are so kind as to promise me, with such indulgence.

I regret that time does not permit me to submit my work for your examination. The opinions and observations of such a person as you would serve as guidance for me and would encourage my first historical endeavor.

With the most profound respect and complete devotion, I have the honor to be, Dear Sir,

Your Excellency's

May 1, 1834.
SPb.

Most humble servant,
Alexander Pushkin.

[494]
To Nikolay Ivanovich Pavlishchev
May 4, 1834. From Petersburg to Warsaw.

Dear Sir, Nikolay Ivanovich,

I thank you for your letter.[1] It is sensible and business-like; consequently it is not hard to answer.

When I consented to take over the management of Father's estate, I demanded a clear accounting of the indebtedness to the government and to private individuals, and of the revenues.

Father answered me that, on the entire estate, there is about 100,000 of debt, that there is about 7000 of interest to be paid, that there is about 3000 of arrears, and that there is about 22,000 of revenues.

I asked that all this be determined with more exactness, and when Father did not succeed in doing it himself, I addressed the Loan Office and ascertained that there is

Of debt to the government	190,750
Of annual interest	11,826
Of arrears	11,045
(Of debts to private individuals I estimate about	10,000)

I am unable to ascertain how much the revenues amount to, but relying on Father's word and placing it at 22,000, it will result that after payment of interest to the government up to 10,000 will be left.

If Father will assign 1500 of this money to Olga Sergeevna, and the same amount to Lev Sergeevich, then 7000 will be left for him. This ought to be enough for him. But there are the arrears to the government, the debts to private individuals, Lev Sergeevich's debts.

And Father has already received and spent part of this year's revenues.

Until I have brought these confused affairs into order and clarified them, I cannot and do not promise anything to Olga Sergeevna. My financial condition permits me to get by without taking anything from the revenues of Father's estates, but I cannot afford to add money *of my own*.

In a few days [. . .]² the 74 serfs which have not been mortgaged [. . .]² *I hope* to receive some [. . .]² thousands, if there are no judgments against the estate. Out of this money, I'll send you what Lev Sergeevich owes you.

With true respect and devotion, I remain,

Your most humble servant,
A. Pushkin.

May 4, 1834.
SPb.

I have not yet received the power of attorney³ from Father, and I have already paid, in one month, 866 [rubles] for Father and 1330 for Lev Segreevich *out of my money*: more I cannot do.

[495]
To Natalia Nikolaevna Pushkina
About May 5, 1834. From Petersburg to Yaropolets.

What's this, wife? Here it has already been five days that I haven't had any news of you. I hope that only the bothers of departure and arrival have prevented you from writing to me, and that you and the children are well. I'm writing to you at Yaropolets. I don't know where to send money for you, whether to Moscow or to Volokolamsk or to Kaluga.¹ In a few days I'll come to some decision. What shall I tell you about myself? My life is very monotonous. I dine at Dumé's about 2 o'clock, so that I won't encounter the bachelor gang. In the evening I'm usually at the club. Yesterday I was at Princess Vyazemskaya's and your Countess [Nadezhda Lvovna] Sollogub was there, too. From there I went to [V. F.] Odoevsky's, who is leaving for Reval. I often see Aunty, who's disturbed that there has been no news about you for a long time. We're having fine weather, but where you are it's probably still better. It's time for you to go to the village for medication, for baths, and for fresh air.

My angel, I have just now received your letter of the first of May. Thank you for deciding to wait until your monthly is over. This proves to me your good sense, and I love you three times as much for it. I rejoice that you're becoming prettier, although that's *du superflu*. Aunty was just now (at five o'clock) sitting with me. She sends you a kiss. The Summer Garden is full. Everybody's promenading. Countess Ficquelmont has invited me to a party. That will be my first appearance in society since your departure. I'm not paying court to Sollogub, Christ be my witness, nor to Smirnova, either. Smirnova has become horribly big-bellied and will bear within a month.[2] Everybody sends regards to you. I'll write some more tomorrow.

Don't you dare go swimming—have you gone out of your mind? Day after tomorrow I'm dining at Spassky's—and I'll complain about you. I didn't go to [Countess] Ficquelmont's, but remained at home; I have reread your letter, and now I'll go to bed. Your brother Ivan [N. Goncharov] is with me. Lev Sergeevich and my father make me very angry, and Olga Sergeevna is already beginning to make me angry. I'll turn the whole thing down[3]—and start living in clover.

[496]
To Natalia Nikolaevna Pushkina
May 12, 1834. From Petersburg to Yaropolets.

What a fool you are, my angel! Of course I'm not going to be disturbed because you let three days go by without writing me a letter, just exactly as I'm not going to be jealous if you waltz three times in a row with a cavalry guardsman. Yet it doesn't follow from this that I'm indifferent and incapable of jealousy. I sent you off from Petersburg with great anxiety; your letter from Bronnitsy has agitated me still more. But when I found out that you had reached Torzhok in good health, a mountain fell from my heart, and I haven't begun being melancholy again. Your letter is very sweet. And your fears with regard to the true reasons of my friendship for Sofia Karamzina are very pleasant for my self-esteem. I answer your questions thus: [Alexandra Osipovna] Smirnova does not go to the Karamzins'—she would not be able to climb that kind of a staircase with her big belly. I think she's already in her summer house,

Countess Sollogub does not go there, either; I saw her at Princess Vyazemskaya's. As for gallivanting, I'm not gallivanting after anybody. My head's going round and round. I rue the day I took over the estate,[1] but what could I do? I did it, not for myself, but for the children. Aunty spent yesterday with me; she sends you a kiss. Yesterday there was a big parade which, they say, didn't turn out well. The Tsar has placed the Heir under arrest.[2] They're expecting the Prussian Prince[3] here and many other guests. I hope to get by without being at a single festival. Your absence has the one advantage for me that I'm not obliged to doze at balls and glut myself on ices. I'm addressing you at Yaropolets, where you should have been since day before yesterday. I send my cordial respects to Natalia Ivanovna [Goncharova]; I kiss you and the children. Christ be with all of you.

Do you know that Princess [Ekaterina N.] Meshcherskaya and Sofia Karamzina are going abroad? Sofia has been weeping for about two weeks already. I'll probably take her as far as Kronshtadt.[4]

[497]
   To Nikolay Vasilievich Gogol
    May 13, 1834. In Petersburg.

I agree with you completely.[1] I shall go this very day to exhort Uvarov, and apropos of the death of *The Telegraph*, I shall also talk about yours.[2] From this, I shall make an imperceptible and skillful transition to the immortality awaiting him. Maybe we shall bring it off.

[498]
   To Natalia Nikolaevna Pushkina
   May 16, 1834. From Petersburg to Yaropolets.

My angel! I have not received any letters from you for a long time. Apparently you haven't had the time. Now you are probably in Yaropolets and are already getting ready for the road again. I miss you so much that, first thing you know, I'll come to you. I've spoken with Spassky about the Pyrmont waters.[1] He wishes you to take them. And he went into details with me which I don't want to write to you about by mail, because I don't want a husband's letters to his wife to circulate among the police.[2] Write me about your health

and the health of the children, whom I send a kiss and my blessing. I send my respects to Natalia Ivanovna. I send you a kiss. In a few days you'll receive letters by an *occasion*. Farewell, my darling.
May 16.

[499]
To Natalia Nikolaevna Pushkina
May 18, 1834. From Petersburg to Yaropolets.

My angel! Best wishes upon Masha's birthday.[1] I kiss you and her. God grant that she have some little teeth, and good health. I wish the same to Sasha, though it's not his name day. You haven't written me for so long, so very long, that although I dislike getting disturbed to no purpose, I am nevertheless disturbed. I should have received at least two letters from Yaropolets. Are you and the children well? Are you calm? I haven't written you, because I've been cross—not with you, but with others. One of my letters has fallen into the hands of the police,[2] and so forth. Look, little wife. I hope that you won't give my letters to anybody to make copies of. If the post has unsealed a husband's letter to his wife, then that's its affair. But there is one unpleasant thing in that: the privacy of family relationships, intruded upon in a foul and dishonorable manner. But if you are to blame, then that would be painful for me. Nobody must know what may take place between us; nobody must be received into our bedroom. Without privacy there is no family life. I write to you, not for the press. And there's no reason for you to accept the public as confidant. But I know that couldn't be. And it has been a long time since swinishness in anybody has astonished me.

Yesterday I was at a concert given for the poor in [D. L.] Naryshkin's magnificent, really magnificent, hall. What a pity that you didn't see it. They sang new music by Vielgorsky, to words by Zhukovsky. I don't see anybody. I don't go anywhere. I've set to work, and I write mornings. Without you, I'm so bored that every minute I think of setting off to see you, if only for a week. Here it's already a month I've lived without you. I'll stick it out until August. And you take care of yourself; I'm afraid of your horseback rides. I still don't know how you ride. Probably fearlessly. But do you sit firmly in the saddle? That's the question. God grant that I find you well and the children safe and sound! And spit on Petersburg, and turn in my resignation, and scamper off to Boldino, and live as a country squire! Dependency is unpleasant, especially for a man who has been independent for some twenty years. This is not a reproach to you, but muttering at my own self. I bless all of you, children.

[500]
    To Alexander Nikolaevich Mordvinov
      May 26, 1834. In Petersburg.
 Dear Sir, Alexander Nikolaevich,
 I make bold to disturb Your Excellency with a most humble request for permission for me to reprint, in one volume, my compositions in prose[1] which have been published up to now, and also for permission to provide Vilgelm Kyukhelbeker with a copy of all my compositions.[2]
 With the deepest respect, I have the honor to be, Dear Sir,
      Your Excellency's
       Most humble servant,
May 26, 1834.   Alexander Pushkin.
SPb.

[501]
    To Natalia Nikolaevna Pushkina
   About (not later than) May 29, 1834.
   From Petersburg to Polotnyany Zavod.
 I thank you, my angel, for the good news about Masha's little tooth. Now I hope she will cut the rest of them without any trouble. Now it's Sasha's turn. Why do you get things mixed up and say, "I'm not writing about myself, because that's not interesting?" It would have been better for you to have written about yourself than about [Countess] Sollogub, about whom you get all kinds of nonsense into your head—to the laughter of all honorable people, and of the police, who are reading our letters.[1] You ask what I'm doing. Nothing worth-while, my angel. However, I stay at home and work until four o'clock. I don't go out into society; I've become unaccustomed to my frock coat; I spend the evenings in the club. The books have come from Paris, and my library is growing and getting crowded. A *Ventriloque*[2] who has made me laugh until I cried, has come to us in Petersburg; I'm truly sorry that you won't get to hear

him. The bothers with regard to the estate[3] infuriate me; with your leave, it will be necessary, I'm afraid, for me to go into retirement[4] and to lay aside with a sigh my Kammerjunker court-dress uniform, which has so pleasantly flattered my self-esteem, and in which I unfortunately haven't had time to play the dandy. You're young, but you're already the mother of a family, and I'm convinced that it won't be more difficult for you to fulfill the duty of a good mother than it is for you now to fulfill the duty of an honest and good wife. Lack of independence and of order in one's domestic affairs is terrible in a household. And no successes of vanity can take the place of tranquillity and content. Here's a moral for you.—You call on me to come to you before August. I'd be glad to go to paradise, but my sins won't let me. Do you really think that swinish Petersburg is not loathsome to me? That I'm having a gay time living in it among the lampoons and denunciations to the police? You ask me about the *Peter*? It's coming along so-so. I'm accumulating materials—bringing them into order—and all at once I'll cast a bronze monument[5] which can't be dragged from one end of the city to the other, from square to square, from alley to alley. Yesterday I saw Speransky, the Karamzins, Zhukovsky, Vielgorsky, Vyazemsky—all send greetings to you. Aunty keeps on spoiling me. For my birthday she sent me a basket of melons, wild strawberries, garden strawberries—so that I'm afraid that I may meet the thirty-sixth year of my stormy life with the flux. Today I'm going to take your letter to her. Meanwhile, farewell, my darling. I am bilious; so excuse my angry letters. I send my kiss and blessing to all of you.

I am sending money in care of Dmitry Nikolaevich [Goncharov].

[502]
To Natalia Nikolaevna Pushkina
June 3, 1834. From Petersburg to Polotnyany Zavod.

What, my darling, is happening to you? This is already the ninth day that I haven't had any news of you. This disturbs me in spite of myself. Let's suppose you have left Yaropolets. All the same you could have taken time to write me a couple of lines. I haven't written you because the swinishness of the post has so chilled me that I haven't had the strength to take a pen in hand. The thought that anybody is eavesdropping on you and me *à la lettre* is driving me mad.

It's quite possible to live without political liberty; without family inviolability (*inviolabilité de la famille*) it's impossible: penal servitude is a lot better. This was written, not for you.[1] But here's what I write for you. Have you begun the mineral baths? Does Masha have any new teeth? And how did she stand cutting her first ones? Guess who is staying with me: Sergey Nikolaevich [Goncharov], who went to his brother's[2] in Tsarskoe Selo, but they quarreled, and he was compelled to flee with all his baggage. I'm very glad to have him. Checkers have been resumed. Aunty left with Natalia Kirillovna [Zagryazhskaya]. I haven't been to see her yet. Dolgorukova-Malinovskaya[3] has had a miscarriage, but she seems to be well. Today I'm dining at Vyazemsky's, whose son is having a name day; Karamzina has left, too. Have I written you that the Meshcherskys have set off for Italy, and that Sofia [Karamzina] simply gushed tears for three days together, accusing herself of hardheartedness, and feeling remorseful that she's leaving Katerina Andreevna [Karamzina] alone? I accompanied them to the steamship. Last Sunday I was presented to the Grand Duchess.[4] I went to Her Highness's on Kamenny Ostrov, in that pleasant mood in which you are accustomed to see me when I put on my magnificent full-dress uniform. But she was so pleasant that I forgot both my unhappy role and my vexation. The censor [A. I.] Krasovsky was presented together with me. The Grand Duchess said to him: *Vous devez être bien fatigué d'être obligé de lire tout ce qui paraît.—Oui, Votre Altesse Impériale*, he answered her, *d'autant plus que ce que l'on écrit maintenant n'a pas le sens commun.*[5] And I was standing beside him. She, as an intelligent woman, somehow managed to smooth it over. Smirnova is about due to have her baby. Her belly is horrible; I don't know how her delivery will be, but she is walking a lot, and she's not like what she was last year. I met Countess Sollogub not long ago. She commanded me to send you a kiss, and her aunt did the same. I'm mostly at home and in the club. I am behaving myself decently; the only thing that's not good is that my stomach has got upset and biliousness is bothering me so. But here you can't safeguard yourself against biliousness. There's no news, and even if there were, I wouldn't tell it. I kiss all of you; Christ be with all of you. My father and mother are going to the village[6] in a few days, and I'm bustling about for them. Lev [Pushkin] goes to Tsarskoe Selo on foot, and Sobolevsky to Oranienbaum. Apparently they don't have anything to do. Farewell, my angel. Don't be angry at the coldness of my letters. I'm having to force myself to write.

June 3.

[503]
To Dmitry Nikolaevich Bantysh-Kamensky
June 3, 1834. From Petersburg to Moscow.

Dear Sir, Dmitry Nikolaevich,

I do not know how to thank you enough for furnishing me with the documents regarding Pugachev.[1] Although I already had a multitude of precious materials in my hands, I found here hitherto unknown details of curious interest, which I shall utilize without fail. I have given Smirdin your excellent article about [P. I.] Panin.[2] He accepted it with thanks. Won't you consent to participate in his journal, and on what conditions?

You have probably heard about Plyushar's commercial and literary undertaking, the Russian *Conversations Lexicon*:[3] a great multitude of biographical articles prepared by you might enter into the make-up of this lexicon. Won't you enter into relationships with Plyushar? In case you will, I request that you choose me as your agent;[4] we are glad to do our best.[5]

With the most profound respect and complete devotion, I have the honor to be, Dear Sir,

Your Excellency's
Most humble servant,
Alexander Pushkin.

June 3, 1834.
SPb.

[504]
To Natalia Nikolaevna Pushkina
June 8, 1834. From Petersburg to Polotnyany Zavod.

My dear angel! I have written you a four-page letter, but it turned out to be so bitter and gloomy that I did not send it to you, and I'm writing you another. I definitely have the spleen.[1] It is boring to live without you and not even to dare to write you everything that comes into my heart.[2] You speak of Boldino. It would be good to settle down there for good, but that is hard to do. We shall have time to talk more about it. Do not be angry, wife, and do not interpret my complaints the wrong way. I have never thought of reproaching you for my dependent state. I had to marry you because without you I would have been unhappy all my life. But I did not have to enter the service, and what is still worse, to entangle myself with financial obligations. The situation of dependency caused by family life makes a man more moral. The situation of dependency which we impose on ourselves from ambition or from need lowers us. Now they look on me as a flunky, whom they may treat as they please. Disgrace is easier to bear than disdain. Like Lomonosov, I do not want to be a clown, even before the Lord God.[3] But you are not to blame in any of this. I am to blame, because of the good nature with which I am filled to the point of stupidity, notwithstanding my experience in life.

I thank you for the scales, a luxurious token of my stinginess. Aunty sent them to me without a note. Probably she is now in the midst of cares and is preparing Natalia Kirillovna for the news of the death of Prince Kochubey, who did not reach you as he had intended, but died in Moscow. I am not sending you any money yet. I have been compelled to outfit my old folks[4] for the road. I am being pestered mercilessly. Probably I shall heed you and soon give up the management of the estate. Let them make a mess of things as they please. It will suffice for their lifetime. And we shall try to leave Sashka and Mashka a piece of bread, shan't we? There is no news. [Count] Fiquelmont is ill and horribly depressed. Vielgorsky is going to Italy to his sick wife.[5] Petersburg is deserted; everybody is in summer houses. I stay at home and write until four o'clock. I dine at Dumé's. In the evening I am at the club. And that is my whole day. I took the notion, for relaxation, to play cards in the club, but I have been compelled to stop. Card playing agitates me—and my biliousness does not abate. I send my kiss and blessing to all of you. Farewell. I am expecting a letter from you about Yaropolets. But be careful . . . your letters are probably being unsealed, too. National security requires it.

[505]
To Natalia Nikolaevna Pushkina
June 11, 1834. From Petersburg to Polotnyany Zavod.

You've found something to scold about! . . . The Summer Garden[1] and Sobolevsky. To be sure, the Summer Garden is my kitchen garden. When I get up after my nap, I go there in my dressing gown and house slippers. After dinner I take a nap in it, I read and write there. I'm at home in it. And Sobolevsky? Sobolevsky is one thing, and I'm another.[2] He makes his schemes, and I make mine. My scheme is to scamper off to the village to you. What is it you write me about Kaluga? Why should you care to see it? Kaluga is a little more loathsome than Moscow, which is much more loathsome than Petersburg. What is there for you to do there? It's your sisters who are prodding you on, and probably my favorite one, at that.[3] That's just like her. I ask you, my darling, not to go to Kaluga. Stay at home. It will be better that way. Aunty's at her summer house, but I haven't been to see her yet. I'm going today with your letters. Natalia Kirillovna [Zagryazhskaya] has learned of Kochubey's death. *Je ne croyais pas*, she said, *que la mort de Kochubey me fît tant de peine*.[4] She is consoling herself that he was the one that died, and not Masha.[5] Today my folks[6] are going to the village, and I'm going to accompany them—to the carriage, not to Tsarskoe Selo, to which place Lev Sergeevich [Pushkin] goes on foot. Oh, how they have pestered me; I was reminded of you, my angel. But there is nothing else to be done. If I don't take over the estate,[7] then it will be lost, with nothing to show for it. Olga Sergeevna and Lev Sergeevich will have to be turned out to graze, and then I'll have them on my hands, and then how much grief and expense I'll have— but a lot they'll care. They'll jeer at me. Oh, my family, my family!

Please, my darling, don't make a trip to Kaluga. Whom do you want to have anything to do with there? The governor's wife?[8] She's very pleasant and intelligent, but I don't see any reason for you to go pay your respects to her. With Dmitry Nikolaevich's fiancée?[9] Now, that's a different matter. You arrange this wedding, and I'll come and be his sponsor at the wedding. Write me, little wife, how you spent your time in Yaropolets, how you got along with your mother and the others. I hope you parted in friendly fashion and didn't manage to quarrel and get jealous of each other. Here the Prussian Prince[10] is expected. Yesterday Ozerov[11] arrived from Berlin with his wife who is three embraces in girth. A real woman. Looking at her, I thought of you and wanted you to return from the Zavod just such a fat slob. Enough of your being lean as a rake. Farewell, wife. My spirits have brightened up. I've received letters from you two days in a row, and with all my heart I've become reconciled with the mails and with the police.[12] The devil take them. What are the children doing? I bless them, and I kiss you.

June 11.
The same day.

Aunty has just now left me. She asks you to write her, and me to pull your ears. She's moving to Tsarskoe Selo, to Prince Kochubey's house, along with Natalia Kirillovna [Zagryazhskaya], who is astonishingly pleasant and kind. Tomorrow I'll go say farewell to her. Why don't you write Aunty? What a scatterbrain you are! She asks me to let you go to Kaluga, but, after all, you'll dash off, even without my permission. You're gifted at that. I have just said farewell to my father and mother. He is depressed, and his thoughts are melancholy. You know what I'm thinking? Shouldn't I come to you for the summer? No, wife, there are things to be done. Let's stick it out another month and a half. And then I'll come to you like a bolt from the blue. If only they will let me. Why should you want to install your sisters in the Palace?[13] In the first place, they'll probably be refused, and in the second, if they are accepted, then think what vile talk will spread over swinish Petersburg. You're too pretty, my angel, to go in for being a petitioner. Wait a little. You'll become a widow, you'll get a little older—then go ahead and be a beggar in rags and tatters, and a titular counsellor's[14] wife. My advice to you and your sisters is to stay as far away from the Court as you can; there's little good in it. You three aren't wealthy. All of you shouldn't tumble in on Aunty. My God! If the Zavod were mine, then you wouldn't lure me to Petersburg even with a Moscow *kalač*.[15] I'd live as a country squire! But you females don't understand the happiness of independence and are ready to bind yourself to eternal servitude, just in order that it might be said about you: *Hier Madame une telle était décidément la plus belle et la mieux mise du bal.*[16] Farewell, *Madame une telle*, Aunty has sent me your letter, for which I thank you very much.

Stay well, intelligent, sweet. Don't ride on spirited horses. Look after the children so that their nursemaids will look after them. Write me oftener. Kiss your sisters for me without ado—and Dmitry Nikolaevich, too. Bless the children for me. I send you a kiss. I'm going on the steamship to accompany Vielgorsky, who probably won't find his wife alive.[17] *Peter I* is coming along; the first thing you know I'll publish the first volume by winter. I've ceased to be angry with *him*,[18] because, *toute réflexion faite*, it's not he that's to blame for the swinishness surrounding him. But if you live in a privy, in spite of yourself you'll get used to s——, and its stench won't bother you, even though you are a *gentleman*.[19] Ugh, I'd like to scamper off to where the air is fresh.

[506]
> To Natalia Nikolaevna Pushkina
> About (not later than) June 19, 1834.
> From Petersburg to Polotnyany Zavod.

I'm sad, little wife. You're sick; the children are sick. How all this will end, God knows. Here I am being pestered and infuriated without mercy. My debts and others' give me no peace. The estate is disorganized, and there is need to cut expenses and bring it into order, but they've taken cheer and begun badgering me. Now it's one thing, now it's another. Here's Spassky's letter for you.[1] If you're well, what do you need baths for? I saw Aunty a few days ago. She's going to Tsarskoe Selo. Farewell, little wife. Pletnev is coming into my room now.

A.P.

I send a kiss to all of you, and my blessing to the children.

[507]
> To Alexander Khristoforovich Benkendorf
> June 25, 1834. In Petersburg.
> (In French)

Count,

Since family matters necessitate my presence, now in Moscow, now in the interior, I am forced to retire from the service, and I beseech Your Excellency to obtain this permission for me.

I would ask, as a last favor, that the permission which His Majesty has deigned to grant me, of visiting the archives, not be withdrawn from me.[1]

I am, respectfully,
Count,
Your Excellency's
Most humble and most obedient servant,
Alexander Pushkin.

June 15.[2]
St. Petersburg.

[508]
To Natalia Nikolaevna Pushkina
About (not later than) June 27, 1834.
From Petersburg to Polotnyany Zavod.

"Your Honor, you always deign to yowl about nothing" (*The Adolescent*).[1]

For pity's sake, what indeed are you scolding me about? Because I missed one post? But, after all, we have the post every day, so that you can write as much as you please and when you please. It's not the way it is from Kaluga, from which letters come every ten days. Your next to the last letter was so sweet that I would have given you a good kissing, and this one is so scatterbrained that I'd like to pull your ears. I'll answer you point by point. When I was presented to the Grand Duchess,[2] the Lady in Waiting on duty was not [Countess] Sollogub, but my cousin by marriage Chicherina,[3] whom I'm not very fond of, and even if Sollogub had been on duty, why then if one is to fall in love.... ——— Oh, little wife! The post prevents, otherwise I would really give you an earful. I wrote you that I've become unaccustomed to a frock coat, and you try to catch me in a lie as in a *petite misère ouverte*,[4] adducing as evidence that I saw this person and that person, and consequently I am going out in society. That doesn't prove anything. The main thing is that I've again become accustomed to Dumé's and to the English Club—and that's nothing to brag about. Smirnova has been delivered successfully, and just imagine: of twins. What do you think of the little woman, and what of the red-eyed rabbit, Smirnov? They so fashioned the first child that he couldn't get out, and this time they had to divide it into two.[5] Today is I think the ninth day—and the report is that the mother and children are well. You write me that you're thinking of marrying off Katerina Nikolaevna to Khlyustin,[6] and Alexandra Nikolaevna to Ubri.[7] Nothing of the sort will happen. Both men will fall in love with you. You are hindering your sisters—because one must be your husband, to court others in your presence, my beauty. Khlyustin is lying to you, and you even believe him. Where does he get the notion that I won't come to you in August? Can it be that he was drunk on cold-fish-and-vegetable-soup-with-onions? One thing is keeping me in Petersburg: mortgaging the Nizhny Novgorod estate.[8] I even intend to entrust my Pugachev to [M. L.] Yakovlev,[9] and tear off to Polotnyany Zavod to you, my angel.

That's where I'd like to scamper away from life, to slip away to! I send you and the children a kiss, and I send my blessing to all of you with all my heart. I'll bet you have grown so good-looking in the village that nobody ever heard of the like. Thank you for the anecdote about Dmitry Nikolaevich.[10] Hasn't he fallen in love? Aunty's in Tsarskoe Selo. I'm going to see her in a few days. *Addio, vita mia; ti amo.*[11]

[509]
    To Natalia Nikolaevna Pushkina
 About June 28, 1834. From Petersburg to Polotnyany Zavod.
 My angel, I have just now sent Count Litta an excuse to the effect that I cannot be at the Petergof celebration,[1] on account of illness. I'm sorry that you won't see it; it's worth seeing. I don't even know whether you'll ever succeed in seeing it. I'm thinking strongly about resigning.[2] We must think about our children's fate. My father's estate, as I have ascertained, is in disorder to the point of impossibility, and only by strict economy can it be straightened out. I may have large sums, but we run through a lot, too. If I were to die today, what would happen to you? It's little consolation that they would bury me in a striped caftan and in the crowded Petersburg cemetery, at that, and not in a church in the open spaces as is fitting for a decent person.[3] You're an intelligent and good woman. You understand what necessity is. Let me become wealthy—and then perhaps we might go on a spending spree to our hearts' content. Petersburg is horribly boring. They say that the world is living on the Petergof road. On Chernaya Rechka are only Bobrinskaya[4] and [Countess]

Ficquelmont. They recieve—but nobody comes. There will be great celebrations after Petergof. But I certainly won't go anywhere. One thing is holding me here: the printing house.[5] My error, one more thing: the mortgaging of the estate.[6] But will it be possible to mortgage it? How right you were, that I ought not to have taken onto myself all these bothers, for which nobody will say thanks, and which have already spoiled so much of my blood that all the leeches in our house couldn't suck it out for me. Apropos of our house: I must tell you that I've quarreled with our landlord,[7] and here's why. A few days ago I was returning home at night. The doors were locked. I knocked and knocked; I rang and rang. With difficulty I at long last succeeded in awakening the yardman. And I had already told him several times not to lock up before I come in. In my anger with him I gave him a father's punishment. The next day I discovered that Olivio was declaiming against me in his yard and had ordered the yardman not to heed me but to lock up the doors about 10 o'clock, so that thieves won't steal the staircases. I immediately ordered that an announcement be nailed to the doors, written in Sergey Nikolaevich's hand, that the apartment is for rent—and I wrote Olivio a letter which the fool hasn't answered up to now. My war with the yardman hasn't ceased, and yesterday I had some trouble with him again. I'm sorry for him, but there's nothing to be done. I'm stubborn, and I want to out-argue the whole household—including thereby even the leeches. I'm entirely at fault toward you, with regard to money. There was money ... and I lost it at cards. But what was I to do? I was so bilious that I had to amuse myself with something. He[8] is to blame for everything. But God forgive him. If he would only let me go to my estate. Your letter isn't before me. It seems that there's something that I'm obliged to object to—but until tomorrow. Meanwhile, farewell. I kiss you and the children, I bless all three. Farewell, my darling. Give my regards to your sisters and brothers. Sergey Nikolaevich was commissioned an officer a few days ago,[9] and he's fussing about, getting a full-dress uniform.

A.P.

[510]
To Natalia Nikolaevna Pushkina
June 30, 1834. From Petersburg to Polotnyany Zavod.

Your Shishkova[1] was mistaken: I have not been paying court to her daughter Polina, because I haven't seen her. But I made a trip to the Academy, to see Alexander Semenovich Shishkov, and I did that, not for a wedding, but for jettons,[2] *pas autrement*.[3] The story about the princesses[4] is entirely correct, but I don't see anything funny in it. Thank you for your sweet, very sweet letter. Of course, my dear, there's no consolation in my life except you—and to live separated from you is just as stupid as it is hard to bear. But what can be done? After tomorrow I'll begin printing my *Pugachev*, which has been lying at Speransky's[5] until now. It will delay me about a month. In August I'll be with you. Tomorrow is the Petergof celebration, but I'll spend it in Pletnev's summer house with him alone. We'll drink to your health. I have quarreled with our landlord, Olivio, once and for all, and we'll have to have another apartment, especially if your sisters come with you. Sergey [N. Goncharov] is still with me; yesterday he came to see me in his officer's full-dress uniform, and he's a fine-looking fellow. The story of how Ivan Nikolaevich quarreled with Yuriev[6] and how they became reconciled is killingly funny, but it would take too long to tell it to you. I have discomfiting news from the village. The new manager whom I sent found everything in such disorder that he refused the management and left.[7] I'm thinking of following his example. He's an intelligent man; Boldino could muss up five more years.

Farewell, little wife. I thank you for promising not to coquette. Even though I have permitted you to do that, all the same it's better not to make use of my permission. I am glad that Sashka has been weaned. It was long overdue. And that the wet nurse would get drunk as she would go off to sleep—that's no misfortune, either. The boy will get used to wine, and will be a fine fellow and favor Lev Sergeevich [Pushkin]. Tell Mashka not to be capricious, or else I'll come, and it'll be bad for her. I bless all of you—I kiss you especially.

June 30.

Please don't demand tender love letters of me. The thought that my letters are being unsealed and read in the post, among the police, and so on, numbs me, and I'm dry and boring in spite of myself. Just you wait. I'll go into retirement, and then corresponding won't be necessary.

[511]
To Mikhail Lukianovich Yakovlev
July 3, 1834. In Petersburg.

Dear Sir, Mikhaylo Lukianovich,[1]

In consequence of the commission which the authorities have entrusted to you with regard to the publishing of my manuscript, entitled *The History of the Pugachev Revolt*, and in accordance with my conversation in person with you on this matter, I hasten to inform you:

1st. I desire that the aforesaid manuscript be printed in 8-vo, with the same kind of format as *The Code of Laws*.

2nd. I fix the number of copies at 3000; I request that paper for 1200 of them be stocked at government expense, and I shall myself deliver to the printing house the necessary quantity of paper for 1800 copies.

3rd. As for the type font and the publishing of the book in general, I rely on your discretion for everything.

I have the honor to be, with the most profound respect,

Dear Sir,

Your most obedient servant,
Alexander Pushkin.

July 3, 1834.
SPb.

[512]
To Alexander Khristoforovich Benkendorf
July 3, 1834. In Petersburg.
(In French)

Count,

Several days ago I had the honor to make application to Your Excellency, in order to obtain permission to retire from the service. This step being improper, I beseech you, Count, not to act upon it. I prefer seeming inconsistent to seeming ungrateful.[1]

However, a leave of absence of several months would be absolutely necessary for me.

    I am, respectfully,
      Count,
        Your Excellency's
          Most humble and most obedient servant,

July 3.   Alexander Pushkin.

[513]
              To Vasily Andreevich Zhukovsky
   July 4, 1834. From Petersburg to Tsarskoe Selo.

When I received your letter, I immediately wrote to Count Benkendorf, asking him to stop my retirement, *ma démarche étant inconsidérée*, and I said *que j'aimais mieux avoir l'air inconséquent qu'ingrat*.[1] But after this I received official notification that I shall receive my retirement, but that access to the archives will be forbidden me.[2] This grieved me in all respects. I submitted my resignation in a moment of spleen and vexation at everybody and everything. My domestic circumstances are difficult. My position is not a cheering one. A change in my mode of living is almost a necessity. I lacked the courage to explain all this to Count Benkendorf—and for this reason my letter must have seemed dry; whereas, it was simply stupid.

But I certainly had no intention of bringing about what has resulted. I don't dare, I swear, to write a letter directly to the Sovereign[3]—especially now. My justifications would be like petitions, and he has already done so much for me. Lizaveta Mikhaylovna [Khitrovo] has just now gone from me. She brought me your two further letters. This, of course, touches me. But just what am I to do! I shall write again to Count Benkendorf.

[514]
            To Alexander Khristoforovich Benkendorf
                 July 4, 1834. In Petersburg.

Dear Sir, Count Alexander Khristoforovich,

I was honored with receiving last evening Your Excellency's letter of June 30.[1] I am extremely grieved that my ill-considered petition, forced from me by unpleasant circumstances and vexing petty cares, could appear to be insane ingratitude and opposition to the will of him who has until now been rather my benefactor than Sovereign. I shall await the determination of my fate, but in any case nothing will change the feeling of my deep devotion to the Tsar or my filial gratitude for his previous favors.

With the most profound respect and complete devotion, I have the honor to be, Dear Sir,

Your Excellency's
Most humble servant,
Alexander Pushkin.

July 4, 1834.
SPb.

[515]
To MIKHAIL LUKIANOVICH YAKOVLEV
July 5, 1834. In Petersburg.
Here, my benefactor, is the first chapter for you[1]—God speed it.

[516]
To VASILY ANDREEVICH ZHUKOVSKY
July 6, 1834. From Petersburg to Tsarskoe Selo.
I myself truly don't know what's happening to me. What crime—what ingratitude—is there in going into retirement when my circumstances, the future fate of my family, and my own peace of mind demand it? But the Sovereign is nevertheless able to see in this something resembling what I cannot understand. In that case I do not submit my resignation, but I ask to be left in the service. Now, why are my letters dry? And just why should they be running like snot? In the depths of my heart I feel myself in the right toward the Tsar. His wrath grieves me, but the worse my position is, the more tongue-tied and numb-tongued I become. What am I to do? Ask forgiveness? All right. But for what? I'll go see Benkendorf and explain to him what I have on my heart—but I don't know wherein my letters are improper. I'll try to write the third.[1]

[517]
>
> To ALEXANDER KHRISTOFOROVICH BENKENDORF
> July 6, 1834. In Petersburg.
> (In French)

Count,

Permit me to speak to you with open heart. In asking to retire,[1] I was thinking only of troublesome and distressing family affairs. I had in view only the inconvenience of being obliged to make a number of trips while attached to the service. I swear on my God and on my soul that that was my only thought; it gives me profound sorrow to see it interpreted so cruelly. The Emperor has showered me with favors since the first moment his royal thought directed itself upon me. Among these favors are some which I cannot think of without profound emotion, for he placed so much straightforwardness and generosity in them. He has always been my providence, and if in the course of these eight years I have happened to murmur, never, I swear it, has a feeling of bitterness been mixed with those feelings which I have pledged toward him. And at this moment, not the idea of losing an all-powerful protector fills me with sorrow, but that of leaving in his mind an impression which, fortunately, I have not deserved.

I repeat, Count, my most humble entreaty that the request which I so thoughtlessly made not be acted upon.

Commending myself to your powerful protection, I make bold to present to you the assurance of my high esteem.

I am, respectfully,
Count,
Your Excellency's
Most humble and most obedient servant,
Alexander Pushkin.

July 6.
SPb.

[518]
>
> To MIKHAIL NIKOLAEVICH ZAGOSKIN
> July 9, 1834. From Petersburg to Moscow.

Dear Sir, Mikhaylo Nikolaevich,

You were kind enough to remember me, and you sent me your

most recent, excellent work,[1] but you have not heard any thanks from me. You have the full right to consider me an ignoramus, a barbarian, and an ingrate, But my friend Sobolevsky is to blame, who every day says he is off for Moscow—but it is already more than six months since he took from me the letter which he promised to deliver to you without delay.[2]

I apply to you about an important matter. M. Alexandre, a very noteworthy person (or even persons)[3] is planning to go to Moscow, and he offers you the following conditions: the gross receipts for the performances to be halved with the management (the expenses of the performance at its expense) and a benefit performance. Honor me with your answer and console little Mother Moscow.

With the most profound esteem and complete devotion, I have the honor to be, Dear Sir,

Your Excellency's
Most humble servant,

July 9.   Alexander Pushkin.

[519]
To Natalia Nikolaevna Pushkina
July 11, 1834. From Petersburg to Polotnyany Zavod.

You, my little wife, are most featherbrained (I had trouble in writing the word). Now you get angry with me over [Countess] Sollogub, now over the briefness of my letters, now over my cold style, now because I don't come to you. Think everything over, and you'll see that toward you I'm not only in the right, but you might even say a saint. I'm not coquetting with Sollogub, because I don't see her at all. I write briefly and coldly on account of circumstances which you are well aware of.[1] I don't come to you on account of business affairs, for I'm printing *Pugachev*, and I'm mortgaging the estates, and I'm in the midst of cares and bothers. And your letter grieved me, but at the same time it gladdened me, too. If you cried from not receiving a letter from me, it follows that you still love me, little wife. For that I kiss your little hands and feet.

If you could see how diligent I have become; how I am reading proofs—how I am hurrying Yakovlev along! Only that I may be with you in August. Now I'll tell you about yesterday's ball. I was at the Ficquelmonts'. You must bear in mind that since your departure I have not been going anywhere except to the club. Here yesterday, when I entered the illuminated hall, with the elegantly dressed ladies, I was as full of confusion as a German professor; with difficulty I found the hostess, with difficulty I muttered a few words. Then I looked things over and saw that not all that many people were there, and that the ball was one without ceremony and not a rout.[2] There were several Prussian ladies whom I didn't know (our ladies are better looking, to say nothing of you), and dressed like Ermolova[3] in desperate days. Then I ate my fill of ices, and I came home—at one. I don't think there's anything to chide me about. In society they inquire about you a lot, and are eagerly awaiting you. I tell them that you went off to Kaluga to dance. All praise you for that. And they say: "'At a girl!" And my heart rejoices. Aunty dropped in to see me yesterday, and she chatted with me in her carriage. I complained to her about my mode of living, and she consoled me. A few days ago I came within a hair's breadth of committing a disastrous thing: I came within a hair's breadth of quarreling with *him*. And how I had to show the white feather! And I became depressed.[4] If I quarrel with this one—I won't live to see another. But I can't be angry with him long—even though he's not in the right. Today I was at Pletnev's summer house; it was his daughter's[5] name day. Only instead of him, I found his one-eyed girl cousin[6]—and nothing else. He had left for Oranienbaum—to teach the Grand Duchess.[7] It was vexing, but there was nothing to be done. Farewell, little wife—I'm sleepy. I send you and the children a kiss—and my blessing to all of you. Christ be with you.

July 11.

[520]
To Praskovia Alexandrovna Osipova
June 29 and July 13, 1834. From Petersburg to Trigorskoe.
(In French)

I thank you with all my heart, dear, good, and kind Praskovia Alexandrovna, for the letter which you were so kind as to write me. I see that you still keep the same friendship and the same interest in me. I am going to answer you frankly, as to what regards Reichman. I know him to be an honest man, and for the moment that is all I need. I cannot have confidence in either Mikhail[1] or Penkovsky, seeing that I know the first and do not know the second. Having no intention to to go Boldino and settle down, I cannot even consider restoring an estate, which, be it said between us, is bordering on complete ruin. I wish only not to be robbed, and to pay the interest to the Loan Office. The improvements will come later. But be calm: Reichman has just written me that the peasants are in such a state of misery and affairs are in such bad condition, that he could not undertake the administering of Boldino, and that at this moment he is at Malinniki.[2]

You cannot imagine how much administering this estate is weighing on me. There is no doubt that Boldino deserves to be saved, if only for Olga and Lev, who have for their prospect beggary or, at the very least, poverty. But I am not rich. I have a family of my own dependent on me, and which without me would fall into destitution. I have taken an estate which will produce only anxieties and unpleasantnesses. My parents do not know that they are on the verge of total ruin. If they could take it upon themselves to remain for several years at Mikhaylovskoe, affairs might be managed, but that will never be.

I am counting on seeing you this summer,[3] and as a matter of course, to stop at Trigorskoe. Please present my regards to all your family and accept once more my thanks and the expression of my respect and unalterable friendship.

June 29.   A.P.
SPb.

July 13. This letter should have been at your house two weeks ago. I do not know why it is not yet on its way. My affairs will keep me in Petersburg for some time yet. But I still plan to present myself at your door.

[521]
            To Natalia Nikolaevna Pushkina
            About (not later than) July 14, 1834.
            From Petersburg to Polotnyany Zavod.

You want to know without fail whether I'll be at your feet soon? Gladly, my beauty. I'm mortgaging my father's estate; that will be finished within a week. I'm publishing *Pugachev*; that will take a whole month. Little wife, little wife, have patience until the middle of August, and then how I'll come to you and embrace you and what a kissing I'll give the children! Do you really think that I like bachelor life so terribly much? I sleep and dream of coming to you. And if only I might remain in one of your villages near Moscow, I would light a candle to God; I'd be glad to go to heaven, but my sins won't permit me.[1] Let me make some money, not for myself but for you. I have little love for money—but I esteem in it the sole means of decent independence. And about which neighbor are you writing me arch letters? With whom are you frightening me? From here I can see what sort of thing it is. A man of some thirty-six years. A retired military man or a civil servant in an elective post. With a paunch and in a military cap. He has three hundred souls and he's en route to remortgage them—on account of a poor harvest. And on the eve of departing he sentimentalizes in front of you. Isn't this correct? And you, my little wench, for lack of *him*[2] or another, choose even him as an adorer: good going. And how is it that balls have not palled on you, that you go even to Kaluga for them. Astonishing!—I must talk to you about my woe. A few days ago the spleen took possession of me; I submitted my resignation. But I received such a tongue-lashing from Zhukovsky and such a dry dismissal from Benkendorf that I had to show the white feather, and I am begging for Christ's and God's sake that they not retire me. And you're even glad of it, aren't you? All right, if I live twenty-five more years; but if I curl up my toes in less than ten, I don't know what you'll do, and what Mashka and especially what Sashka will say. There will be little consolation for them in little papa's having been buried as the court jester and in their little mama's having been terribly pretty at the Anichkov balls.[3] Well, there's nothing to be done. God is great; the most important thing is that I don't want them to be able to suspect me of ingratitude. That's worse than liberalism.[4] Stay well. Kiss the children and bless them for me. Farewell; I send you a kiss.

A.P.

[522]
To Natalia Nikolaevna Pushkina
July 14, 1834. From Petersburg to Polotnyany Zavod.
All you ladies are cut to the same pattern. How very interesting

are the little fool D.'s[1] adventures and his family quarrels! But how glad you are of them. How you've burst out coquetting, too, I'll bet. How about Kaluga? So you will reign there a while? Little wife, I'm not chiding you for that, though. All that's in the nature of things. Be young, because you are young—and reign, because you're beautiful. I kiss you with all my heart. Now let's talk about a serious matter. If you really have taken the notion of bringing your sisters here, then it's impossible for us to remain at Olivio's.[2] There's no room. But are you bringing both your sisters? Hey, little wife, look here. ... My opinion is that a family must be *alone* under *one* roof: the husband, the wife, the children while they're small; the parents, when they have become very aged. Otherwise there will be no end of bothers, and there'll be no domestic tranquillity. We'll talk some more about this, though. Yakovlev promises to let me go to you in August. I'll leave *Pugachev* in his care. August is close. Thank God, we've waited it out. I hope you're pure and innocent toward me and that we'll meet as we parted. It seems to me that you are beginning to like Sashka. I am glad. He's a lot nicer than Mashka, who'll lead you a merry dance. Smirnova again came within a hair's breadth of dying. She became angry with the doctor, and her blood rushed to her head; thank God it wasn't her milk.[3] She's receiving now, but I haven't been to see her yet. Today there are fireworks—Sergey Nikolaevich [Goncharov] is going to see them, but I'll stay in the city. With us it's the third day of terrific heat—and we don't know what to do. I sleep and dream of getting away from Petersburg to you. But you don't believe me, and you scold me. Today I'll make a trip to Pletnev's. We'll talk about you. I'm having great bothers with regard to Boldino. In a year I'll spit on the whole thing—and I'll get busy on my own affairs. Lev Sergeevich is behaving very badly. Of money, he doesn't have a single kopek, but he loses fourteen bottles of champagne at a time at dominoes at Dumé's. I don't say anything to him, because, thank God, the fellow is thirty. But I'm sorry for him, and I'm vexed. Sobolevsky is directing him, and just what they do, God only knows. Both are empty-headed enough. Aunty is in Tsarskoe Selo. I keep on planning to go to see her, but I don't ever get there. Farewell. I hug you tight—I bless the children —you, too. Do you pray every day, standing in the corner?

July 14.

[523]
To Natalia Nikolaevna Pushkina
About (not later than) July 26, 1834.
From Petersburg to Polotnyany Zavod.

My angel Natasha, do you know what? I'm taking the story[1] now being occupied by the Vyazemskys. The Princess is going abroad; her daughter[2] is seriously ill; they're afraid it's consumption. God grant that the South help her. Today I dreamed she had died, and I awoke in horror. For God's sake, take care of yourself. Woman, says Galiani, *est un animal naturellement faible et malade*.[3] What kind of helpers or workers are the lot of you? You work only with your little feet at balls, and you help your husband squander. And thank you for that. Please don't be angry with me because I'm slow in coming to you. Truly, my soul is longing, but my purse forbids. I'm working my pants off.[4] I'm reading the proofs of the two volumes[5] at once, writing notes, mortgaging villages—sending Lev Sergeich packing to Georgia.[6] I'll take care of everything—and I'll come galloping headlong to you.—Just now proofs were brought to me, and I left you for *Pugachev*. I have read in the proofs that "Pugachev entrusted to Khlopusha the plundering of the factories."[7] I'm entrusting to you the plundering of the Factories—do you hear, my Khlo-Pushkina? Plunder the Factories and return with the booty.[8] I don't go out in society. Smirnova has commanded that I be told that she's writing me into the category of foreigners who are not to be received. She's well, but she came within a hair's breadth of dying (*animal naturellement faible et malade*). I kiss Masha, and I laugh at her pranks, sight unseen. She's an intelligent wench. But for the time being it's not intelligence I want of her, but health. Are you satisfied with your German woman and the wet nurse? You did badly in not getting rid of the wet nurse. How can you believe the promises and tears of a drunkard, and keep her with the children? Hush, I'll settle all that. Nine sheets remain between me and you. That is, when I have examined nine printed sheets and have written at the bottom *print*, then I'll dash off to you. And meanwhile I'll request a leave of absence. There is no news of any kind—except that poor Marshal Maison[9] came very near to getting crushed to death on maneuvers. See what fine fellows ours are! I kiss you and them. The Lord bless all of you.

[524]
To Natalia Nikolaevna Pushkina
About (not later than) July 30, 1834.
From Petersburg to Polotnyany Zavod.

What does this mean, wife? Here it's already more than a week since I've received any letters from you. Where are you? How are you? In Kaluga? In the village? Respond. What could so occupy and amuse you? What balls? What conquests? You aren't ill, are you? Christ be with you. Or do you simply want to make me hurry and come to you? Please, little wife, away with these military stratagems which, all joking aside, torment me, seven hundred miles away from you. I'll come to you as soon as Yakovlev lets me off. My affairs are progressing well. The two volumes[1] are being printed at once. For one week's difference, don't make me abandon everything and then moan a whole year, if not two or three. Be sensible. I'm very busy. I work all morning—until four o'clock—and I don't allow anybody in to see me. Then I dine at Dumé's. Next I play billiards in the club. I return home early, hoping to find a letter from you—and every day I'm disappointed. How lonesome I am.

I've already come to an agreement with Prince Vyazemsky. I'm taking his apartment.[2] By August 10 I'll have 2500 rubles laid up for him. I'll have our things moved, and I myself will gallop off to you. There's not long to wait.

Farewell. All of you, keep well. I kiss your portrait,[3] which somehow seems at fault. Look to it ——

[525]
To Natalia Nikolaevna Pushkina
August 3, 1834. From Petersburg to Polotnyany Zavod.

You ought to be ashamed, little wife. You get angry with me, without investigating which is at fault—I or the post—and you leave me for two weeks without any news about you and the children. I have been so disturbed that I haven't known what to think. Your letter calmed me, but it didn't console me. The description of your trip to Kaluga, however comic, is not at all amusing to me. Why should you want to gad about to a foul, provincial little town, in order to see vile actors vilely performing an old, vile opera? Why should you want to stop at an inn, go visiting merchants' daughters, observe with the mob the provincial fireworks, when in Petersburg you would never even think of paying any attention to the Karatygins[1] and you wouldn't be lured into a carriage by any fireworks. I asked you not to make trips to any Kalugas, but that's apparently just the kind of nature you have. There's nothing for me to say with regard to your coquettish relationships with your neighbor. I myself gave you permission to coquette—but I don't at all need to read a sheet covered on both sides with detailed description of it. After chiding you, I take you tenderly by the ears and kiss you—thanking you that you pray to God on your knees in the middle of the room. I pray to God too little, and I hope that your pure prayer is better than my prayers are, both for me and for us. You are expecting me at the beginning of August. Here it's already the third now, and I still am not getting under way; Yakovlev will let me off about the middle of the month. But even then I won't be completely free. I've taken the Vyazemskys' apartment.[2] I'll have to move myself and the furniture and books, and then I'll cross myself and set off on the trip. God grant that I arrive by your name day;[3] that would make me happy.

The Vyazemskys are here. Poor Polina[4] is very weak and pale. It's pitiful to look at her father. How crushed he looks. They're all going abroad. God grant that the climate may help her. Maria [Vyazemskaya] has grown prettier, and in poor and slighted Moscow she has produced a great effect. Talk is still clattering about you, after your momentary appearance. They found that you had become thin—I'll bring you back a fat slob, as you promised. Look to it! Don't make a liar of me. A few days ago I met Mme. George. She stopped me on the street and asked about your health; I said that in a few days I'm going to you *pour te faire un enfant*. She began to curtsey, and said over and over: *Ah, Monsi, vous me ferez une grande plaisir*.[5] However, I'm afraid of a lying-in for you, after you've had a miscarriage. I hope, however, that you've rested up. I've seen Smirnoya; she's begun to recuperate, but she looks bad and yellow. Aunty has returned from Tsarskoe Selo, and she has been to see me. She's very sweet, but she has become completely fed up with Natalia Kirillovna [Zagryazhskaya]. Natalia Kirillovna is angry with everybody, especially with Prince Kochubey: how could he die and thereby grieve her Masha?[6] She pouts at the Princess, too, and says: *Mon Dieu, mais nous toutes nous avons perdu nos maris et cependant nous nous sommes consolées.*[7] Aunty says that you don't write her at all. That's not good. And she is always putting herself to trouble for you. Sergey [Goncharov] is in camp. I do not see your brother Ivan. Farewell; Christ be with you. I kiss all of you, you especially. They've brought some proof sheets.[8]

August 3.

[526]
     To Mikhail Lukianovich Yakovlev
 About (not later than) August 12, 1834. In Petersburg.

And just why? Voltaire was a very respectable man, and his relations with Catherine are a matter of history.[1]

[527]
     To Mikhail Lukianovich Yakovlev
 Between August 10 and 20, 1834. In Petersburg.

Here's the eighteenth sheet.[1] I've checked it against the other copies,[2] and I didn't find any sense there, either. Voltaire's name (you're right, favorite of the Muses!)[3] will have to be removed from the Preface,[4] though I love him very much.

Notes to Part XI

Letter 476
1. As a result of this letter and a visit to Benkendorf, Pushkin received from the Tsar a loan of twenty thousand rubles, to pay for the publication of his *History of Pugachev*.

Letter 477
1. Stepan Dmitrievich Nechaev (1792-1860) was the Head Procurator of the Holy Synod, and also a poet and archaeologist.
2. Fedor Fedotovich Lebedev. This letter gives another instance of Pushkin's generous willingness to use his influence in favor of almost anyone who sought it.

Letter 478
1. This letter is Pushkin's official request for a loan for the publication of his *History of Pugachev*. It was written after Pushkin's personal conference with Benkendorf on February 26. See Letter 476.

Letter 478a
1. This letter was discovered and first published in 1956. It is the only letter which has been so far discovered, from Pushkin to Countess Vorontsova. Pushkin had been in love with her in 1824 ("Elise" is included in his "Don Juan List"), but their relationships are still not entirely clear. Pushkin is responding to Countess Vorontsova's letter of December 26, 1833, in which she requested something from his pen for an almanac sponsored by her for the benefit of the poor in Odessa. Countess Vorontsova's letter was signed, almost illegibly, "E. Wilbemans[?]," which has been interpreted as being an anagram of her name. Pushkin recognized her handwriting or deciphered the anagram, and he fulfilled her request, in the midst of his fuming over being made a Kammerjunker, and in his concern over the health of his pregnant wife—who had a miscarriage on the night of this letter (see Letter 481). Under the entirely "correct" words can be sensed a warm personal attachment.

What work Pushkin sent Countess Vorontsova is not known. Perhaps it was his *Rusalka*, which he was working on at this time, and which he never finished. Pushkin's manuscript arrived too late for inclusion in Countess Vorontsova's almanac, which was signed by the censorship on March 8, 1834.

Letter 479
1. Pushkin and Odoevsky attended, at Grech's invitation, a meeting at Grech's house to discuss participation in the compilation of *The Encyclopedic Lexicon*, to be published by the Petersburg bookseller Adolf Plyushar and edited by Grech. The encyclopedia was, planned for twenty-four volumes, of which only seventeen ever appeared (1835-1841). See Letter 480.

Letter 480
1. *The Encyclopedic Lexicon* (see Letter 479). Pushkin calls it by the title of the famous *Konversations-Lexikon*, published by Brockhaus in Leipzig in 1809.
2. That is, of the literary proletariat, in contradistinction to the literary aristocracy, to which Pushkin and Odoevsky belonged.
3. Pushkin and Odoevsky attended the meeting at Grech's and both agreed to par-

ticipate in the compilation of the encyclopedia, but they made such reservations that their participation was rejected. Pushkin speaks of the meeting and enterprise in his diary (under March 17) as follows: "Yesterday at Grech's there was a literary conference concerning the publication of a Russian *Konversations Lexikon*. Of us there were about a hundred great Russian people, most of whom were unknown to me. Grech told me as a preliminary, 'Plyushar in this business is a charlatan, and I am his stooge: I drink his medicine and praise him.' Thus it turned out. I detected much charlatanry and very little sense. An enterprise of a million rubles, but I see nothing to be gained from it. I do not speak yet of honor. But why should one want to crawl into the slough where Bulgarin, Polevoy, and Sviniin are splashing about." In commenting about the "exclusion" of Odoevsky, Pushkin, and others who had made reservations about participating in the encyclopedia, Pushkin in his diary (under April 2), adds: "An honorable man, says Odoevsky, can be deceived once, but only a fool is deceived a second time. This lexicon will be nothing but *The Northern Bee* and *A Library for Reading*, with a new arrangement and scope."

Letter 481

1. Nashchokin had finally abandoned his gypsy mistress, Olga Andreevna, and had married Vera Alexandrovna Narskaya.

2. V. V. Nashchokin.

3. The terms have to do with card playing: fifteen times the stake and twice the stake, respectively.

4. On March 4, 1834. Pushkin's account of it in his diary, under the date of March 6, is as follows: "Thank God! Carnival has ended, and, with it, the balls. A description of the last day of Carnival (March 4) will give an understanding of the others. Selected ones were invited to the palace for a matinee ball, at 12:30. Others, to the evening ball, at 8:30. I arrived at 9. They were dancing the mazurka, with which the matinee ball was ending. The ladies were assembling, and those who had been in the palace since morning changed their finery. There was a world of displeased ones; the ones who were invited for the evening envied the matinee lucky ones. . . . All this ended with my wife having a miscarriage. That's what all the dancing led to."

5. Mme. Goncharova was living on the estate Polotnyany Zavod, together with her still unmarried daughters, Alexandra Nikolaevna Goncharova and Ekaterina N. Goncharova.

6. Iosif Matveevich Penkovsky (d. 1885 or 1886), manager of Boldino.

7. Pushkin was made Kammerjunker on December 31, 1833. At this time, this rank was given to young nobles in their early twenties. Pushkin felt insulted that this rank was conferred upon him instead of the superior rank of Chamberlain, a rank which his friend Vyazemsky and his Lyceum classmate Korf, for example, already had. Pushkin had not attained a rank in government service commensurate with his age; his official rank in the service was allowed by the Tsar to determine the court rank given him. Pushkin's humiliation and his fury at this "honor" are clear in subsequent letters.

Letter 482

1. The Moscow Society of Lovers of Russian Literature. Pushkin had been elected a member in 1829 (see Letter 269). Pogodin had been insisting that Pushkin send the Society one of his poems to be read there before it would appear in print.

2. Pushkin's attack on Bulgarin, in the guise of an article on Vidocq (see Letter 277, and note).

3. *The Moscow Record*, edited by Prince P. I. Shalikov, commented approvingly in

1830 of the election of the men of letters, Pushkin, Baratynsky, Bulgarin, and the composer Verstovsky, as members of the Society.

4. The heroine's father, Famusov, so greets the hero, Chatsky, in Griboedov's *Woe from Wit*.

5. That is, his historical researches on Peter the Great.

6. Pogodin had recently been promoted from adjunct to professor at Moscow University (see Letter 446).

Letter 483

1. Joachim Lelewel (1786-1861), Polish historian and politician, a leader in the Polish Revolution of 1830-1831, and President of the Polish National Committee. He continued his revolutionary activities after the revolution was crushed.

2. Count Grigory Alexandrovich Stroganov (1770-1857), a member of the State Council, Mme. Pushkina's great-uncle. Count Stroganov was noted as an extremely handsome man in his youth; in Byron's *Don Juan*, Julia held out even against his attractiveness. Count Stroganov to a considerable degree took the side of d'Anthès and Heeckeren against Pushkin in the events leading up to Pushkin's death, but after Pushkin's death, he became one of his children's guardians.

3. Count Stroganov had sent Pushkin the *Journal de Francfort*, No. 101, of April 24 (April 12, Old Style), 1834, which gave an account of Lelewel's reading aloud one of Pushkin's early, revolutionary poems and attributing revolutionary ideas to him. The article was a corrective to Lelewel's remarks: it pointed out Pushkin's recent anti-Polish poems and his being in good standing with the Tsar and the Court. How Pushkin was struck by the event is indicated by the fact that he copied part of the article in his diary. Scholars have noted the violence of Pushkin's remarking in this letter that to be accepted by a Pole as continuing to be a believer in the revolutionary ideas of his youth was worse than to be in exile in Siberia as a Decembrist revolutionary.

4. Countess Yulia Pavlovna Stroganova (d. 1864).

Letter 484

1. This letter marks Pushkin's officially taking over the financial management of his father's estate, Boldino. Pushkin gave Penkovsky another power of attorney on October 30, 1834. Managing his father's estate was a source of continuing harrassment to Pushkin from the time he took it over until he gave it up in June or July, 1835.

Letter 485

1. Ivan Ivanovich Lazhechnikov (1792-1869), author of historical novels, and at this time Director of Educational Institutions of the Province of Tver. The manuscript which Lazhechnikov sent Pushkin was the description of Pugachev's siege of Orenburg, by Peter Ivanovich Rychkov (1712-1777). Pushkin received copies of this manuscript from Spassky, Yazykov, and Lazhechnikov. He published Rychkov's account in one of the Appendices to his *History of Pugachev*.

2. Lazhechnikov's first novel was *The Last Novik* (1831-1833). His "new" novel was *The House of Ice* (1835). In Muscovite Russia, a *novik* was a young nobleman who had recently begun obligatory service at court.

3. *Dawn* for 1834.

Letter 486

1. Natalia Nikolaevna Pushkina and the Pushkin children left to visit their Goncharov relatives in Moscow, Yaropolets, and Polotnyany Zavod, on April 15. They spent the summer visiting.

2. Pushkin also wrote in his diary of how Count Litta, Head Chamberlain, "dressed down" the Kammerjunkers, insisting that there were " fixed rules" for the "Gentlemen of the Court," and how Kirill Alexandrovich Naryshkin (1786-1838), Head Marshal of the Court, answered that Litta was mistaken, that the rules were for the Ladies in Waiting. There is an untranslatable pun on *règles* "rules, periods."
3. Probably S. D. Bezobrazov.
4. Nikolay Fedorovich Remer (1806-1889), who was made a Kammerjunker, along with Pushkin, in 1833.
5. "I would rather be whipped in front of everybody."—In Molière's *Bourgeois gentilhomme*.
6. Probably the *Correspondence littéraire* (1753-1773) of Baron Friedrich Melchior von Grimm, French critic and *Philosophe*.
7. Pushkin probably means that he was expecting the postman to ring with a letter from Mme. Pushkina.
8. "Madam" of a "fashionable" house of prostitution.
9. A servant of the Pushkins'.
10. Pushkin's English and spelling.

Letter 487
1. That is, their family physician's instructions. Mme. Pushkina's trip was for convalescence from her miscarriage on March 4, 1834. See Letter 481.
2. Pushkin's English and spelling.

Letter 488
1. Pushkin shows his contempt for his court rank of Kammerjunker as being for younger men of his class, by using the term *Kammerpaž*, or Chamber Page, granted only to boys.
2. The three tsars were Paul I, Alexander I, and Nicholas I.
3. Pushkin's "namesake" was Alexander I. The "namesake" of Pushkin's son became Alexander II; at this time he was Grand Duke Alexander, the "Heir" to the throne. The celebrations were upon the "Heir's" attaining his sixteenth birthday (on April 17, 1834) and hence his legal majority, and upon his taking the oath of fealty.
4. Pushkin is thinking of his father-in-law's madness.
5. Prince Viktor Pavlovich Kochubey (1768-1834), statesman, Senator, and Chairman of the Committee of Ministers of the State Council. The rank of chancellor was the highest civil rank, and it corresponded with the military rank of field marshal.
6. Natalia Andreevna Ozerova, nee Obulenskaya (1812-1901), wife of Sergey Petrovich Ozerov (1809-1884).
7. Princess Maria Petrovna Vyazemskaya.
8. Karl Karlovich Merder (1788-1834), tutor of the Heir, died on March 24, 1834.
9. Count A. A. Arakcheev died on April 21, 1834. He was hated by all Russian liberals as the symbol, instigator, and administrator of the reactionary policies of the last ten years of the reign of Alexander I, and especially for the establishment of the military colonies in 1817. Though Nicholas I continued many of the policies of Arakcheev, he considered him a "monster" (*izverg*).
10. This letter, with its expression of clear displeasure at the court rank of Kammerjunker, with its admission of giving lying excuses for avoiding court functions, and with its critical approach to tsars in general, was opened by the Moscow postmaster, Bulgakov, and the contents reported to Nicholas I, who did not hesitate to speak of the letter to members of the court. Pushkin's rage at this action, clearly stated in subsequent letters,

led him to attempt, unsuccessfully, to resign from the service and retire to the country. These events are climactic in Pushkin's life.

Pushkin speaks thus of the event in his diary, under the date of May 10, 1834: "A few days ago I received from Zhukovsky a note from Tsarskoe Selo. He was informing me that a certain letter of mine was circulating about the city, and that the Sovereign had spoken to him about it. I imagined that the point was foul verses, full of repulsive obscenity, which the public was indulgently and graciously attributing to me. But it proved otherwise. The Moscow post unsealed a letter written by me to Natalia Nikolaevna, and, finding in it an account concerning the oath of the Grand Duke, written, apparently, not in the official style, made a report about it to the police. The police, without making out the meaning, presented the letter to the Sovereign, who flared up and did not understand it, either. Fortunately, the letter was shown to Zhukovsky, who then explained it. Everything quieted down. It did not please the Sovereign that I referred to my becoming a Kammerjunker, without tender emotion and without gratitude. However, I can be a subject, even a slave, but I shall not be a flunky and a clown even before the Tsar of Heaven. But what profound immorality there is in the customs of our government. The police unseal a husband's letters to his wife, and take them for reading to the Tsar (a well-bred and an honorable man), and the Tsar is not ashamed to admit it—and to set in motion an intrigue worthy of Vidocq and Bulgarin! No matter what you say, being an autocrat is hard."

Letter 489
1. Sofia Fedorovna Timiryazeva (b. 1799) and her husband, General Ivan Semenovich Timiryazev (1790-1867), were among Pushkin's good friends in the last years of his life.

Letter 490
1. Another reference to her father's madness.
2. The ball was in celebration of the attaining of his "majority" by the Heir to the throne, Grand Duke Alexander, who was born in 1818. It was given by the nobility of the Petersburg Province, at the home of Dmitry Lvovich Naryshkin (1764-1838). Pushkin did not attend. (See following letter.)
3. "Tell me what you drink, and I'll tell you what you are." Pushkin substitutes the word "drink" for "eat" in the aphorism of the French gastronome, Anthelme Brillat-Savarin, in his *Physiology of Taste* (1826).

Letter 491
1. See Letter 490, and note 2.
2. Pushkin was mistaken. See Letter 492.
3. That of Princess Tatiana Vasilievna Golitsyna (1782-1841), wife of the Governor General of Moscow, Prince D. V. Golitsyn.
4. Henriette Gertrude Walpurgis Sontag (1806-1854), wife of Count Rossi. She was a well-known singer of the time.
5. Pushkin again speaks of himself as a Chamber Page instead of a Kammerjunker. See Letter 488, note 1.

Letter 492
1. See Letter 490, and note 2.
2. Nestor Vasilievich Kukolnik (1809-1868), author of romantic and patriotic dramas in blank verse in a bombastic style.
3. See Letter 491.

4. Ekaterina Pavlovna Bakunina (d. 1869) married Alexander Alexandrovich Poltoratsky (1792-1855), a cousin of Anna Petrovna Kern, on April 30, 1834.

5. Count Ivan Illarionovich Vorontsov-Dashkov (1790-1854) married Countess Alexandra Kirillovna Naryshkina (1817-1856), daughter of Kirill Alexandrovich Naryshkin.

6. Novomlensky, probably a student and admirer of Mme. Pushkina before her marriage, as was also Sorokhtin.

Letter 493

1. In a letter of April 10, 1834, the historian Dmitry Nikolaevich Bantysh-Kamensky (1788-1850) sent Pushkin a sketch of Pugachev's seal and offered to send him a biography of Pugachev. In response to Pushkin's letter, Bantysh-Kamensky sent Pushkin a biography of Pugachev, twenty short biographies of followers of Pugachev, and a biography of Count Peter Ivanovich Panin.

Letter 494

1. Pushkin's brother-in-law, Pavlishchev, in his letter asked Pushkin, who had taken over the management of his father's estate Boldino, to send the money owed Pavlishchev by Lev Pushkin and also asked for information as to when he would receive the 1500 rubles annually which Pushkin's sister Olga had been promised after her marriage. Lev Pushkin owed Pavlishchev some 500 rubles. From the time Pushkin took over his father's estate, Pavlishchev continually peppered him with long, detailed, complaining letters, which provided one of the major irritations of Pushkin's management of the estate.

2. The sheet is torn at this point.

3. For managing Boldino and for disposing of the revenues from it. Pushkin managed his father's estate from April, 1834, until June or July, 1835.

Letter 495

1. That is, to the Goncharovs' Moscow house, to their estate Yaropolets in the Volokolamsk District, or to the estate Polotnyany Zavod in the Kaluga District.

2. Alexandra Osipovna Smirnova (nee Rosset) bore twin daughters on June 18, 1834.

3. The management of his father's estate Boldino.

Letter 496

1. His father's estate of Boldino.

2. Pushkin wrote in his diary that Nicholas I was dissatisfied because his son "galloped instead of trotted."

3. Frederick William (1795-1861), who as Frederick William IV was King of Prussia from 1840 to 1861, the brother of the Russian Empress Alexandra Fedorovna. He arrived in Russia on June 13 and left on August 1, 1834.

4. Pushkin notes in his diary that on May 26 he "was on the steamship, and accompanying the Meshcherskys, who were setting off for Italy."

Letter 497

1. Gogol was trying to obtain the post of professor in Kiev University, his request being motivated by bad health. He asked Pushkin to speak of Gogol's poor health to the Minister of Education, S. S. Uvarov.

2. Polevoy's *Moscow Telegraph* was closed down on April 3, 1834, as the result of a deposition by Uvarov. Pushkin's remark is mordantly ironic. Pushkin wrote thus in his diary of the closing down of this journal: "Zhukovsky says, 'I'm glad that *The Telegraph*

is forbidden, though I regret that they forbade it.' *The Telegraph* deserved its lot; it would be hard to preach Jacobinism with greater impudence under the nose of the government, but Polevoy was a pet of the police. He was able to assure them that his liberalism was only an empty mask."

Letter 498
1. Mineral waters and muds in the town of Pyrmont, Principality of Waldeck, Germany, on the Emmer River.
2. The last clause of this sentence was struck out but is still legible. Pushkin had discovered that Letter 488 (q.v., and note) has been intercepted.

Letter 499
1. May 19.
2. Letter 488.

Letter 500
1. *Tales Published by Alexander Pushkin* appeared in 1834. The edition included Pushkin's *Tales of Belkin, The Blackamoor of Peter the Great,* and "The Queen of Spades."
2. Special permission was required for sending his works to his friend Kyukhelbeker, the Decembrist.

Letter 501
1. See Letters 498 and 499.
2. Alexandre Vattemare, a French ventriloquist, actor, and mimic.
3. Boldino.
4. Pushkin made the official request a month later (Letter 507).
5. The allusion is to the monument of Peter the Great in Petersburg; this monument forms the center of Pushkin's *Bronze Horseman.* Pushkin was again working on the history of Peter the Great. Pushkin's comment here is reminiscent of his "Monument" ("I have erected myself a monument, not made by human hands"), which he wrote two years later.

Letter 502
1. Pushkin's strong language was for those who intercepted his private letters and for those who read them. Pushkin was well aware that in this number were included not only post officials, but also the secret police and the Tsar himself.
2. Ivan Nikolaevich Goncharov was then an officer and stationed in Tsarskoe Selo.
3. Princess Ekaterina Alexeevna Dolgorukova, nee Malinovskaya.
4. Elena Pavlovna, wife of Grand Duke Mikhail Pavlovich. Pushkin was presented to her on May 27, 1834. He quotes the conversation a little differently in his diary entry of June 2.
5. "You must be quite tired of being obliged to read all that appears." "Yes, Your Imperial Highness, . . . the more so that what is being written now has no common sense."
6. Pushkin's parents left on June 11 to spend the summer at Mikhaylovskoe (see Letter 505).

Letter 503
1. See Letter 493, and note.
2. In response to Pushkin's Letter 493, Bantysh-Kamensky sent Pushkin the article about Panin, for publication if found suitable.

3. See Letter 480, and note 1. Pushkin's spelling.
4. At this time Pushkin was interested in becoming literary agent for people such as Bantysh-Kamensky.
5. Pushkin jokingly concludes with the tsarist soldier's conventional response to a commendation.

Letter 504
1. Pushkin transliterates the English word into Russian orthography.
2. The allusion is to Pushkin's letters being intercepted and read (see Letter 488, and note 10).
3. On May 10, Pushkin had written almost exactly the same thing in his diary (see Letter 488, note 9). The quotation from Lomonosov is from a letter to Shuvalov, dated January 19, 1761.
4. His parents.
5. Countess Luiza Karlovna Vielgorskaya (1791-1853).

Letter 505
1. The Pushkins' Petersburg apartment was near the Summer Garden, near the Summer Palace of Peter the Great. It was a center for court life.
2. *Sobolevskij sam po sebe, a ja sam po sebe.* Pushkin jokingly adapts the proverbial soldier's distinction between a cannon and a mortar: *puška sama po sebe, a edinorog sam po sebe.* The remark is particularly apt, because Pushkin's own surname comes from *puška,* "cannon."
3. Pushkin's "favorite" of Mme. Pushkina's sisters was Alexandra Nikolaevna Goncharova.
4. "I would not have believed . . . that Kochubey's death would grieve me so."
5. Princess Maria Vasilievna Kochubey (1779-1844), Kochubey's widow, and Natalia K. Zagryazhskaya's niece.
6. Pushkin's parents.
7. Boldino.
8. The governor of Kaluga at the time was Illarion Mikhaylovich Bibikov (d. 1861), and his wife was Ekaterina Ivanovna Bibikova (1795-1849).
9. Pushkin is jokingly referring to Countess Nadezhda Grigorievna Chernysheva. See Letter 457.
10. Frederick William (see Letter 496).
11. Sergey Petrovich Ozerov and his wife, Natalia Andreevna Ozerova, nee Obolenskaya.
12. Another allusion to his letters being opened and read.
13. That is, to have them made Ladies in Waiting.
14. Pushkin's rank in the government service.
15. A *kalač* is a kind of roll. Pushkin is playing on the Russian saying, "You couldn't lure me, even with a *kalač*," meaning "nothing would induce me to come," by adding a particular place to which he could not be lured (Petersburg), and a special kind of *kalač* (Moscow).
16. "Yesterday Madame such-and-such was definitely the most beautiful and best dressed at the ball."
17. Mme. Vielgorskaya died in 1853.
18. Nicholas I.
19. Pushkin's English.

Letter 506

1. Spassky's letter no doubt contained medical advice for Mme. Pushkina, who was convalescing.

Letter 507

1. Pushkin's request to be allowed to retire was prompted by his indignation at the interception of his letters by the police, by the humiliation of his "promotion" to Kammerjunker, and by his ever-worsening financial situation in Petersburg. The letter itself was naturally considered by Nicholas I and Benkendorf to be "dry," for it lacked any explanation or justification for the request. On June 30, Pushkin received Benkendorf's answer, that "His Imperial Majesty [did not] wish to keep anyone against his will," and hence Pushkin might retire, but that permission to use archive materials could not then be granted, "for this right can belong solely to people enjoying the especial trust of the authorities." Zhukovsky and Mme. Khitrovo pleaded Pushkin's case with the authorities. He eventually felt compelled to take back his request (see Letters 512, 516, 517, and notes).

2. Slip of the pen for June 25.

Letter 508

1. This is a good example of the way Pushkin uses an epigraph for a letter. The quotation is from Fonvizin's *Adolescent*, Act IV, and it is addressed to the block-headed "hero" of the play.

2. Elena Pavlovna. See Letter 502.

3. Ekaterina Petrovna Chicherina (d. 1874), one of the Grand Duchess Elena Pavlovna's Ladies in Waiting. She was a third cousin of Pushkin's.

4. The second highest bid in the card game of Boston: the bidder contracts to discard one card and lose the twelve tricks. Eighty white counters would be won from or lost to each of the other players, depending upon the success of the play.

5. Alexandra O. Smirnova was unable, in 1832, to bear her first child, in seventy-two hours of labor; the child had to be destroyed before it could "get out."

6. Semen Semenovich Khlyustin (1810-1844), a nephew of Tolstoy the American.

7. Sergey Pavlovich Ubri, then in exile in Kaluga.

8. His father's estate of Boldino.

9. Yakovlev saw Pushkin's book through the press. A number of the succeeding letters are to him in this connection.

10. The anecdote is unknown.

11. "Farewell, my life; I love you."

Letter 509

1. In the beginning of June, Nicholas I and his court went to Petergof, a suburb of Petersburg. Special celebrations and amusements occurred.

2. Pushkin had already sent in his letter of resignation three days earlier (Letter 507) and was awaiting its results. It will be seen that Pushkin is not candid with his wife on this matter.

3. Pushkin died less than three years later in Petersburg, but he was buried by "a church in the open spaces," at the monastery Svyatye Gory, near his mother's estate of Mikhaylovskoe.

4. Countess Anna Vladimirovna Bobrinskaya. Pushkin, on December 18, 1834, wrote in his diary that "she always lies for me and gets me out of scrapes."

5. The printing of his *History of Pugachev*.

6. Boldino, of which Pushkin was his father's financial manager at the time.
7. Alexander Karlovich Olivio.
8. Nicholas I.
9. On June 22, 1834.

Letter 510
1. Ekaterina Vasilievna Shishkova; her daughter "Polina" was Praskovia Dmitrievna Shishkova.
2. Metal tokens were given upon members' attendance at meetings of the Russian Academy, and they were redeemed later. Alexander Semenovich Shishkov was President of the Russian Academy. Pushkin had been a member since January 7, 1833. Though Pushkin attended several sessions of the organization in 1833, he attended only one in 1834, that on December 8.
3. "Not otherwise."
4. Unknown.
5. That is, at the printing plant.
6. Perhaps V. G. Yuriev.
7. Karl Reichman refused the management of Boldino, in his letter of June 22, 1834.

Letter 511
1. Pushkin's old friend M. L. Yakovlev was at this time the head of the printing house of the Second Section of His Majesty's Chancellery. Yakovlev saw Pushkin's *History of Pugachev* through the press for him. The letter is written in the form of an official note.

Letter 512
1. See Letter 507. Zhukovsky had undertaken to smooth things out between the Tsar and Pushkin, after Pushkin's attempted resignation. The present letter is the direct result of a letter by Zhukovsky to Pushkin (of July 2, 1834), in which Zhukovsky gives the Tsar's response to Zhukovsky's question "Can't all this be corrected somehow?" The Tsar answered as follows: "Why not? I never hold anybody back, and I shall give him his retirement. But in that case all is finished between us. He can, however, still ask for his letter to be returned." Pushkin realized what reason he had to fear the Tsar's words "in that case all is finished between us."

Letter 513
1. "My step being ill-considered . . . that I prefer seeming inconsistent to seeming ungrateful." See Letter 512, and note. Pushkin quotes himself a little imprecisely.
Zhukovsky, in addition to his letter of July 2, had written Pushkin a long letter on July 3, in which he roundly berated Pushkin for sending in his resignation without having consulted in advance either with him or Prince Vyazemsky, and advised him to "accuse" himself for his "stupid deed" in a letter to the Tsar, and to explain what moved him to send in the resignation. Zhukovsky says that if Pushkin does not so act, he will harm himself for his "whole life," and that he will earn his friends' "disapprobation"—at least Zhukovsky's. Zhukovsky also sent a second version of the letter, one that could be shown to Benkendorf.
2. See Letter 507, and note 1.
3. Pushkin did not write directly to Nicholas I, but, instead, again to Benkendorf.

Letter 514
1. See Letter 513, and notes.

Letter 515
1. This note was written on the manuscript of *The History of Pugachev*.

Letter 516
1. This letter was written hurriedly, like Letter 517, upon Pushkin's receiving still another letter from Zhukovsky, likewise dated July 6, complaining that neither of Pushkin's letters to Benkendorf (Letters 512, 514) is satisfactory, because the first does not say whether he wishes to continue in the service, and the second "is so dry that it might seem to the Sovereign to be a new impropriety." Zhukovsky emphasized that Nicholas I considered Pushkin's resignation as "ingratitude" and insisted that Pushkin write what his "heart will say." The "third" letter was Letter 517.

Letter 517
1. See Letter 507. Nicholas I's response to this letter, made to Benkendorf, was as follows: "I forgive him, but you summon him again to explain to him the senselessness of his behavior and what all this could end with; what might be forgiven a twenty-year-old madcap cannot be applied to a man of thirty-five years, a husband and father of a family." Pushkin understood this hint of another exile, and he tersely wrote in his diary on July 22: "The last month has been stormy. I came within a hair's breadth of quarreling with the Court—but everything came out all right. Just the same, I won't get away with it."

Pushkin did not get away with it. His last chance of living as he chose disappeared when he submitted to the Tsar's desire that he remain in Petersburg. After Pushkin's death, three years later, Zhukovsky changed his opinion considerably with regard to Pushkin's reasons for "gratitude" towards Nicholas and his "ingratitude" in wanting to get away, when Zhukovsky, given the task of reading and sorting all Pushkin's papers, became so aroused at the suspicious treatment of Pushkin during Nicholas' reign, that he wrote an indignant letter to Benkendorf.

Letter 518
1. Zagoskin's novel, *Askold's Tomb* (1833).
2. No such letter survives.
3. Alexandre Vattemare, the ventriloquist, and hence "persons." Vattemare had asked Pushkin to write to Zagoskin, in the latter's capacity as Director of the Moscow Imperial Theater. Zagoskin's answer is unknown.

Letter 519
1. Namely, that some of Pushkin's letters had been opened and read by post officials, the police, and the Tsar.
2. "Routs" were fashionable in Russia at the time. See Letter 243 and note 8.
3. Josephine Charlotte Ermolova, nee Comtesse de Lasalle. Pushkin comments about the filthiness of her clothing, in his diary, under the date of December 5, 1834: "N.N. said, 'Here is Mme. Yermolova *la sale* (Lassale).' "
4. Pushkin is referring to his submitting his resignation to Nicholas I, and the upshot. Pushkin's attitude toward his wife's judgment, and his opinion of what her attitude would be toward his wishing to retire is clear from the dates of his letters to her during the "stormy month." His letters to her, during her trip, had been dated, on the average, about four days apart, until the letter of June 11, in which he expressed clear displeasure with the Tsar and his desire to get away to "fresh air." His next letter, dated June 19. was only a brief note. Obviously the desire to resign was growing and growing

in him. Then he sent in his resignation on June 25. While he was waiting for the answer, he wrote his wife three letters in about four days. Then, on June 30, when he received the Tsar's curt acceptance of his resignation, the second act of the drama began—of his trying to take back the resignation. Pushkin did not write his wife again until July 11, almost two weeks later, when the drama was completed.

5. Olga Petrovna Pletneva.
6. Unidentified.
7. Grand Duchess Elena Pavlovna.

Letter 520
1. M. I. Kalashnikov.
2. Reichman was manager of Mme. Osipova's estate of Malinniki; she had suggested him as manager of Boldino. He refused this management in a letter of June 22, 1834.
3. Pushkin next visited Trigorskoe in 1835.

Letter 521
1. The equivalent English proverb is less colorful: If wishes were horses, beggars would ride.
2. Nicholas I.
3. Court balls in the Anichkov Palace. Pushkin wrote in his diary, under January 1, 1834, that he was made a Kammerjunker because "the court wanted Natalia Nikolaevna to dance in the Anichkov."
4. "Liberalism" was the charge leading to Pushkin's exile under the guise of an administrative transfer in 1820.

Letter 522
1. Unidentified.
2. Pushkin's landlord.
3. In Letter 508, of June 27, 1834, Pushkin had reported that Mme. Smirnova had recently borne twins.

Letter 523
1. Pushkin moved there in the middle of August, 1834. The house was on the Gagarinskaya Embankment, and it was owned by Sila Andreevich Batashev.
2. Princess Praskovia Petrovna Vyazemskaya; she died in Rome on March 11, 1835.
3. Woman "is a naturally feeble and sickly animal."
4. *Do nizlozenija riz*. It has proved impossible to preserve the biblical flavor of the expression, which has to do with Noah's taking off his clothes while drunk after the Flood (Genesis 9:21). The quotation has humorous connotations in Russian.
5. Of his *History of Pugachev*.
6. Lev S. Pushkin re-entered the military service and went to Caucasian Georgia to serve, but not until 1836.
7. Khlopusha was the nickname of Afansy Timofeevich Sokolov, one of Pugachev's military leaders. The incident is recounted in the first volume of Pushkin's *History of Pugachev*.
8. Pushkin makes a double pun, on Khlopusha's name and his own, and on the name of the Goncharov estate, Polotnyany Zavod, "Linen Factory."
9. Count Joseph Maison (1771-1840), French ambassador at the Russian court. Pushkin wrote of the event in his diary (under the date of July 22), as follows: "Marshal Maison fell from his horse on maneuvers and came very near to being crushed by the

Obraztsov Regiment. Arendt has announced that he is out of danger. At Austerlitz he smashed our cavalry guards. One good turn deserves another."

Letter 524
1. Of Pushkin's *History of Pugachev*.
2. See Letter 523.
3. Probably the portrait of Mme. Pushkina as a bride, by A. P. Bryullov, in water colors. See Illustration opposite Letter 350.

Letter 525
1. The actor Vasily Andreevich Karatygin and his wife, the dramatic actress Alexandra Mikhaylovna Karatygina, nee Kolosova. Pushkin knew both personally.
2. See Letters 523 and 524.
3. August 26.
4. Princess Praskovia Petrovna Vyazemskaya. See Letter 523, and note 2.
5. "To make a baby for you." "Oh, Sir, you will give me great pleasure."
6. Princess Maria Vasilievna Kochubey (see Letter 505).
7. "Good Lord, but we have all lost our husbands, and yet we have consoled ourselves."
8. Of Pushkin's *History of Pugachev*.

Letter 526
1. This note and the following one show the strictness of the censorship under which Pushkin operated. This note was written on the manuscript of the Preface of Pushkin's *History of Pugachev*, in response to Yakovlev's question, "Can't Voltaire be dispensed with?" Pushkin had included Voltaire's name in the list of historical figures "whose names are met" in Pushkin's work, a "historical page," which "must not be lost for posterity." Pushkin was forced to remove Voltaire's name from the Preface (see Letter 527).

Letter 527
1. Of the proofs of Pushkin's *History of Pugachev*.
2. The other copies of Rychkov's description of the siege of Orenburg by Pugachev (see Letter 485, note 1).
3. A quotation from Batyushkov's poetic epistle to I. M. Muraviev-Apostol (already quoted in Letter 184).
4. See Letter 526, note.

PART XII

CARES AND WOES—PETERSBURG

August, 1834—December, 1835

Natalia Nikolaevna Pushkina, 1844.

[528]
>   To Ivan Ivanovich Lazhechnikov
>   About August 20, 1834. From (?) to Tver.

I have kept on hoping, honored and amiable Ivan Ivanovich, to thank you in person for your favorable attitude toward me, for the two letters, for the novels, and for the Pugachev materials,[1] but unsuccess pursues me. I'm passing through Tver by post chaise, and in such an appearance that I simply dare not come to see you and renew our ancient, momentary acquaintance. I postpone it to September, that is, until my return trip. Meanwhile, I commend myself to your indulgence and good will.

>   One who heartily esteems you,
>   Pushkin.

[529]
>   To Natalia Ivanovna Goncharova
>   About (not later than) August 25, 1834.
>   From Polotnyany Zavod to Yaropolets.

Dear Madame, Mother, Natalia Ivanovna,

How I regret that I didn't drop in to Yaropolets on my way from Petersburg. I would have had the happiness of seeing you, and I would have shortened the trip by several miles. Besides, I would have missed Moscow, which I am not very fond of, and in which I spent several hours too many. Now I'm at the Zavod, where I found all my family well, except Sasha. I'm leaving them for several more weeks and going on business for my father to his Nizhny Novgorod village,[1] and I'm sending my wife off to you, where I myself will come as soon as possible. My wife is sad that she won't spend with you the name day[2] of you both. What's to be done! I'm sorry, too, but it can't be helped. Meanwhile I congratulate you upon the day of August 26—and I heartily thank you for the 27th.[3] My wife is charming, and the longer I live with her the more I love this sweet, pure, kind creature, whom, before God, I have in no way deserved. I have been seeing my brother-in-law Ivan Nikolaevich often in Petersburg, and Sergey Nikolaevich was even living with me almost up to my departure. He's now bustling around, outfitting himself.[4] Both of them, thank God, are well.

I kiss your little hands, and I commend myself and all my family to your favor.

A. Pushkin.

[530]

To Alexander Ivanovich Turgenev
About (not later than) September 9, 1834. In Moscow.

My wife has selected the pins, and she cordially thanks you. It goes without saying that you'll be the first to receive my *Pugachev*,[1] as soon as it comes forth from the press. Simbirsk was besieged not by him but by one of his confederates, nicknamed Firska. I shall leave the book at my wife's, who will pass it on to you. All yours—goodby.

A.P.

In 1671 Simbirsk held out against Stenka Razin,[2] the Pugachev of that time.

[531]

To Sergey Alexandrovich Sobolevsky
September 9, 1834. From Moscow to Petersburg.

Moscow, September 9.

Please, dear Sergey Alexandrovich, explain to my wife[1] where *notre ami l'usurier*[2] lives. I am relying on your sluggishness, and I consider it a certainty that you are still in Paris[3]—and that I shall even find you're there upon my arrival in Petersburg.

[532]

To Alexander Ivanovich Turgenev
September 9 or 10, 1834. In Moscow.

I already have all this—and it will be printed in an appendix.[1] I am grateful to Polevoy[2] for his being kindly disposed toward the historiographer of Pugachev, the Kammerjunker,[3] etc. I am leaving right now. The horses are already harnessed up.

[533]
    To Natalia Nikolaevna Pushkina
 September 15 and 17, 1834. From Boldino to Petersburg.
            September 15.

 The post goes on Tuesday, but today is still only Saturday. And so this letter won't reach you very soon. I arrived day before yesterday, Thursday, in the morning—that's how one creeps along the provincial roads—and, at that, I have paid almost everywhere double the post-horse fee. True, horses had been taken from everywhere for the Sovereign, who must go from Moscow to Nizhny. The first snow met me in the village,[1] and now the yard in front of my little window is all white; *c'est une très aimable attention*.[2] However, I haven't got down to writing yet, and I'm taking my pen for the first time, in order to have a little chat with you. I'm glad that I have got to Boldino; it looks as though there will be less bother than I expected. I should very much like to write something or other. I don't know whether inspiration will come. Here I found Bezobrazov[3] (just why are you so astonished? It wasn't your adorer,[4] but my cousin Margaritka's husband). He's bustling about and managing the estate and probably will buy half of Boldino. Oh! If I only had a hundred thousand! How I would get all that settled. But Pugachev, my little peasant on quitrent, won't bring me even half of that, and, besides, you and I will squander every kopeck he brings in, won't we? Well, nothing can be done about it. If I live, there'll be some money, too.... Here's Bezobrazov coming to see me—farewell.

 Ugh! I had difficulty in getting rid of him. He stayed with me for two hours. We both tried to outsmart each other—God grant that I outsmarted him in deed; in words, I think, I outsmarted him. I can see from here your mistrustful smile. You think I'm a tomfool, and that they'll hoodwink me again. We'll see. When I get to Moscow, I'll finish the deal in two days, and I'll come to Petersburg with a "well done," the owner of the village Boldino....[5]

 Just now some peasants came to see me, with a petition. I was forced to try to outsmart them, but they probably will outsmart me. ... Even though I've become an awfully clever politician since I've been reading *Conquêtes de l' Angleterre par les Normands*.[6] What's this, now? A peasant woman with a petition. Farewell; I'll go listen to her.

Well, little wife, some humor. A soldier's wife asks that her son be registered as one of my peasants. However, she says, he has been registered as a bastard, though she gave birth to him, she says, only thirteen months after husband was sent off as a recruit. So how, then, can he be a bastard? I shall do what I can for the honor of the insulted widow.[7]

17th.

Now you're probably in Yaropolets, and you're probably already thinking about departing. I'm impatiently awaiting a letter from you. Don't forget my address: *in the Arzamas District*, to the village Abramovo, thence to the village Boldino. I'm all right here, but I'm bored, and when I'm bored, I feel drawn to you, just as you cuddle up to me when you're frightened. I kiss you and the children, and I bless all of you. I haven't begun writing yet.

[534]

To Natalia Nikolaevna Pushkina

Between September 20 and 25, 1834. From Boldino to Petersburg.

Here it will soon be two whole weeks that I've been in the village, and I still haven't received a letter from you. I'm bored, my angel. Verses won't come into my head, and I'm not copying the novel.[1] I'm reading Walter Scott and the Bible, and I keep on thinking of you. Is Sashka well? Have you given his wet nurse the sack—have you gotten rid of the damned German woman? How were you when you reached there? There are many things that I'm disturbed about. Apparently I'm not to stay long in Boldino this autumn. I have settled my affairs some way or other. I'll hang around a little and see whether I won't get into a writing vein. If not—then Godspeed, and onto the road. I'll stay in Moscow three days, at Natalia Ivanovna's twenty-four hours—and then I'll come to you. And, indeed, can it really be that near you I won't get into a writing vein? Nonsense. I've been expecting [A. M.] Yazykov to come see me, but apparently he won't make it.

Tell me, please, whether you aren't with child. If you are with child, I ask you, my darling, to be careful, not to jump, not to fall, not to kneel in front of Masha (or even in prayer). Don't forget that you've had a miscarriage, that you must take care of yourself. Oh, if only you were already in Petersburg. But according to all my calculations, you won't reach there before October 3. And how are things going to be for you there? Without money, without Amelian,[2] with your two fool nurses and slatternly maidservants (let this not be said in anger to Pelagea Ivanovna,[3] whom I kiss, sight unseen). I'll bet your head's going round and round. There's one hope: Aunty. But you can't make two Aunties out of one—it's obvious that I must hurry. Farewell; Christ preserve all of you. A big kiss to you—all of you keep well.

[535]
To Nikolay Mikhaylovich Yazykov
September 26, 1834. From Boldino to Yazykovo.

I was delighted, in my solitude, at the coming of Alexander Mikhaylovich [Yazykov], who, unfortunately, spent only a few hours with me. He tempts me with his proposal to go to the village Yazykovo[1] with him to be a witness of his wedding, promising to make good use of me. But it is impossible for me—my wife and children. . . .

In conversing about various subjects, we decided that it would not be at all bad for me to begin an almanac, or better yet, a journal.[2] I have nothing against it, but if I am to do so I must be assured of your collaboration. What do you think, sir? You see, yourself: the hack writers are getting the better of us. It's time, by golly it's time, to give them a sizable repulse. I am setting off for Petersburg in a few days. If you have the leisure to write me a couple of lines, address them to the Dvortsovaya Naberezhnaya, to the house of Batashev—at the Prachechny Bridge. Alexander Mikhaylovich is in a hurry—and I am ending my letter by commending myself to your good will.

One who prays for you,
A. Pushkin.

September 26.
V[illage] Boldino.
My sincere respects and my greetings to Peter Alexandrovich [Yazykov].

[536]
>
> To Mikhail Lukianovich Yakovlev
> October 19, 1834(?). In Petersburg.
>
> It's at your house we're celebrating the Anniversary, isn't it?
> October 19.   No. 14.[1]

[537]
>
> To Alexandra Andreevna Fuchs
> October 19, 1834. From Petersburg to Kazan.
> October 19, 1834. SPb.

Yesterday, upon returning to Petersburg after three months of boring traveling over the provinces, I was delighted by an unexpected boon; a letter and a parcel[1] from Kazan. I avidly read your charming poems and, among them, your epistle to me, the unworthy admirer of your Muse. In exchange for the productions of your imagination, which are filled with charm, intelligence, and sensitiveness, I hope in a few days to deliver to you the repulsively horrible *History of Pugachev*. Do not scold me. Poetry seems to have dried up for me. I am doing nothing but prose, and what kind at that! . . . I am truly ashamed, especially before you.

You wrote that Baron Lützerode[2] should have delivered to me a letter as long ago as last year. To my extreme regret I have not received it, probably because Baron Lützerode was no longer in Petersburg when I returned from Orenburg. He had already been recalled to Dresden. E. P. Pertsov,[3] whom I had the pleasure of seeing for a moment in Petersburg, was telling me that he had at his house a letter from you to me, but it has not reached me, either. He has left Petersburg, without delivering to me this valuable token of your kind remembrance of me. I understand his distractedness under his circumstances of that time, but I cannot help complaining. I forgive him magnanimously, but only on condition that he send me the letter which he forgot to deliver to me here.

Please take the trouble, dear Madame, to present my most profound respects to Karl Fedorovich [Fuchs], whose amiability and favorable inclination will be eternally memorable to me.

With the most profound respect and cordial devotion, I have the honor to be [. . . .][4]

[538]
To Nikolay Vasilievich Gogol
The second half of October, 1834. In Petersburg.

I have reread it with great pleasure. It all, I should think, can be passed. It would be a pity to have to omit the flogging;[1] I think it necessary for the full effect of the evening's mazurka. Maybe God will bring it through. Godspeed!

A.P.

[539]
To Iosif Matveevich Penkovsky
November 10, 1834. From Petersburg to Boldino.

I have received your letter of October 30, and I hasten to answer you. I myself shall pay *my* debt to the Guardian Council, but not a single kopek must be spent from the Boldino revenues. As regards the 1270 which are demanded for an extension of Father's debt, if you can find such a sum, then pay it. I am sending you the power of attorney by the next post. You have done well in that up to now you have not started selling the grain. Prices are bound to rise. Fortunately, I can wait a while longer.[1]

A.P.   November 10.

[540]
To Alexander Khristoforovich Benkendorf
November 23, 1834. In Petersburg.

Dear Sir, Count Alexander Khristoforovich,

The History of the Pugachev Revolt has been printed, and I have been awaiting Your Excellency's permission for its release. Meanwhile, permit me to trouble you with one more humble request. I should like to have the happiness to present to the Sovereign Emperor the first copy of the book, augmenting it with certain notes which I decided not to publish, but which may be of interest to His Majesty. I make bold to have recourse to Your Highness in order to receive this permission.

The bookseller Smirdin wants to publish in one book my poems which have already appeared in print;[2] I have made bold to send them to the chancellery of His Excellency A. N. Mordvinov, according to the prescribed form for so doing.

With the most profound respect, complete devotion, and gratitude, I have the honor to be,
      Dear Sir,
       Your Excellency's
November 23, 1834.   Most humble servant,
 SPb.   Alexander Pushkin.

[541]
    To Alexander Ivanovich Turgenev
   Between December 1 and 11, 1834. In Petersburg.

I don't have a *French* copyist, but as many Russian ones as you like. Tomorrow I'll scare one up. For the time being, I don't need anything from Paris,[1] unless maybe Maistre's *Pope*.[2]

[542]
   To Alexander Khristoforovich Benkendorf
     December 17, 1834. In Petersburg.
       (In French)

I am in despair at having to trouble Your Excellency again, but M. Speransky has just had me informed that, since *The History of the Pugachev Revolt* has been in his section by order of His Majesty the Emperor, it is impossible for him to deliver the edition *bez vysočajšego na to soizvolenija*.[1] I beseech Your Excellency to pardon me and to extricate me from this difficulty.

 I am, with the most profound respect,
  Count,
   Your Excellency's
    Most humble and most obedient servant,
December 17, 1834.   Alexander Pushkin.

[543]
    To Alexey Alexeevich Bobrinsky
     January 6, 1835. In Petersburg.
       (In French)

We have received an invitation from Countess Bobrinskaya:[1] M. and Mme. Pushkin *and her sister*, etc. There is a great clamor among the females over it (as W. Scott's Antiquary[2] says): *which*?[3] Since I suppose it is simply an error, I take the liberty of addressing you in order to remove us from the quandary and to restore peace in my household.

>I am, respectfully, Count,
>Your most humble and most obedient servant,

January 6, 1835.   A. Pushkin.

[544]
To Pavel Voinovich Nashchokin
About (not later than) January 8, 1835.
From Petersburg to Moscow.

Dear Pavel Voinovich,

You can't imagine with what pleasure I have finally received a letter from you. But first of all, let's talk about business. Sobolevsky, with whom I have financial dealings, *without delay* will deliver to you the two thousand rubles. Consequently, don't be uneasy. I could find a lot to tell you in excuse for my insolvency, but to write that by the post would be a superfluous thing; God grant that my belated money may arrive at a good time for you. I congratulate you upon your daughter Katerina Pavlovna;[1] I wish good health to the recently confined mother. (You don't write me when her confinement was.) All summer I scoured Russia, but I couldn't find you anywhere. You had been driven out of Tula by the fires. A whole week in Moscow I couldn't find you. In Torzhok nobody could give me news of you. I'm glad, Pavel Voinovich, of your letter, by which I see that your astonishing good nature and your sensible, patient indulgence have undergone no change, neither from the bothers of a life new for you, nor from your friend's culpability toward you. If only we might see each other! I would tell you a lot of things; this year much has piled up that it wouldn't be bad to have a chat with you about, at your place on the divan, with a pipe between my teeth, far from gypsy tempests[2] and Rokhmanov's forays![3] Write me, if you can, a little oftener: *On the Dvortsovaya Naberezhnaya* to the house of Batashev at the Prachechny Bridge (where Vyazemsky used to live), and not to Smirdin's, who keeps your letters for whole months, and sometimes, probably, even mislays them. I would take a peep at your domestic and village life with curiosity. I have always known you tempest-tossed. What kind of effect is tranquillity having on you? Have you ever seen horses unloaded on the Petersburg

Exchange? They stagger and can't walk. Isn't it that way with you, too? I don't want to talk to you about myself, because I have no intention of taking as my confidant the Moscow post, which this present year has committed astonishing swinish acts with regard to me;[4] I'll write you by an *occasion*. Meanwhile I embrace you with all my heart, and I kiss the hands of the recently confined mother.

[545]
              To Pavel Voinovich Nashchokin
       January 20, 1835. From Petersburg to Moscow.

I'm sending you, dear Pavel Voinovich, fifteen hundred rubles; the remaining five hundred would have gotten to you, but yesterday a young man touched me for them as a loan, for a stake at cards. Commiserating with a state in which you and I, too, have chanced to get caught on occasion, you'll probably be magnanimous and forgive me. However, please send me a full reckoning of my debt.[1]

My wife sends her cordial greetings to your Vera Alexandrovna [Nashchokina]; at Mme. Sichler's she has ordered her a hat, which today is being sent off to Moscow. My wife says that *comme Mme. Nashchokin est brune et qu'elle a un beau teint*,[2] she has chosen for her a hat of such-and-such a color, and not of another. But that's a ladies' affair.

You probably have seen my *Pugachev*, but I hope you haven't bought it. I am keeping a special copy for you. What do you think of these times? Pugachev has become a good, punctual payer of his quitrent—Emelka Pugachev, my peasant on quitrent! He has brought me in money enough, but since I had been living on credit for a couple of years, I'm keeping nothing hidden in my bosom, but everything's going for paying off debts. Now I embrace you with all my heart, kiss Vera Alexandrovna's little hand, and I'm setting off for the post.

                                    January 20, 1835.
                                      SPb.

[546]
 To Alexander Khristoforovich Benkendorf
 January 26, 1835. In Petersburg.
Dear Sir, Count Alexander Khristoforovich,
I have the honor to forward to Your Highness certain observations which could not enter into *The History of the Pugachev Revolt* but which may be of interest. I asked for permission to present them to the Sovereign Emperor, and I have had the happiness to receive the Highest's assent to my so doing.[1]

Along with this I make bold to ask Your Excellency to solicit a favor which is important for me: the Sovereign's authorization for me to read the Pugachev dossier, which is in the archives.[2] In my free time I would be able to make a brief excerption from it, if not for publication, then at least in order to make complete my work, which without this is imperfect, and in order to set my historian's conscience at rest.

With the most profound respect and with complete devotion, I have the honor to be,
        Dear Sir,
           Your Highness's
              Most humble servant,
                  Alexander Pushkin.
January 26, 1835.
 SPb.

[547]
 To Dmitry Nikolaevich Bantysh-Kamensky
 January 26, 1835. From Petersburg to Moscow.
Dear Sir, Dmitry Nikolaevich,
With gratitude I am returning to you the articles which your good will toward me has allowed me to utilize in the compilation of my *History*.[1] Along with them I am also forwarding a copy of the *History* itself. Your opinion of it, whatever it may be, is precious to me. Praise from a genuine historian, and not from a superficial narrator or transcriber, would be flattering for me; whereas, from censure I would learn a great deal (which you know, yourself, I cannot expect to do from the observations of our inveterate critics).

I ask you to take upon yourself the labor of correcting two errors which have been justly noted in *The Son of the Fatherland*:² On page 128 *was already* 10 *miles* should read 35. And in a note to the fifth chapter (16), instead of *Tobolsk*, *Tabinsk*.

With the most profound respect and gratitude, I have the honor to be,

      Dear Sir,
       Your Excellency's
January 26.   Most obedient servant,
 SPb.   Alexander Pushkin.

[548]
     To Ivan Ivanovich Dmitriev
   February 14, 1835. From Petersburg to Moscow.

Dear Ivan Ivanovich, young [Andrey Nikolaevich] Karamzin showed me Your High Excellency's letter, in which you reproach me with unforgivable impoliteness. I hasten to justify myself. I have not delivered you my tribute¹ until now, because I have been momentarily expecting the portrait of Emilian Ivanovich [Pugachev], which is being engraved in Paris; I have wanted to present my book to you in perfect condition. Not to fulfill that would be, on my part, not only stinginess, but also ingratitude: my chronicle is indebted to you for a striking and vivid passage,² for the sake of which much will be forgiven me by even the severest readers.

You scoff at our generation, and of course you have full right to do so. I am not going to take up for the historians³ and versifiers of my time. In olden days the historians had less charlatanry and more erudition and diligence, the versifiers, more sincerity and spiritual warmth. As regards financial profits, permit me to observe that Karamzin was the first among us to show an example of large enterprise in the trade of literature.⁴

I do not know whether you feel interested in the fate of our academy, which not long ago lost its secretary,⁵ who died on his shield—that is, on the last proof sheet of its dictionary.⁶ It is not known who will be his successor. The holy place will not remain empty—but the place of the permanent secretary was empty enough, even before it was vacated.

Your contemporary,⁷ whom you mention in your letter to Andrey

Nikolaevich Karamzin, is well, thank God, and continues to visit Smirdin's bookshop daily and the academy on Saturdays. In the bookshop he takes his own works which are still unsold, and he gives them out to his fellow members of the academy with touching financial disinterestedness.

With the most profound respect and devotion, I have the honor to be, Dear Sir, Your High Excellency's most humble servant.

February 14, 1835.   Alexander Pushkin.
SPb.

[549]
To Pavel Alexandrovich Katenin
April 20, 1835. From Petersburg to Stavropol.
(Fragment)

I am at fault toward you, in not having answered your letter for so long. The point is that I had nothing good to tell you in answer. Your "Sonnet" is exceedingly good, but I was not able to publish it. Now the censorship has become just as arbitrary and muddle-headed as in the times of the blessed[1] Krasovsky and Birukov: it passes things for which it deservedly gets a dressing-down, and then, out of fright, it will no longer pass anything. Your next to the last verse was enough to arouse all the censorship committee against your[2] sonnet.[3]

[550]
To Lev Sergeevich Pushkin
April 23 or 24, 1835. From Petersburg to Tiflis.
(In French)

I have delayed answering you because I have not had much to tell you. Since I had the weakness to take my father's affairs in hand, I have not touched 500 rubles of the revenues; and as for the loan of 13,000, it has already been spent. Here is the accounting which concerns you.[1]

    to Engelgardt[2]   1,330
    to the restaurant   260
    to Dumé   220 (for wine)
    to Pavlishchev   837
    to the tailor   390

to Pleshcheev³	1,500
Besides, you have received; in bills	280
(*In August*, 1834) in gold	950
	5,767

Your promissory note (10,000) has been redeemed.⁴ Thus, in addition to rent, board, and the tailor, which have cost you nothing, you have received 1230 rubles.

In view of the fact that my mother has been very sick, I am still taking care of affairs, in spite of a thousand unpleasantnesses. I am counting on giving them up at the first opportunity. I shall try, at that time, to arrange for you to receive your share of the lands and the peasants. Probably then you will busy yourself with your affairs and you will lose your indolence and the ease with which you allow yourself to live from one day to the next. From this moment on, address yourself to your parents. I have not paid your petty gambling debts, because I have not gone to seek out your companions—they should have addressed themselves to me.

[551]
To Ivan Ivanovich Dmitriev
April 26, 1835. From Petersburg to Moscow.

Dear Sir, Ivan Ivanovich, I want to express my sincere gratitude to Your High Excellency for your friendly word and for your consoling encouragement to my historical fragment.¹ It is being berated,² and deservedly: I wrote it for myself, not thinking that I would be able to publish it, and I strove only for a clear exposition of occurrences which were involved enough. Readers love anecdotes, the peculiarities of the locality, etc.—but I thrust all that back into the notes. As regards those thinkers who are indignant with me because Pugachev is presented in my book as Emelka Pugachev and not as Byron's Lara,³ I willingly refer them to Mr. Polevoy, who probably for a suitable sum will undertake to idealize this personage according to the very latest fashion.

You ask who is the secretary in our academy. I do not think it has been decided yet. Ulysses Lobanov and Ajax Fedorov are quarreling over the arms of Achilles. But they may very well fall to Yazykov-

Nestor (at least to the publisher of Nestor).[4] You are a prophet in your own country.

A black year has come onto our academies; scarcely had Sokolov passed away in the Russian Academy when Dondukov-Korsakov[5] appeared in the Academy of Sciences as the Vice President. Uvarov is a clown, and Dondukov-Korsakov is his stooge. Somebody said that where one goes, there goes the other; one turns flips on the rope, and the other, under him on the floor.

With the most profound respect and with complete devotion, I have the honor to be, Dear Sir, Your High Excellency's most humble servant,

Alexander Pushkin.

April 26, 1835.
SPb.

[552]
To Vasily Alexeevich Perovsky
March or April, 1835. From Petersburg to Orenburg.

I am sending you *The History of Pugachev*, in memory of our jaunt to Berdy;[1] and three more copies for Dal,[2] Pokatilov, and for the hunter[3] who compares woodcocks with Wallenstein or with Caesar. I regret that in Petersburg we succeeded in meeting only at a ball. Good-by until we meet again, in the steppes or high in the Urals.

A.P.

[552a]
To Gustav Nordin
After the middle of April, 1835. In Petersburg.
(In French)

Sir, please accept my most sincere thanks for your kind contraband.[1] Will you pardon my importuning you once more? I very much need the work on Germany[2] by that scapegrace, Heine. May I dare to hope that you will have the kindness to obtain it, too?

Accept, Sir, the assurance of my high esteem.

A. Pushkin.

[553]
To Iosif Matveevich Penkovsky
May 1, 1835. From Petersburg to Boldino.

All your arrangements meet with the full measure of my approval. I am thinking of being there in July. My affairs in Petersburg have taken a bad turn, but I hope to set them straight. According to my agreement with Father, the revenues from Kistenevo from now on are assigned exclusively to my brother Lev Sergeevich and my sister Olga Sergeevna.[1] Consequently, send all the revenues from my share to wherever my sister or her husband Nikolay Ivanovich Pavlishchev requests; and send the revenues from the other half (except the interest which is due to the government Loan Office) to Lev Sergeevich, wherever he may direct. Boldino will remain for Father.

In a few days I shall write you in more detail.

May 1.   A. Pushkin.

[554]
To Lev Sergeevich Pushkin
May 2, 1835. From Petersburg to Tiflis.

Father has agreed to give you complete control of half of Kistenevo. I am yielding my own share to our sister (i.e., only the revenues). I have already written to this effect to the manager.[1] You will have a net income of about two thousand rubles. I advise you to leave up to the manager the payment of the interest—and that you yourself receive only this sum. Two thousand is not a great deal, but all the same one can live on it. Our Mother was dying; now she is better, but not completely well. I don't think she can live long.

[555]
To Nikolay Ivanovich Pavlishchev
May 2, 1835. From Petersburg to Warsaw.

Dear Sir, Nikolay Ivanovich,

I have not answered you for a long time, because I could write nothing definite. I am answering both your letters today. You are right about almost everything, and there's no use discussing what you're not right about. Let's talk about business. You demand a sister's lawful share. You know our family circumstances; you know how difficult it is for us to proceed to anything sensible or business-like. Let us postpone this until another time. Here are the arrangements which I proposed to Father a few days ago, and to which, thank God, he agreed. He is letting Lev Sergeevich have half of Kistenevo; I am yielding my half to my sister (i.e., the revenue), with the proviso that she receive the revenues and pay the interest to the government Loan Office: I have already written to this effect to the manager.[1] Boldino remains Father's. Of course, this is neither a sacrifice nor a favor on my part, but a consideration for the future. My own family and my affairs are not in good condition. I am thinking of leaving Petersburg and going to the village, if only I can avoid incurring displeasure in so doing.

For the clasp and the pin I am offered 850 rubles.[2] What do you want me to do? It would not be a bad idea for you to come to Petersburg, but we still have time to exchange letters about it.

I have been still managing the estate up to now, but I am thinking of giving it up by July. Mother is better, but she is by no means so well as she thinks; the doctors have no hope for a complete recovery.

I send cordial greetings to you and my sister.

May 2.   A. Pushkin.

[556]
To Mikhail Petrovich Pogodin
The beginning of May, 1835. From Petersburg to Moscow.
(Rough draft)

Dear Sir, Mikhaylo Petrovich,

I have just now received the most recent issue of *A Library for Reading*, and in it I have noticed some tale with the signature *Belkin*[1]—and I ran across your name. Since I shall not read the story, I hasten to announce to you that this Belkin is not my Belkin, and that I am not answerable for any absurdities of his.

This letter will be delivered to you by Mr. Semen,[2] the editor of *The Pictorial Annual*. He is planning to describe Moscow, and I am sending him to one who loves her.

Tell the Observers[3] that they should be a little more punctual in delivering.

[557]
To Natalia Ivanovna Goncharova
May 16, 1835. From Petersburg to Yaropolets.
Dear Madame, Mother, Natalia Ivanovna,

I have the happiness to congratulate you upon your grandson Grigory[1] and to commend him to your favor. Natalia Nikolaevna gave birth to him successfully. But she was in pain longer than usual. And her condition now is not exactly good—though, thank God, there is no danger whatever. I was absent when the baby was born; I had been forced to make a trip to the Pskov village on personal business,[2] and I returned the day after her delivery. My arrival disturbed her, and she suffered all day yesterday; today she is better. She has commissioned me to solicit your blessing on her and the new-born child.

Yesterday the hatbox was received from you, together with the note, which I have not shown my wife, so as not to cause her pain, in her condition. She seems not to have carried out your errand satisfactorily, and she might conclude from the note that you have become angry with her.

I kiss your little hands, and I have the happiness to be, with the most profound respect and heartfelt devotion,

      Your most humble
       Servant and son-in-law,
        A. Pushkin.

[558]
To Semen Semenovich Khlyustin
May 25, 1835(?). In Petersburg.
(In French)

I beseech you to excuse me. It will be impossible for me to come and dine at your house. My wife has suddenly become very ill. Please be so kind as to send me the address of M. de Circourt.[1]

      All yours,
May 25.   Pushkin.

[559]
　　　　　To Vladimir Fedorovich Odoevsky
　　　　　April or May, 1835. In Petersburg.
What do you take me for? I heard the fool¹ once in Moscow, and I'm not going to any more. One must listen to him, however, in order to berate him properly in the Chronicler.² And so, subscribe, Prince! Be so kind as to pay up, Your Highness—you'll get used to it and come to love it. Don't be stingy. And shall we see each other some fine day?
　　　　　　　　　　　　　　　　　　　　　　　　　A.P.

[560]
　　　　　To Alexander Khristoforovich Benkendorf
　　　　　April or May, 1835. In Petersburg.
　　　　　(Rough draft; in French)
I make bold to submit for Your Excellency's decision the following:

In 1832 His Majesty deigned to grant me the permission to be the publisher of a political and literary journal.¹

This profession is not mine, and it is distasteful to me in quite a few respects, but circumstances oblige me to have recourse to a measure which until now I believed I could avoid. I am living in Petersburg, where, thanks to His Majesty, I can devote myself to pursuits which are more important and more to my taste. But the life I am leading entails expenses, and my family affairs are so disorganized that I find myself in the necessity of either abandoning historical labors,² which have become dear to me, or of having recourse to the Emperor's kindnesses, to which I have no claim other than the benefactions which he has already showered upon me.

A journal offers me the means of living in Petersburg and of meeting my sacred obligations. I therefore should like to be the editor of a gazette similar in every way to *The Northern Bee*, and I should like permission to publish separately items of a purely literary nature (such as long and detailed critiques, tales, short novels, long poems, etc.), for which room could not be found in a *feuilleton* (a volume every three months in the manner of the English *Reviews*).³

I beg your pardon, but I am obliged to tell you everything. I have had the misfortune to incur the enmity of the Minister of Public Instruction,[4] and also that of Prince Dondukov, born Korsakov. Both of them have already made me feel this in a rather disagreeable manner. In entering upon a field of endeavor where I shall be dependent upon them, I would be lost without your immediate protection. I therefore make bold to beseech you to grant my journal a censor drawn from your chancellery. This is all the more indispensable to me in that, since my journal is to appear at the same time as *The Northern Bee*, I must have time to translate the same articles, under the penalty of otherwise being obliged to republish on the morrow the news already published the preceding evening—which would indeed suffice to ruin the whole undertaking.

[561]
To ALEXANDER KHRISTOFOROVICH BENKENDORF
April or May, 1835. In Petersburg.
(Second rough draft; in French)

When I asked for permission to become the publisher of a literary and political gazette, I myself felt all the objections to this undertaking. I was compelled to do so by painful circumstances. Neither I nor my wife, so far, has an estate; that of my father is so disorganized that I have been obliged to take over the direction of it, in order to assure a future to the rest of my family. I wanted to become a journalist only so as not to reproach myself with having neglected a means which, by giving me an income of 40,000, would deliver me from my difficulties. I confess that, my plan not meeting with His Majesty's approval,[1] I was relieved of a great burden. But I am, as a consequence, obliged to have recourse to the kindnesses of the Emperor, who is now my only hope. I ask your permission, Count, to explain my situation to you and to entrust my request to your protection.

Finding a way to borrow 100,000 would suffice me to pay my debts and to be able to live, to arrange my family affairs and finally to be free to devote myself without any worries to my historical labors and to my pursuits. But in Russia it is impossible.

The Emperor, who up to the present has never wearied of showering me with favors, but what is painful to me [. . . .],[2] in deigning to take me into his service, he did me the favor of setting my salary at 5,000. This sum represents the interest on a capital of 125,000. If, instead of my salary, His Majesty would do me the favor of giving me the capital as a *loan* for ten years and without interest—I would be perfectly happy and tranquil.[3]

[562]
To ALEXANDER KHRISTOFOROVICH BENKENDORF
June 1, 1835. In Petersburg.
(In French)

Count,

I am ashamed of always troubling Your Excellency, but the indulgence and the interest which you have always deigned to display toward me will be the excuse for my indiscretion.

I have no property; neither I nor my wife has yet the portion which is to come to us. Up to the present I have lived on only the fruits of my labor. My fixed income is the salary which the Emperor has deigned to grant me. Working in order to live has, most certainly, no humiliation for me. But it is completely impossible for me, accustomed to independence, to write for money; and that idea alone is enough to reduce me to inaction. Life in Petersburg is horribly expensive. Up to the present I have looked rather indifferently upon the expenditures which I have been obliged to make, because a political and literary journal—a purely commercial undertaking—would give me immediately the means of having an income of 30,000–40,000. However, this work was so repugnant to me that I have considered having recourse to it only as the last resort.

I see myself in the necessity of cutting short expenditures which only entail my making debts and which are preparing for me a future of anxiety and cares, if not of destitution and despair. Three or four years of retirement to the country would make it possible for me again to come and resume in Petersburg the pursuits for which I am still indebted to the favors of His Majesty.

I have been showered with benefactions by the Emperor; I would be in despair if His Majesty could suppose, in my desire to depart from Petersburg, any other motive than that of absolute necessity. The least sign of displeasure or of suspicion would suffice to keep me in the status where I now am, because, in short, I would rather be in financial difficulties than be ruined in the opinion of the one who has been my benefactor, not as Sovereign, not from duty or justice, but from a free feeling of noble and generous benevolence.[1]

Entrusting my fate into your hands, I have the honor to be, with the most profound respect,

    Count,
        Your Excellency's
            Most humble and most obedient servant,

June 1.   Alexander Pushkin.
  SPb.

[563]
        To Nikolay Ivanovich Pavlishchev
    June 3, 1835. From Petersburg to Warsaw.
Dear Sir, Nikolay Ivanovich,

You wish to know just what Father's estate consists of. I am sending you a listing of it:

In the village of Boldino, according to the seventh revision, 564 souls.

In the little village of Kistenevo (also called Timashevo), 476.

The late Vasily Lvovich [Pushkin] owned *the other half of Boldino*, in which there were also about 600 souls. This part was sold three years after the heir himself renounced the inheritance. I was not able to take upon myself the debts of the deceased, because I was already hard up, even without doing that.[1] And I should think that Lev Sergeevich [Pushkin] could not have even thought of it, for, the very first thing, one would have had to pay at least 60,000. It's a pity that you did not get in touch with me at that time. If I could have supposed that you would take over the management of this estate, I might not have renounced it.

You want to have a power of attorney[2] for managing that part of Kistenevo, the income of which I am yielding to my sister. Gladly. Only write me whether I am to send it to you or whether you yourself will come for it. It would not be a bad idea to talk everything over.

June 3, 1835.   All yours, A. Pushkin.

[564]
> To VASILY ANDREEVICH DUROV
> June 16, 1835. From Petersburg to Elabuga.

Dear Sir, Vasily Andreevich,[1]

I was sincerely gladdened by receiving your letter, which reminded me of our old, pleasant acquaintanceship, and I hasten to answer you. If the author of the Notes[2] will agree to entrust them to me, then I shall willingly undertake the cares of their publication. If he is thinking of selling them in manuscript, then let him set the price himself. If the booksellers do not agree to it, I shall probably buy them. I should think their success can be vouched for. The author's fate is so curious, so well known and so mysterious, that the solution of the riddle cannot help producing a powerful, a general impression. As for the style, the simpler it is, the better. The most important thing is truth, sincerity. The subject in itself is so interesting that it needs no adornments. They would even harm it.

I congratulate you upon your new mode of living; I am sorry that of your hundred thousand ways to obtain a hundred thousand rubles, not one seems to have been employed by you with success. But money will come with time. The main thing: may we stay alive.

Farewell—I am awaiting your answer with impatience.

With the most profound respect and complete devotion, I have the honor to be,
>
> Dear Sir,
> Your most humble servant,

June 16, 1835.   A. Pushkin.
SPb.
On the Dvortsovaya Naberezhnaya, the house of Batashev.

[565]
> To ANDREY ALEXANDROVICH KRAEVSKY
> June 18, 1835. In Petersburg.

I have not written anything to the Moscow brotherhood. But do me the favor of correcting the next to the last verse in "The Cloud."[1]

And the wind, *caressing the little leaves* of the trees [. . . .]

[566]
To Alexander Khristoforovich Benkendorf
July 4, 1835. In Petersburg.

Dear Sir, Count Alexander Khristoforovich,

It was the Sovereign's pleasure to jot down on my letter to Your Highness[1] that I may not leave for several years in the village, unless I first resign. I commit my fate completely to the Tsar's will, and I wish only that His Majesty's decision[2] be not a sign of disfavor toward me, and that access to the archives not be forbidden me, when circumstances permit me to be in Petersburg.

With the most profound respect, devotion, and gratitude, I have the honor to be,

Dear Sir,
Your Highness's
Most humble servant,
Alexander Pushkin.

July 4, 1835.
SPb.

[567]
To Natalia Ivanovna Goncharova
July 14, 1835. From Petersburg to Yaropolets.

Dear Madame, Mother, Natalia Ivanovna,

I sincerely thank you for the present which you have been so kind as to bestow upon my new-born son,[1] and which arrived very opportunely. We expected Dmitry Nikolaevich [Goncharov] for the christening, but he didn't get here. He writes that his affairs detained him, and that his anticipations with regard to Countess N.[2] were not fulfilled. He does not seem to be in despair. As you instructed, I kissed my wife with all possible tenderness; she kisses your little hands and is intending to write you. We are now living in a summer house, on Chernaya Rechka, and we are thinking of moving from here to the village and even for several years.[3] Our financial circumstances require it. However, I am awaiting the decision of my fate by the Sovereign, who has been very gracious to me, and whose wish will be my law.

I have a request and domestic explanations to address to you: Until now our chief bothers have come from our not being able to cope with our male cooks, who in Petersburg, are spoiled and excessively expensive. If you have any male cook in Yaropolets whom you do not need (if only he be of good, honorable, and undebauched conduct), then you would do us a true benefaction by sending him to us—especially in case we leave for the village. Forgive me for speaking to you without ceremony and directly, relying on your indulgence and good will.

My wife, children, and sisters-in-law[4]—all, thank God, at my house are well, and they kiss your little hands. Masha is asking to go to a ball, and she says she has already learned to dance from the little doggies. You see how precocious they are among us; the first thing you know she will be marriageable.

With the most profound respect and devotion, I have the happiness to be,

        Dear Madame, Mother,
            Your most humble servant and son-in-law,

July 14.   A. Pushkin.

[568]
        To Alexander Khristoforovich Benkendorf
           July 22, 1835. In Petersburg.
               (In French)

Count,

I have had the honor of waiting upon you at Your Excellency's door, but I did not have the good fortune to find you in.

Showered with favors by His Majesty, I, Count, am writing you now in order to thank you for the interest which you have been so kind as to display toward me, and to explain my situation frankly to you.

During my last five years' residence in Petersburg, I have incurred debts of close to sixty thousand rubles. Moreover, I have been obliged to take in hand my family's affairs, which have so encumbered me that I have been obliged to forego a legacy,[1] and so that the only means that I had of putting my affairs in order were either to retire to the country, or else borrow, once and for all, a large sum of money. But this latter course is almost impossible in Russia, where the law grants too weak a guarantee to the creditor, and where loans are almost always debts between friends and on one's word.

Gratitude is not for me a painful feeling, and most certainly my devotion to the person of the Emperor is not troubled by any mental reservations of shame or of remorse. But I cannot conceal from myself that I have absolutely no right to benefactions from His Majesty and that it is impossible for me to ask for anything.[2]

It is therefore to you, Count, that I entrust once more the deciding of my fate, and beseeching you to accept the assurance of my high esteem, I have the honor to be, with respect and gratitude,
        Count,
           Your Excellency's
July 22, 1835.   Most humble and most obedient servant,
St. Petersburg.   Alexander Pushkin.

[569]
        To Vladimir Dmitrievich Volkhovsky
        July 22, 1835. From Petersburg to Tiflis.

I have a friendly and most humble request to make of you, my honored Vladimir Dmitrievich:[1] Count Zabela is en route to Georgia to serve under your command. His friends and relatives ask, on his behalf, your protection and good will, which of course he needs in his situation. I know that my intercession is completely superfluous in this instance, but I rejoice at the chance to remind you from afar of your Lyceum comrade, who is sincerely devoted to you.

I am sending you my most recent composition, *The History of the Pugachev Revolt*. In it I was trying to investigate the military actions of that time, and I was thinking only of the clear exposition of them, which cost me no little labor, for the commanders, who operated confusedly enough, wrote their reports still more confusedly, boasting or justifying themselves equally unintelligibly. It was necessary to check all this, to verify, etc. Your opinion regarding my book would be precious to me in every respect.

Be healthy and happy.

July 22, 1835.   A. Pushkin.
   SPb.

[570]
>   To Alexander Khristoforovich Benkendorf
>   July 26, 1835. In Petersburg.
>   (In French)

Count,

It pains me, at the moment when I am receiving an unexpected favor, to ask for two more, but I have resolved to have recourse in all frankness to the one who has deigned to be my Providence.

Of my sixty thousand in debts, half are debts of honor. In order to pay them, I see myself under the necessity of contracting usurious debts, which will redouble my difficulties, or even place me in the necessity of having recourse again to the generosity of the Emperor.

I therefore beseech His Majesty to do me a full and complete favor: first, to grant me the possibility of paying off these thirty thousand rubles; and, second, to deign to permit me to regard this sum as a loan and, accordingly, to have the payment of my salary suspended until my debt be paid off.[1]

Commending myself to your indulgence, I have the honor to be, with the most profound respect and with the most heartfelt gratitude,

>   Count,
>   Your Excellency's,
> July 26, 1835.   Most humble and most obedient servant,
> St. Petersburg.   Alexander Pushkin.

[571]
>   To Alexandra Andreevna Fuchs
>   August 15, 1835. From Petersburg to Kazan.
>   August 15, 1835. SPb.

I have long delayed delivering your tribute to you, while I was awaiting the portrait of Pugachev from Paris. Finally I have received it, and I hasten to forward my book to you.[1] Relying on your indulgence, I have made bold to send in care of you a copy for delivery to Mr. Rybushkin,[2] from whom I had the honor to receive his interesting history of Kazan.

I commend myself to your precious good will, and to the friendship of honored Karl Fedorovich [Fuchs] (to whom I apologize for the imperfections in the publishing of my book).

With the most profound respect and devotion, I have the honor to be [. . . .]³

[572]
To Efim Petrovich Lyutsenko
August 19, 1835. In Petersburg.

Dear Sir, Efim Petrovich!¹

I am truly ashamed for the bothers which I am letting Your Excellency in for. Smirdin has not kept his word; I suspect that actually his circumstances are in a muddle. The printing of your poem² cannot cost fifteen hundred rubles; he is mistaken. My departure for the village prevents me from undertaking the business myself. I have just now written to Baron Korf, asking him to intercede for you, as for one connected with the Lyceum. I hope that on his part he will do everything possible.

With genuine respect and complete devotion, I have the honor to be, Dear Sir, Your Excellency's most humble servant.

August 19, 1835.   A. Pushkin.

[573]
To Vasily Alexeevich Polenov
August 28, 1835. In Petersburg.

Dear Sir, Vasily Alexeevich,¹

I have the honor to make a most humble request of Your Excellency.

The Sovereign Emperor has been so kind as to empower me to unseal the Pugachev dossier, in order to compile a Historical Extract.² In the eight binders provided me from the St. Petersburg Senate, I have not found the most important document: the deposition taken from Pugachev himself, in the Committee of Inquiry established in Moscow. I make bold most humbly to request Your Excellency that you have this matter referred to A. F. Malinovsky,³ who probably knows where this essential document is located.⁴

With the most profound respect and with complete devotion, I have the honor to be,
                    Dear Sir,
                        Your Excellency's
August 28, 1835.   Most humble servant,
    SPb.   Alexander Pushkin.

[574]
To Egor Frantsevich Kankrin
September 6, 1835. In Petersburg.

Dear Sir, Count Egor Frantsevich,

Having a most humble request to make of Your Highness, I make bold to burden your attention with a preliminary explanation of my piece of business.

As a consequence of domestic circumstances, I was compelled to request retirement, in order to go to the village for several years. The Sovereign Emperor most graciously deigned to say that he does not want me to be torn away from my historical labors, and he commanded that I be given 10,000 rubles,[1] as a grant in aid. This sum was not sufficient to rectify my financial status. Remaining in Petersburg, I could not avoid either further muddling my affairs by the hour, or having recourse to grants in aid and to favors, an expedient to which I am not accustomed, for until now, thank God, I have been independent and have lived by my labors.

And so I have made bold to ask His Majesty for two favors: (1) that I be given, *instead of a grant in aid, a loan of 30,000 rubles, every ruble of which I need* for payment of debts which must be paid; (2) that my salary be withheld until this sum has been repaid. The sovereign has been kind enough to consent to both.[2]

But from the State Treasury I was given, instead of 30,000 rubles, only 18,000, for there was a deduction of various amounts of interest and of the 10,000 (ten thousand rubles) which had been given me as a loan for the publishing of a certain book.[3] Thus I am in a more constrained position than ever, for I am compelled to remain in Petersburg, with my debts not paid and deprived of my 5000 rubles of salary.

I make bold to request Your Highness for the authorization for me to receive in full the sum which I was forced to request of the Sovereign, and for permission to pay the interest on the sum which was given me in 1834, until my circumstances permit me to pay the sum itself in full.[4]

Commending myself to Your Highness's good will, with the

most profound respect and with complete devotion, I have the honor to be,

Dear Sir,
Your Highness's
Most humble servant,

September 6, 1835. Alexander Pushkin.

[575]
To Natalia Nikolaevna Pushkina
September 14, 1835. From Mikhaylovskoe to Petersburg.

You and I are fine ones. I didn't give you my address, and you didn't ask me for it. Here it is: to the Pskov Province, to Ostrov, to the village Trigorskoe.[1] Today is September 14. Here it has already been a week since I left you, my darling, but I have seen no benefit in having done so. I haven't begun writing, and I don't know when I'll begin. Instead, I think of you constantly, and I won't think up anything worth while. I'm sorry I didn't bring you along with me. What weather we're having! Here I've just spent three whole days jaunting about—now on foot, now on horseback. Thus I'll jaunt away my whole autumn, and if God doesn't send some decent frosts, I'll return to you without having accomplished anything. Praskovia Alexandrovna [Osipova] isn't here yet. She's either in the village at Begicheva's,[2] or she's fussing around in Pskov. She's expected in a few days. Today I saw the moon over my left shoulder,[3] and I began to be very much disturbed about you. How's our expedition?[4] Have you seen Countess Kankrina, and what's the answer? As a last resort, if Count Kankrin turns us off, we have Count Yuriev[5] left; I direct you to him. Write me as often as you can; and write everything you're doing, so that I may know whom you're coquetting with, where you go, whether you're behaving yourself well, what your gossiping is like, and whether you're waging war successfully with your surnamesake.[6] Farewell, darling: I kiss Maria Alexandrovna's[7] little hand, and I ask her to be my intercessor with you. I kiss Sashka on his round forehead. I bless all of you. To Aunts Azya and Koko,[8] my cordial greeting. Tell Pletnev to write me about our mutual affairs.

[576]
>To Peter Alexandrovich Pletnev
>Between September 1 and 15, 1835.
>From Mikhaylovskoe to Petersburg.
>(Rough draft)

You advise me to continue *Onegin*, assuring me that I haven't finished it [. . . .][1]

[577]
>To Alexandra Ivanovna Bekleshova

Between September 11 and 18, 1835. From Trigorskoe to Pskov.

My angel,[1] how sorry I am that I found you were no longer here, and how glad Evpraxia Nikolaevna [Vrevskaya, nee Vulf] made me, by telling me that you intend to come to our parts again! Do come, for God's sake; at least by the 23rd. I have heaps of confessions, explanations, and all sorts of stuff for you. We might, at our leisure, even fall in love. I am writing you, and cater-cornered from me you yourself are sitting, in the form of Maria Ivanovna [Osipova].[2] You wouldn't believe how she calls to mind a former time

>And journeys to Opochka[3]

and so forth. Forgive me my friendly chatter. I kiss your little hands.
>A.P.

[578]
>To Natalia Nikolaevna Pushkina

September 21, 1835. From Mikhaylovskoe to Petersburg.

My wife, here it's already the 21st, and I haven't received a single line from you yet. This disturbs me in spite of myself, though I know that you probably didn't learn my address before the 17th, in Pavlovsk. Did you? Besides, the mail from Petersburg comes only once a week. However, I am constantly uneasy, anyhow, and I'm not writing anything. And time is passing. You can't imagine how vividly the imagination operates when we sit alone within four walls, or when we walk in the woods, when nobody hinders us from thinking—from thinking until the head begins to whirl. And what do I think about? Here's what: what are we going to live on? My father won't leave me the estate; he has already squandered half of it. Your estate is within a hair's breadth of ruin. The Tsar doesn't permit me to join the ranks of the landowners or the journalists. God sees that I can't write books for money. We don't have a penny of sure income, but a sure outgo of thirty thousand. Everything hangs on me and Aunty. But neither I nor Aunty is eternal. How all this will come out, God knows. Meanwhile, it's sad. Just give me a kiss; maybe the woe will pass. But it's no use—your little lips won't stretch two hundred fifty miles. I just sit and pine—what would you have! Now listen to my diary: I was at the Vrevskys[1] day before yesterday, and spent the night there. Praskovia Alexandrovna [Osipova] was expected, but she didn't come. Vrevskaya is a very kind and sweet little woman, but she's as fat as Mefody, our Pskov bishop. And you'd think, looking at her, she's with child; she's still just the same as when you saw her. I borrowed Walter Scott from them, and I'm reading him. I'm sorry that I didn't bring the English along with me. By the way: send me, if you can, *Essays de M. Montagne* [sic][2]—four dark blue books on my long shelves. Look them up. Today the weather is gloomy. Autumn is beginning. Maybe I'll set to work. I'm expecting Praskovia Alexandrovna, who probably will arrive in Trigorskoe today.—I walk a lot, I ride horseback a lot, on jades which are very glad of it, for in reward they're given oats, to which they're not accustomed. I eat baked potatoes, like a Finn, and soft-boiled eggs, like Louis XVIII. That's my dinner. I lie down at 9 o'clock; I get up at 7. Now I require of you a similar detailed accounting. I kiss you, my darling, and all the children. I bless all of you with all my heart. Stay well, all of you. To my sisters-in-law, my greeting. How must one say it: *bel' sery* or *bel' seri*?[3] Farewell.

[579]
To Natalia Nikolaevna Pushkina
September 25, 1835. From Trigorskoe to Petersburg.

I am writing you from Trigorskoe. What's this, little wife? Here it's already the 25th, and all this time I haven't had a single line from you. This angers and disturbs me. How are you addressing your letters to me? Write *To Pskov*, to Her Honor, Praskovia Alexandrovna Osipova, for delivery to A.S.P., the well-known writer—and that's all there is to it. That way it'll be surer that I'm reached by your letters, without which I will get completely stultified. Are you well, my darling? And how are my young ones? How's our home, and how well are you managing it? Just imagine, I haven't written a line up till now, and all because I'm not tranquil. In Mikhaylovskoe I found everything as of old, except that my nursemaid[1] is no longer here, and that near the old familiar pines there has grown up during my absence a young pine family which it's vexing for me to look at,[2] just as it's sometimes vexing for me to see young cavalry guardsmen at balls, at which I no longer dance. But there's nothing to be done. Everything around me says that I'm growing old, and sometimes even in plain Russian. For example, yesterday I was met by a peasant woman I know, whom I couldn't help telling that she had changed. Then she, to me: "And you, too, my provider, you've grown old and ugly." Though I can say of myself, as my deceased nursemaid used to, that I never was good-looking—but I once was young. All that is no great matter. There is one great matter: don't notice, my darling, what I am noticing all too well. What are you doing, my beauty, in my absence? Tell me what occupies you, where you go, what new gossip there is, etc. [Sofia Nikolaevna] Karamzina and the Meshcherskys, I've heard, have arrived.[3] Don't forget to give them my cordial greeting. It's roomier now at Trigorskoe: Evpraxia Nikolaevna [Vrevskaya, nee Vulf] and Alexandra Ivanovna [Bekleshova, nee Osipova] are married, but Praskovia Alexandrovna [Osipova] is still the same, and I love her very much. I am behaving myself with modesty and decency. I go on jaunts on foot and horseback. I'm reading Walter Scott's novels, which I'm in rapture over, and I am moaning for you. Farewell. I give you a big kiss; I bless you and the children. How are Koko and Azya?[4] Are they married, or not yet? Tell them not to get married without my blessing. Farewell, my angel.

[580]
 To Natalia Nikolaevna Pushkina
 September 29, 1835. From Mikhaylovskoe to Petersburg
 My darling, yesterday I received two letters from you; they grieved me very much. What's Katerina Ivanovna [Zagryazhskaya] ill of? You write *terribly ill*. Consequently there's danger? With impatience

I am awaiting your *bulletin*. All that proceeds from her inhuman mode of living. Will we live to see the day when Countess Polier has finally married her prince?[1] Kankrin jokes—but I'm in no mood for jokes. The Sovereign promised me a *Gazette*,[2] but then he forbade it; he makes me live in Petersburg but does not give me the means of living by my own labors. I am wasting my time and spiritual powers, I'm throwing my hard-earned money out the windows, and I don't see anything in the future. My father is squandering his estate away, without pleasure and without prudence; your folks are losing theirs on account of the stupidity or the heedlessness of the deceased Afanasy Nikolaevich [Goncharov]. What will come of all this? The Lord knows. Your fire occurred probably from the negligence of your Ladies in Waiting; may they thrive in my absence! Thank God that the affair was limited to the curtains. You have sent me a note from Mme. Kern; the fool has taken it into her head to translate [George] Sand,[3] and she asks that I act the pander for her with Smirdin. The devil take them both! I have commissioned Anna Nikolaevna [Vulf] to answer her for me that if her translation is as faithful as she herself is a faithful copy of Mme. Sand, then her success is undoubtable, but that I have no business connections with Smirdin.—What about Pletnev? Is he thinking about our mutual piece of business?[4] Probably not. I am spending my time very monotonously. Mornings I am not getting anything done, but I am merely milling the wind. In the evening I ride to Trigorskoe, burrow in old books, and nibble on nuts. But I'm not even thinking of writing either poetry or prose. Tell Sashka that I have white plums here which there's no comparing with the ones he steals from you, and that I ask him to eat some with me. How's Mashka? What do you think of her friendship with the little *Peassant*?[5] And what do you think of her conquests? Write me the political news, too. I don't read newspapers here—I don't go to the English Club or see [Elizaveta M.] Khitrovo. I don't know what's happening in the great wide world. When will the Tsars be there? And isn't there something to be heard about a war, etc.? I bless all of you—stay well. I kiss you. How stupidly you addressed your letter to me; what a dainty dish! "To the Pskov Province, to the village Mikhaylovskoe." Oh you, you dove! But you didn't say what district. And I'll bet there is more than one village Mikhaylovskoe. And even if only one, then just who knows where it is? What a featherbrain! You see that I keep on grumbling, but what's to be done? There's nothing to be glad about. Write to me about Aunty—and about your mother. *Je remercie vos soeurs*,[6] as Natalia Ivanovna [Goncharova] writes, although, truly, there's nothing to thank them for.

[581]
To Natalia Nikolaevna Pushkina
October 2, 1835. From Mikhaylovskoe to Petersburg.

My dear little wife, we have a filly here which takes either harness or the saddle. She's good in every way, but just let something frighten her on the road, and she will take the bit in her teeth and she'll take you six or eight miles over mounds and ravines—and then there is no way you can curb her in until she herself is all fagged out.

I have received, angel of skittishness and beauty! your letter, where you see fit to take the bit in your teeth and kick out your dainty and shapely little hoofs shod by Mme. *Katherine*.[1] I hope that now you are all fagged out and have calmed down. I am awaiting from you some decent letters wherein I may hear you and your voice—and not abuse, which I have not deserved at all, for I am behaving myself like a fairy-tale maid. Since yesterday I have begun to write (but knock on wood). Our weather is becoming worse and worse, and fall seems to be approaching in earnest. Perhaps I shall get in a writing vein. From your angry letter I conclude that Katerina Ivanovna [Zagryazhskaya] is better;[2] you wouldn't have abused me so spiritedly if she were seriously ill. All the same, write me about everything, and in detail. Why don't you write anything about Masha? After all, though Sashka is my favorite, I still love her pranks. I look out the window and think: it wouldn't be bad if suddenly a carriage entered the yard—and Natalia Nikolaevna were sitting in the carriage! But no, my darling. Stay in Petersburg, and I'll try to hurry up and come to you sooner than the appointed time. How about Pletnev?[3] How are the Karamzins, the Meshcherskys, etc.?—Write me about everything. I kiss you, and I bless the children.

[582]
>
> To Peter Alexandrovich Pletnev
> About (not later than) October 11, 1835.
> From Mikhaylovskoe to Petersburg.

I was made glad by receiving from you a letter (a sensible one, as yours usually are). I shall try to answer point by point and in detail: You have received the *Journey*[1] from the censorship, but what did the committee decide with regard to my most humble petition?[2] The little ass Nikitenko won't kick and the bull Dunduk[3] butt me to death, will they? They won't get rid of me so easily, though. My thanks, my great thanks to Gogol for his "Calash";[4] the almanac can travel a long way in it. However, my opinion is this: don't accept "The Calash" for nothing, but set a price for it; Gogol needs money. You ask a name for the almanac: let's call it Arion or Orion. I love names which don't make any sense; there's nothing for jokes to stick to. Have Langer[5] also sketch a vignette without any sense. There should be some little flowers, and lyres, and chalices, and ivy, as in Alexander Ivanovich's apartment in Gogol's comedy.[6] That will seem very natural. I would be glad to come to you in November; all the more that I've never had such a fruitless autumn in my life. I'm writing, but bungling the job. For inspiration one must have spiritual tranquillity, and I'm not tranquil at all. You're doing badly in becoming indecisive. I have always found that everything which you have devised has succeeded for me. Let's begin the almanac with the *Journey*. Send the proofs along to me, and I'll send you some poems. Who will be our censor? I rejoice that Senkovsky is trafficking on the name of Belkin. But can't we (of course stealthily and unobtrusively, for example, in *The Moscow Observer*) announce that the real Belkin is dead and refuses to accept responsibility for the sins of his homonym?[7] That truly wouldn't be a bad thing to do.

[583]
>
> To Egor Frantsevich Kankrin
> October 23, 1835. In Petersburg.

Dear Sir, Count Egor Frantsevich,

Upon returning from the village,[1] I discovered that Your Highness had been so kind as to inform me of the Sovereign's approving my most humble request, which I conveyed to you. I want to express to Your Highness my sincere, profound gratitude for the indulgent attention with which you, in the midst of your labors, have honored me, and for your well-disposed intercession, to which I am obligated for the success of my piece of business.[2]

With the most profound respect and with complete devotion, I have the honor to be,

Dear Sir,
Your Highness's
Most humble servant,
Alexander Pushkin.

October 23.
St. Petersburg.

[584]
To Alexander Khristoforovich Benkendorf
About (not earlier than) October 23, 1835. In Petersburg.
(Rough draft)

I address myself to Your Excellency with a complaint and a most humble request.

On the occasion of the censorship's finding difficulties in authorizing the publication of one of my poems, I was compelled during your absence to direct a petition to the Censorship Committee that the misunderstanding which had arisen be resolved. But the Committee has not honored my petition with an answer.[1] I do not know how I could have deserved such neglect—but not a single Russian writer has been more oppressed than I.

My compositions, approved by the Tsar, have been stopped at their appearance—they are published with arbitrary emendations by the censor; my complaints have been left without attention. I do not dare to publish my compositions—for I do not dare [. . . .][2]

[585]
To Praskovia Alexandrovna Osipova
About (not later than) October 26, 1835.
From Petersburg to Trigorskoe.
(In French)

Here I am, Madame, arrived in Petersburg. Just imagine, my

wife's silence proceeded from her having taken it into her head to address her letters to Opochka. God knows how she came to do that. In any case I beseech you to send one of our servants there, so that the post master will be informed that I am no longer in the country and that he should forward to Petersburg all the mail he has for me.

I have found my poor mother at death's door.[1] She had come from Pavlovsk to seek lodgings, and suddenly fell in a faint at Mme. Knyazhnina's,[2] where she had stopped. Raukh[3] and Spassky have no hope. In this sad situation I also have the affliction of seeing my poor Natalia the object of the hatred of society. Everywhere it is being said that it is dreadful that she should be such a woman of fashion when her father-in-law and her mother-in-law do not have the wherewithal to eat, and that her mother-in-law is dying at the home of outsiders. You know how things really stand. Strictly speaking, no one can say that a man who has twelve hundred peasants is poverty-stricken. It is my father who has something and I who have nothing. In any case, Natalia has nothing to do with all this; I am the one who should be answerable. If my mother had come to take up her abode at my house, Natalia, as a matter of course, would have taken her in. But a cold house, full of little ones, and crowded with company, is hardly suitable for an ill person. My mother is better off at her own house. I have found her already moved.[4] My father is in a very pitiable state. As for me, I am in a fret, and I am completely dumbfounded.

Believe me, dear Madame Osipova, all life, *süsse Gewohnheit*[5] that it is, has a bitterness which ends by rendering it disgusting, and society is a nasty pile of filth. I prefer Trigorskoe. I greet you with all my heart.

[586]
To Ivan Ivanovich Lazhechnikov
November 3, 1835. From Petersburg to Moscow.

Dear Sir, Ivan Ivanovich!

In the first place, I must ask your forgiveness for my laggardliness and unpunctuality. I received the portrait of Pugachev a month ago,[1] and upon returning from the village I discovered that until now your copy of the *History* of him has not been delivered to you. I am returning to you Rychkov's manuscript,[2] which, by your benevolence, I was able to utilize.

Permit me, Dear Sir, to thank you now for the excellent novels which we all have read with such avidity and with such enjoyment. Perhaps, as regards artistry, *The House of Ice* stands even higher than *The Last Novik*, but it does not abide by historical truth, and that, in time, when the Volynsky[3] affair is made available to the public, will of course harm your work. But poetry will always remain poetry, and many pages of your novel will live as long as the Russian language is not forgotten. On behalf of Vasily Trediakovsky,[4] I confess, I am ready to argue with you. You injure a person who is in many respects worthy of our esteem and gratitude. In the Volynsky affair he plays the role of a martyr. His report to the Academy is extremely touching. It is impossible to read it without indignation at his tormentor. One might also discuss Biron a little. He had the misfortune to be a German; on him has been dumped all the horror of Anna's reign, which was in accordance with the spirit of its time and the mores of the populace. Incidentally, he had great intelligence and great talents.

Permit me to pose for you a philological question, the resolving of which is important for me: in what sense did you use the word *xobot* in your last work, and according to what dialect?[5]

Commending myself to your favor, I have the honor to be, with the most profound respect,

    Dear Sir,
      Your most obedient servant,
November 3, 1835.   Alexander Pushkin.
St. Petersburg.

[587]
    To Praskovia Alexandrovna Osipova
   December 26, 1835. From Petersburg to Pskov.
       (In French)

Madame, I have finally had the consolation of receiving your letter of November 27. It was almost four weeks on the way. We did not know what to think of your silence. I do not know why I am assuming that you are at Pskov, and I am addressing this letter to you there. My mother's health has improved, but there is not yet a convalescence. She is weak; however, the malady has subsided.

My father is very much to be pitied. My wife thanks you for remembering her and commends herself to your friendship. *Rebjatuški takže*.[1] I wish you health and merry holidays, and I say nothing to you of my unalterable devotion.

The Emperor has just granted a pardon to the majority of the conspirators of 1825, to, among others, my poor Kyukhelbeker. *Po ukazu dolžen on byt' poselen v južnoj časti Sibiri.*[2] It is a beautiful region, but I should like to have him closer to us; and perhaps he will be permitted to withdraw to the lands of Mme. Glinka, his sister. The government has always treated him with gentleness and indulgence.

When I consider that ten years have elapsed since these unfortunate disturbances,[3] it all seems a dream. How many occurrences, how many changes in everything, beginning with my own ideas—my situation, etc., etc. Actually, only my friendship for you and your family do I rediscover in my soul still the same, still unaltered and undiminished.

December 26.

Your promissory note[4] is ready, and I shall send it to you next time.

Notes to Part XII

Letter 528
1. Lazhechnikov's novels were *The Last Recruit* and *The House of Ice*. The "Pugachev materials" were in Rychkov's manuscript. See Letter 485, and note 1.

Letter 529
1. Boldino.
2. August 26.
3. Mme. Pushkina's birthday.
4. Sergey Nikolaevich Goncharov had been made an army officer on June 22, 1834.

Letter 530
1. It appeared at the end of December, 1834. There is information about the seige of Simbrisk by Firska in the eighth chapter.
2. Pushkin's various mentions of Stenka Razin show that Pushkin was very much interested in his uprising, in the seventeenth century, as well as that of Pugachev, in the eighteenth, and the Decembrist Uprising, in the nineteenth.

Letter 531
1. This letter was probably delivered by Pushkin's wife.
2. What pawnbroker Pushkin meant is not known.
3. Pushkin often joked at his friend Sobolevsky's "sluggishness" and laggardliness. Sobolevsky had been planning for years to make a trip to Paris. He did not make it until 1837.

Letter 532
1. The reference is obviously to Pugachev materials.
2. Probably K. A. Polevoy, who managed the book trade of the brothers Polevoy and who offered to co-operate with Pushkin in selling Pushkin's *History of Pugachev*.
3. Pushkin's allusions are to K. A. Polevoy's brother N. A. Polevoy, author of *The History of the Russian People*, and also to the fact that the Polevoys belonged to the literary proletariat or bourgeoisie, rather than the literary aristocracy, to which Pushkin belonged.

Letter 533
1. Pushkin left Petersburg on August 25. He spent a few hours in Moscow, and then went to Polotnyany Zavod, where his wife was visiting relatives. After spending about two weeks there, he returned with Mme. Pushkina to Moscow, where they spent a few days. Then she left for Petersburg, and he to visit his father's estate of Boldino. He arrived there on September 13. He returned to Petersburg on October 18.
2. "That is very nice of it."
3. Peter Romanovich Bezobrazov (1797-1856), husband of Vasily Lvovich Pushkin's natural daughter, Margarita Vasilievna Bezobrazova. The Bezobrazovs did not succeed in keeping Mme. Bezobrazova's inherited share of Boldino. Pushkin's father owned the other half share of it. Pushkin uses the contemptuous form, Margaritka, in referring to his cousin.
4. S. D. Bezobrazov.

5. Pushkin did not buy all or part of Boldino.
6. By Augustin Thierry. The third edition (Paris, 1830) was in Pushkin's library.
7. A recruited peasant's service as a soldier was so long (twenty-four years) that, if married, his wife was left, in effect, a widow and usually without resources. Such "widows" often resorted to prostitution.

Letter 534
1. Probably his *Captain's Daughter*.
2. That is, Emelian, apparently a servant.
3. Unknown.

Letter 535
1. The three brothers Yazykov were still living together on their estate of Yazykovo in the Province of Simbirsk.
2. Pushkin's idea of a journal finally materialized, in his *Contemporary*, in 1836. N. M. Yazykov contributed to it.

Letter 536
1. Members of the first class continued to celebrate faithfully October 19, the anniversary of the founding of the Tsarskoe Selo Lyceum. The celebration in 1834 was at Yakovlev's house. Pushkin's room at the Lyceum was number 14.

Letter 537
1. *The Poems of Alexandra Fuchs* (Kazan, 1834).
2. Baron Karl Theodore Lützerode, then Ambassador from Saxony to Russia. The letter in point has not survived, nor has the other letter mentioned.
3. One Erast Petrovich Pertsov.
4. The original of this letter has not survived—only the form in which Mme. Fuchs later published it, with the omission of the complimentary close and signature.

Letter 538
1. The reference is to Gogol's tale, "The Nevsky Prospect." The scene of Pirogov's being flogged by the German shopkeepers was taken out by the censor. The word Pushkin uses for "flogging," *sekutija*, is a humorous formation from the Russian verb "to flog" (which has the root of *sek*) and based on the analogy of the Russian transliteration, *èksekucija*, of the French word *exécution*.

Letter 539
1. The letter has to do with financial and legal arrangements for Penkovsky to manage Boldino and Kistenevo, under the direction of Pushkin, who was still his father's business manager. Pushkin is keeping his own finances, in connection with Kistenevo, carefully separate from his father's, in connection with Boldino. Penkovsky paid the 1270 rubles alluded to. Pushkin signed the power of attorney for Penkovsky to manage Boldino and Kistenevo, on November 20, 1834. The Guardian Council was the government office through which the serfs were mortgaged.

Letter 540
1. Pushkin received the desired permission.
2. *The Long Poems and Verse Tales of Alexander Pushkin* appeared in 1835.

Letter 541
1. Turgenev was about to set off for Paris.
2. Count Joseph de Maistre's *Du pape* appeared in 1817.

Letter 542
1. "Without the Sovereign's authorization to do so." The Russian passage was underlined, and it is apparently a direct quotation. Nicholas I gave permission for the book to be released, "if there is nothing besides what I have read." Benkendorf, on December 23, authorized the issuance of the book. Speransky was the head of Section II of His Imperial Majesty's Chancellery, which included the typography.

Letter 543
1. Countess Sofia Alexandrovna Bobrinskaya (1799-1866), wife of Count Alexey Alexeevich Bobrinsky.
2. Oldbook, a character in Sir Walter Scott's *Antiquary* (1816).
3. When Mme. Pushkina returned to Petersburg from her visit to her relatives in 1834, she brought both her sisters along. They continued to live in Petersburg with the Pushkins.

Letter 544
1. Nashchokin, in a letter written a month earlier, had informed Pushkin of Mme. Nashchokina's having given birth to their daughter Ekaterina Pavlovna Nashchokina (b. 1834), had asked Pushkin to pay at once the two thousand rubles Pushkin owed him, and had asked that Mme. Pushkina buy a hat and some dress materials (see Letter 545) in Petersburg for Mme. Nashchokina.
2. The allusion is to Nashchokin's earlier tempestuous life with his former mistress, the gypsy Olga Andreevna.
3. Rokhmanov had been an agent of Pushkin and of Nashchokin in 1831-1832, and 1833. For example, he was given the task of redeeming Mme. Pushkina's pawned diamonds.
4. Another allusion to the interception of Letter 488 by the post officials and the police.

Letter 545
1. See Letter 544 and note 1.
2. "Since Mme. Nashchokina is a brunette and has a beautiful complexion."

Letter 546
1. See Letter 540, and note 1.
2. Pushkin received the requested permission. On February 21, the Minister of Justice reported that the Pugachev dossier had been transferred to the State Archive for Pushkin's use.

Letter 547
1. Pushkin's *History of Pugachev*. See Letter 503, and note 2.
2. In January, 1835.

Letter 548
1. A copy of Pushkin's *History of Pugachev*.

2. Dmitriev's description, as a spectator, of the execution of Pugachev. Pushkin quotes this description in a note to Chapter VIII.

3. The allusion is to Polevoy's *History of the Russian People* and perhaps also to Kachenovsky and his skeptical attitude towards the genuineness of *The Lay of the Host of Igor.*

4. Russian editors have pointed out that Pushkin is mistaken. Nikolay Ivanovich Novikov (1744-1818), in the period between 1769 and 1791, had made excellent profits publishing satirical and other periodicals, a historical dictionary of Russian writers, a series of old Russian chronicles, and other things.

5. Peter Ivanovich Sokolov.

6. *The Dictionary of the Russian Language.* As an old Arzamasian, Pushkin here takes a sarcastic attitude toward the Russian Academy and its activities, though he was at this time a member.

7. Count D. I. Khvostov. Pushkin often laughs at the way he bought up copies of his own works at booksellers and donated them to his acquaintances.

Letter 549

1. The implication of the word here is "idiotic." The term "blessed" was a common appellative for the *jurodivye*, wandering holy fools.

2. Variant reading: "the whole."

3. Katenin had requested that Pushkin print his sonnet "Caucasus Mountains" in *A Library for Reading.* The next-to-the-last verse reads as follows: "The thicker the darkness around, the brighter the shining of the star."

Letter 550

1. When Pushkin took over the managing of his father's estate Boldino (see Letter 494), he agreed to pay the debts of his brother, L. S. Pushkin. Pushkin's brother-in-law, Pavlishchev, who watched the Pushkin family's finances like a hawk, pointed out that Pushkin by January, 1835, had already paid eighteen thousand rubles of his brother's debts.

2. L. S. Pushkin had rented an apartment from V. V. Engelgardt for the staggering sum of two hundred rubles per week.

3. L. S. Pushkin had gone into debt with Alexander Pavlovich Pleshcheev in Warsaw.

4. A promissory note given in November, 1833, to Ilia Alexandrovich Boltin, with a term of four years, for a gambling debt.

Letter 551

1. Pushkin's letter is a point-by-point answer to Dmitriev's letter of April 10, 1835.

2. In his diary, Pushkin further notes, "and what is worse, they are not buying it."

3. Hero of Byron's verse tale of the same name; Byron's romantic verse tales continued to be in vogue in Russia in the 1830's, and romantic tales in prose with Byronic heroes, but authors such as Bestuzhev-Marlinsky and Polevoy, were extremely popular.

4. The question was who would succeed P. I. Sokolov, "Achilles." The play on the names of Greek heroes from Homer's *Iliad* was suggested to Pushkin by the fact that Dmitry Ivanovich Yazykov (1773-1845), writer and translator, who, as Pushkin predicts, received the post, had published a translation of Schlözer's *Nestor: Russian Chronicles in the Ancient Slavic Language* . . . (Petersburg, 1809-1819). The other two contenders were Mikhail Estafievich Lobanov and Boris Mikhaylovich Fedorov.

5. He was appointed on March 7, 1835.

Letter 552

1. During Pushkin's visit to the Ural region, while doing research on Pugachev, in 1833. See Letter 466.

2. Vladimir Ivanovich Dal (1801-1872), write, lexicographer, and physician, most famous as the compiler of the four-volume *Dictionary of the Great-Russian Language* (1861-1868). Dal was present, as physician, at Pushkin's suffering and death, in January, 1837, after Pushkin received his mortal wound.

3. Konstantin Demianovich Artyukhov, an army captain of engineers. Dal recounts how Artyukhov gave Pushkin a lively account of hunting the woodcock, including how, after being shot, the bird would "pause stock-still in the air, dying, like Brutus." Pushkin puns on the name Wallenstein and the Russian word for woodcock, *val'dšnep* (German, *Waldschnepfe*). Pushkin wrote in his presentation copy, "To the officer who compares a woodcock with Wallenstein."

Letter 552a

1. This letter was first published in 1956. Gustav Nordin (1799-1867) was in 1835 secretary of the Swedish Embassy in Petersburg. It is not known what "contraband," i.e., foreign book prohibited in Russia, Nordin had given Pushkin.

2. The reference is to the fifth and sixth volumes of a French-language edition of Heine's *Works*, published in Paris in 1834-1835; the two volumes have the title "On Germany." The term "scapegrace," as has been noted, does not necessarily reflect Pushkin's own opinion of Heine, but the disfavor with which he was looked upon by official Russia. This is the only mention of Heine in Pushkin's letters. Apparently Pushkin's request to Nordin was fulfilled; the two volumes "on Germany" were in Pushkin's library, one of them with a presentation note from Count Ficquelmont, dated April 27, 1835, referring to the "two volumes of contraband."

Letter 553

1. This letter announces Pushkin's giving up the managing of his father's estate of Boldino. Pushkin directly informed his brother and his sister in Letters 554 and 555, respectively.

Letter 554

1. See Letters 553 and 555. Pushkin had received his "share" (half) of Kistenevo just before his marriage.

Letter 555

1. Letter 553. See also Letter 554 and note.

2. In addition to continually peppering Pushkin with letters querulously demanding Olga's "lawful share," Pavlishchev asked Pushkin to see about the sale of some of her valuables.

Letter 556

1. The tale was "A Tale Lost to the World," and it was really by Senkovsky. It contained ironical comment about a story by Pogodin. Pushkin is informing Pogodin that the author of *The Tales of Belkin* (Pushkin) did not write this tale.

2. Avgust Semen, bookseller and publisher of the Moscow publication, *Pictorial Review of Memorable Objects from the Sciences, Fine Arts, Trade, and Society*.

3. Publishers of the journal *The Moscow Observer* (1835-1837), edited by Pogodin and Shevyrev, and with contributors, the same group who had supported *The Moscow*

Messenger and *The European*. Pushkin contributed to the journal when it began to appear, but his relationships with it and its editors and contributors cooled in 1836.

Letter 557
1. Pushkin's son, Grigory Alexandrovich Pushkin, was born on May 14, 1835.
2. Pushkin left for the village of Mikhaylovskoe on May 5 and returned on May 15.

Letter 558
1. Count Adolphe de Circourt, French publicist, who was well acquainted with Russian men of letters of the day, including for example, A. I. Turgenev, Zhukovsky, and Chaadaev. Count Circourt was the husband of Khlyustin's sister, Anastasia Semenovna de Circourt.

Letter 559
1. Unidentified.
2. Pushkin wrote and then crossed out the word "Review" in English. In May, 1835, Pushkin was trying to establish a periodical; it was to have had a supplement called "The Contemporary Chronicler of Politics, the Sciences, and Literature." Pushkin obtained permission to establish a journal, which he called *The Contemporary*, in 1836 (see Letters 560, 561, and 568).

Letter 560
1. The projected periodical, *Diary*. See Letter 429, and note 2.
2. The work on Peter the Great.
3. The word "Review" is in English in the original. Pushkin was eventually given permission to publish a literary, but not a political journal (see Letter 588).
4. S. S. Uvarov, against whom Pushkin directed his satirical "On the Convalescence of Lucullus." About this time Pushkin wrote in his diary: "Uvarov is a great scoundrel. He screams about my book [*The History of Pugachev*] as being a subversive work. His stooge Dundukov (a fool and the dregs of society) persecutes me with his censorship committee. He does not consent for me to print my works with the consent of the Sovereign alone. The Tsar likes, but the whipper-in dislikes."

Letter 561
1. See Letter 560, and note 3.
2. The phrase was left unfinished.
3. Pushkin may not have sent this letter; it may have been replaced with Letter 568. Pushkin's debts were becoming more and more crushing, and he was forced to project and to take more and more radical actions to cope with them.

Letter 562
1. Pushkin's request for a lengthy leave of absence (or a temporary retirement) from the service was rejected by Nicholas I, with a threatening note recalling Pushkin's attempt to retire a year earlier. Pushkin had to give in. It may be noted that this request to retire, thus presented, strengthened Pushkin's position in his request to be allowed to publish a journal and also in his efforts to borrow money from the government, for its rejection deprived him of one of the alternatives.

Letter 563
1. For Pushkin's unrealized idea of taking over the inheritance of his uncle, Vasily Lvovich Pushkin, see Letters 475 and 533.
2. Pushkin did not give it to him.

Letter 564
1. Vasily Andreevich Durov (b. 1799). Pushkin had made Durov's acquaintance in the Caucasus in 1829. Pushkin wrote in his "Table Talk" a character-sketch of Durov, including examples of his "hundred thousand schemes to obtain a hundred thousand rubles."
2. Nadezhda Andreevna Durova, by marriage Chernova (1783-1866), sister of Durov. Disguised as a man, she fought as a Russian soldier and officer in the wars against Napoleon from 1807 to 1814. She wrote under the masculine penname of Alexander Andreevich Alexandrov and hence here and elsewhere Pushkin uses the masculine pronoun in speaking of or to her.

Letter 565
1. Andrey Alexandrovich Kraevsky (1810-1889), journalist and later well known as editor of the journal, *Memoirs of the Fatherland* (1839-1884). At this time he was an intermediary between Pushkin and Moscow journals, particularly *The Moscow Observer*, in which "The Cloud" appeared. As always, Pushkin takes great interest in his works being published accurately, including minor textual revisions.

Letter 566
1. Letter 562 (q.v., and note).
2. The original word, struck out in the rough draft, was "retiring [me]." Obviously Pushkin had not given up all hope of being allowed to retire for several years, but he nevertheless was careful to remove the word.

Letter 567
1. Grigory Alexandrovich Pushkin.
2. Countess Nadezhda Grigorievna Chernysheva.
3. See Letters 562 and 566. The request was denied.
4. Mme. Pushkina's two sisters were still living with the Pushkins.

Letter 568
1. That of his uncle, Vasily Lvovich Pushkin. See Letters 475, 533, and 563.
2. Nicholas I offered Pushkin a loan of ten thousand rubles and a six-month leave of absence, during which he would see "whether he needed to go into retirement or not."

Letter 569
1. Vladimir Dmitrievich Volkhovsky (1798-1841), a Lyceum comrade of Pushkin's, at this time a general in the Russian army in the Caucasus. This letter shows another instance of Pushkin's willingness to help others with what influence he had. Nothing is known of the Count Zabela for whom "protection and good will" are sought.

Letter 570
1. Pushkin's request was granted by Nicholas I.

Letter 571
1. The portrait of Pugachev, engraved in Paris, was received considerably later than the appearance of Pushkin's *History of Pugachev*.
2. Mikhail Samsonovich Rybushkin (1792-1849), an Adjunct Professor of Kazan University. His book was *A Brief History of the City of Kazan* (1834).

3. The original of the letter has not survived. In the published form, the complimentary close and signature were omitted.

Letter 572
1. Efim Petrovich Lyutsenko (1776-1854), an official and man of letters. From 1811 to 1813 he had been an official at the Tsarskoe Selo Lyceum.
2. Lyutsenko wished Smirdin to publish his translation of Wieland's verse tale, *Die Wünsche oder Pervonte*. The deal with Smirdin fell through. Then Pushkin himself published it, without the name of the translator, and with the title page reading as follows: "Vastola, or Desires: A Tale in Verse, Composed by A. Wieland, Published by A. Pushkin, Petersburg, 1836." Pushkin obviously hoped that his name as publisher would attract more purchases than Lyutsenko's name would have attracted as translator. Misunderstanding resulted, and Pushkin was attacked by his journalist enemies as being the uninspired translator of the poem (see Letter 592 and notes).

Letter 573
1. Vasily Alexeevich Polenov (1776-1851), Director of the State Archives.
2. Pushkin had requested this permission in Letter 546 (q.v.).
3. Alexey Fedorovich Malinovsky was Director of the Moscow Archives of the Ministry of Foreign Affairs.
4. It is noteworthy that Pushkin continued his researches in the Pugachev affair after his book had been published, compiling materials which he had no hope of publishing.

Letter 574
1. See Letter 568, note 2.
2. See Letter 570, and note.
3. Pushkin's *History of Pugachev*. The loan was twenty thousand rubles, instead of ten thousand. See Letter 476 and note.
4. Pushkin's request was granted. Pushkin wrote the letter to Kankrin as Minister of Finance.

Letter 575
1. Pushkin left Petersburg for Mikhaylovskoe on September 7. He remained there until October 20, when he departed for Petersburg, upon hearing of his mother's poor health. Pushkin is asking that his mail be sent to Mme. Osipova's address.
2. Mme. Osipova's niece, Anna Ivanovna Begicheva.
3. In Pushkin's poem, "Portents" (1829), he makes poetic utilization of the superstition that seeing the moon over the left shoulder is associated with sadness and despondency.
4. The "expedition" was to Countess Ekaterina Zakharovna Kankrina (1796-1879), the wife of the Minister of Finance, Count Kankrin. Pushkin was hoping through Mme. Kankrina to influence her husband with regard to the business of Letter 574, that none of the loan of thirty thousand rubles, which Nicholas I granted Pushkin, be withheld.
5. Count Vasily Gavrilovich Yuriev, an officer who lent money.
6. Probably Countess Emilia Karlovna Musina-Pushkina.
7. His three-year-old daughter. Pushkin gives a special effect by using the mode of address of a young lady for his daughter, and following it immediately with the rough-affectionate diminutive for his son.
8. Mme. Pushkina's sister, Alexander N. Goncharova, and Ekaterina N. Goncharova, respectively.

Letter 576
  1. Only this small fragment of the letter exists, if indeed it is a letter. It was first published among Pushkin's letters in the Academy of Sciences of the Soviet Union editions of Pushkin's *Works*, both large (XVI [1949], 431), and small (X [1949], 546). In the Index volume to the large Academy *Works*, which became available while this edition was already in the press, it is stated (p. 76) that what was printed as a letter is really a sketch of the plan of the uncompleted poem "To Pletnev" ("You Advise Me, Dear Pletnev," 1835).
  One of the interesting problems in Puskin criticism is whether his novel in verse, *Evgeny Onegin*, is a completed work. "Onegin's Journey," at first projected as Chapter VIII, was not completed and was omitted by Pushkin. Pushkin began a Chapter X, but it exists only in fragments. He is reported as having said in 1829 that Onegin was to have become a Decembrist and to have died in the Caucasus.

Letter 577
  1. Alexandra Ivanovna Bekleshova, nee Osipova, had been, since 1833, the wife of the Pskov Chief of Police, Peter Nikolaevich Bekleshov.
  2. Maria Ivanovna Osipova was the half-sister of Alexandra Ivanovna Bekleshova and of Evpraxia Nikolaevna Vrevskaya.
  3. Pushkin quotes a verse from his love poem, "Confession," which he had written to the addressee of this letter nine years earlier. The time called to mind is that of Pushkin's exile in Mikhaylovskoe, when almost all of the Osipova-Vulf family were more or less in love with him and/or he with them.

Letter 578
  1. Baron Boris Alexandrovich Vrevsky and his wife, Evpraxia Nikolaevna Vrevskaya, nee Vulf. Pushkin visited them on September 19.
  2. Pushkin's library contained a copy of the Paris, 1828, edition of Montaigne's essays.
  3. Pushkin's question has to do with the plural form, in Russian orthography, of the French expression, *belle-soeur*.

Letter 579
  1. Arina Rodionova.
  2. The next day, September 26, 1835, Pushkin wrote his lyric, "Again I Visited...," in which is presented the experience of his revisiting Mikhaylovskoe after ten years. He speaks there of his nursemaid "who is no more," and of the "green family" of pines that has grown up, and which he will not live to see mature.
  3. They had gone abroad in May, 1834 (see Letter 470).
  4. Mme. Pushkina's two sisters.

Letter 580
  1. Countess Varvara Petrovna Polier married the Neapolitan ambassador in Petersburg, Prince Giorgio Butera di Ridali, in 1836.
  2. See Letter 429, note 2.
  3. Anna Petrovna Kern had translated George Sand's novel, *André* (1835).
  4. Probably a projected joint publication of an almanac (see Letter 582).
  5. *Muzjk* (instead of *mužik*).
  6. "I thank your sisters."

Letter 581
1. Perhaps her sister, Ekaterina Nikolaevna Goncharova; perhaps the proprietress of a fashionable shop.
2. See Letter 580, regarding her illness.
3. Apparently the allusion is to a projected almanac. See Letter 580.

Letter 582
1. Pushkin's *Journey to Erzurum*, a travel-account of his trip to the Caucasus and Erzurum in 1829. It appeared in the first issue of Pushkin's journal, *The Contemporary*, in 1836.
2. Pushkin had made an official petition to the Chief Directorate of the Censorship, on August 28, 1835, for clarification of his position with regard to the double censorship: of the ordinary censorship, on the one hand, and that of Benkendorf and Nicholas I, on the other. See also Letter 584.
3. Pushkin usually calls Prince M. A. Dondukov-Korsakov *Dunduk*, "muddlehead." Pushkin used the term in an epigram on him. Alexander Vasilievich Nikitenko (1805-1877) was a censor and Dondukov-Korsakov an official in the censorship.
4. Gogol's tale, "The Calash," was published in the first issue of Pushkin's *Contemporary* in 1836.
5. Valerian Platonovich Langer, an artist.
6. Part of Gogol's play *Vladimir, Third Class* was also published in the first issue of *The Contemporary*.
7. Under Pushkin's pseudonym of Belkin, Senkovsky had published "A Tale Lost to the World." (See Letter 556). In *The Russian Invalide* there appeared a vitriolic critique in 1836, showing that Pushkin could not be the author of the tale, and hinting at Senkovsky as the author.

Letter 583
1. Pushkin left Mikhaylovskoe on Occtober 20, after a month and a half's absence from Petersburg, upon hearing of his mother's serious illness.
2. See Letter 574. Pushkin received, as a four-year loan, the entire thirty thousand rubles he had requested.

Letter 584
1. The censorship refused to pass the "second, corrected" edition of Pushkin's *Angelo*, an adaptation into a poem, of Shakespeare's *Measure for Measure*, though Nicholas I himself had approved the original manuscript. Pushkin's petition of August 28, 1835 (see Letter 582, note 2) was left unanswered. Thus Uvarov was avenging Pushkin's epigram on him.
2. No fair copy of this letter survives. Whether it was sent is not known.

Letter 585
1. See Letter 583, note 1.
2. Princess Varvara Alexandrovna Knyazhnina (1774-1842), a childhood friend of Pushkin's mother.
3. Egor Ivanovich Raukh (1789-1864), like Spassky, a physician.
4. Pushkin's parents had moved into a small and uncomfortable apartment in the home of his sister, Olga Sergeevna Pavlishcheva.
5. "Sweet habit."

Letter 586

1. See Letters 548 and 571. Apparently Pushkin received the portrait in February, 1835.
2. See Letter 485, where Pushkin also mentions Lazhechnikov's novels alluded to below. *The House of Ice* appeared in 1835.
3. Artemy Petrovich Volynsky (1689-1740), Russian statesman and diplomat, was executed as head of the "Russian" opposition to "German" influence of Count Ernst Johann Biron (1690-1772), favorite of the Russian Empress Anne (reigned 1730-1740).
4. Eighteenth-century neo-classical poet.
5. In a lengthy letter of November 22, 1835, Lazhechnikov defends his conception of Volynsky, Trediakovsky, and Biron against Pushkin's objections. He further states that the word *xobot*, in the expression *kakim-to xobotom*, was still used in the "Great Russian dialect" by narrators of folk tales to mean *kakim-to putem, kakim-to obrazom,* "in a certain way, manner."

Letter 587

1. "The youngsters, likewise."
2. "According to the ukase he must be settled in the southern part of Siberia." Pushkin cites the ukase of December 14, 1835, according to the provisions of which the punishment of several Decembrists was somewhat eased. Kyukhelbeker was allowed to settle in the Irkutsk Province of Eastern Siberia. He was not permitted to live in the village of his sister, Yustina Karlovna Glinka, nee Kyukhelbeker.
3. The Decembrist Uprising of 1825.
4. Apparently Pushkin must have borrowed some money from Mme. Osipova.

PART XIII

CONTEMPORARY JOURNALIST—PETERSBURG

December, 1835 — October, 1836

[588]
>   To ALEXANDER KHRISTOFOROVICH BENKENDORF
>   December 31, 1835. In Petersburg.

Dear Sir, Count Alexander Khristoforovich,

I have the happiness to submit for His Majesty's inspection the memoirs of the Brigadier Moreau de Brasey[1] about the expedition of the year 1711, along with my notes and introduction. These memoirs are interesting and sensible. They are an important historical document, and they very well may be the sole one (except for the journal of Peter the Great himself).

I make bold to disturb Your Excellency with a most humble request. I should like during next year, 1836, to publish four volumes of items of a purely literary (e.g., of tales, poems, etc.), historical, scholarly nature, and also critical analyses of Russian and foreign literature; something on the order of the English quarterly *Reviews*.[2] In refusing to participate in all our journals, I have been deprived also of my own revenues. The publication of such a *Review* would again provide me with independence, and, along with that, the means of continuing the labors which I have begun. This would be a new benefaction for me on the part of the Sovereign.

Commending myself to the favor which you always show toward me, I have the honor to be, with the most profound respect and with complete devotion,

>   Dear Sir,
>   Your Excellency's
> December 31, 1835.   Most humble servant,
> SPb.   Alexander Pushkin.

[589]
>   To NADEZHDA ANDREEVNA DUROVA
>   January 19, 1836. From Petersburg to Elabuga.

Dear Sir, Alexander Andreevich,[1]

I have been exceedingly disturbed by your last letter, of January 6. I have not received your manuscript, and here is what I suspect to be the reason. Though I left for three months in the village, I spent only three weeks there, and then was compelled to return hastily to Petersburg. Your manuscript has probably been sent to Pskov. Do me the favor not to be angry with me. I am going now to take what steps I can with regard to it; I shall try to make up for the delays.

I was about to be in complete despair of ever receiving the Memoirs, which I have been awaiting so impatiently. Thank God that now I have managed to get on their trail.

With the most profound respect and with complete devotion, I have the honor to be,

>Your most zealous and most humble servant,
>January 19, 1836. A. Pushkin.

[590]
To Pavel Voinovich Nashchokin
Between January 10 and 20, 1836. From Petersburg to Moscow.
My dear Pavel Voinovich,

I have not written you because I am at odds with the Moscow post.[1] I have heard that you were planning to come see me at my village. I rejoice that you didn't come, because you would not have found me there. The illness of my mother has forced me to return to the city. There have been various rumors about you with regard to your winnings; but what has truly consoled me is that all people have been unanimously justifying you, and you alone. I am thinking of spending some time in Moscow, if I don't croak on the road. Have you a corner for me? Then wouldn't we chatter to our heart's content! But here there's nobody to do it with. My financial circumstances are bad—I have been forced to undertake a journal.[2] I don't know yet how it will go. Smirdin is already offering me fifteen thousand to renounce my undertaking and become again a collaborator of his *Library [for Reading]*. But though that would be profitable, I nevertheless cannot agree to it. Senkovsky is such a knave and Smirdin such a fool that one cannot have anything to do with them. I should like to get a glimpse of your family life and rejoice at it. After all, I had something to do with it, for I had an influence on the decisive turning point of your life.[3] My family is increasing, growing, being noisy about me. Now, I should think, there's no reason to murmur at life or to fear old age. For a bachelor it's boring in society: he's vexed to see new, young generations. Only the father of a family looks without envy at the youth surrounding him. From this it follows that we did well in getting married. How are your affairs? How are Knörzer and your little Jewish doctor[4] whom Natalia Nikolaevna so dislikes? And she has a most perceptive heart. Look, get rid of him; your really must. But let's talk all this over later. Good-by, my friend.

[591]
   To Alexander Nikolaevich Mordvinov (?)
The second half of January or the beginning of February, 1836.
     Petersburg.
   (Rough draft; in French)
I beseech you to pardon my obtruding myself upon you, but, since yesterday I was not able to make my justification to the minister[1] [. . . .][2]

My ode was sent to Moscow without any explanation. My friends had no knowledge of it. Any sort of allusion in it has been carefully removed. The satirical part strikes at the vile avidity of an heir, who at the moment of his relative's illness, already has seals affixed to the effects which he covets. I confess that a similar story had been widely spread and that I have picked up a poetical expression which has slipped out on this theme.

It is impossible to write a satirical ode without the malign immediately finding innuendoes in it. Derzhavin in his "Noble Lord" portrayed a sybarite plunged in voluptuousness, deaf to the cries of the people, and who exclaims,

> To me a moment of my tranquillity is more pleasing than centuries in history.

These verses were applied to Potemkin and to others[3]—however, all these declamations were commonplaces, which had been repeated a thousand times. That is to say, in the satire of the basest and the most common vices, portrayed [. . . .][2]

Fundamentally they were the vices of the great lord, and I have no way of knowing to what degree Derzhavin was innocent of indulging in personalities.

In the portrait of a vile miser, of a foxy fellow who steals wood belonging to the Crown, who presents to his wife inaccurate accounts, of a toady who becomes children's nursemaid at great lords' houses, etc.—the public has recognized, it is said, a certain great lord, a rich man, a man honored with an important office.[4]

So much the worse for the public—it is enough for me that I not only have not named names, but have not even hinted to anyone whatever that my ode [. . . .][2]

I ask only that anyone prove to me that I have named him, what feature of my ode could be applied to him, or even what I have insinuated.

All this is very vague; all these accusations are commonplaces.

It matters little to me whether the public is wrong or right. What matters much to me is to prove that never in any manner have I *insinuated* to anyone that my ode was leveled against anyone whatever.[5]

[592]

To Semen Semenovich Khlyustin
February 4, 1836. In Petersburg.
(In French)

Sir,

Permit me to correct several points where you appear to me to be in error.[1] I do not remember having heard you quote anything from the article in question. What prompted me to express myself, perhaps with too much heat, is the remark which you made to me, that I was wrong last evening to take Senkovsky's words to heart.

I answered you: *Ja ne seržus' na Senkovskogo; no mne nel'zja ne dosadovat', kogda porjadončye ljudi povtorjajut neleposti svinej i merzavcev.*[2] To put you on the same footing with *svin'i i merzavcy*[3] is certainly an absurdity, which could neither have entered my head nor have escaped me, even in all the heat of an altercation.

To my great surprise, you replied to me that you take complete responsibility for Senkovsky's injurious article, and in particular for the expression *obmanyvat' publiku.*[4]

I was all the less prepared for such an assertion coming from you *in that neither last evening nor at our last interview did you say anything whatever to me which related to the article in the journal.* I believed that I did not understand you and I requested you to be so kind as to explain yourself, which you did in the same terms.

I then had the honor to make the observation to you that what you have just put forth turns the question into something quite different, and I held my tongue. Leaving you, I told you that I could not leave things thus. That can be regarded as a provocation, but not as a threat. Wherefore, to sum things up, I am obliged to repeat: I can pay no attention to the words of a Senkovsky, but I cannot disdain them when a man like you adopts them. In consequence, I have commissioned M. Sobolevsky to request of you in my name to be so kind as to retract the words purely and simply, or else to grant me the customary satisfaction. The proof of how repugnant this last course was to me is that I have specifically told Sobolevsky that I shall not insist upon an apology. I am sorry that M. Sobolevsky has displayed his usual negligence in all this.

As for the incivility which I showed in not bowing to you when you left me, I pray you to believe that it was a completely involuntary inadvertence, and I ask your pardon for it with all my heart.

I have the honor to be, Sir, your most humble and most obedient servant.

February 4.

A. Pushkin.

[593]

To Nikolay Grigorievich Repnin-Volkonsky
February 5, 1836. In Petersburg.
(In French)

Prince,

To my regret I am compelled to trouble Your Excellency.[1] But as a gentleman and the father of a family, I must watch over my honor and the name which I am to leave to my children.

I do not have the honor to be personally acquainted with Your Excellency. Not only have I never offended you, but for certain reasons known to me, up to the present I have had for you a true feeling of respect and of gratitude.

However, a M. Bogolyubov[2] has publicly repeated remarks which I consider insulting, and as coming from you. I pray Your Excellency to be so kind as to let me know what to believe.

No one knows better than I the distance which separates me from you: but I hope that you who are not only a great lord, but also a representative of our ancient and genuine nobility, to which I too belong—I hope that you will understand without difficulty the imperious necessity which has dictated this step to me.

    I am, respectfully,
      Your Excellency's
        Most humble and most obedient servant,
February 5, 1836.   Alexander Pushkin.

[594]
    To Vladimir Alexandrovich Sollogub
   The first days of February, 1836. In Petersburg.
     (Rough draft; in French)

You[1] have put yourself to useless trouble in giving me an explanation which I have not asked of you. You have permitted yourself to address improper remarks to my wife, and you have boasted that you have *uttered impertinences* to her.

Circumstances do not permit me to set out for Tver before the end of the month of March.[2] Please excuse me [. . . .][3]

[595]
   To Nikolay Grigorievich Repnin-Volkonsky
    February 11, 1836. In Petersburg.
Dear Sir, Prince Nikolay Grigorievich,

I want to express to Your Highness my sincere, most profound gratitude for the letter which you were so kind as to honor me with.

I cannot help acknowledging that Your Highness's opinion with regard to compositions which are insulting to the honor of a private person is completely just. It is difficult to excuse them even when they are written in a moment of chagrin and blind vexation. As an amusement for an idle or depraved mind, they would be unforgivable.[1]

With the most profound respect and with complete devotion, I am,
    Dear Sir,
      Your Highness's
        Most humble servant,
February 11, 1836.   Alexander Pushkin.

[596]
To ALEXANDRA ANDREEVNA FUCHS
February 20, 1836. From Petersburg to Kazan.
Dear Madame, Alexandra Andreevna,

I am so much to blame toward you that I do not make bold even to try to justify myself. Not long ago I returned from the village[1] and I found at my house the letter which you were so kind as to honor me with. I do not understand how it can be that my tramp Emelian Pugachev[2] has not reached Kazan, a memorable place for him; apparently he has made side excursions and has gone on a spree, according to his wont. Now Count Apraxin[3] has indulgently undertaken to deliver my book to you. Along with this, permit me, Dear Madame, to forward to you also a subscription for *The Contemporary*, which I am publishing. Dare I hope that you will embellish it some time with the productions of your pen?[4]

I testify my most profound respect toward amiable, honored Karl Fedorovich [Fuchs], commending myself to your and his good will.

I have the honor to be, with the most profound respect and complete devotion,

Dear Madame,
Your

SPb.
February 20, 1836.

Most humble servant,
Alexander Pushkin.

[597]
To VASILY DMITRIEVICH SUKHORUKOV
March 14, 1836. From Petersburg to Pyatigorsk.
My very dear Vasily Dmitrievich,[1]

I am writing you in the room of a compatriot of yours, a pleasing young man[2] from whom I not infrequently receive news of you. He has just now told me that you are married.[3] I congratulate you with all my heart; I wish you happiness, which you deserve in all respects. I send my respects to Olga Vasilievna and my regrets that I cannot tell her all that I think, and everything good that I know, about you.

Have I written you since our separation in the Erzurum Palace? I don't think I have written; forgive my eternal lack of leisure, and don't attribute my procrastination to anything else. Now let us talk about business. You know that I have become a journalist (which reminds me that I have not sent you *The Contemporary*;[4] excuse me—I'll try to make up for my fault). And so, having become a confrere of Bulgarin and Polevoy, I address you with astonishing shamelessness and ask for *some articles* from you. Really, do send me something out of your sensible, conscientious, interesting works. In the vicinity of Beshtau and Elbrus both leisure and inspiration dwell. Meanwhile, it wouldn't be a bad idea to talk about value (monetary). I pay two hundred rubles per printed sheet. Shan't we enter into commercial relationships, too?

Farewell; all yours,
March 14, 1836.   A.P.
SPb.

[598]
To Vladimir Fedorovich Odoevsky
The end of February or the first half of March, 1836.
In Petersburg.

I am highly, very highly pleased and grateful.[1] If it will be possible to print five sheets per week, that's capital—and our business is in the bag. However, have the proofs of my *Journey*[2] sent to me. There are many mistakes in the manuscript. What about your tale "Zizi"?[3] It's a capital thing.

A.P.

[599]
To Peter Andreevich Vyazemsky
About (not later than) March 17, 1836. In Petersburg.

Hurrah! We have won![1] Kozlovsky's article[2] came through all right; I am beginning to print it now. But poor [A. I.] Turgenev! ... all his political gossip has been stopped. Even the names of Fieschi and of all the ministers have been blotted out; only the orthodox spelling of the names of our Russian Catholic women and diplomats' wives remains.[3] However, I shall address myself to Benkendorf—won't he intercede? You spoke to me about your verses to Pototskaya.[4] Have you obtained them? Can't you at least recall them?

A.P.

[600]
>   To MIKHAIL ALEXANDROVICH DONDUKOV-KORSAKOV
>   March 18, 1836. In Petersburg.

Dear Sir, Prince Mikhail Alexandrovich,

Utilizing the permission granted me by Your Highness, I make bold to have recourse to you with a most humble request.

The Censorship Committee could not pass the "Letters from Paris," as an item containing political news. Will you permit me, Dear Sir, in order that I may receive this permission to address myself to Count Benkendorf? Or will you command that this be left to the Committee?[1]

With the most profound respect and with complete devotion, I have the honor to be,

>   Dear Sir,
>   Your Highness's
>   Most humble servant,
> March 18, 1836.   Alexander Pushkin.
> SPb.

[601]
>   To ALEXANDER LUKICH KRYLOV
>   Between March 20 and 22, 1836. In Petersburg.
>   (Rough draft)

Dear Sir, Alexander Lukich,

Prince M. A. Korsakov has written me that the "Letters from Paris" will be examined in the Highest Committee. I am forwarding them to you. One observation: Turgenev's "Letters from Paris" are being published in *The Moscow Observer* not as political, but as literary, articles.[1]

[602]
>   To ALPHONSE JOBARD
>   March 24, 1836. From Petersburg to Moscow.
>   (In French)

Sir, I have received with genuine pleasure your charming translation of the "Ode to Lucullus" and the very flattering letter accompanying it.[1] Your verses are as pretty as they are barbed, which is saying a great deal. If it is true, as you say in your letter, that the attempt was made to establish legally that you have lost your mind, one must acknowledge that since then you have devilishly found it again!

The good will which you apparently bear me, and which I am proud of, justifies my speaking to you in full trust. In your letter to the Minister of Public Instruction, you seem inclined to publish your translation in Belgium, supplementing it with some notes, which are necessary, you say, for comprehending the text: I make bold to beseech you, Sir, to do nothing of the kind. I am sorry for having published a piece which I wrote in a moment of bad humor. With its publication I have incurred the displeasure of a certain one[2] whose opinion is dear to me, and whom I cannot defy without ingratitude and without folly. Be so good as to sacrifice the pleasure of publicity to the idea of obliging a brother-writer. Do not revive, with the aid of your talent, a production which otherwise would fall into the oblivion which it deserves. I make bold to hope that you will not refuse me the favor which I am asking of you, and I pray you to be so kind as to receive the assurance of my complete esteem.

I have the honor to be, Sir, your most humble and most obedient servant.

March 24, 1836.   A. Pushkin.
St. Petersburg.

[603]
To Vasily Andreevich Durov
March 17 and 27, 1836. From Petersburg to Elabuga.
Dear Sir, Vasily Andreevich,

I thank you very much for sending the memoirs and for the trust which you have shown in me. Here are my proposals. (I) I publish a journal; in the second issue of it (i.e., in the month of July) I am publishing *The Memoirs of* [18]12 (all or a part of them), and I shall send you money at once, at the rate of two hundred rubles per printed sheet. (II) Now that I have finally received your brother's other memoirs, I am thinking of combining *The Memoirs of* [18]12 with them.[1] In this way the book will be thicker, and consequently more expensive.

The Complete Memoirs will probably sell well, after I trumpet them in my journal. I am ready either to buy or to print them on the author's behalf—whichever he likes and is most profitable for him. In any case, be assured that I shall exert every possible effort for the success of our mutual piece of business.

Your brother writes that he will be in Petersburg this summer. I await him with impatience. Farewell. Be happy, and God grant that you grow rich on the lucky little hand of brave Alexandrov, which little hand I ask you to kiss for me.

All yours,

March 17, 1836.   A. Pushkin.
SPb.

I have just now read the *Memoirs* copied out: it's charming. It's lively, original, and the style is excellent. Its success is indubitable. March 27.[2]

[604]
To George Borrow
Between the end of October, 1835, and March, 1836.
In Petersburg.

Alexander Pushkin has received Mr. Borrow's book with the most profound gratitude, and he heartily regrets that he has not had the honor of becoming personally acquainted with him.[1]

[605]
To Vladimir Fedorovich Odoevsky
The beginning of April, 1836. In Petersburg.

In my first issue there won't be a single line from your pen. That grieves me. But we lacked the time—and my friends had made a vow to the public, in my name, that *The Contemporary* would be issued in St. Thomas' Week.[1]

I am thinking of beginning the second issue with your sensible, intelligent, and powerful article—which I should like to entitle "Of Enmity Toward Enlightenment,"[2] for I should like to put in the same issue, as well, a critique of *The Inn*, under the title "Of Certain Novels."[3] Do you permit it?

The censorship seems to have fallen into a quandary over "Segeliel."[4] But I am not very content with the work—besides, printing it as a fragment might harm the publication of your complete work.

I am leaving on Tuesday.[5] Shall I see you before then?

All yours,
A.P.

I did not include "The Conversation of the Discontented Ones,"[6] because I already had Gogol's "Scenes"[7] in type—and because you two might damage the effect of each other.

[606]
To Mikhail Alexandrovich Dondukov-Korsakov
April 6, 1836. In Petersburg.

Dear Sir, Prince Mikhail Alexandrovich,

I make bold to make a most humble request of Your Highness.

Of course I do not have the right to complain of strictness on the part of the censorship: all the articles which have gone into my journal were passed. But I am obliged for the authorizing of them solely to Your Highness's good-natured indulgence, for the censor, Mr. [A. L.] Krylov, in and of himself could not make up his mind to pass them. Though I feel in full measure the value of the protection which you have shown toward me, I nevertheless make bold to observe, in the first place, that it is shameful and unseemly for me to disturb Your Highness every moment with paltry requests, whereas I should like to utilize the right which you have granted me, only in cases which are truly difficult and which really require the authorization of the higher authorities; in the second place, that such a double censorship takes an excessive amount of time for me, so that my journal cannot come out on schedule. I do not complain of superfluous mistrustfulness on the part of my censor. I know that on him lies a responsibility which is perhaps not delimited by the Censorship Regulations. But I make bold to request Your Highness for the authorization to choose myself an additional censor, in order that thus the examining of my journal may be made twice as rapid. Without this, it will come to a halt and fail.[1]

With the most profound respect and with complete devotion, I have the honor to be,

Dear Sir,
Your Highness's

April 6, 1836.
SPb.

Most humble servant,
Alexander Pushkin.

[607]
           To Mikhail Petrovich Pogodin
       April 14, 1836. From Mikhaylovskoe to Moscow.
Dear Sir, Mikhaylo Petrovich,
I am writing to you from the village, where I have come in consequence of mournful circumstances.[1] My journal came out in my absence,[2] and you have probably already received it. The article about your aphorisms[3] was not written by me, and I had neither the time nor the strength to examine it decently. Do not be angry with me if you are dissatisfied with it. Won't you enter into literary and commercial relationships with me? In case you will, I ask you to state your demands, with no beating around the bush. If you should see Nadezhdin, thank him for me for his *Telescope*. I shall send him *The Contemporary*. Today I am going to Petersburg. But I shall be in Moscow in May—to do some burrowing in the archives and to see you.
    April 14.   All yours, A.P.
    Mikhaylovskoe.

[608]
           To Nikolay Mikhaylovich Yazykov
       April 14, 1836. From Golubovo[1] to Yazykovo.
Guess where I'm writing you from, my dear Nikolay Mikhaylovich. From the land

   —where the free ones used to dwell, etc.[2]

where exactly ten years ago we three were feasting—you, [Alexey N.] Vulf, and I; where your verses chimed and also our capacious goblets, where now we are remembering you—and old times. A greeting to you from the hills of Mikhaylovskoe, from the portals of Trigorskoe, from the waves of the blue Sorot, from Evpraxia Nikolaevna, once upon a time a semi-ethereal maid, and now a plump wife, and already with child for the fifth time, and at whose house I'm a guest. A greeting to you from everything and everybody devoted to you in heart and memory!
   Alexey Vulf is here, a retired student and hussar, a mustachioed

agriculturalist, the Lovelace of Tver[3]—pleasant as before, but he has already crossed the threshold of his thirtieth year. My visit in Pskov is not so boisterous and merry now as during my exile, in the days when Alexander reigned; but it has reminded me of you so keenly that I could not help writing you a few words in the expectation that you will respond, in turn. You will receive my *Contemporary*; I hope that it may merit your approbation. One of the critical articles is mine: about Konissky.[4] Do be my collaborator, without fail.[5] Your verses are living water, ours are dead water.[6] We have doused *The Contemporary* with ours; besprinkle it with your seething drops. Your "Epistle to Davydov" is charming! Our warrior with black curls had dyed his gray hair and had tinted his white forelock, too, but after your verses he washed it out again—and he did well.[7] This is a mark of veneration for poetry. Farewell—write me, and, by the way, do send to Vyazemsky, as well, an answer to his epistle which was printed in *The Housewarming*[8] (as I remember), and which you haven't said a word about to him. Stay well, and write. That is: *Live and let live*.[9] All yours, A.P.

April 14.

Send me, for God's sake, *The Verses About Alexey, Man of God*[10] and some other legend—*it's essential*.

[609]
To Alexander Nikolaevich Mordvinov
April 28, 1836. In Petersburg.

Dear Sir, Alexander Nikolaevich,

I hasten to forward to Your Excellency the letter which I received. It was delivered to me about a week ago. Upon my return from a walk, I discovered that it had been given to my servants without any verbal message, I do not know by whom. I supposed that the letter had been delivered to me with your knowledge.[1]

With the most profound respect and with complete devotion, I have the honor to be,

Dear Sir,
Your Excellency's
Most humble servant,
Alexander Pushkin.

April 28, 1836.
SPb.

[610]
To MIKHAIL ALEXANDROVICH DONDUKOV-KORSAKOV
Between April 19 and 30, 1836. In Petersburg.
(Rough draft)

I have had the happiness to receive the letter with which Your Highness has honored me,[1] and the article about the Occupation of Dresden.[2]

Although the censorship could not pass for publication General Davydov's justification—nevertheless, Dear Sir, I am grateful to Your Highness for the attention with which you have been so kind as to honor my most humble request.

With the most profound respect
And complete devotion [. . . .]

[611]
To NATALIA NIKOLAEVNA PUSHKINA
May 4, 1836. From Moscow to Petersburg.

May 4. Moscow at Nashchokin's—opposite Stary Pimen,[1] the house of Mme. Ivanova.

Here is a detailed report for you, my Tsaritsa: my trip[2] went all right. I spent the night of May 1 in Tver, and I arrived here on the night of the 2nd. I have stopped at Nashchokin's. *Il est logé en petite maîtresse.*[3] His wife is very sweet. He is happy, and he has plumpened up a little. We were, it goes without saying, very glad to see each other, and yesterday we chattered the whole day through, about God knows what. I have already succeeded in visiting Bryullov. I found him in the studio of some sculptor, at whose house he's living.[4] I was greatly taken with him. He has a fit of the spleen, he is afraid of the Russian cold, etc., he yearns for Italy, and he's very much discontented with Moscow. At his place I saw several sketches which he has begun, and I thought of you, my charming one. It can't be that I won't have a portrait of you, painted by him! It's impossible that, upon seeing you, he wouldn't want to paint you; please don't drive him off, the way you drove off the Prussian Kridner.[5] I very much want to bring Bryullov to Petersburg.[6] Why, he's a genuine artist, a fine fellow, and he's ready for everything. Here Perovsky[7] made a prisoner of him; he took him to his own house, shut him up under lock and key, and made him work. Bryullov had difficulty in getting away from him. Nashchokin's little house[8] has been brought to perfection—the only thing lacking is some living tiny people. What fun Masha would have with it! Here is some local news for you. Okulova, the long-nosed singer, yesterday was married to the widower Diakov.[9] Her sister Varvara has gone mad of love. She was in love and had hoped to get married. Her hope was not realized. She fell into melancholy, began to talk incoherently. Her sister's wedding completely addled her brains. She ran off to Troitsa.[10] They had difficulty in catching her and in taking her away. I am very sorry for her. They hope that what she has is only fever with delirium,[11] but that's hardly it. I have seen our match-maker, [F. I.] Tolstoy. His daughter[12] is almost mad, too. She lives in a dream world, surrounded by visions, translates from the Greek of Anacreon, and is being given homeopathic treatments. I have not yet succeeded in seeing Chaadaev, [M. F.] Orlov, [A. N.] Raevsky, and the Observers[13] (whom Nashchokin calls *les treize*). I intend to coquette with the Observers and the booksellers, and I'll try to take care of *The Contemporary* as best I can.—Here is Nashchokin coming, and I'm leaving you for him. I kiss and bless you and the children. I greet your ladies. Here they're already talking about Maria Vyazemskaya's wedding[14]—I'm being secretive for the time being. Farewell. My dear—I kiss you again.

[612]
To Natalia Nikolaevna Pushkina
May 6, 1836. From Moscow to Petersburg.

Here I have already been in Moscow three days, and I still have not done anything. I have not seen the archives,[1] have not struck a bargain with the booksellers, have not paid all my calls, have not been to the Solntsevs[2] to pay my respects. What would you have me do? Nashchokin gets up late, I start chattering with him—look, it's time to dine, and then to have supper, and then to sleep—and the day is gone. Yesterday I was at [I. I.] Dmitriev's and at [M. F.] Orlov's, [F. I.] Tolstoy's; today I'm planning to go see the others. The poet [A. S.] Khomyakov is getting married to Yazykova,[3] the sister of the poet. A wealthy groom, a wealthy bride. What Moscow gossip should I pass on to you? There seems to be a lot of it, but I can't remember. What Moscow says about Petersburg is killingly funny. For example: "In Petersburg there is a certain *Saveliev*, a cavalry guardsman, an excellent young man. He's in love with Idalia Poletika, and on account of her he has slapped Grinvald in the face. Saveliev, in a few days, will be shot. Imagine how pathetic Idalia is!"[4] And about you, my darling, some talk is going about which isn't reaching me in its entirety, because husbands are always the last in the city to discover about their wives. However, it seems that you have driven a certain person[5] to such despair with your coquetry and cruelty that he has acquired himself in solace a harem of theatrical trainees. That is not good, my angel. Modesty is the best adornment of your sex. In order to regale, with something or other, Moscow, which expects some fresh news from me, as a visitor, I tell them that Alexander [N.] Karamzin (the son of the historiographer) wanted to shoot himself, from love *pour une belle brune*, but that fortunately the bullet only knocked out a front tooth.[6] However, enough nonsense. Send for Gogol, and read him the following: I have seen the actor Shchepkin,[7] who asks him, for Christ's sake, to come to Moscow and read *The Inspector General*.[8] Without him the actors won't put it over. He says that the comedy will be a caricature and *filthy* (toward which Moscow has always had a sneaking inclination). For my part, my advice to him is the same; *The Inspector General* must not crash in Moscow, where they love Gogol more than in Petersburg. Enclosed is a *packet* for Pletnev, for *The Contemporary*. If the censor [A. L.] Krylov won't pass it, give it to the committee,[9] and for God's sake print it in the second issue. I await a letter from you with impatience. How about your belly,[10] and how about your money? I don't regret coming to Moscow, but I feel nostalgia for Petersburg. Are you at the summer house? How did you make out with the landlord? How are the children? Woe is me! I see that I absolutely must have an income of eighty thousand. And I shall have it. It's not for nothing that I have let myself in for speculating on a journal—after all, that's the same thing as *honey bucketing*, which [S. D.] Bezobrazov's mother wanted to get farmed out to her: to clean up Russian literature means to clean out privies and to depend on the police. The first thing you know.... The devil take them! My blood is turning to bile. I kiss you and the children. I bless them and you. I greet the ladies.[11]

[613]
>To Peter Andreevich Vyazemsky
>May 7, 1836. In Moscow.

Here is the point:

A recommendation (No. 11,483) has been made by the governor of Ryazan regarding the pension which is due to the widow of Stepan Savelievich Gubanov, provincial land surveyor. His wife is in dire need and requests that they hasten the day when she will receive the pension.

Please, my dear fellow, accomplish this through D. V. Dashkov, whom this matter depends on. You will also oblige Okulov, at whose house I am writing you this note, and who makes the same request of you.[1]

May 7. A. Pushkin.

[614]
>To Natalia Nikolaevna Pushkina
>May 10, 1836. From Moscow to Petersburg.

I have just now received a letter from you, and it has so touched me that I hasten to send you nine hundred rubles. I'll write you an answer later on; now for the time being, farewell. Ivan Nikolaevich [Goncharov] is sitting with me.

[615]
>To Natalia Nikolaevna Pushkina
>May 11, 1836. From Moscow to Petersburg.

I thank you very, very much for your letter. I can imagine your bothers, and I ask your forgiveness for myself and the booksellers. They are horribly bad tone, as Gogol says,[1] i.e., worse than swindlers. But God will help us. I thank [V. F.] Odoevsky, too, for his typographical bothers.[2] Tell him to print however he takes the notion—the sequence is of no importance. How about the memoirs of [Nadezhda A.] Durova?[3] Have they been passed by the censorship? They are essential for me—without them I'm sunk. You write about the *Goltsov* article. What's that? One by Koltsov[4] or by Gogol? Print the Gogol,[5] but scrutinize the Koltsov. That's not important, though. Yesterday Ivan Nikolaevich [Goncharov] was at my place. He assures me that his affairs are going well. Dmitry Nikolaevich [Goncharov] knows that better than he does, though. My life is most dissipated. I am not staying at home—I am not burrowing in the Archives. Today I'm going to Malinovsky's[6] for the second time. A few days ago I dined at [M. F.] Orlov's, at whose house the Moscow Observers gathered together, and among others, [A. S.] Khomyakov, the engaged. Orlov is an intelligent man and a very fine fellow, but I'm somehow not overly fond of him, on account of our old relationships. Raevsky (Alexander), who last time seemed to me to have grown a bit stultified, seems to have livened up again and become more intelligent. His wife[7] is no beauty—they say she's very intelligent. Since being a journalist has now been added to my other merits, I have a new charm for Moscow. Not long ago, I was told that Chertkov[8] had come to see me. We had never visited each other in our lives. But on this reliable opportunity he remembered that his wife is kin to me, and therefore he brought me a copy of his *Journey to Sicily*. Oughtn't I give him a good scolding *en bon parent*? Yesterday I had supper at Prince Fedor Gagarin's and I returned at 4 o'clock in the morning—in just such a good mood as if it had been from a ball. Nashchokin is my only solace here. But he sleeps until noon, and in the evening he goes to the club, where he plays until dawn. I have seen Chaadaev only once in all. My letter is like one of Turgenev's[9]—and it can prove to you the difference between Moscow and Paris. I'm going out to see what I can do about the affairs of *The Contemporary*. I'm afraid the booksellers may take advantage of my softheartedness and wheedle some concessions in spite of your strict instructions. But I'll try to show a noble firmness. I have been at Solntseva's.[10] He is not here, he's in the village. She is inviting Father to their village for the summer. My little cousins are squealing like jackdaws. I have been at Perovsky's, who showed me some unfinished pictures of Bryullov's. Bryullov, who had been imprisoned at his house,[11] escaped from him and has quarreled with him. Perovsky, as he was showing me "The Taking of Rome by Genseric" (which is as good as his "Last Day of Pompeii")[12] kept saying: "Notice how excellently that scoundrel, such a swindler, has painted this horseman. How he managed, the swine, to express his rascally, brilliant idea, the rogue, the knave. How he has painted this group, the drunkard, the cheat." Killingly funny. Well, farewell. I kiss you and the youngsters. Stay well, all of you. Christ be with you.

May 11.

[616]
To Ksenofont Alexeevich Polevoy
May 11, 1836. In Moscow.

Dear Sir, Ksenofont Alexeevich,

I have not answered your last letter, for I have been hoping to see you in person. The bookseller Farikov[1] has provided me with the book[2] which you have done me the honor to send addressed to me. As regards *The Contemporary*, Farikov did not want to take it from me for you, for he had already sent it to you himself.[3] The money (275 rubles)[4] about which you were so kind as to write was not delivered to me by him, either. I most humbly request that if henceforth you should choose to have business with me, you not entrust anything to Mr. Farikov—for he seems an undependable and unpunctilious person.

With true respect, I have the honor to be

Your most humble servant,

A. Pushkin.

May 11.

[617]
To Natalia Nikolaevna Pushkina
May 14 and 16, 1836. From Moscow to Petersburg.

What's this, little wife? You began so well, and have ended so badly. Not a line from you. You haven't had the baby already, have you? Today is Grishka's[1] birthday. Many happy returns of the day to him and to you. I shall drink to his health. He doesn't have a new little brother or little sister, does he? Wait until I arrive. And I'm already preparing to come to you. I've been in the Archives, and I shall be compelled to burrow into them for some six months. What'll happen to you then? I'll bring you with me, if you like. My life in Moscow is staid and respectable. I stay at home—I see only the male sex. I don't go out walking, I don't cut capers—and I'm getting fat. A few days ago [A. D.] Chertkov invited me for dinner. I arrived there—and his wife had had a miscarriage. This didn't prevent us from dining very boringly and very badly. I am playing the coquette with Moscow literature as well as I know how. But the Observers hold me in no high esteem. Nobody except Nashchokin loves me. But *tintere*[2] is my rival with him, and I'm being sacrificed to it. When I listen to the small talk of the local men of letters, I am astonished at how decent they can be in print and how stupid in conversation. Confess: Is that the way it is with me? Truly, I'm afraid it is. Baratynsky, however, is very pleasant. But somehow we're cold towards each other. I'm pressing Bryullov to come to Petersburg—but he's ill and is having a fit of the spleen. Here they want a bust of me to be sculptured.[3] But I don't want it. Then my Negro ugliness would be committed to immortality in all its dead immobility; I tell them that I have a beauty at home, whom we'll sculpture some time. I have seen Khomyakov's betrothed.[4] I couldn't get a good look at her in the twilight. As the late Gnedich used to say, she is *pas un bel femme*, but *une jolie figurlette*.[5] Good-by for a minute. Two buffoons are coming in to see me. One is a major and a mystic;[6] the other is a drunkard and a poet.[7] I am leaving you for them.

May 14.

I had difficulty in getting rid of the buffoons—including Norov. Everybody is inviting me to dinner, but I am refusing everybody. I'm beginning to think about departing. You are probably already in your suburban swamp.[8] Just how are my children and my books? Just how was the moving of the former and the hauling of the latter? And however did you manage to get your belly hauled? I bless you, my angel. God be with you and the children. Stay well, all of you. I greet your equestriennes.[9] I kiss Katerina Ivanovna's [Zagryazhskaya] little hands. Farewell.

A.P.

I have received an extremely sweet letter from you—I haven't the time to answer it. I thank you and kiss you, my angel.

May 16.

[618]

To Natalia Nikolaevna Pushkina

May 18, 1836. From Moscow to Petersburg.

Wife, my angel, though thanks for your nice letter, all the same

I'll scold you a little. Why did you write: "This is my last letter; you won't receive any more"? You want to compel me to come to you before the twenty-sixth. That's not the thing to do. God will help; *The Contemporary* will come out even with me away. But you won't give birth with me away. Can you give Odoevsky five hundred out of the money you have received? No? Well, let them wait until I get there—and that's all there is to it. Your new dispositions regarding your own revenues are your affair. Do as you like, though, I should think, it's better to have dealings with Dmitry Nikolaevich [Goncharov] than with Natalia Ivanovna [Goncharova]. This I say only *dans l'intérêt de M. Durier et Mme. Sichler*;[1] it's all the same to me. Your Petersburg news is horrible. What you write about Pavlov has reconciled me with him. I am glad he had challenged Aprelev.[2]— With us murder can be a vile way of settling scores: it saves one from a duel and exposes one to only a penal sentence—but not to capital punishment. Stolypin's drowning is horrible![3] Was it really impossible to help him? With us, here in Moscow, everything, thank God, is quiet: Kireev's fight with the Yar has produced great indignation in our prim local public. Nashchokin takes Kireev's[4] part very simply and very sensibly: what matter that a hussar lieutenant got drunk and beat up an innkeeper, who undertook to defend himself? In our day, when we used to beat the Germans in the Red Tavern,[5] didn't we, too, get what for, and did the Germans take being shoved around, with their arms folded? In my opinion Kireev's brawl is much more excusable than the fine dinner of your cavalry-guards, and the prudence of the young men, whose eyes get spit in, and they wipe them with a batiste handkerchief, opining that if an unpleasantness results, they won't be invited to the Anichkov Palace.[6] Bryullov has just now left me. He's going to Petersburg reluctantly; he fears the climate and lack of freedom. I try to console and encourage him. But at the same time my own heart drops into my boots when I recall that I'm a journalist. Though still a decent person, I have received police reprimands, and I have been told, *Vous avez trompé*,[7] and such like. What will happen to me now? Mordvinov will look on me as he does Faddey Bulgarin and Nikolay Polevoy—as a spy. The devil prompted my being born in Russia with a soul and with talent! It's great fun, I must say. Farewell; stay well, all of you. I kiss you.

[619]
To Pavel Voinovich Nashchokin
May 27, 1836. From Petersburg to Moscow.

My dear Pavel Voinovich,

I arrived home at my summer cottage on the twenty-third at midnight, and on the threshold I learned that Natalia Nikolaevna had given birth successfully to a daughter, Natalia, a few hours before my arrival. She was asleep. The next day I congratulated her and gave her, instead of a ten-ruble gold piece, your necklace, which she is in raptures over. Knock on wood; all's going well. Now let's talk about business. I left you two extra copies of *The Contemporary*. Give one to Prince [F. F.] Gagarin, and send the other from me to Belinsky[1] (N.B.: but keep it secret from the Observers), and have him told that I regret very much that I didn't succeed in seeing him. *Secondly*, I forgot to bring along your Memoirs[2] with me; do me the favor to hurry and send them. *Thirdly*, money, money! I need it desperately.

My trip went all right, though I had to repair the calash three times, but thank God, I did it on the spot, i.e., at a station, and it didn't take over two hours *en tout*.

The second issue of *The Contemporary* is very good, and you will thank me because of it. I am beginning to love it myself, and I'll probably start working at it actively. Farewell, be lucky at *tintere* and all else. I send my cordial greetings to Vera Alexandrovna [Nashchokina]. I have not yet succeeded in carrying out her commissions. In a few days I'll see what I can do about them.

May 27.

Here's an anecdote about my Sashka for you. He is being forbidden (I don't know why) to ask for what he wants. A few days ago he says to his aunt: "Azya![3] Give me some tea! I shan't ask."

[620]
To Denis Vasilievich Davydov
Between May 24 and 30, 1836. From Petersburg to Moscow.
(Rough draft)

I have just now arrived from Moscow—

I cannot send you your article about Dresden[1] until it has been printed, for it is a censored document. You will have time to look at its noble wounds to your heart's content.

Meanwhile, I thank you for the permission to publish it in its present form. But it's a pity. Why didn't we print it in the second issue of *The Contemporary*, which will be all full of Napoleon?[2] How fitting it would have been, in the same place, to slaughter General Wintzengerode[3] at the foot of the Vendôme Column,[4] as a propitiatory sacrifice! I was about to roll up my sleeves to do it! He got away, damn him. God be with him, the devil take him.

Vyazemsky advises me to publish "Your Eyes"[5] without your permission. I would be glad to, but I'm a little afraid. What do you think? Mayn't I—without your name? . . .

I'm expecting some letters from Yazykov.

[621]
To Lev Sergeevich Pushkin
June 3, 1836. From Petersburg to Tiflis.

Here for you is a brief accounting of our proposed apportioning.[1]

The 80 souls and 1900 acres of land in the Pskov Province are worth (at the rate of 500 rubles per soul, instead of the usual price of 400 rubles)

	—40,000 rubles
From them is excluded a 7th share for our father	5,714
And a 14th share for our sister	2,857
Total	8,571—

Our father has declined his own share and granted it to our sister.

For our share, it remains to divide equally	31,429 rubles
For your share will come	15,715.

We shall not have time to get anything done before the month of September.

Write what debts you have in Tiflis, and if you have time, buy up your notes of hand before your creditors find out about your inheritance.

I see from your letter to Nikolay Ivanovich [Pavlishchev] that you don't know anything about your own affairs. Your note of hand, given to Boltin, has been bought up by me. The debt to Pleshcheev[2] has been paid (except 300 rubles which he wrote me about after I had already given up the management of the estate). The debt to Nikolay Ivanovich [Pavlishchev] has also been paid. Of the petty ones, your debt to Gut[3] has not been paid, *nor have certain others which you know of*, Nikolay Ivanovich tells me.

June 3.

My opinion: to spread out the payment of these 15,000 to you over three years, for you probably need money, and you couldn't consent to receive only the revenues from half of Mikhaylovskoe. About what has been assigned to you by Father I shall talk with him, although that will probably lead to nothing. When I gave the estate back to him,[4] I thought I had bespoken for you the net revenues from half of Kistenevo.[5] But apparently our father has changed his mind. As for me, under no circumstances do I want to meddle in the administration, or ruination, of our father's estate.

[622]

To Andrey Alexandrovich Kraevsky
June 6, 1836. In Petersburg.

In Vyazemsky's article about Julius Caesar and Napoleon there are errors against the nature of the language in the proper names. For example, *Tarkvin* instead of *Tarkvinij* [Tarquin], *Parfy* instead of *Parfjane* [Parthians], *Tiverij* instead of *Tiberij* [Tiberius]—and others. Do me the favor of correcting them, if you run across them.[1]

June 6.

[623]

To Nadezhda Andreevna Durova
About June 10, 1836. From Petersburg to Elabuga.

Here is the beginning of your notes. All the copies have already been printed and are now being bound. I do not know whether it would be possible to stop the edition.[1] My sincere and disinterested opinion is, leave it as it is. "The Memoirs of an Amazon" is a little too far-fetched, precious; it reminds one of German novels. "The Memoirs of N. A. Durova" is simple, sincere, and noble. Be brave— step onto the literary field of endeavor just as courageously as onto the one which has made you famous. Half measures are good for nothing.

All yours, A.P.

My house is at your service. On the Dvortsovaya Naberezhnaya, the house of Batashev at the Prachechny Bridge.

[624]
To Ivan Ivanovich Dmitriev
June 14, 1836. From Petersburg to Moscow.

Dear Sir, Ivan Ivanovich, upon returning to Petersburg I had the good fortune to find at my house a letter from Your High Excellency. Father has entrusted me with testifying of his most profound gratitude for the sympathetic interest which you take in the misfortune which has come upon us.[1]

Your favorable comment about *The Contemporary* encourages me in a field of endeavor which is new for me. I shall try also henceforth to justify your kind opinion.

The observation about your homonym[2] will adorn the second issue of *The Contemporary* and will be printed word for word. Your Sosie is no son of Jupiter,[3] and his encounter with you is unprofitable for him in all respects.

God grant you health and many years! Outlive our young literary men, just as your poetry will outlive our young literature.

With the most profound respect and with complete devotion, I have the honor to be, Dear Sir, Your High Excellency's most humble servant.

June 14.   Alexander Pushkin.
SPb.

[625]
To Iosif Matveevich Penkovsky
June 14, 1836. From Petersburg to Boldino.

Upon returning from Moscow, I found your letter at my house. I hope that you have already received the receipt from the Moscow Council.[1] There is no need to increase the quitrent. If it is possible and financially advantageous to put Kistenevo to the plow,[2] then go to it. But it will hardly be possible.

Father plans to spend this year there, but it is hardly likely that he will really do it. He probably will not consent to reside in Boldino. If he does not remain in Moscow, then I think he will settle down in Mikhaylovskoe.

I am very grateful to you for taking care of our estate. I know that last year you halted Father in his intention of selling this estate and thereby depriving, if not me, then my children, of their last dependable crust of bread. Be assured that I shall never forget it.

June 14, 1836.   A.P.
   SPb.

I shall write you about Mikhaylo and his family.[3]

[626]
To Nikolay Ivanovich Ushakov
About June 14, 1836. In Petersburg.
(Rough draft)

Upon returning from Moscow, I had the honor to receive your book[1]—and I have read it avidly.

I shall not undertake to judge it as the work of a learned military man, but I am delighted with the clear, eloquent, picturesque account. From now on the name of the subjugator of Erivan, Erzurum, and Warsaw[2] will be coupled with the name of his brilliant historian. With astonishment I noticed that you have also granted me immortality—with one stroke of your pen. You have admitted me to the Temple of Glory, just as once upon a time Count Erivansky permitted me to enter conquered Erzurum after him.[3]

With the most profound, etc.

[627]
To Nadeziida Andreevna Durova
About (not earlier than) June 25, 1836.
From Petersburg to Elabuga.

I thank you very much for your frank and decisive letter.[1] It is very pleasing, because it bears the genuine stamp of your fiery and impatient character. I shall answer you *item by item*, as the court clerks say.

(1) Your notes are still being copied out. I felt obliged to give them only to someone I could depend on. Because of this, the business has been held up.

(2) The Sovereign has seen fit to be my censor. That's true. But I do not have the right to submit *others'* works for his examination. You of course will be an exception, but a pretext is necessary for doing so, and that is what I should like to talk with you about, in order that the business not be spoiled by our being hasty.

(3) You have passed through one field of endeavor with glory; you are entering upon a new one, still foreign to you. The bothers of the writer are still incomprehensible to you. It is impossible to publish a book in one week; at least some two months are required for that. The manuscript must be copied, presented to the censorship, one must apply to the printing house, etc., etc.

(4) You write me: "Take action or let me take action." As soon as I receive the copied-out manuscript, I shall begin immediately. This cannot and must not prevent you from taking action on your part. My aim is to provide you with as much profit as possible, and not to leave you a victim of the mercenary and careless booksellers.

(5) It is impossible for me to go see the Tsar on maneuvers for many reasons. I had even thought of applying to him *as a last resort*, if the censorship does not pass your notes. I shall explain all this to you when I have the pleasure of seeing you in person.

I shall have the honor of delivering the remaining five hundred rubles to you by July 1.[2] With me, payment usually (as with other journalists) occurs only when the article purchased is issued.

I know a man who would have willingly bought your memoirs; but his terms probably would have been more profitable for him than for you. In any case, whether you sell them or whether you have them printed yourself, please entrust me with all the troubles of the publication, of the proofs, etc. Be assured of my devotion, and for God's sake do not be hasty and blame me as lacking in zeal.

With the most profound respect and with devotion, I have the honor to be, Dear Sir,[3]

Your most humble servant,
Alexander Pushkin.

P.S. In a few days the second issue of *The Contemporary* will come out. Then I shall be more free and in funds.

[628]
To Ivan Alexeevich Yakovlev
July 9, 1836. In Petersburg.

Dear Ivan Alexeevich,

I am so much at fault toward you that I shall not even try to justify myself. Money has been coming to me and slipping through my fingers. I have been paying others' debts, trying to buy up others' estates[1]—and my own debts have remained on my neck. My extremely disordered affairs have made me insolvent . . . and I am compelled to ask of you another extension until autumn. Meanwhile I congratulate you upon your arrival. Where may we see you? I am in mourning[2] and do not go anywhere, but I would be glad to meet you, even though you are my creditor.[3] I am relying on your only too well tried magnanimity.

July 9, 1836.
Kamenny Ostrov.

All yours,
A. Pushkin.

[629]
To Nikolay Ivanovich Pavlishchev
July 13, 1836. From Petersburg to Mikhaylovskoe.

I well knew that the steward[1] was a swindler, although, I confess, I had not suspected him of such impudence. You have done well in dismissing him and taking over the management of the estate yourself. One thing is bad. From your letter I see that, in defiance of my orders, the steward had already succeeded in selling off everything. What are you going to live on meanwhile? By golly, I don't know. Your Polonsky[2] has not come to see me. But since I do not yet have a power of attorney from Lev Sergeevich [Pushkin],[3] I have not tried to look him up. However, where am I to find him when I need him? Father left Petersburg on July 1—and I have not received any news of him. I shall forward Sister's letter to him as soon as I find out where to write him. How is her health? With all my heart I embrace her. I also send my greetings to dear and honored Praskovia Alexandrovna [Osipova], who has forgotten me completely. Here my head's going round and round. I am thinking of coming to Mikhaylovskoe, as soon as I have brought my affairs into a little order.

July 13.

[630]
To Nikolay Ivanovich Pavlishchev
About (not later than) August 13, 1836.
From Petersburg to Mikhaylovskoe.

Do me the favor to compose on the spot the *announcement of the sale* of Mikhaylovskoe,[1] and send it to me; and I shall print it that way. But try to talk it over with the *best* buyers there on the spot. One of our neighbors here, who knows both the region and our land, has offered me 20,000 rubles for Mikhaylovskoe. I confess that it is hardly likely that anyone will give twice that, and I don't dare even to think of 60,000. I cannot agree to the transaction you propose,[2] and here is why: Father will never consent to give Olga her share of his estate while he is alive, and I can't rely on Boldino. Father has already lived up and lost, through poor management, half of the estate, and has even wanted to sell the remainder already. You write that for me Mikhaylovskoe would be only a toy. So it would—for me. But my children are not a bit richer than your Lelya,[3] and I cannot play jokes with their future and their property. If you took Mikhaylovskoe and then it should become necessary for you to sell it, then it wouldn't be a toy for me, either. Your appraisal of 64,000 is a good price, but one must find out whether so much would be given. I might even give it, but I don't have the money, and if I had it, I could use the capital more advantageously. I send greetings to Olga. God grant her good health—and us good buyers. This fall I shall be in Mikhaylovskoe—probably for the last time. I should like to find you still there.

A.P.

[631]
To Andrey Andreevich Zhandr
July or August, 1836. In Petersburg.
(Rough draft)

I make bold to trouble you with a request for a young man whom I am not acquainted with, but who finds himself in circumstances which require immediate aid. Mr. Khmelnitsky[1] arrived from Little Russia a few days ago. He is here without money and without protectors. He is twenty-three years old. Judging from his conversation and a letter which I received from him, he is intelligent and has noble feelings. Here is the point: he wishes to get a place in the Navy, but up to now he has not had admission to see Prince Menshikov.[2] I have promised to introduce him to you, vouching for your readiness to do him a good turn, if only it be possible.

[632]

To Denis Vasilievich Davydov
August, 1836. From Petersburg to Maza.
(Rough draft)

You thought your article "Of Partisan Warfare"[1] would pass through the censorship whole and unharmed. You were mistaken: it did not get by without some red ink. Really, the military censors seem to blot out, to prove that they read.

It's hard, one must say. With one censorship you have to dance a merry tune; but what is it like to depend on all four?[2] I do not know what offense has been committed by Russian writers, who not only are mild but are even, in and of themselves, in accord with the spirit of the government. But I know that never have they been so oppressed as now, not even in the last five years of the reign of the late Emperor,[3] when all literature remained in manuscript, thanks to Krasovsky and Birukov.

The censorship is a civilian matter; the *opričina* has been separated from it—but the members of the *opričina* are guided, not by the code, but by their extreme notions.[4]

[633]

To Peter Alexandrovich Korsakov
About (not later than) September 27, 1836.
In Petersburg.

Dear Sir, Peter Alexandrovich,

Once upon a time, when I was taking my first steps in the literary field of endeavor, you gave me a friendly hand.[1] Now I make bold to have recourse again to your indulgent protection.

You alone among us have been able to combine the ticklish duty of the censor with the feeling of a man of letters (the best ones—not those of the present times). I know how burdened you are with your duties. I am ashamed to trouble you. But you are the only one to whom we can have recourse with full confidence and with sincere esteem for your ultimate decision. You have only yourself to blame.

I make bold to forward to you the first half of my novel for authorization; I ask you to preserve the secret of my name.

With the most profound respect and with complete devotion, I have the honor to be,
>Dear Sir,
>>Your most humble servant,
>>>A. Pushkin.

[634]
>To Nikolay Ivanovich Grech
>October 13, 1836. In Petersburg.

Dear Sir, Nikolay Ivanovich,

I sincerely thank you for your kind word about my "Great Leader."[1] The stoic figure of Barklay is one of the most remarkable in our history. I do not know whether he can be fully justified with respect to military art, but his character will remain eternally worthy of astonishment and admiration.

With sincere respect and with devotion, I have the honor to be,
>Dear Sir,
>>Your most humble servant,

October 13, 1836.   Alexander Pushkin.

[635]
>To Modest Alexandrovich Korf
>October 14, 1836. In Petersburg.

What you sent me yesterday[1] is valuable to me in all respects and will remain with me as a memorial. I am truly sorry that the governmental service has deprived us of a historian. I have no hope of replacing you. Upon reading this list of names, I became frightened and ashamed: a great part of the books cited are unknown to me. I shall exert all possible efforts to obtain them. What a field modern Russian history is! And when you reflect that it is as yet completely untilled, and that except for us Russians nobody can even undertake it! But history is long, life is short, and worst of all, human nature is lazy (Russian nature especially). Good-by. Tomorrow we shall probably see each other at Myasoedov's.[2]

Devoted to you in heart,

October 14.   A.P.

[636]
To Mikhail Lukianovich Yakovlev
Between October 9 and 15, 1836. In Petersburg.

I agree with the opinion of No. 39.[1] There is no point in changing the ancient customs of the Lyceum for the twenty-fifth anniversary. That would be a bad omen. It has been said that even the last Lyceum student will celebrate October 19 *alone*.[2] It is not a bad idea to call that to mind.

No. 14.

[637]
To Peter Yakovlevich Chaadaev
October 19, 1836.
(In French)

October 19.

I thank you for the booklet which you sent me. I was delighted to read it again, although very much astonished at seeing it translated and published. I am pleased with the translation; it has preserved the energy and the unconstraint of the original. As for the ideas, you know that I am far from being entirely of your opinion.[1] There is no doubt that the Schism separated us from the rest of Europe and that we have not participated in any of the great occurrences which have agitated it. But we have had our own special mission. Russia, in its immense expanse, was what absorbed the Mongol conquest. The Tatars did not dare to cross our western frontiers and leave us to their rear. They withdrew to their deserts, and Christian civilization was saved.[2] For this purpose we were obliged to have a life completely apart, one which though leaving us Christians left us such complete strangers to the Christian world that our martyrdom did not provide any distraction to the energetic development of Catholic Europe. You say that the well to which we went to draw Christianity was contaminated, that Byzantium was contemptible and contemned, etc. Well, now, my friend! Was not Jesus Christ himself born a Jew, and was not Jerusalem the laughing-stock of nations? Are the Gospels the less wonderful for that? We have taken the Gospels and traditions from the Greeks, but not the spirit of puerility and controversy. The customs of Byzantium were never those of Kiev. The Russian clergy, up to Feofan,[3] was worthy of respect; it was never besmirched by the infamies of papism, and most certainly it would never have provoked the Reformation at the moment when humanity had the most need of unity.[4] I acknowledge that our present-day clergy is behind the times. Do you want to know the reason why? Because it wears the beard; that is all. It does not belong to good society.[5] As for our history being nil, I absolutely cannot be of your opinion. The Wars of Oleg and of Svyatoslav, and even the wars of appanage—are these not that life of adventurous effervescence and of ruthless, pointless activity which characterizes the youth of all peoples? The invasion by the Tatars is a sad and a grand picture. What? Are the awakening of Russia, the development of its power, its march toward unity (Russian unity, of course), the two Ivans,[6] the sublime drama begun at Uglich and concluded at the Ipatiev Monastery[7]—is all this to be not history, but a pallid and half-forgotten dream? And Peter the Great, who in himself alone is a universal history! And Catherine II, who placed Russia on the threshold of Europe? And Alexander, who led us to Paris? And (cross your heart) do you find nothing impressive in the present-day situation of Russia, nothing which will strike the future historian? Do you believe that he will place us outside Europe? Although I personally am sincerely attached to the Emperor, I am far from admiring all that I see around me; as a man of letters, I am embittered; as a man of prejudices,[8] I am offended. But I swear to you on my honor that not for anything in the world would I be willing to change my fatherland, nor to have any other history than that of our ancestors, such as God gave it to us.

This is a very long letter. After having taken issue with you, I must tell you that many things in your letter are profoundly true. One must admit that our social life is a sad thing. The absence of public opinion, the indifference toward all duty, justice, and truth, the cynical disdain for human thought and dignity are truly distressing. You have done well to say it out loud. But I fear that your historical opinions may do you harm ... in a word, I am vexed that I was not near you when you delivered your manuscript to the journalists. I do not go anywhere, and I cannot tell you whether your article is attracting attention. I hope that it will not be puffed. Have you read the third issue of *The Contemporary*? The article "Voltaire" and the "John Tanner"[9] are mine. Kozlovsky would be my providence if he were to consent once and for all to become a man of letters. Farewell, my friend. If you see [M. F.] Orlov and [A. N.] Raevsky, remember me kindly to them.—What are the lukewarm Christians saying of your letter?[10]

[638]
To Sergey Lvovich Pushkin
October 20, 1836. From Petersburg to Moscow.
(In French)

My dear Father, here, first of all, is my address: *On the Moyka at the Konyushenny Bridge, in the house of Princess Volkonskaya.*[1] I have been obliged to leave Batashev's house, the caretaker of which is a rascal.

You ask me for news of Natalia and the youngsters. Thank God, all are healthy. I have no news of my sister, who left the country, ill. Her husband, after having put me out of patience with his perfectly useless letters,[2] is giving no further signs of life, when the thing to be done is to straighten up his affairs. Do send him a *power of attorney* for the share which you have given Olga. It is needed. Lev has entered the service,[3] and is asking me for money, but I am not in position to support everybody. I myself am in very disordered circumstances, burdened with a numerous family, supporting them by dint of hard work, and not daring to look to the future. Pavlishchev reproaches me with the expenditures I make, though I am not a burden upon anyone, and though I do not have to give an accounting to anyone but my children. He asserts that all the same they will be richer than his son. I know nothing of the sort. But I neither can nor will be generous at their expense.

I had counted on going to Mikhaylovskoe; I have not been able to. This will upset my affairs for another year, at least. In the country I would have worked a great deal. Here I do nothing but fret.

Farewell, my dear Father. I kiss your hands and embrace you with all my heart.

October 20, 1836.

[639]
To Peter Alexandrovich Korsakov
October 25, 1836. In Petersburg.

Dear Sir, Peter Alexandrovich,

I hasten to answer your questions.[1] The name of the maiden Mironova is fictitious. My novel is based on a tradition I once heard, that one of the officers, who was unfaithful to his duty and went over to Pugachev's gangs, was pardoned by the Empress at the request of his aged father, who threw himself at her feet. The novel, as you see, departed far from the truth. I would ask you not to mention the real name of the author, but to state that the manuscript was delivered via P. A. Pletnev, whom I have already informed in advance.

Permit me, Dear Sir, to testify again of my most profound respect and my cordial gratitude.

                I have the honor to be,
                Dear Sir,
                Your most humble servant,

October 25.   Alexander Pushkin.

[640]
To Vladimir Fedorovich Odoevsky
1835 or 1836. In Petersburg.

I am at home, ill, with a cold in the head. I am ready to receive a dear guest in my cubicle—but I myself shall not come out of my cubicle.[1]

                A.P.

[641]
To Anna Petrovna Kern
1835 or 1836 (?). In Petersburg.
(In French)

My pen is so poor that Mme. Khitrovo cannot use it, and so I have the privilege of being her secretary.[1]

[642]
>To Anna Petrovna Kern
>1835 or 1836 (?). In Petersburg.
>(In French)

Here is Sheremetev's[1] answer. My wish is that it be agreeable to you. Mme. Khitrovo has done what she could. Farewell, beautiful lady. Be calm and happy, and believe in my devotion.

[643]
>To Anna Petrovna Kern
>1835 or 1836 (?). In Petersburg.
>(Fragments; in French)

When you could not obtain anything, you, a pretty woman, what, then, will I be able to do, I who am not even a handsome lad? [...] All that I can advise is to turn again to the expedient [....][1]

[644]
>To Peter Andreevich Vyazemsky
>In the second half of 1835 or in 1836.
>In Petersburg.

Arab (does not have a feminine), a dweller or native of Arabia, an Arabian. *Karavan byl razgrablen stepnymi arabami* [The caravan was plundered by the Arabs of the steppes].

Arap, feminine *arapka*; this is what negroes and mulattoes are usually called. *Dvorcovye arapy*, negroes serving in the palace. *On vyezžaet s tremja narjadnymi arapami* [He is leaving with three finely dressed negroes].

Arapnik, from the Polish *Herapnik* (*de* **harap**), *cri de chasseur pour enlever aux chiens la proie. Reiff*).[1] N.B.: **harap** *vient de* **Herab** [down].

Really, it wouldn't be a bad idea to get busy on a Lexicon or at least a critique of lexicons.[2]

[645]
>To Mikhail Lukianovich Yakolev
>1836(?). In Petersburg.

Smirdin has plunged me into misfortune; this tradesman is

always going back on his word, and a promised day, with him, means God knows when.[1]

Tomorrow I shall receive the money at 2 o'clock in the afternoon. And in the evening I shall deliver it to you.

All yours, A.P.

[646]
To Achille Tardif de Mello
1836(?). In Petersburg.
(In French)

You have made me find my verses very beautiful,[1] Sir. You have reclothed them in that noble garment in which poetry is truly a goddess, *vera incessu patuit dea*.[2] I thank you for your precious packet.

You are a poet and you are teaching youth; I invoke two benedictions upon you.

A. Pushkin.

Notes to Part XIII

Letter 588
 1. Pushkin's edition of "The Memoirs of Brigadier Moreau de Brasey" was published in *The Contemporary* in 1837, after Pushkin's death.
 2. Pushkin uses the English word "Review" here and below. This official request resulted in Pushkin's obtaining permission to publish a literary journal, *The Contemporary*, which began to appear in April, 1836.

Letter 589
 1. Pushkin addresses Mme. Durova, the "Amazon" who fought, disguised as a man, in Russia's wars against Napoleon, by her masculine pseudonym, Alexander Andreevich Alexandrov (see Letter 564, and note). Pushkin printed a fragment from her memoirs in his *Contemporary* in 1836, but he did not publish the edition in book form.

Letter 590
 1. Pushkin's wrath had not cooled in the almost two years since the Moscow postmaster had intercepted one of his letters and given it to the police, who gave it to the Tsar (see Letter 488, and note).
 2. *The Contemporary*.
 3. The allusion is to Nashchokin's abandoning his mistress, Olga Andreevna, and marrying.
 4. A certain V—— who called himself doctor, and who practiced alchemy. Nashchokin spent considerable money on his experiments to produce gold.

Letter 591
 1. Probably Benkendorf. This letter concerns Pushkin's clash with Uvarov, Minister of Public Education, over Pushkin's "Ode on the Convalescence of Lucullus," in which Uvarov is satirized and the charges are leveled against him as indicated in this letter. Benkendorf asked Pushkin in person at whom the satire was directed. Pushkin replied, "At you." Benkendorf laughed at the absurdity. Then Pushkin inquired why people thought it might be about Uvarov.
 2. Pushkin did not complete the sentence.
 3. That is, to favorites of Catherine the Great. Derzhavin's poem was written in 1794, two years before Catherine's death.
 4. In his diary in February, 1836, Pushkin makes these specific charges—and worse—against Uvarov.
 5. It may be noted that Pushkin does not deny that the poem is a personal satire on Uvarov. He only says that the charges are commonplace and that he has never told anyone that the poem was a satire on anyone.

Letter 592
 1. Pushkin's letter is in answer to a letter of the same day from Khlyustin, challenging Pushkin to a duel. The challenge resulted from hot words of Pushkin's upon hearing Khlyustin repeat Senkovsky's charge that Lyutsenko's translation of *Vastola* was Pushkin's own (see Letter 572). Khlyustin demanded satisfaction on three points: (1) that Pushkin included him among the "swine and scoundrels" he accuses, (2) that Pushkin made threats equal in significance to a challenge and then did not send a

challenge, and (3) that Pushkin was impolite in not bowing when he left Khlyustin. In this letter Pushkin answers all three points, but Khlyustin was satisfied with the answer to only the third. Further negotiations and conversations, with Sobolevsky as intermediary, were necessary to prevent a duel. The last twelve months of Pushkin's life begin with him in an irritated mood and making intemperate charges. This is the first of several almost-duels which were averted in 1836, before the fatal duel occurred in January, 1837.

2. "I am not angry with Senkovsky, but I cannot help being vexed when decent people repeat the absurdities of swine and scoundrels." Pushkin's self-quotation in Russian shows that the conversation in point had been in Russian, though Khlyustin's challenge and Pushkin's reply are both in French. Pushkin could consider Senkovsky a "swine and a scoundrel," but he was not "angry" with him, that is, he would not challenge him to a duel, as a member of a lower social class.

3. "Swine and scoundrels."

4. "To deceive the public." Pushkin left himself open for this charge by publishing Lyutsenko's translation of *Vastola*, without the name of the translator, but with his own name as publisher on the title page—with the result that it could be assumed that Pushkin was the translator.

Letter 593

1. Prince Nikolay Grigorievich Repnin-Volkonsky (1778-1845), a member of the State Council and brother of the Decembrist S. G. Volkonsky.

2. Varfolomey Filippovich Bogolyubov (ca. 1785-1842), an official serving in the Collegium of Foreign Affairs, and a man close to Uvarov. He informed Pushkin that Repnin-Volkonsky considered Pushkin's satire on Uvarov, "On the Convalescence of Lucullus" (see Letter 591, and note), as directed at him, Repnin-Volkonsky. Repnin-Volkonsky had been removed from the post of Governor-General of Little Russia in 1834, because of irregularities in his accounts, and hence he might very well feel that he had reason to think that Pushkin's poem was about him. (See Letter 595.)

Letter 594

1. Count Vladimir Alexandrovich Sollogub, later a well-known writer of short stories. At a ball in December, 1835, or January, 1836, Sollogub answered some bantering comments of Mme. Pushkina's with a remark which she considered offensive. Pushkin, sensitive about his wife's honor, immediately sent off a challenge to Sollogub, but it remained undelivered, because Sollogub had left to serve under the Governor of Tver. When Sollogub learned of the challenge, which has not survived, he wrote a letter of explanations, which Pushkin is here answering. The affair ended without a duel. Pushkin was "satisfied" when Sollogub, after extended personal negotiations, wrote a letter asking Mme. Pushkina's pardon. Though Pushkin was willing to fight, his attitude toward dueling at this time is clear from one thing he said to Sollogub: "Surely you don't think it's fun for me to duel? But what can I do? I have the misfortune to be a public man, and, you know, that's worse than being a public woman." Sollogub, after this event, was in very friendly relations with Pushkin. Pushkin chose him as his second for negotiations with Georges Charles d'Anthès-Heeckeren (1812-1895) with regard to a duel in November, 1836. This duel did not take place, and Sollogub had no part in the arrangements for Pushkin's fatal duel two months later.

2. Pushkin traveled through Tver on May 1, 1836, and tried to have a meeting with Sollogub, but Sollogub was then out of town. Three days later Sollogub went to Nashchokin's house in Moscow, where Pushkin was then on a visit, and the satisfactory explanations took place.

3. The sentence was left uncompleted. The fair copy of this letter is unknown. In the version published from memory by Sollogub in 1865, the following sentence occurs, which is not in this rough draft: "The name which you bear and the society which you frequent oblige me to demand of you the reason for the impropriety of your conduct." Like Pushkin, Sollogub was an aristocrat and a Kammerjunker.

Letter 595
1. Repnin-Volkonsky, in his letter (in Russian) of February 10, 1836, in answer to Letter 593, stated that he had never spoken of Pushkin at all in the presence of Bogolyubov. He added that "to you I shall sincerely say that your genius and talent will bring benefit to the fatherland and glory to you, in lauding the Russian faith and loyalty, rather than in insulting honorable men." Repnin-Volkonsky was "grieved" that Pushkin had not "contemned tales so repugnant to [his] principles."

Letter 596
1. Pushkin's letter is a tardy answer to Mme. Fuch's letter of November 15, 1835. Pushkins last previous trip to the "village" had been in September and October, 1835.
2. Pushkin's *History of Pugachev*.
3. Unidentified.
4. Mme. Fuchs sent various works to Pushkin, as a result of this invitation, but he did not print any of them in *The Contemporary*.

Letter 597
1. Vasily Dmitrievich Sukhorukov (1795-1841), army officer and writer, implicated in, but not a participant of the Decembrist Uprising of 1825. Materials which he collected for a history of Don troops and, later, of the Russian expedition to Erzurum in 1829, were confiscated by the authorities and never returned to him. Pushkin met him in the Caucasus, "in the vicinity" of the mountains of Beshtau and Elbrus, when Pushkin also took part in the expedition to Erzurum. In his *Journey to Erzurum*, Pushkin mentions meeting Sukhorukov (Chapter V).
2. Possibly one F. I. Shumkov.
3. To Olga Vasilievna Shvetsova.
4. Pushkin no doubt means a notification that Sukhorukov would receive it. Pushkin was sending such announcements to his friends and prospective contributors at the time. No articles by Sukhorukov appeared in the journal during Pushkin's lifetime.

Letter 598
1. Odoevsky was Pushkin's closest collaborator in *The Contemporary*. The discussion here is about the first issue.
2. Pushkin's *Journey to Erzurum*.
3. Odoevsky's tale "Princess Zizi" did not appear in Pushkin's *Contemporary*, but in *Memoirs of the Fatherland* (1839).

Letter 599
1. The letter has to do mainly with difficulties with the censorship in connection with articles for Pushkin's *Contemporary*. All the items mentioned in this letter appeared in the first issue of *The Contemporary*.
2. Prince Peter Borisovich Kozlovsky (1783-1840), writer and diplomat. His article was "Review of the Paris Mathematical Annual for 1836."
3. The reference is to A. I. Turgenev's "Letters from Paris," which contained comment about social and political events of the time, including the unsuccessful

attempt on the life of King Louis Philippe of France, made by Giuseppi Fieschi, Corsican conspirator, on July 28, 1835. Brief mentions of Fieschi and several French ministers, including among others Guizot and Thiers, were nevertheless permitted to occur in the printed "Letters."

4. Vyazemsky's poem, "The Rose and the Cypress," addressed to Princess Maria Alexandrovna Pototskaya (d. 1845).

Letter 600
1. Pushkin's point is that, after the Censorship Committee made substantial cuts in A. I. Turgenev's "Letters from Paris," Pushkin wished to present them at once to Benkendorf for approval, thus by-passing the Chief Directorate of the Censorship. Prince Dondukov-Korsakov answered, however, that the article would be presented to the Chief Directorate of the Censorship. Pushkin noted on the back of Dondukov-Korsakov's letter, "With the censorship you can quarrel, he says, but not with His Grace."

Letter 601
1. See Letters 599 and 600. Alexander Lukich Krylov (1798-1853), professor of history at Petersburg University, as the censor of A. I. Turgenev's "Letters from Paris," had made cuts which Pushkin wished restored. This letter calls attention again to the close scrutiny which the censorship under Nicholas I kept over all foreign news of any political interest.

Letter 602
1. Alphonse Jean Jobard (1793—after 1845) had been professor of Latin and Greek at Kazan University in the 1820's. He was expelled from Russia in 1836, as the result of clashes with Uvarov, Minister of Public Education. On March 16, 1836, Jobard sent his own translation of Pushkin's satire on Uvarov, "On the Convalescence of Lucullus," to Pushkin, along with a copy of a letter addressed to Uvarov, in which Jobard proposed that Uvarov accept the translation and publish it as his own, as he was in the habit of doing with others' work. Upon receiving Pushkin's letter, Jobard agreed not to publish the translation and letter to Uvarov "for a time," but he stated that he had sent copies to relatives in France and Belgium, and that they might be published there if Jobard did not receive "justice" in Russia.
2. Nicholas I.

Letter 603
1. Pushkin published only a part of Nadezhda Andreevna Durova's memoirs in his journal, *The Contemporary*. Durova was Durov's sister; Pushkin calls her Durov's "brother" and "him" because she wrote under a masculine pseudonym, Alexander Andreevich Alexandrov, in recounting her experiences of serving in the army disguised as a man.
2. The letter was sent off only on April 18.

Letter 604
1. This is the only known letter of Pushkin's to an English man of letters. The book in question is Borrow's *Targum, or a Metrical Translation from Thirty Languages*, which he published in English in Petersburg in 1835. It contains some translations from Pushkin.

Letter 605
1. The first issue of Pushkin's *Contemporary* appeared on April 11, 1836. St. Thomas' Week is the second week after Easter.
2. Odoevsky's article, "Of Enmity Toward Enlightenment, as Observed in Most Recent Literature," was published in the second issue of *The Contemporary*, but not at the beginning of it.
3. Odoevsky's critique of the novel, *The Inn* (1835), by Alexander Petrovich Stepanov (1781-1837), was published in the third issue of *The Contemporary*, under the title "How Novels Are Written Among Us."
4. Odoevsky's "fragment" remained unfinished; it did not appear in *The Contemporary*.
5. Pushkin left for Mikhaylovskoe on April 7 or 8, 1836, for the burial of his mother, who died on March 29.
6. A dramatic fragment by Odoevsky. It did not appear in *The Contemporary*.
7. Gogol's "Morning of a Man of Business: Petersburg Scenes," which appeared in the first issue of *The Contemporary*.

Letter 606
1. As a result of this request, an additional censor was named for Pushkin's *Contemporary*, Pavel Ivanovich Gaevsky. Gaevsky proved so severe a censor that Pushkin soon had reason to regret having made the request.

Letter 607
1. The death of his mother on March 29.
2. The first issue of *The Contemporary* appeared on April 11, during the first week of Pushkin's absence from Petersburg.
3. The review of Pogodin's *Historical Aphorisms* (Moscow, 1836) was written by Gogol. During Pushkin's lifetime one article by Pogodin appeared in *The Contemporary*.

Letter 608
1. The estate of the Vrevskys. Pushkin was visiting the family of Evpraxia Nikolaevna Vrevskaya, nee Vulf.
2. The quotation is from Yazykov's poem "Trigorskoe."
3. In 1829, Pushkin had called Vulf "Lovelace Nikolaevich" (Letter 254), and in another letter he called himself "the Lovelace of Tver" and Vulf "Valmont" (Letter 238).
4. An unsigned article about *The Collected Works* of Georgy Konissky (1717-1795), Belorussian Archbishop.
5. Yazykov, in response to this request, contributed "A Dramatic Tale About Ivan Tsarevich . . . " to *The Contemporary* in 1836.
6. In Russian fairy tales, "dead water" causes the parts of a dismembered body to grow back together, and "living water" then brings it back to life. Puskin utilized this folklore motif in *Ruslan and Lyudmila*.
7. In Yazykov's poetic "Epistle to Davydov," which had been published in *The Moscow Observer* during the previous year, he alludes to a well-known physical trait of D. V. Davydov, as he says, "You are a warrior with curly black hair, with a white lock on your forehead."
8. Yazykov's answer to Vyazemsky's poem, "To Yazykov" (1834), was published in 1844.
9. The quotation is from Derzhavin, "On the Birth of Tsaritsa Gremislava: To Lev Alexandrovich Naryshkin."
10. Yazykov answered that he had sent the work to his brother to be given to

Pushkin, but that Pushkin should obtain a copy of the work from Peter Vasilievich Kireevsky, whose copy had been collated with many copies.

Letter 609
 1. The letter in question was from Kyukhelbeker, whose prison sentence in connection with the Decembrist Uprising had been commuted to permission to settle in Eastern Siberia (see Letter 587). Pushkin is answering Mordvinov's letter stating that Benkendorf wanted the letter from Kyukhelbeker and wanted to know via whom Pushkin received it.

Letter 610
 1. Dondukov-Korsakov's letter of April 10, 1836, in which he named Gaevsky as second censor of Pushkin's *Contemporary*, in response to Pushkin's request (Letter 606).
 2. Denis V. Davydov's essay, "The Occupation of Dresden . . .," which contained criticism of certain military leaders and self-justification by Davydov. Because of the military matters involved, it had to be sent to the military censorship. See Letter 620.

Letter 611
 1. A church in Moscow.
 2. Pushkin left on April 28 for what turned out to be his last trip to Moscow. He went there to work in the archives and to accomplish certain business with regard to his *Contemporary*.
 3. Pushkin is playing on the idiom "he is lodged foppishly," so as to include the idea that "he is lodged with a little mistress."
 4. The painter Karl Pavlovich Bryullov (1799-1852). The sculptor he was living with was probably Ivan Petrovich Vitali (1794-1855).
 5. Probably an error, for Alexander Julius Klinder, a portraitist.
 6. Bryullov visited Petersburg at the end of May or the beginning of June, 1836, after Pushkin returned from Moscow.
 7. The writer, Alexey Alexeevich Perovsky. Bryullov was painting his portrait at the time, but did not finish it.
 8. Nashchokin's play house (see Letter 412 and notes). Some "tiny people" were added later, including a figurine of Pushkin.
 9. Elizaveta Alexeevna Okulova and Varvara Alexeevna Okulova were sisters of Nashchokin's brother-in-law. The former married Alexey Nikolaevich Diakov (1790-1837) on May 3, 1836.
 10. The Troitse-Sergieva Lavra (Monastery).
 11. *Belaja gorjačka.*
 12. Sarra Fedorovna Tolstaya (1820-1838). She died of tuberculosis.
 13. The publishers of the journal, *The Moscow Observer*.
 14. Princess Maria Petrovna Vyazemskaya married Peter Alexandrovich Valuev (1815-1880) on May 22, 1836.

Letter 612
 1. To work on materials regarding Peter the Great.
 2. Pushkin's aunt and uncle and their family.
 3. Ekaterina Mikhaylovna Yazykova (1817-1852). The wedding took place a month later.
 4. Judging from Pushkin's tone, Moscow gossip must have had the story all wrong. According to other information, Peter Yakovlevich Saveliev (1801—after 1838), a Cavalry Guard Officer, was made a private in the Nizhny Novgorod Dragoon Regiment

three days after this letter was written, as the upshot of a quarrel with one Staff-Captain Gorgoli. There is no evidence that he slapped the face of Rodion Grigorievich Grinvald (1797-1877), the commander of the regiment in which he had been serving as an officer. What interest Idalia Poletika took in Saveliev is not known.

5. Nicholas I.

6. No other record of the love of Alexander Nikolaevich Karamzin (1815-1888) for a beautiful brunette or attempt at suicide is known.

7. Mikhail Semenovich Shchepkin (1788-1863), who became perhaps the most famous Russian realistic actor. He became famous in the role of the Town Mayor in Gogol's *Inspector General*. That the first Moscow performance of the play was by no means a complete success is attributed to the fact that Shchepkin, denied a free hand in directing the play, refused to continue as its director.

8. Gogol's *The Inspector General*, one of the greatest of all Russian dramas, had been presented for the first time less than a month earlier, on April 19, 1836, in the presence of Nicholas I himself, who joined in the praise of the satire. There were also attacks on it by the journalists Senkovsky, Bulgarin, and Polevoy, and they contributed to Gogol's going abroad on June 9, 1836.

9. The Censorship Committee.

10. Pushkin is, as usual, unceremonious in his query concerning his wife's pregnancy. The expected child was born on May 23.

11. Mme. Pushkina's aunt, Mme. Zagryazhskaya, and her two sisters.

Letter 613

1. This letter shows Pushkin's continued willingness to exert his influence on behalf of anyone who requested him to. Nothing more is known about Stepan Savelievich Gubanov and his widow. The Governor of Ryazan at the time was Stepan Vasilievich Perfiliev (1796-1878). The surveying office, in which Gubanov had served, was administratively subordinate to the Ministry of Justice, of which the head was Pushkin's old friend Dashkov. What interest Matvey Alexeevich Okulov (1793-1853) may have had in the affair is not known.

Letter 615

1. Gogol's *The Inspector General*, Act V.
2. For his work in seeing the second issue of *The Contemporary* through the press.
3. See Letter 589.
4. Alexey Vasilievich Koltsov (1809-1842), self-taught poet, particularly effective in folk-type lyrics on peasant subjects. His poem, "The Harvest," appeared in the second issue of *The Contemporary*.
5. Gogol's tale "The Nose" was also published in the second issue of *The Contemporary*.
6. Alexey Fedorovich Malinovsky, Director of the Archives in Moscow.
7. Ekaterina Petrovna Raevskaya, nee Kindyakova (1812-1839). The marriage had taken place on November 11, 1834.
8. Alexander Dmitrievich Chertkov (1789-1858), historian and archaeologist. His *Recollections of Sicily* had been published in Moscow during the preceding year.
9. That is, like A. I. Turgenev's "Letters from Paris," which were being published in *The Contemporary*. See Letters 599, 600, and 601, and notes.
10. Pushkin's aunt, Elizaveta Lvovna Solntseva, his father's sister. "He" in the next sentence is her husband, M. M. Solntsev, and the "little cousins" referred to further along are their children.

11. See Letter 611.

12. Paintings by Bryullov. "The Taking of Rome by Genseric" (1836), remained an unfinished sketch. His "Last Day of Pompeii" (1833) was a sensational success when it was shown in 1834, the same year that Edward Bulwer-Lytton's novel *The Last Days of Pompeii* appeared.

Letter 616

1. One of the minor Petersburg booksellers.
2. Ksenofont Polevoy's *Mikhail Vasilievich Lomonosov* (Moscow, 1836).
3. Apparently Pushkin wished to give K. A. Polevoy a free subscription to *The Contemporary*, but Farikov wished K. A. Polevoy to subscribe to it through him.
4. K. A. Polevoy had offered to be Pushkin's agent in obtaining subscriptions for *The Contemporary*. The reference here is apparently to payment for subscriptions to Pushkin's journal.

Letter 617

1. Rough-affectionate diminutive for Grigory (Alexandrovich Pushkin), Pushkin's second son.
2. A card game.
3. Apparently the sculptor I. P. Vitali proposed that he sculpture Pushkin. This was accomplished only after Pushkin's death, and at the behest of Nashchokin.
4. Ekaterina Mikhaylovna Yazykova.
5. Pushkin is laughing at the commoner Gnedich's self-acquired French.
6. Avraam Sergeevich Norov (1795-1869), minor poet whose left leg had been torn off in the Battle of Borodino in 1812. He later (1853-1854) published accounts of his travels in Europe, Egypt, Nubia, and Palestine.
7. Unidentified.
8. In their summer home on Kamenny Ostrov.
9. Mme. Pushkina's two sisters.

Letter 618

1. M. Durier and Mme. Sichler were proprietors of fashionable shops. The point of reference is Mme. Pushkina's own income from family estates. Pushkin thinks she would do better to deal with her oldest brother, Dmitry, than with her mother.
2. Alexander Fedorovich Aprelev (1798-1836) seduced the sister of one Pavlov. After Aprelev refused either to marry the girl or to give "satisfaction" in a duel, Pavlov, on May 8, 1836, stabbed Aprelev to death on the church porch on the day of Aprelev's wedding with another woman.
3. Pavel Grigorievich Stolypin (1806-1836), retired cavalry officer, drowned on May 9, 1836.
4. Nothing is known of Kireev in addition to what Pushkin says here.
5. A restaurant in Petersburg.
6. The Court balls were presented in the Anichkov Palace in Petersburg.
7. "You have deceived."

Letter 619

1. Vissarion Grigorievich Belinsky (1811-1848), who was to become the greatest of all Russian critics and the greatest literary power in his own day. During the 1840's his perceptive criticism of Pushkin, Lermontov, and Gogol resulted in their being generally accepted in the esteem they have held ever since; he lived to hail and champion many of the later great Russian realistic writers, including Turgenev, Goncharov, and

Dostoevsky, among others. Belinsky had sharply attacked *The Moscow Observer*. Pushkin wished to attract Belinsky to work on his *Contemporary*, but he did not wish to arouse the "Observers" prematurely. Pushkin did not live to accomplish the hope of adding Belinsky to his collaborators.

2. Nashchokin began writing his memoirs at this time, after long insistence on the part of Pushkin (see Letter 441). The manuscript survives, with Pushkin's extensive corrections, a good sample of the kind of editorial work Pushkin did for his journal.

3. The child's aunt, Alexandra Nikolaevna Goncharova.

Letter 620

1. Davydov's article, "The Occupation of Dresden . . .," which was published in the fourth issue of *The Contemporary*, suffered considerably from the censorship. See Letter 610 and note.

2. Napoleon figures in two articles by Vyazemsky, "Napoleon and Julius Caesar" and an article on Edgar Quinet's poem "Napoleon" (1836), both in the second issue of Pushkin's *Contemporary*.

3. Baron Ferdinand von Wintzengerode (1770-1818), German-born field marshal and diplomat in Russian service, had been the military superior of the famed guerilla leader, D. V. Davydov, in the War Against Napoleon of 1812-1813. Davydov had clashed with Wintzengerode when Davydov took Dresden without orders from his superior. Davydov's defense of this action was excised by the censorship from the published article.

4. Napoleon had the Vendôme Column constructed (1806-1810) to celebrate the defeat of the Russians and Austrians at Austerlitz in 1805. The statue of Napoleon which was placed on it in 1812 was replaced with another of him in 1833.

5. Davydov's poem here referred to, "I Remember—Deeply . . .," was first published four years later.

Letter 621

1. The point of discussion of this letter is the apportionment of the estate of Mikhaylovskoe after the death of Pushkin's mother. Pushkin's father inherited a seventh share of the estate and his sister a fourteenth; Pushkin and his brother Lev shared equally the remainder. Pushkin here discusses buying his brother's share. Lev S. Pushkin answered with a power of attorney for Pushkin to manage the estate, and he gave Pushkin his blessing to buy or mortgage the estate, for all he was interested in was the money. Pushkin did not, however, manage to buy the estate, because of disagreement with his brother-in-law Pavlishchev about the value of it.

2. For Lev S. Pushkin's debts to Boltin, Pleshcheev, and Pavlishchev, see Letter 550.

3. Unidentified person.

4. That is, when Pushkin gave up the financial management of his father's estate of Boldino and half of Kistenevo. See Letter 553 and notes.

5. See Letter 554, and also Letters 553 and 555.

Letter 622

1. This is another instance of Pushkin's insistence upon accuracy and purity in the use of language, and also of his editorial conscience and care. Kraevsky made the corrections which Pushkin here enumerates, in Vyazemsky's article, "Napoleon and Julius Caesar," in the second issue of *The Contemporary*.

Letter 623

1. Nadezhda Andreevna Durova was vexed that Pushkin had entitled her recollections

of serving in the Russian army while disguised as a man as "The Memoirs of N. A. Durova," instead of "Notes by the Own Hand of the Russian Amazon Known Under the Name of Alexandrov." See Letter 589.

Letter 624
1. In a letter of May 5, 1836, Dmitriev had expressed sympathy to Pushkin and his father upon the death of Pushkin's mother. In the same letter, Dmitriev gave an extremely favorable estimate of the first issue of Pushkin's *Contemporary*.
2. Dmitriev's "observation" was that "your journal moved and refreshed me for a whole week and made me forget my step-brothers." By "step-brothers" Dmitriev alludes to an article signed "I.D." and a poem signed "Ivan Dmitriev" which had recently appeared in *The Moscow Record* and in *The Russian Invalide*, respectively. Pushkin did as he said and published the comment in the second issue of his *Contemporary*.
3. The allusion here is to Molière's play *Amphitryon*, in which the servant confuses his master with Jupiter, in the form of his master. Pushkin uses the term conventionally for a double being mistaken for the original.

Letter 625
1. The Loan Office where Kistenevo was mortgaged.
2. Pushkin means, if it is more profitable to cultivate the entire estate on the basis of *barščina* (with the serfs working part-time, usually half, on the owner's part and the remainder of the time on their own), instead of quitrent (money payment in lieu of part-time work for the owner).
3. M. I. Kalashnikov, his son Vasily, and his daughter Olga.

Letter 626
1. *The History of the Military Activities in Asiatic Turkey in* 1828 *and* 1829 (Moscow, 1836), by General Nikolay Ivanovich Ushakov (1802-1861), a military writer and historian.
2. General Paskevich-Erivansky.
3. In a footnote, Ushakov remarks that "our glorious poet" Pushkin participated in the cross fire of June 14, 1829. Pushkin recounts the campaign in detail, including his entering Erzurum, in his *Journey to Erzurum*.

Letter 627
1. In a letter of June 25, 1836, the self-styled Amazon, Durova, expressed impatience with Pushkin for the delays in the appearance of her memoirs. When difficulties with the censorship arose, she insisted that Pushkin show her memoirs to the Tsar himself, and even take them to him on maneuvers, threatening otherwise to take other action. After this polite but firm refusal, she made other arrangements for their publication; they appeared in 1838.
2. The money was in payment for a fragment from her notes, published in the second issue of *The Contemporary*, which had not yet appeared.
3. As in other letters to Durova, Pushkin addresses her in accordance with her masculine pseudonym, Alexander Andreevich Alexandrov. She used the masculine pronoun to refer to herself in her letter to him.

Letter 628
1. Pushkin is alluding to his projected purchase of his brother's share of his late mother's estate of Mikhaylovskoe. See Letter 621.
2. Because of his mother's death, some three and a half months earlier.

3. Pushkin had owed Yakovlev six thousand rubles since 1828-1829.

Letter 629
1. The steward at Mikhaylovskoe, a German named Ringel. Pavlishchev dismissed him, after discovering many irregularities in the accounts.
2. One Vasily Ivanovich Polonsky.
3. Early in July, 1836, Lev Pushkin sent a power of attorney for Pushkin to manage or dispose of the estate of Mikhaylovskoe; however, Pushkin had not yet received it. See Letter 621.

Letter 630
1. In his letter of July 11, 1836, Pavlishchev proposed that Pushkin buy the estate of Mikhaylovskoe at the price of 64,000 rubles, and pay Olga and Lev their shares in that case, or else advertise and sell the estate. Pushkin himself had evaluated the estate at 40,000 rubles in Letter 621.
2. The "transaction" proposed by Pavlishchev was that he, Pavlishchev, buy the estate of Mikhaylovskoe for 64,000 rubles, and that Pushkin assume his sister Olga's share of the inheritance of their father's estate, Boldino, for Pushkin's share in Mikhaylovskoe, which would thus be counted at 25,000 rubles. Pushkin was well aware that his sister Olga was hardly likely to inherit 25,000 rubles from their father.
3. Pavlishchev's son, Lev Nikolaevich Pavlishchev.

Letter 631
1. Alexander Ivanovich Khmelnitsky, later a journalist. Whether Pushkin's request was of avail is not known. Pushkin's old friend Zhandr was at this time Director of the Chancellery of the Ministry of the Navy.
2. Vice Admiral Alexander Sergeevich Menshikov (1787-1849). Khmelnitsky's appointment in the Navy depended upon him.

Letter 632
1. Davydov's article was published in the third issue of *The Contemporary* in 1836. Being on a military subject, it had to be passed by the military censorship, as well as the usual one.
2. The various censorships included the usual one, the religious censorship, the censorship of the Ministry of Foreign Affairs, and the military censorship; for Pushkin there was a fifth, that of the Court.
3. Alexander I.
4. Ivan the Terrible divided Russia into the *zemščina* and the *opričina*. The latter were his special bodyguard and troops and were greatly favored; they were used by Ivan to subjugate the nobles to his will and were allowed liberty to pillage and persecute the *zemščina*, the remainder of the populace. Pushkin is comparing the depredations of the military censors on Davydov's article to the arbitrary lawlessness of the *opričina* under Ivan the Terrible.

Letter 633
1. Peter Alexandrovich Korsakov (1790-1844), a writer, translator, and censor, and brother of Prince M. A. Dondukov-Korsakov. In 1817, Korsakov had published some of Pushkin's poems in *The Northern Observer*. His reputation of being a mild and reasonable censor was immediately justified, as he passed Pushkin's novel, *The Captain's Daughter*, and kept the secret of its authorship.

Letter 634
 1. Grech, in a letter of October 12, 1836, had given a rapturous appreciation of Pushkin's poem on Barklay de Tolly, which had appeared in the third issue of Pushkin's *Contemporary*. Pushkin's poem aroused considerable controversy. The praise of Barklay, who was replaced in the war against Napoleon of 1812 as Commander-in-Chief of the Russian Army of the West by Kutuzov, as a result of dissatisfaction with his refusal to come to decisive battle with Napoleon's forces, seemed directly contradictory to the traditional Russian patriotic view of praise of Kutuzov and blame of the "foreigner" Barklay de Tolly. Pushkin was forced, in self-defense, to prove his own admiration for Kutuzov by publishing part of his poem written earlier to Kutuzov, "Before the Sacred Tomb" (1831).

Letter 635
 1. A bibliography, which Korf had compiled, of foreign books relating to Peter the Great and his time, and which he sent Pushkin in connection with the latter's historical labors.
 2. Pavel Nikolaevich Myasoedov (1799-1868), like Korf, a Lyceum schoolmate of Pushkin's. He gave a dinner for his old Lyceum comrades on October 15, 1836, and attended the anniversary celebration of the opening of the Lyceum, on October 19.

Letter 636
 1. That is, with the opinion of Yakovlev, that the celebration on October 19, 1836, the twenty-fifth anniversary of the opening of the Tsarskoe Selo Lyceum, should be limited to members of the first graduating class. The numbers were those of the rooms at the Lyceum. Yakovlev's room was number 39, and Pushkin's number 14.
 2. A self-quotation from Pushkin's own poem, "October 19" (1825).

Letter 637
 1. The " booklet " was a copy of the issue of *The Telescope* (1836) containing a Russian translation of the first of Chaadaev's *Philosophical Letters* (the original was in French). In the "Philosophical Letter," Chaadaev, postulating religion as the prime historical moving force and Roman Catholicism as the proper form of Christianity, argued that Russia, having received Christianity from Byzantium and having fallen on the side of Greek Orthodoxy in the Great Schism of 1054, had no real history, culture, or tradition; he includes a devastating attack on contemporary Russian society, based on serfdom. The result of the publication of this letter was that the editor of the journal, Nadezhdin—who had published the letter in order to publish later refutations of it—was exiled to Siberia. The censor, Alexey Vasilievich Boldyrev (1780-1842), who had passed it, was discharged. Chaadaev was declared mad, and put under the daily observation of a physician.
 Chaadaev's letter may be considered the opening gun in the Westerner-Slavophile controversy, which became the central ideological controversy in Russia in the nineteenth century. Later Westerners, like Alexander Herzen (1812-1870), rejected Chaadaev's arguments regarding religion, but agreed with his interpretation of the status of Russia at the time. The Slavophiles rejected his arguments *in toto*, arguing that Orthodoxy is the only true form of Christianity and that Russia's culture before its Westernization under and after Peter the Great had been in essence far superior to the culture of Western Europe. To the government party, under Uvarov's motto of "Orthodoxy, autocracy, and nationality," all of Chaadaev's opinions were anathema.
 Chaddaev's first "Philosophical Letter" was dated December 1, 1829. Pushkin read

it probably soon after it was written; in the summer of 1831, he read the second and third of these letters (see Letter 376). Pushkin respected Chaadaev's ideas, though he by no means agreed with all of them. Pushkin's letter in answer to Chaadaev is the most important of all his letters, from the point of view of social and political ideas. It shows how, as a historian, he was interested in a broad view of history, how as a patriot he defended Russian history as it was, and how as a man of his own day, he was in substantial agreement with Chaadaev in his criticism of Russian society of the time.

Pushkin did not send the letter to Chaadaev. On October 22, 1835, Pushkin received a letter from K. O. Rosset, informing him of the action being taken against Chaadaev, Nadezhdin, and Boldyrev, and advising him to "reread" his own letter, or "still better," that he "defer" sending it by the post. Pushkin kept the letter, noting on it, " 'A falcon does not peck out another falcon's eye,' a saying quoted by Walter Scott in *Woodstock*."

Vyazemsky, like Pushkin, basically disagreed with Chaadaev, but it is interesting that in a letter he made an attempt to minimize Chaadaev's "guilt" (see Letter 662). Vigel presented the denunciation which led immediately to the action against Chaadaev, Boldyrev, and Nadezhdin.

2. Pushkin had already developed this idea in his unfinished article "Of the Nullity of Russian Literature" (1834), where he indignantly rejects the idea that it was Poland that thus saved Europe during the time of the Tatar yoke in Russia (1240-1480).

3. Feofan Prokopovich (1681-1736) drew up the "Spiritual Regulation" (1721) which abolished the patriarchate and established the Holy Synod, making the Russian Church subordinate to the Russian state. The Over-Procurator of the Holy Synod, a government appointee, obtained almost complete authority in Church administration.

4. That is, at the time of the invasion of Europe by the Turks, who besieged Vienna in 1529 and 1683.

5. Peter the Great had forced noblemen, but not the clergy, to shave, and thereby separated the clergy from "good society."

6. Pushkin is thinking of Ivan III (the Great), ruler of Russia from 1462 to 1505, under whose rule the Tatar yoke was thrown off, who annexed Novgorod, who married Sophia Paleologue, niece of the last Byzantine emperor, and who adopted the Byzantine double-headed eagle, and gave a basis to the claim of Moscow as the "Third Rome"; and Ivan IV (the Terrible), who ruled from 1533 to 1584, who first took the title of "Tsar" (Caesar), who conquered Kazan, and in whose reign western Siberia was annexed to Russia. It may be noted that under each of the rulers mentioned here by Pushkin there were added sizable conquests.

7. The greatest drama in the history of the Russian government before 1917 had to do with the ending of the house of Ryurik and the accession of the house of Romanov. The drama began with the murder of Dimitry, son of Ivan the Terrible, at Uglich in 1591, leaving no descendant of Ryurik to ascend the throne upon the death of Tsar Fedor in 1598. Boris Godunov, son-in-law of Ivan the Terrible, ruled as elective Tsar until 1605. Then the Time of Troubles began, with two False Dimitrys and invasions by Poland and Sweden before the house of Romanov (reigned 1613-1917) was established with the election of Michael Romanov, which was announced to him in the Ipatiev Monastery in 1613.

8. Pushkin's "prejudices" are those of a member of the old aristocracy against the aristocracy of service, established by Peter the Great in his Table of Ranks in 1722. See rough-draft variant of this letter, note 10 below.

9. The latter article is a review of the memoirs of John Tanner, a white American who was captured as a boy and brought up by the American Indians. The book was published in New York in 1830, and a French edition was published in Paris in 1835.

Pushkin begins his article with the expression of distaste for democracy in the United States, as depicted in Alexis de Tocqueville's *De la Démocratie en Amérique* (1835).

10. The rough-draft variants to this letter are interesting and important enough to justify quoting at length:

> [Peter the Great] tamed the nobility by promulgating the *Table of Ranks*, and the clergy, by abolishing the patriarchate (N.B.: Napoleon said to Alexander: "You are *Pope* at home; that is not so stupid"). But it is one thing to make a revolution, and another to enshrine the results. Up to Catherine II, Peter's revolution was continued among us, instead of being consolidated. Catherine II was still afraid of the aristocracy; Alexander was a Jacobin himself.[a] The *Table of Ranks* has already been doing away with the nobility for 140 years, and the present emperor was the first to place a dike (very feeble, so far) against inundation by a democracy worse than that of America. (Have you read Tocqueville? I am still all hot and bothered and quite frightened by his book.)
>
> As for the clergy, it is outside society, it is still bearded. One does not see it anywhere, not in our salons, not in literature; it does not belong to good society. It is not above the people, it does not wish to be of the people. Our sovereigns have found it convenient to leave it where they found it. Like eunuchs, it has no passion but for power. Consequently it is dreaded. And, I know, a certain one, in spite of all his energy, yielded to it on one grave occasion. I was enraged by this at the time.[b]
>
> Religion is, fortunately, foreign to our thoughts and to our habits, but there is no need to say so.
>
> Your booklet appears to have produced a great sensation. I do not speak of it the society I frequent.
>
> What needed saying and what you have said is that our present society is as contemptible as stupid. That this absence of public opinion, this indifference toward all duty, justice, right, and truth, this cynical disdain for all that is not necessity. This cynical disdain for thought and the dignity of man.[c] It was necessary to add (not as a concession, but as the truth) that the government is still the only European in Russia, and that as brutal and cynical as it is, it could have been a hundred times worse. Nobody was paying the slightest attention to it.
>
> The conquest of Ryurik[d] is as important as that of the Norman Bastard.[e] The youth of Russia passed joyfully in the invasions of Oleg and of Svyatoslav, and even in the wars of appanage, which were nothing but continual duels—the result of this effervescence and of this activity springing from the youth of peoples, of which you speak in your letter. The invasion is a sad and a grand picture. Oh, isn't the invasion of the Tatars a memory.

Notes to rough-draft variants (Note 10).

a. In a conversation with Grand Duke Michael in 1834, Pushkin went so far as to tell him that "all the Romanovs have been revolutionaries and levellers," and he expressed his objections to the nobility of service (see his Diary, under December 22).

b. Pushkin is apparently speaking of the removal of Gerasim Petrovich Pavsky (1787-1863) as teacher of divine law to Grand Duke Alexander (later Alexander II), on the complaint of the Moscow Metropolitan Filaret. (See Pushkin's Diary, under February, 1835.) The "certain one" was Nicholas I.

c. The sentence fragments are Pushkin's.

d. Original reading: "of Igor, of Ryurik, and of Oleg." All three were heroes of Kievan Rus. Ryurik (d. 879) was the reputed Varangian, or Scandinavian, founder of the empire of Russia and the ruling house, which lasted until 1598. Igor (d. 945, ruled 912-945) and Oleg (see Letter 101, note) were princes of Kiev.

e. The reference is to the conquest of England by William the Conqueror in 1066.

Letter 638

1. Pushkin gives the address, as usual, in Russian spelling. The house was owned by Princess Sofia Grigorievna Volkonskaya.

2. See Pushkin's answers to Pavlishchev's letters: Letters 494, 555, 563, 629, 630.

3. Lev S. Pushkin had re-entered the military service and left for Caucasian Georgia for active duty, in July, 1836.

Letter 639

1. In a letter of the same date, Korsakov agreed to be the censor of Pushkin's novel, *The Captain's Daughter* (see Letter 633). He also raised two questions regarding the novel: (1) whether the heroine Mironova was a historical person and whether she actually went to see Catherine the Great, and (2) whether Pushkin, who wanted authorship of the novel to remain unknown, wished Korsakov to tell the Censorship Committee that Pushkin had delivered the manuscript to him. In the case of an anomymous manuscript, someone had to take responsibility for it. In order the better to preserve his anonymity, Pushkin asked Pletnev to do this for him.

Letter 640

1. Russian editions place Letters 640 through 646 at the end of the letters of 1836. It has seemed best for this edition to place these letters, all of which were apparently written before Letter 647, in this position, in order to make a separate chapter of the letters of the final stage of Pushkin's life.

Letter 641

1. This short note is a postscript to a brief note by Elizaveta M. Khitrovo to Anna Petrovna Kern, sent in Pushkin's hand. Like the following two letters, it shows Pushkin's continuing friendly relationship with Mme. Kern, with whom he had been so much in love a decade earlier. This letter and the following two have to do with Mme. Kern's unsuccessful attempt to buy up the estate given her as dowry and then sold by her father to a Count Sheremetev—probably Dmitry Nikolaevich Sheremetev.

Letter 642

1. See Letter 641, note. Sheremetev's answer was a refusal.

Letter 643

1. *Revenir à la charge*, "to renew an attempt, to become again a dependant." Mme. Kern quoted this note in her *Memoirs*, adding, "etc., etc., and playing on the last word." This letter also has to do with Mme. Kern's attempts to buy back her family estate from Sheremetev (see Letter 641 and note).

Letter 644

1. "Hunter's cry, to call dogs off their prey." Pushkin is quoting from Philipp Reiff's *Russo-French Dictionary . . . or Etymological Dictionary of the Russian Language*, the first volume of which (A-O) appeared in Petersburg in 1835. Pushkin used the word *arap* in the title of his own uncompleted novel about his Abyssianian ancestor: *Arap Petra Velikogo (The Blackamoor of Peter the Great)*.

2. Pushkin has in mind a critique of the Russian Academy *Dictionary* and Plyushar's *Encyclopedic Lexicon*.

Letter 645

1. Pushkin's little poem includes play on words on two idioms relating to the days of the week. It reads, literally, as follows:

Smirdin has plunged me into misfortune. With this tradesman there are seven Fridays in a week, and his Thursday is really Thursday after a little rain.

Letter 646

1. Achille Tardif de Mello, French man of letters, very much interested in Russian literature, especially in the works of Pushkin. In a letter to Pushkin, he had enclosed his own translation of Pushkin's *Prisoner of the Caucasus*.

2. "A true goddess appears in her gait."

PART XIV

SOLE DEFENDER OF HONOR — PETERSBURG

November, 1836 — January, 1837

Pushkin in His Coffin. *Painting by A. Kozlov.*

[647]
To Egor Frantsevich Kankrin
November 6, 1836. In Petersburg.

Dear Sir, Count Egor Frantsevich,

Encouraged by the indulgent attention which Your Highness has already been so kind as to honor me with, I make bold to disturb you again with a most humble request.

According to arrangements of which Your Highness's ministry is aware, I stand indebted to the Treasury (without security) for 45,000 rubles, of which 25,000 must be repaid by me in the course of five years.

Now, wishing to repay my debt in full and immediately, I discover that to my so doing there is one obstacle, which can be easily removed, but only by you.

I have 220 souls in the Nizhny Novgorod Province, of which 200 are mortgaged for 40,000. According to the arrangements of my father, who has bestowed this estate upon me, I do not have the right to sell them during his lifetime, although I may mortgage them either to the Treasury or to private individuals.[1]

But the Treasury has the right to recover what is due it, regardless of any private individual's agreements, unless they are confirmed by the Sovereign.

As payment of the aforesaid 45,000, I make bold to give over this estate, which surely is worth that much, and probably even more.

I make bold to burden Your Highness with still another request, which is important for me. Since this matter is quite unimportant and may fall within the scope of a customary procedure, I most earnestly request Your Highness not to bring it to the notice of the Sovereign Emperor, who in his magnanimity probably would not wish such a repayment (although it is not at all burdensome to me), and he might even order that my debt be forgiven me, which would place me in an extremely painful and embarrassing situation: for in such a case I would be compelled to refuse the Tsar's favor, and that might seem an impropriety, vaingloriousness, and even ingratitude.[2]

With the most profound respect and complete devotion, I

have the honor to be, Dear Sir, Your Highness's most humble servant.

November 6, 1836.   Alexander Pushkin.

[648]
To Nikolay Borisovich Golitsyn
November 10, 1836. From Petersburg to Artek.
(In French)

St. Petersburg, November 10, 1836.

Thank you very much, dear Prince,[1] for your incomparable translation of my piece of verse leveled against the enemies of our country. I have already seen three translations,[2] one of which is by a powerful personage *from among my friends*, but none is so good as yours. Why didn't you translate the piece at the opportune time;[3] I would have sent it off to France, to throw it in the teeth of all the noisy clamorers of the Chamber of Deputies.

How I envy you your excellent Crimean climate:[4] your letter has awakened in me many memories of all kinds. It is the cradle of my *Onegin*, and you are sure to have recognized certain personages.[5]

You give me notice of a verse translation of my *Fountain of Bakhchisaray*. I am sure that you will succeed in it, as in all that comes from your pen, although the genre of literature which you are taking up is the most difficult and the most thankless I know of. In my opinion nothing is more difficult than to translate Russian verses into French verses, because, owing to the conciseness of our language, one can never be so brief. Honor, then, to the one who performs it as well as you do.

Farewell. I do not despair of seeing you soon in our capital, considering your aptitude for travel. Truly yours,

                                                 A. Pushkin.

[649]
To Vladimir Alexandrovich Sollogub
November 17, 1836. In Petersburg.
(In French)

I do not hesitate to write what I can declare verbally. I have challenged M. G. Heeckeren to a duel, and he has accepted, without entering into any explanations. I am the one who now prays the witnesses of this affair to be so kind as to consider this challenge as not having taken place, for I have learned from popular report that M. Georges Heeckeren has decided to declare his intentions of marriage with Mlle. Goncharova, after the duel. I have no reason to attribute his resolve to considerations unworthy of a man of gallant soul.[1]

I request, Count, that you make whatever use of this letter you judge appropriate.

Accept the assurance of my complete esteem.

November 17, 1836. A. Pushkin.

[650]
To Mikhail Lukianovich Yakovlev
November 19, 1836. In Petersburg.

My dear and honored Mikhaylo Lukianovich! Excuse me! I invited you to dine at my house today, but I shall not be at home. Until another time, forgive me magnanimously. Do not forget to deliver the note about the saints,[1] to me, a sinner.

[651]
To Louis van Heeckeren
Between November 17 and 21, 1836. In Petersburg.
(Reconstructed text of unsent letter; in French)

Baron,

First of all, permit me to summarize everything that has just taken place.[1] The behavior of your son had been fully known to me for a long time and could not be a matter of indifference to me, but since it was kept within the bounds of the proprieties and since, moreover, I knew how much on that score my wife deserved my trust and my respect, I contented myself with the role of an observer free to intervene when I might think proper. I well knew that a handsome face, an unlucky passion, two years' perseverance always may end by producing some effect on a young woman's heart, and that then the husband, at least if he is not a fool, becomes quite naturally the confidant of his wife and the master of her conduct.[2] I shall admit to you that I was not without misgivings. An incident, which at any other moment would have been very disagreeable, came quite fortunately to rescue me from the difficulty: I received anonymous letters. I saw that the moment had come, and I availed myself of it. You know the rest: I made your son play a role so ludicrous and pitiful that my wife, astonished at so much truckling,³ could not refrain from laughing, and that the emotion which she had perhaps come to feel in response to this great and sublime passion, faded into the coolest and most deserved disgust.

But you, Baron, will permit me to observe that your role in all this affair is not of the most seemly. You, the representative of a crowned head, have paternally acted as the pander of your bastard, or the one so called; all the behavior of this young man has been directed by you. You dictated the sorry jokes which he has just been reciting and the vacuous things which he has taken a hand in writing. Like an obscene old woman you would go and lie in wait for my wife in every corner, in order to speak to her of your son, and when, ill with the syphilis, he was kept at home for treatments, you would say, vile man that you are, that he was dying of love for her. You would murmur to her, "Give me back my son." That is not all.

You see that I know all about it. But wait, that is not all: I have told you that the affair was getting complicated. Let us return to anonymous letters. You well surmise that they may be of interest to you.

On November 2 you received a piece of news from your son which gave you much pleasure. He told you that I was angry, that my wife was afraid . . . that she was losing her head. You decided to strike a blow which you thought would be decisive. An anonymous letter was composed by you.

I received three copies of the half a score which were delivered. This letter had been fabricated with so little caution that at the first glance I was on the trail of the author. I did not trouble myself about it further; I was sure of finding my knave. Sure enough, in less than three days of searching, I knew positively what to believe.

If diplomacy is only the art of knowing what is done at others' houses and of making game of their plans, you will do me the justice to admit that you have been vanquished on all points.

Now I am arriving at the object of my letter. Perhaps you desire to know what has prevented me up to the present from dishonoring you in the eyes of our court and of yours. I shall tell you.

I am, you see, a good, unsophisticated person, but my heart is sensitive. A duel is no longer enough for me, and whatever may be its outcome, I shall not consider myself sufficiently avenged, either by the death of your son, or by his marriage, which would seem to be a good joke (which, it must be added, troubles me very little), or finally by the letter which I have the honor to be writing you, and a copy of which I am keeping for my personal use. I want you yourself to take the trouble to find the reasons which would suffice to make me pledge not to spit in your face, and to annihilate even the last traces of this miserable affair, from which it will be easy for me to make an excellent chapter in my history of cuckoldry.[4]

I have the honor to be, Baron,
Your most humble and most obedient servant,
A. Pushkin.[5]

[652]
To Alexander Khristoforovich Benkendorf
November 21, 1836. In Petersburg.
(In French)

Count!

I have just cause and I believe myself obliged to inform Your Excellency of what has just taken place in my family. On the morning of November 4 I received three copies of an anonymous letter, injurious to my honor and that of my wife. From the appearance of the paper, from the style of the letter, from the manner in which it was worded, I recognized from the first moment that it was written by a foreigner, by a man of high society, by a diplomat.[1] I started making inquiries. I learned that seven or eight persons had received, on the same day, a copy of the same letter, in a double envelope, the inner of which was sealed and addressed to me. The majority of the persons who received them, suspecting a vile deed, did not send them on to me.

People in general were indignant at such a despicable, such an unprovoked insult. But while repeating that the conduct of my wife has been irreproachable, they said that the pretext of this infamy was the assiduous court which M. d'Anthès has been paying her.

It did not suit me to see the name of my wife linked on this occasion with the name of anyone whatever.[2] I had M. d'Anthès so informed.

The Baron de Heeckeren came to my house and accepted a duel for M. d'Anthès, asking for a delay of fifteen days.

It turns out that in the interval granted, M. d'Anthès fell in love with my sister-in-law, Mlle. Goncharova, and that he made her a marriage proposal. Public report having informed me of this, I had the request made to M. d'Archiac (M. d'Anthès' second) that my challenge should be regarded as not having taken place.[3] Meanwhile I made sure that the anonymous letter was from M. Heeckeren, which I believe it my duty to call to the attention of the government and of society.

Being the sole judge and defender of my honor and that of my wife, and consequently asking for neither justice nor vengeance, I neither can nor will provide anyone whatever with the proofs for what I assert.

In any case, I hope, Count, that this letter is a proof of the respect and of the trust which I bear toward you.[4]

With these feelings, I have the honor to be,
  Count,
    Your most humble and most obedient servant,
November 21, 1836.   A. Pushkin.

[653]
To Egor Frantsevich Kankrin
About (after) November 21, 1836. In Petersburg.
(Rough draft)

I have had the happiness to receive the letter with which Your Highness was so kind as to honor me. I regret extremely that the expedient which I have made bold to propose has proved to be unsuitable.[1] In any case, I shall count it a duty to rely absolutely in everything on Your Highness's good judgment.

Expressing to Your Highness my sincere gratitude for the consideration with which you were so kind as to honor me, with the most profound [. . . .]

[654]
To Vladimir Fedorovich Odoevsky
December 7, 1836(?). In Petersburg.

I am very grateful to you. I am always at home, and I am completely at fault toward you—but the devil knows how lazy I have become.

December 7.

[655]

To Amable Guillaume Barante
December 16, 1836. In Petersburg.
(In French)

Baron,

I hasten to send Your Excellency[1] the information which you wished to have, concerning the regulations which treat of literary property in Russia.

Literature has become with us an important branch of industry only during the last score of years or so. Up till then it was regarded as only an elegant and aristocratic pursuit. Madame de Staël said in 1811: "In Russia a few gentlemen have engaged in literature" (*Ten Years of Exile*).[2] Nobody dreamed of deriving any other fruit from his works than triumphs in society. Authors themselves encouraged reprinting without authorization and prided themselves upon it, and our academies, at the same time, were setting the example of this offense with a clear conscience and in freedom from apprehension. The first complaint for such reprinting was lodged in 1824.[3] It was discovered that the case had not been foreseen by the law-giver. Literary property has been recognized in Russia by the present sovereign. Here are the terms of the law:

"Every author or translator of a book has the right to publish and to sell it as acquired (non-hereditary) property.

"His legitimate heirs have the right to publish and to sell his works (provided that the property has not been alienated) during the period of twenty-five years.

"After twenty-five years from the date of his death have passed, his works and his translations become public property."
(*The law of April* 22, 1828.)

The amendment of April 28 of the same year explains and supplements these regulations. Here are its principal articles.

"A literary work, either in printed or in manuscript form, may not be sold either during the lifetime of the author or after his death, in order to satisfy creditors, unless he insists upon it himself.

"The author has the right, notwithstanding any previous agreement, to make a new edition of his work if two-thirds of it have been altered or else completely recast.

"He will be regarded as pirate (1) who in reprinting a book does not observe the formalities required by the law; (2) who sells a manuscript or the right to publish it to two or more persons at once, without having their consent for his so doing; (3) *who publishes a translation of a work printed in Russia (or else one which has been approved by the Russian censorship), while at the same time adding to it the original text itself*; (4) *who reprints in a foreign country a work published in Russia, or else one which has been approved by the Russian censorship, and sells copies of it in Russia.*"

These regulations are far from resolving all questions which might arise in the future. The law stipulates nothing with regard to posthumous works. The legitimate heirs ought to have sole property in them, with all the privileges of the author himself. Does the author of a pseudonymous work, or else one attributed to a known writer, lose his property rights, and what is the rule to be followed in this event? The law says nothing about it.

The reprinting of foreign books is not prohibited and ought not be. Russian booksellers will always have a great deal to gain, when they reprint foreign books, and the sale of them will always be assured for them, even without exporting; whereas, the foreigner would not be able to reprint Russian works, for lack of readers.

The statute of limitations for the offense of pirating is fixed at two years.

The question of literary property is very much simplified in Russia, where nobody can present his manuscript to the censorship without giving the name of its author, and without placing it, by this same token, under the immediate protection of the government.

   I am, respectfully,
    Baron,
     Your Excellency's,
      Most humble and most obedient servant,
December 16, 1836.   Alexander Pushkin.
SPb.

[656]
To Nikolay Mikhaylovich Konshin
December 21 or 22, 1836. From Petersburg to Tsarskoe Selo.

Your letter made me very glad, dear and honored Nikolay Ivanovich,[1] as a sign that you still have not forgotten me. I shall set your memorandum going this very day.[2] I shall see Zhukovsky and I shall turn you over from my hands to his. Alas! I am not in such friendly relationships with Uvarov, but Zhukovsky will, I hope, fix everything up. Upon taking over the place of Lazhechnikov, won't you, too, on the example of your predecessor, take up writing novels? How good that would be! All the same, you had forgotten me, although finally you did remember me. And I permit myself to give you a little friendly reproach because of that.

Aren't you going to be in Petersburg? In the event you are, I hope I shall see you. I shall try to provide you with an answer as soon as possible.

A.P.

[657]
To Praskovia Alexandrovna Osipova
December 24, 1836. From Petersburg to Trigorskoe.
(In French)

You won't believe, my dear Praskovia Alexandrovna, how much pleasure your letter has given me. I had not had any news of you in more than four months; and only day before yesterday M. Lvov[1] gave me some. On the same day I received your letter. I had been hoping to see you in the autumn, but I was prevented from doing so partly by my affairs, partly by Pavlishchev, who has put me in such bad humor that I have not wished to seem to be coming to Mikhaylovskoe in order to arrange the partition of it.

With much regret I have been obliged to give up the idea of being your neighbor, but I still hope not to lose that place, which I prefer to many another. *Vot v čem delo*:[2] At first I proposed to take over the estate at once for myself alone, agreeing to pay my brother and my sister the shares which are due them, at the rate of five hundred rubles per soul. *Pavliščev ocenil Mixajlovskoe v* 800 *r. dušu—ja s nim i ne sporju, no v takom slučae prinužden byl otkazat'sja i predostavil imenie prodat'. Pered svoim ot"ezdom pisal on ko mne, čto on imenie ustupaet mne za* 500 *r. dušu,* **potomu čto emu den'gi nužny.**³ I have sent him about his business, telling him that if the estate is worth twice that much, I would not wish to profit at the expense of my sister and my brother. There the matter dropped. Do you want to know what my wish would be? I would have liked you to be the proprietress of Mikhaylovskoe and to reserve for myself the *usad'ba*,⁴ together with the garden and a half score of *dvorovye*.⁵ I have a great longing to come to Trigorskoe for a little while this winter. We would speak of all that. Meanwhile, I greet you with all my heart. My wife thanks you for remembering her. *Ne privezti li mne vam ee?*⁶ My regards to all your family—to Evpraxia Nikolaevna⁷ especially.

[658]
To Vladimir Fedorovich Odoevsky
About (not later than) December 29, 1836.
In Petersburg.

It is just as caustic as sensible.¹ I don't think, though, that the censorship will destroy it all. In any event, there is no harm in asking. Shan't we see each other at the Academy of Sciences, where sits Prince Dunduk?²

[659]
To Adolf Alexandrovich Plyushar
December 29, 1836. In Petersburg.
(In French)

Sir,

I am completely in agreement on all the conditions which you are so obliging as to propose to me concerning the publication of a volume of my long poems¹ (in your letter of December 23, 1836). It is, then, agreed that you will have 2500 copies printed on paper which you will choose, that you alone will be encharged with the sale of the edition, for the consideration of 15 percent discount, and that proceeds of the first volumes sold will be used to reimburse you for all the costs of publication, as well as the 1500 rubles in bills which you have been so kind as to advance me.

Please accept, Sir, the assurance of my complete esteem.

December 29, 1836.   A. Pushkin.
St. Petersburg.

[660]
 To Vladimir Fedorovich Odoevsky
The end of November or in December, 1836. In Petersburg.

Of course, "Princess Zizi" has more truth in it and is more entertaining than "The Sylphide."¹ But any gift of yours is a benefaction. The father-in-law's letter seems cold and too insignificant. On the other hand, in the others there is much that is charming. I have noted one place with the mark (?)—it seemed to me unintelligible. In any case, whether it is "The Sylphide" or whether it is the "Princess," finish it and send it off. Without you *The Contemporary* is done for.

A.P.

[661]
 To Vladimir Fedorovich Odoevsky
The end of November or in December, 1836. In Petersburg.

Mr. Volkov's article¹ is indeed very noteworthy, sensibly and intelligently written, and interesting for everybody. However, I shall not put it in, because in my opinion there is no need at all for the government to get mixed up with the project of this Gerstner. Russia cannot afford to throw away 3,000,000 on the attempt. The business of the new railroad is one for private persons: let them be the ones to take the necessary steps. All that they can be promised is the franchise for twelve or fifteen years. A railroad from Moscow to Nizhny Novgorod may be needed still more than one from Moscow to Petersburg—and my opinion would be: start with it....

I am of course not against railroads. But I am against the government undertaking this matter. Several objections to the project are irrefutable. For example: the snowdrifts. To take care of that a new machine must be *invented*, a *sine qua non*. There's no use thinking of sending out people or hiring laborers for clearing away the snow. That is an absurdity.

Volkov's article is written in a lively, pointed manner. Otreshkov is polished off very humorously. But one must not forget that many members of the State Council have been against railroads, and so the *tone* of the article in general must be softened greatly. I should like for the article to be published separately or in another journal; then we might present an advantageous account of it, with an abundance of excerpts.

I agree with you that the epigraph chosen by Volkov is unfitting. The words of Peter I [the Great] would be the most fitting ones, but for this time send me the following: "But ask the German, doesn't he want to f—— us?"

[662]

To Peter Andreevich Vyazemsky
December, 1836. In Petersburg.

Your letter is excellent: I should think that whether the form is *Dear Sergey Semenovich*, or *Of*, etc.,[1] is of no significance: the main thing is to give the article as wide circulation and as much vogue as possible. But in any event the censorship will not dare to pass it, and Uvarov will not provide the birches to be used on himself. It would be difficult, and awkward, to mix Benkendorf up in this matter. Just what is to be done? I think: leave the article as it is, and at some later time extract from it all that can be gotten by with, as you once used to do in *The Literary Gazette* with the articles which Shcheglov would not pass. It's a pity that you didn't criticize Ustryalov according to the formula devised by Voeykov for Polevoy.[2] How good it would have been! I am copying the verses for you.

[663]

To Vladimir Fedorovich Odoevsky
December, 1836. In Petersburg.

Saints alive, Your Highness! Have some fear of God: I'm neither kith nor kin to Lvov, Ochkin, or the children.[1] Why should I play the fool[2] for *The Children's Journal*? As it is, they're already saying that I am falling into my second childhood. Unless maybe for the money? Oh, that's not a childish—but a sensible matter. At any rate, let's talk it over.

[664]
To Sergey Lvovich Pushkin
The end of December, 1836. From Petersburg to Moscow.
(In French)

It has been a very long time since I have had any news of you. Venevitinov[1] has told me that he found you sad and agitated, and that you are planning to come to Petersburg. Is it true? I need to go to Moscow. In any case I hope to see you soon. Well, the new year is almost upon us. God grant that it may be happier for us than that which has just passed. I have no news of my sister or Lev. The latter must have been a member of the expedition, and all that is sure is that he has not been killed or wounded.[2] What he wrote about General Rozen[3] has turned out to be unfounded. Lev is touchy, and spoiled by the familiarity of his former superiors. General Rozen did not ever treat him like a dog, as he said, but like a staff captain, which is a completely different thing. We are having a wedding. My sister-in-law Katerina is getting married to Baron Heeckeren, the nephew and adopted son of the ambassador of the King of Holland.[4] He is a very handsome and fine fellow, very much in fashion, rich, and four years younger than his intended. Preparations for the trousseau are occupying and amusing my wife and her sisters much, but they are driving me wild. For the house has the air of a millinery and lingerie shop. Venevitinov has presented his report on the state of the province of Kursk. The Emperor was impressed by it, and has made a lot of inquiries about Venevitinov; he said to I don't remember whom: "Introduce him to me the first time we are together." There's a career made. I have received a letter from Peshchurov's cook,[5] who proposes that I take his apprentice back. I have answered him that I shall await your commands as to that. Do you wish to keep him? And what were the conditions of his apprenticeship? I am very busy. My journal and my Peter the Great are taking a lot of time. This year I have managed my affairs badly enough; next year will be better, I hope. Farewell, my very dear father. My wife and all my family embrace you and kiss your hands. My respects and my best wishes to my aunt and her family.[6]

[665]
To Nikolay Ivanovich Pavlishchev
January 5, 1837. From Petersburg to Warsaw.
(Fragment)

Let Mikhaylovskoe be sold. If a good price is given for it, then it will be better for you. I shall see whether I shall be able to keep it for myself.

[666]
To Fedor Afanasievich Skobeltsyn
January 8, 1837. In Petersburg.

Can't you, dear Fedor Afanasievich, lend me for three months, or obtain for me, three thousand rubles?[1] You would oblige me extremely, and you would save me from the hands of the booksellers, who are glad to give me the squeeze.

January 8, 1837. A. Pushkin.

[667]
To Alexander Ivanovich Turgenev
January 16, 1837. In Petersburg.

Here are your letters for you. It will be necessary to blot out the stereotyped official phrases and also certain sincere, cordial words, for don't cast,[1] etc. Try to write as legibly as you can whatever you insert. Here is the sort of title I am thinking of giving to all this: "The Labors, Researches, of *Such-and-Such*, or of *A. I. T.*, in the Archives of Rome and Paris." The article is profoundly interesting.[2]

Here are my verses to Vyzemsky for you:

> So the sea, the ancient killer of man, is inflaming your genius; with golden lyre you glorify the trident of awesome Neptune. . . . Do not glorify him: in our vile age Gray Neptune is the ally of Land. In all the elements, man is tyrant, traitor, or prisoner.[3]

January 16.

[668]
> To Alexandra Osipovna Ishimova
> January 25, 1837. In Petersburg.

Dear Madame, Alexandra Osipovna,[1]

A few days ago I had the honor to call at your home, and I regret extremely that I did not find you there. I hoped to talk over a matter of business with you. Peter Alexandrovich [Pletnev] has given me hope that you will be kind enough to collaborate in the publication of *The Contemporary*. I agree in advance to all your terms, and I hasten to take advantage of your good will: I should like to acquaint the Russian public with the works of Barry Cornwall.[2] Won't you consent to translate several of his Dramatic Sketches? In that case I shall have the honor of forwarding his book to you.

With the most profound respect and with complete devotion, I have the honor to be,

> Dear Madame,
> Your most humble servant,

January 25, 1837.   A. Pushkin.

[669]
> To Lyubov Matveevna Alymova
> Between March, 1833, and January 25, 1837.
> In Petersburg.

Dear Madame, Lyubov Matveevna,

I most humbly request that Mr. Yuriev be permitted to take out of your yard the bronze statue which is there.[1]

With true respect and with devotion, I have the honor to be, Dear Madame,

> Your most humble servant,
> Alexander Pushkin.

[670]
> To Louis van Heeckeren
> January 26, 1837. In Petersburg.
> (In French)

Baron!

Permit me to summarize what has just taken place.[1] The behavior of your son had been known to me for a long time, and could not be a matter of indifference to me. I contented myself with the role of an observer free to intervene when I might think proper. An incident which at any other moment would have been very disagreeable came quite fortunately to rescue me from the difficulty: I received the anonymous letters.[2] I saw that the moment had come, and I availed myself of it. You know the rest: I made your son play a role so pitiful[3] that my wife, astonished at so much cowardice and truckling, could not refrain from laughing, and that the emotion which perhaps she had come to feel in response to this great and sublime passion faded into the coolest disdain and the most deserved disgust.

I am obliged to point out, Baron, that your role has not been altogether seemly. You, the representative of a crowned head, have paternally acted as your son's pander. It appears that all his behavior (clumsy enough, at that) has been directed by you. You probably dictated the sorry jokes he has just been reciting and the vacuous things which he has taken a hand in writing. Like an obscene old woman, you would go and lie in wait for my wife in every corner, in order to tell her of the love of your bastard, or the one so called, and when, ill with the syphilis, he was kept at home, you would say that he was dying of love for her. You would murmur to her, "Give me back my son."

You well realize, Baron, that after all this I cannot permit my family to have anything at all to do with yours. On this condition I consented not to follow up this filthy business and not to dishonor you in the eyes of our court and of yours, as I had the power and the intention of doing. I do not care for my wife to hear any more of your paternal exhortations. I cannot permit your son, after the despicable conduct which he has demonstrated, to dare to speak a word to my wife, nor still less to recite guardhouse puns[4] to her and play at devotion and unlucky passion, for he is only a coward and only a soundrel. I am therefore obliged to address myself to you, in order to pray you to put an end to all this little game, if you desire to avoid a new scandal, from which most certainly I shall not shrink.

        I have the honor to be, Baron,
            Your most humble and most obedient servant,
                Alexander Pushkin.

January 26, 1837.

[671]
                    To ALEXANDER IVANOVICH TURGENEV
                         January 26, 1837. In Petersburg.
    I can't get away. I expect you before 5 o'clock.[1]

[672]
                          To KARL FEDOROVICH TOL
                         January 26, 1837. In Petersburg.
    Dear Sir, Count Karl Fedorovich,
    The letter with which Your Highness[1] has been so kind as to honor me will remain for me a precious memorial of your good will, and the attention with which you have honored my first historical effort fully rewards me for the indifference of the public and the critics.
    I was no less gladdened by Your Highness's opinion of Mikhelson,[2] who has been too much forgotten among us. His services have been obscured by slander; it is impossible to see without indignation what he was forced to endure on account of the jealousy or the incompetence of his peers and his superiors. I am sorry that I did not succeed in placing in my book a few strokes of your pen for the full justification of the meritorious warrior. No matter how strong may be the prejudice of ignorance, no matter how avidly slander may be accepted, one word spoken by such a person as you destroys them forever. Genius discloses the truth at the first glance, and "the truth is mightier than the Tsar," says the Holy Writ.[3]
    With the most profound respect and with complete devotion, I have the honor to be,
                                Dear Sir,
                                   Your Excellency's
                                       Most humble servant,
    January 26, 1837.   Alexander Pushkin.

[673]
                          To AUGUSTE D'ARCHIAC
          Between 9:30 and 10:00 A.M. January 27, 1837. In Petersburg.
                                (In French)
       Viscount,
       I do not have the slightest desire to let Petersburg idlers into the

secrets of my family affairs; therefore I reject all negotiations between seconds. I shall bring mine only to the place of meeting. Since it is M. Heeckeren who is challenging me and who is offended, he can choose one for me, if that is agreeable to him; I accept him in advance, even though he be his lackey. As for the time and the place, I am completely at his command. According to our Russian customs, that is enough. I pray you to believe, Viscount, that this is my last word, and that I have nothing more to say in reply to anything concerning this affair, and that I shall not budge again, except to go to the place.[1]

Please accept the assurance of my complete esteem.

January 27.   A. Pushkin.

[674]
To ALEXANDRA OSIPOVNA ISHIMOVA
January 27, 1837. In Petersburg.

Dear Madame, Alexandra Osipovna,

I regret extremely that it will be impossible for me to come at your invitation today.[1] Meanwhile I have the honor to forward the Barry Cornwall.[2] You will find at the end of the book some pieces marked with a pencil; translate them as you can—I assure you that your translating couldn't be better. Today I chanced to open your *History in Tales*,[3] and I couldn't help becoming engrossed in them. That is how writing should be done!

With the most profound respect and with complete devotion, I have the honor to be,

Dear Madame,
Your most obedient servant,

January 27, 1837.   A. Pushkin.

Pushkin. Death Mask.

Notes to Part XIV

Letter 647

1. On November 4, 1836, Pushkin received several copies of a fake "certificate" in French, which read as follows:

> The Grand-Cross Commanders and Chevaliers of the Most Serene Order of Cuckolds, convened in plenary assembly under the presidency of the venerable Grand Master of the Order, His Excellency D. L. Naryshkin, have unanimously elected M. Alexander Pushkin coadjutor of the Grand Master of the Order of Cuckolds and historiographer of the Order.
> Perpetual Secretary, I. Borkh.

Dmitry Lvovich Naryshkin was husband of the acknowledged mistress of Alexander I. The mention of Naryshkin in the "certificate" and the designation of Pushkin as "historiographer" could be interpreted as a scarcely concealed hint at his own position, receiving a salary from the government for doing historical research and holding the court rank of Kammerjunker, and attending court functions, where the popularity of Mme. Pushkina extended, as the Letters indicate, to the Tsar himself.

Pushkin attributed the writing of the letter to Louis van Heeckeren (1791-1884), Dutch ambassador to the Russian court, who had recently legally adopted Georges Charles d'Anthès, French legitimist exile then in Russian service. D'Anthès-Heeckeren had been paying court, ever more openly, to Mme. Pushkina for two years (see Letters 651, 652, and 670).

Pushkin immediately took two actions: he challenged d'Anthès-Heeckeren to a duel, and he made the attempt through this letter to settle his financial accounts with the government of Nicholas I. In this letter, Pushkin is proposing that the government buy the estate of Kistenevo, in settlement of Pushkin's debt. Pushkin's father had given him the right to manage Kistenevo and to receive the revenues and to mortgage the serfs there (see Letter 349), but Pushkin had no legal right to sell it before his father's death.

2. Kankrin answered on November 21 that he considered the government's acquiring private lands "unsuitable in general" and that in any case it could not be done without His Majesty's command.

Letter 648

1. Prince Nikolay Borisovich Golitsyn (1794-1866), a retired army officer and musician, who translated Russian poetry into French. His French translation of Pushkin's "To the Calumniators of Russia" was published in Moscow in 1839, and of Pushkin's *Fountain of Bakhchisaray*, in 1838.

2. The three translations include the one sent him by Elizaveta M. Khitrovo (see Letter 400), the translation done by Baron B. A. Vrevsky or Countess Alexandra Grigorievna Laval, and the translation done by Uvarov (see Letter 404).

3. That is, while the Polish Revolution of 1830-1831 was going on.

4. Prince Golitsyn was then living in his summer house in the Crimea, which recalled to Pushkin his own visit to the Crimea in 1820 (see Letters 11, 169).

5. Apparently members of the Raevsky family.

Letter 649
  1. D'Anthès-Heeckeren was out of Petersburg when Pushkin sent him a challenge to a duel, on November 5, 1836, the day after Pushkin received anonymous letters. Heeckeren, d'Anthès-Heeckeren's adoptive father, persuaded Pushkin to postpone the duel for fifteen days. In the meantime, he made all possible efforts to get Pushkin to take back his challenge. Pushkin was willing to take back his challenge only when he learned that d'Anthès-Heeckeren wished to marry Mme. Pushkina's sister, Ekaterina Nikolaevna Goncharova. D'Anthès-Heeckeren insisted that Pushkin make no allusion to the forthcoming marriage in his letter taking back the challenge. Pushkin had no real faith that d'Anthès-Heeckeren would really marry Mme. Pushkina's sister, and he flatly refused to omit mention of the marriage in the letter necessary to prevent the duel. However, he consented to add phraseology to the effect that d'Anthès-Heeckeren was not acting dishonorably in deciding to marry Mme. Pushkina's sister. The enraged Pushkin intended to make d'Anthès-Heeckeren the laughing stock of Petersburg, by setting up a situation in which d'Anthès-Heeckeren would appear a coward. Pushkin was successful at this point.

Letter 650
  1. Probably about Yakovlev's and Eristov's *Historical Dictionary of the Saints* (1836). A review of this book was published in the third issue of *The Contemporary*.

Letter 651
  1. Though Pushkin had just taken back his challenge to d'Anthès-Heeckeren (Letter 649), his anger now turned toward d'Anthès-Heeckeren's adoptive father, Heeckeren, whom Pushkin considered the author of the "anonymous letter" which Pushkin received on November 4 and the abettor of d'Anthès-Heeckeren, as the latter paid open court to Mme. Pushkina.
  2. This passage indicates that Mme. Pushkina was seriously attracted to d'Anthès-Heeckeren, that d'Anthès-Heeckeren had been paying marked court to her for a long time, and that Mme. Pushkina had admitted "everything" to her husband.
  3. This is a plain hint at cowardice in that d'Anthès-Heeckeren was satisfied with Pushkin's taking back his challenge on the basis of rumors of the approaching marriage of d'Anthès-Heeckeren and Ekaterina Goncharova.
  4. The allusion is to Pushkin's being called, in the "anonymous letter" of November 4, the "historiographer" of the order of cuckolds.
  5. Pushkin showed this letter to Zhukovsky and to Sollogub, his second in the negotiations with d'Anthès-Heeckeren regarding the duel, but he did not send it, probably as the result of advice from Benkendorf (after sending Letter 652) and of Nicholas I himself, with whom Pushkin had an audience on November 23. However, Pushkin kept the letter, and he used it as the basis for Letter 670, the provocation which resulted in the duel which was mortal for him. Pushkin tore the final version of this letter to shreds as he utilized phrases for the composition of Letter 670. The letter in the form here presented is a reconstruction from two existing versions, and the final form is to some degree conjectural. It should be compared with Letter 670.

Letter 652
  1. Pushkin is hinting here that Heeckeren, the Dutch Ambassador, was the author of the "anonymous letter" of November 4.
  2. Pushkin may possibly be alluding here, not only to d'Anthès-Heekeren, but to Nicholas I himself.

3. Letter 649. Vicomte Auguste d'Archiac, attaché at the French consulate and first cousin of d'Anthès-Heeckeren, was d'Anthès-Heeckeren's second, not only in connection with the duel in November, 1836, which did not take place, but also in the duel of January 27, 1837.

4. Two days after this letter, Pushkin had an audience with Nicholas I in the presence of Benkendorf on November 23. Apparently Nicholas I persuaded Pushkin not to send Letter 651 to Heeckeren nor to take any further action with regard to anonymous letters or his suspicions.

Letter 653
1. Pushkin's letter is in response to Kankrin's refusal of his petition for the government to buy Kistenevo (Letter 647).

Letter 655
1. Baron Amable Guillaume Barante, French writer, historian, and, at this time, Ambassador to Russia. Barante had written Pushkin on December 11, 1836, requesting information regarding copyright laws in Russia from Pushkin, as the person in Russia best qualified to speak on the subject, and informing Pushkin that the whole question of authors' rights, including those of translation, was then under consideration in France.
2. Her *Ten Years of Exile* was published in 1821.
3. Pushkin is referring to himself and the Oldekop "swindle," when with impunity Oldekop published Pushkin's *Prisoner of the Caucasus*, together with Oldekop's German translation of it. See Letter 77.

Letter 656
1. Pushkin errs in Konshin's patronymic.
2. In a letter of December 20, 1836, Konshin had asked Pushkin to obtain Zhukovsky's intercession with Uvarov, Minister of Public Education, for Konshin's receiving the post of Director of the Tver Gymnasium and the Educational Institutions of the Province of Tver, a position which had become vacant upon the retirement of the historical novelist Lazhechnikov. Though Pushkin often laughed at the minor poet Konshin in his letters, Pushkin immediately fulfilled Konshin's request. Konshin obtained the appointment early in 1837.

Letter 657
1. Possibly one Alexey Ivanovich Lvov.
2. "Here is the situation."
3. "Pavlishchev appraised Mikhaylovskoe at eight hundred rubles per soul. I have no intention of quarreling with him, but that being the case I was forced to refuse and I offered the estate for sale. Before his departure, he wrote me that he is letting me have the estate for five hundred rubles per soul, 'because he needs the money.'"
4. "Manor house and outbuildings."
5. "House serfs."
6. "Shouldn't I bring her along for you?"
7. Baroness Vrevskaya, nee Vulf.

Letter 658
1. "It" is probably an article by Vigel against Bulgarin, on the occasion of fierce attacks on Pushkin in an article in *The Northern Bee* in 1836.
2. The last sentence of the letter is a paraphrase of Pushkin's epigram on Prince M. A. Dondukov-Korsakov: "In the Academy of Sciences sits Prince Dunduk. They say such

an honor is not fitting for Dunduk. Why is he sitting there? Because he has an a———."
The conclusion of the epigram is double-edged—it includes allusion to the suspected homosexual relationships between Prince Dondukov-Korsakov and his superior, Uvarov. *Dunduk* means a muddle-headed person. Pushkin's reference to the meeting of the Academy of Sciences is to that of December 29, 1836. Pushkin attended it, and according to the testimony of Kraevsky, there he pointed at Dondukov-Korsakov and alluded to the epigram.

Letter 659
1. Pushkin here is accepting the proposal made by the bookseller and publisher Plyushar for the publication of a one-volume edition of Pushkin's long poems. The edition did not materialize, because of Pushkin's death.

Letter 660
1. Stories by Odoevsky, which Pushkin wished for the fifth issue of *The Contemporary*. Odoevsky rewrote the father-in-law's letter as a result of Pushkin's comment.

Letter 661
1. This letter shows Pushkin's interest in contemporary civic developments, and it also shows the peculiar difficulties of publishing in Russia in Pushkin's day. The article in question is one by Matvey Stepanovich Volkov (1802-1878), engineer and professor, in objection to an article, by N. I. Tarasenko-Otreshkov, which favored the construction of a railroad from Petersburg to Moscow, as proposed by the German-Czech engineer František Gerstner (1793-1840). Gerstner proposed in 1835 that the Russian government finance the construction of three railroads, from Petersburg to Moscow, from Moscow to Nizhny Novgorod, and from Petersburg to Tsarskoe Selo and Pavlovsk. This third railroad was authorized, and completed in the summer of 1836. Then sharp discussion arose about the desirability of the longer railroads. Gerstner attempted to obtain a monopoly on railroad construction in Russia. He advanced, among other proposals, that foreign capital be used for constructing railroads in Russia. He did not receive permission for the construction of any railroad except the short line from Petersburg to Pavlovsk. Pushkin later consented to publish Volkov's article, but he died before it could appear. Then Tarasenko-Otreshkov became one of the guardians of Pushkin's family, and the article could not be published in Pushkin's journal.

Letter 662
1. Vyazemsky's article was written in the form of a letter; Pushkin means that it does not matter whether a letter-form or article-form is used. Vyazemsky's article-letter was addressed to Uvarov, Minister of Education, and was directed against the doctoral dissertation, "Of the System of Pragmatic Russian History," by Nikolay Gerasimovich Ustryalov (1805-1870), in which Ustryalov attacked the historian Karamzin. Vyazemsky, in the article, accuses Uvarov of retreating from his famous formula of "Orthodoxy, autocracy, and nationality" by allowing such a dissertation, and of "allowing and even encouraging historical skepticism." The letter is an indirect defense of Chaadaev and his presentation of his historical views (see Letter 637), for which Chaadaev had been declared mad. Vyazemsky, however, was far from sharing Chaadaev's opinions. Vyazemsky's letter was not published until 1879.

2. Voeykov, in the journal, *The Slav* (1827-1830), in a section called "The Chameleonist," published a collection of stupid expressions from articles by Polevoy and sharp criticisms on Polevoy, in the form of a "wreath, plaited by a brigadier's wife."

Letter 663
1. Odoevsky apparently suggested that Pushkin contribute to the journal, *A Child's Library*, published by Prince Vladimir Vladimirovich Lvov (1804-1856) and Amply Nikolaevich Ochkin (1791-1865). Odoevsky participated actively in the journal in 1836. Pushkin declined.
2. Pushkin's expression is an untranslatable bilingual pun: *sot-dejstvovat'*, "to co-operate" and "to play the fool."

Letter 664
1. Alexey Vladimirovich Venevitinov, brother of the poet, D. V. Venevitinov.
2. Pushkin means that if Lev Pushkin, who was serving in the army in the Caucasus, had been killed or wounded, they would have received the information from official reports.
3. General Baron Grigory Vladimirovich Rozen (1782-1841), Lev Pushkin's commanding officer in the Caucasus at the time.
4. The wedding of Ekaterina Nikolaevna Goncharova and d'Anthès-Heeckeren took place on January 10, 1837. Pushkin refused to attend, but sent Mme. Pushkina, instead. Pushkin refused to receive the couple after their marriage.
5. The cook of A. N. Peshchurov, the Opochka Marshal of the Nobility.
6. The Solntsevs, in Moscow.

Letter 666
1. Fedor Afanasievich Skobeltsyn (b. 1781), a rich landowner and gambler, was then staying at Vyazemsky's, in the same house where Pushkin was living. Skobeltsyn refused Pushkin's request.

Letter 667
1. Pushkin was fond of the biblical injunction against casting pearls before swine (see Letter 435).
2. At the command of Nicholas I, A. I. Turgenev had been doing research in materials relating to Russian history of the sixteenth to eighteenth centuries, in the state archives of France and the Papal States. His article was intended for publication in Pushkin's *Contemporary* in 1837, but it did not appear.
3. Pushkin had written the poem in 1826, upon hearing the rumor, which turned out to be false, that A. I. Turgenev's brother, N. I. Turgenev, had been arrested in London in connection with the Decembrist Uprising of 1825. A. I. Turgenev heard of the poem only in 1837. He was, naturally, interested in the poem because of its connection with his brother, to whom he sent it on January 21, 1837. Pushkin had quoted the poem in his letter to Vyazemsky of August 14, 1826 (Letter 188). This time Pushkin quotes the poem without division into stanzas, and he makes changes in the punctuation.

Letter 668
1. Alexandra Osipovna Ishimova (1806-1881) became well known as a writer for children.
2. Pushkin had been very much interested in the works of Barry Cornwall, pseudonym of the English poet and dramatist Bryan Waller Procter, since 1830. Pushkin borrowed from him the form of the dramatic scene for his "little tragedies" in blank verse, which include some of his best works. Pushkin had in his library a copy of *The Poetical Works of Milman, Bowles, Wilson, and Barry Cornwall* (Paris: Galignani, 1829).

Wilson's *City of the Plague*, in the same volume, was the source of Pushkin's *Feast in Time of Plague* (see Letter 406, and note 1). See Letter 674 and notes.

Letter 669

1. Lyubov Matveevna Alymova (b. 1808) was sister of the owners of the house on Furshtatskaya Street, where Pushkin lived from May to December, 1832. He apparently had the statue of Catherine II (see Letter 287) brought to Petersburg at that time. Pushkin hoped to sell it to Vasily Gavrilovich Yuriev, probably in settlement of a gambling debt.

Letter 670

1. D'Anthès-Heeckeren did not cease his attentions to Mme. Pushkina after his own marriage on January 10, 1837. He continued to attempt to monopolize her at balls, though he was refused admittance into the Pushkins' home. Mme. Pushkina recounted to her husband their conversation, but she was unwilling or unable to take such action that d'Anthès would cease his attentions to her. She even consented to a rendezvous with him, in the home and presence of her friend Idalia Poletika. Mme. Poletika slipped away, on some excuse, and d'Anthès-Heeckeren pressed his case, but one of Poletika's children interrupted them, and Mme. Pushkina slipped away. A curious point is that an officer, Peter Petrovich Lanskoy (1799-1877), who stood guard outside Poletika's house while this meeting was taking place, married Mme. Pushkina seven years later. Pushkin received an anonymous letter on the following day, telling of this "assignation." He then proceeded to write this letter, reworking Letter 651. As he rewrote the earlier letter, Pushkin tore it to shreds, piecing together many of the expressions he had written earlier into this final form. This method of composition, plus the surviving rough-draft variations, show that Pushkin wrote this letter in cold rage. He made his letter as insulting as possible, in order that a duel would be inevitable. It is possible that Pushkin really wrote and sent the letter on January 25 and inadvertently misdated it. The letter was sent to Heeckeren so as to implicate him in the whole business; Pushkin was aware that the duel would be with d'Anthès-Heeckeren.

2. Pushkin still considered Heeckeren the author of the anonymous letters of November 4, 1836, and he is here hinting at him as the author.

3. The assertion here is of cowardice, upon d'Anthès-Heeckeren's accepting Pushkin's letter taking back his challenge of November 5, 1836. See Letter 651, note 2.

4. Mme. Pushkina dutifully reported to her husband what d'Anthès-Heeckeren said to her. A sample of his "guardhouse puns" is the following: Mme. Pushkina and her sister, now Mme. d'Anthès-Heeckeren, had the same chiropodist, which gave him the occasion to tell Mme. Pushkina: *Je sais maintenant que votre cor est plus beau, que celui de ma femme* [I know now that your corn is more beautiful than my wife's], with a pun on *cor* "corn" and *corps* "body."

Letter 671

1. A. I. Turgenev noted on this letter, "Pushkin's last note to me, on the eve of the duel." This is Pushkin's last letter to an old friend. A. I. Turgenev, who had been to a considerable degree responsible for Pushkin's attending the Tsarskoe Selo Lyceum, and who had been Pushkin's friend all his life, was the person who was permitted to accompany Pushkin's corpse from Petersburg to the burial place at the Svyatye Gory Monastery, near Mikhaylovskoe.

Letter 672

1. Adjutant General Karl Fedorovich Tol had participated notably in the wars against

Napoleon and the Polish Revolution of 1830-1831. Pushkin is answering Tol's letter thanking him for a copy of Pushkin's *History of Pugachev*.

2. Ivan Ivanovich Mikhelson (1740-1807), who took an important part in putting down the Pugachev uprising. Tol's opinion was that history would finally give Mikhelson his due.

3. I have been unable to trace this quotation.

Letter 673

1. This letter was written in answer to insistent demands by d'Archiac, d'Anthès-Heeckeren's second, that Pushkin send a second for negotiations about the conditions of the duel between Pushkin and d'Anthès-Heeckeren. Pushkin asked Arthur Magenis, secretary of the English embassy, to be his second, but Magenis declined when Pushkin refused to tell him the reasons for the quarrel. Pushkin had been infuriated that his second in November, Sollogub, had attempted to enter into negotiations, and this time he meant to make it impossible. A few hours later, Pushkin met his old Lyceum comrade and friend, Konstantin Karlovich Danzas (1801-1871), and half-persuaded, half-commanded him to be his second, but he did not permit any further negotiations at all.

Letter 674

1. This letter, written a few hours before Pushkin's fatal duel with d'Anthès-Heeckeren, contains the last words he wrote. The calm tone of the letter, discussing in a matter-of-fact manner business regarding his *Contemporary*, and also the polite praise of the work that Ishimova had previously done, show Pushkin's control of himself. Perhaps it was most fitting that he died on his literary shield, like his uncle, Vasily Lvovich Pushkin (see Letter 313).

The duel took place in knee-deep snow at Chernaya Rechka, in the suburbs of Petersburg, about 4:30 p.m. on the same day. D'Anthès-Heeckeren fired first and Pushkin fell, wounded in the abdomen. Pushkin summoned enough strength to fire his shot, which wounded d'Anthès-Heeckeren only slightly, but was enough to knock him down. Pushkin's doctors, Spassky, Arendt, and Dal, never had hopes of his recovery, nor did he. During the two days he lay dying, he was surrounded by his old friends the Vyazemskys, Zhukovsky, Ekaterina Karamazina, and Danzas. Though he tried to hide his suffering from his wife, he wished it not to be concealed from her that his wound was mortal. He died at 2:45 p.m. on January 29.

2. Mme. Ishimova translated, from the book containing the works of Barry Cornwall (see Letter 668), five dramatic scenes marked by Pushkin, including *Ludovico Sforza, Love Cured by Kindness, The Way to Conquer, Amelia Wentworth,* and *The Falcon*. They were published in *The Contemporary* in 1837.

3. Ishimova's *History of Russia in Tales for Children*, the first volume of which appeared in December, 1836. The work went through several editions.

INDEX

INDEX

Abakumov, Faddey Ivanovich, II, 463
  Letter to, II, 415
Academic Calender, The (Akademičeskij kalendar'), I, 196, 276
Academy, Russian. *See* Russian Academy
Academy of Sciences, Petersburg, III, 706-7, 736, 812, 823-24
Addison, Joseph (1672-1719), English man of letters, I, 221
Aderkas, Boris Antonovich (d. 1831), governor of Pskov, I, 188, 189, 228, 239, 259, 262, 271, 272, 273, 288, 290, 295
  Letter to, I, 185
Adrian, undertaker, II, 436, 470
Aeschylus, ancient Greek tragedian, I, 95
Agrafena, II, 417, 464
Aladiin, Egor Vasilievich (1796-1860), man of letters, I, 205, 279
Album of the Northern Muses, The (Al'bom severnyx muz), II, 388
Alcyone (Al'ciona) for 1832, II, 534, 545, 577, 581
Alexander I (1777-1825), Emperor (Tsar) of Russia (1801-1825), I, 28, 33, 36, 38, 46, 49, 59, 67, 70, 104, 108, 119, 120, 125, 127, 128, 149, 161, 172, 173, 176, 177, 185, 196, 207, 218, 223, 228-29, 233, 234, 236, 241, 244, 251, 253, 257, 265, 271, 274, 276, 284, 286, 289, 290, 291, 293, 294, 296, 297, 301, 302, 303, 307, 312, 316; II, 446, 452, 458, 472, 474, 476; III, 643, 681, 760, 777, 789, 795, 798
  Letters to, I, 217-18, 255-56
Alexander II (1818-1881), Emperor (Tsar) of Russia (1855-1881), II, 497, 509; III, 643, 644, 648, 651, 681, 682, 683, 798
Alexander Nevsky (1220-1263), Great Prince of Novgorod, I, 48
Alexandra Fedorovna, Tsaritsa (1798-1860), wife of Nicholas I, I, 79, 118, 317; II, 502, 511, 517, 519, 571, 579; III, 683
Alexandrov, Alexander Andreevich. *See* Durova, Nadezhda Andreevna
Alexandrov, Pavel Konstantinovich (1808-1857), II, 559, 586; III, 614
Alexeev, Nikolay Stepanovich (1789—1850's-1860's), I, 140, 169; II, 336, 385, 473
  Letters to, II, 335, 448
Alexey, servant of ASP, II, 539, 540, 579
Alexey (Lelenka), unidentified, III, 620, 622, 629
Alfieri, Vittorio (1749-1803), Italian dramatist, I, 215, 221, 237, 285, 303; II, 367
  Of the Prince and of Literature, I, 303, 317
Alfred, actress, II, 400
Ali Pasha (1741-1822), Turkish pasha of Jannina, Albania, I, 80, 81, 119
Alymov, Pavel Matveevich (1810-1891), II, 550, 582
Alymova, Ekaterina Petrovna, house owner, II, 550
Alymova, Lyubov Matveevna (b. 1808), III, 827
  Letter to, III, 817
Amphion (Amfion), journal, I, 62, 67, 68
Anacreon, III, 762
Ancelot, Jacques Arsène François (1794-1854), French poet and dramatist, I, 310-11, 319
Andrieux, restaurateur, II, 340, 371, 397
Anna Bogdanovna, servant, I, 239, 290
Anne (1693-1740), Empress (Tsaritsa) of Russia (1730-1740), I, 131; III, 731, 743
Annette. *See* Vulf, Anna Nikolaevna
Anrep, Roman Romanovich (d. 1830), officer, III, 601, 623
Antipin, Ivan Fomich, II, 463
  Letter to, II, 415
Antiquity. See: Russian Antiquity
Apostol. *See* Muraviev-Apostol, I. M.
Apraxin, Count, unidentified, III, 753
Aprelev, Alexander Fedorovich (1798-1836), III, 768, 792
Arakcheev, Alexey Andreevich (1769-1834), statesman, I, 49, 290; III, 644, 681

INDEX

Arbenieva, Nenila Onufrievna, servant of ASP, II, 557, 585
Arendt, Nikolay Fedorovich (1785-1859), physician and surgeon, II, 350, 390; III, 690, 827
Aretino, Pietro (1492-1557), Italian author, I, 144, 145, 171
Wandering Harlot, The, I, 145, 171
Arina Rodionovna (1754-1828), ASP's nursemaid, I, 51, 193, 195, 237, 244, 275, 291; II, 332, 384; III, 725, 741
Ariosto, Ludovico (1474-1533), Italian poet, I, 94, 221, 223, 227
Orlando Furioso, I, 124, 197, 276
Aristarchus, ancient Greek grammarian and critic, I, 88, 93, 122
Aristides the Just, ancient Athenian statesman, I, 107, 128
Aristippus, ancient Greek philosopher, I, 163, 177, 258
Aristotle, ancient Greek philosopher, I, 164, 177; II, 500
Arkhip, serf, I, 205, 279; II, 541, 580
Arnault, Antoine Vincent (1766-1834), French poet, I, 276
"Solitude," I, 276
Artyukhov, Konstantin Demianovich, army officer, III, 707, 737
Arzamas, literary society, I, 32, 44, 48, 60, 61, 67, 68, 69, 70, 117, 118, 121, 126, 129, 169, 171, 174, 176, 198, 229, 262, 271, 284, 288, 293; II, 362, 521, 522-23, 525, 573; III, 736
Letter to members of, I, 77-78
Asiatic Messenger, The (*Aziatskij vestnik*), I, 283
ASP. *See* Pushkin, Alexander Sergeevich
Athenaeum (*Atenej*), journal, II, 351, 390, 391
Augustus Caesar, Roman Emperor, I, 83, 104, 120, 286
L'Avenir, French newspaper, II, 504

Bakhtin, Nikolay Ivanovich (1796-1869), I, 317
Bakunin, Nikolay Modestovich (1801-1838), II, 569, 590
Balsh, Todoraki, Moldavian nobleman, I, 165, 178

Balzac, Honoré de (1799-1850), French novelist, I, 169; II, 563
Fatal Skin, The, II, 588
Woman of Thirty, The, II, 588
Bantysh-Kamensky, Dmitry Nikolaevich (1788-1850), III, 683, 684, 685
Letters to, III, 647-48, 656, 703-4
Baranov, Dmitry Osipovich (1773-1834), minor poet, II, 569, 589
Barante, Guillaume (1782-1866), French author and diplomat, III, 823
Letter to, III, 809-10
Baratynskaya, Anastasia Lvovna, nee Engelgardt (1804-1860), wife of E. A. I, 318
Baratynskaya, Sofia Mikhaylovna. *See* Delvig, Sofia Mikhaylovna
Baratynsky, Evgeny Abramovich (1800-1844), poet, I, 89, 96, 97-98, 99, 102, 106, 107, 113, 122, 127, 142, 148, 151, 183, 194, 202, 207, 214, 220, 222, 278, 280, 305, 310, 318; II, 351, 360, 361, 387, 401, 431, 438, 446, 455, 457, 460, 501, 535, 546, 560, 563, 576, 581, 587; III, 608, 609, 626, 680, 767
Concubine, The (*Naložnica*), II, 452, 474, 546, 581
"Declaration" (*Priznanie*), I, 148
Eda, I, 189, 190, 193, 194, 197, 202, 271, 273, 274, 275, 305, 310, 317, 318
"Herons" (*Capli*), II, 331, 383
"To Gnedich, Who Advised the Poet to Write Satires" (*Gnediču, kotoryj sovetoval sočinitelju pisat' satiry*), I, 142, 170
"To * *" (*K **), II, 362, 394
Barber of Seville, The. *See* Beaumarchais; Rossini
Barklay de Tolly, Mikhail Bogdanovich (1761-1818), general, I, 265, 297; II, 575; III, 778, 796
Barkov, Dmitry Nikolaevich (1796-after 1855), I, 101, 126
Barkov, Ivan Semenovich (1732-1763), poet, I, 314, 319
Batashev, Sila Andreevich, III, 689, 772, 781
Batyushkov, Konstantin Nikolaevich (1787-1855), poet, I, 48, 60, 62, 67, 68, 89, 96, 99, 106, 122, 125, 126, 197, 226, 276; II, 382, 401, 552, 583

Batyushkov, Konstantin Nikolaevich, contd.
Attempts in Verse and Prose (*Opyty v stixax i proze*), I, 208, 280
"Epistle to I. M. Muraviev-Apostol" (*Poslanie I. M. Murav'evu-Apostolu*), I, 310, 318; II, 484, 505; III, 677, 690
Beaumarchais, Pierre Caron de (1732–1799), French dramatist, II, 453, 474
Barber of Seville, The, I, 64, 69
Marriage of Figaro, The, II, 523, 573
Bee. See: *Northern Bee, The*
Begicheva, Anna Ivanovna, niece of Mme. Osipova, III, 722, 740
Bekleshov, Peter Nikolaevich, husband of Alexandra, III, 741
Bekleshova, Alexandra Ivanovna, nee Osipova (d. 1864), step-daughter of Mme. Osipova, I, 184, 272; II, 368; III, 601, 624, 725, 741
Letter to, III, 723
Belinsky, Vissarion Grigorievich (1811–1848), literary critic, III, 769, 792, 793
Bellizard, Ferdinand (d. 1863), bookseller, II, 457, 476, 482, 500, 510
Benkendorf, Alexander Khristoforovich (1783–1844), head of Secret Police under Nicholas I, I, 33, 41, 51, 52; II, 345, 362, 378, 384, 385, 386, 387, 388, 389, 395, 397, 400, 401, 411, 413, 418, 420, 424, 429, 461, 462, 472, 481, 482, 483, 498, 504, 509, 510, 519, 540, 553, 557, 561, 566, 573, 576, 578, 580, 581, 582, 587; III, 619, 623, 629, 666, 667, 672, 678, 686, 687, 688, 735, 742, 754, 755, 785, 788, 790, 814, 822, 823
Letters to, II, 334, 338–39, 340–41, 343–44, 347, 353, 355–56, 369–70, 371–72, 373, 380, 380–81, 407–8, 413–14, 416, 454, 532, 535–36, 546–47, 548–49, 549, 550, 551, 552; III, 599, 621, 633, 634, 660–61, 665–66, 666–67, 668, 699–700, 700, 703, 711–12, 712–13, 713–14, 716, 717–18, 719, 729, 747, 807–8
Beranger, Pierre Jean de (1780–1857), French poet, II, 469, 556

Bon Dieu, Le, tr. by V. L. Pushkin, I, 227, 287
Bernikov, Alexander Sergeevich, house owner, II, 531
Bertrand, Henri Gratien (1773–1844), French general, I, 202, 278
Bestuzhev, Alexander Alexandrovich (pen-name, Marlinsky) (1797–1837), man of letters and Decembrist, I, 94, 96, 104, 107, 109, 123, 124, 125, 127, 130, 170, 172, 173, 190, 196, 197, 199, 202, 205, 207, 274, 276, 277, 281, 283, 285, 286, 317; II, 564, 588; III, 736
"Ah, Where Are the Islands . . ." (*Ax, gde te ostrova . . .*), I, 149, 173
"Castle Neuhausen" (*Zamok Nejgauzen*), I, 151, 172, 173
"Evening at a Bivouac" (*Večer na bivuake*), I, 113, 130; II, 524, 573
"Glance at Old and New Literature in Russia, A" (*Vzgljad na staruju i novuju slovesnost' v Rossii*), I, 109, 113, 129, 130, 224, 286
"Glance at Russian Literature in the Course of 1824 and at the Beginning of 1825, A" (*Vzgljad na russkuju slovesnost' v tečenie 1824 i načale 1825 godov*), I, 221–24, 281, 285
"Novel in Seven Letters, A" (*Roman v semi pis'max*), II, 524, 573
"Roman and Olga" (*Roman i Olga*), I, 113, 130
"Tournament of Reval" (*Revel'skij turnir*), I, 224, 286
"Traitor, The" (*Izmennik*), I, 224, 286
Letters to, I, 92–93, 113–15, 147–48, 151–52, 162–63, 200–1, 209–10, 221–24, 264–65
Bestuzhev, Nikolay Alexandrovich (1791–1855), man of letters, I, 151, 152, 173
Bestuzhev-Marlinsky. See Bestuzhev, A. A.
Bestuzhev-Ryumin, Mikhail Alexeevich (1800–1832), journalist and writer, II, 522, 672
Bezobrazov, Peter Romanovich (1797–1856), III, 695, 733
Bezobrazov, Sergey Dmitrievich (1801–1879), army officer, II, 559, 562, 586;

Bezobrazov, Sergey Dimitrievich, contd. III, 614, 615, 628, 640, 681, 695, 733, 763
Bezobrazova, mother of S. D., III, 763
Bezobrazova, Lyubov Alexandrovna, nee Khilkova (1811-1859), III, 614, 615, 627, 628
Bezobrazova, Margarita Vasilievna, nee Vasilieva (1810-1889), natural daughter of V. L. Pushkin, III, 622, 630, 695, 733
Bibikov, Ilarion Mikhaylovich (d. 1861), governor of Kaluga, III, 658, 685
Bibikova, Ekaterina Ivanovna (1795-1849), wife of I. M., III, 658, 685
Bible, I, 146, 156, 189, 192; II, 500; III, 696
  Genesis, I, 139-40, 165, 169, 178, 189, 190, 273; II, 382, 401, 450, 473, 557, 584; III, 674, 689
  Exodus, II, 407, 509
  I Kings, II, 542
  Job, I, 139, 163, 169, 177, 277
  Psalms, I, 77, 118, 160, 176, 306, 317; II, 437, 470, 500, 542
  Ecclesiastes, II, 501, 510
  Jonah, II, 481, 504
  Ecclesiasticus, I, 205, 279
  Gospels, I, 141, 148, 155, 255; III, 780
  Matthew, I, 94, 124, 200, 294; II, 556, 584; III, 816, 825
  Mark, I, 94, 124
  Luke, I, 85, 94, 120, 124, 146, 171, 246; II, 419, 464
  John, I, 94, 124
  I Corinthians, I, 305, 317
  I Peter, I, 165, 178, 199, 277
  Revelation, Book of (Apocalypse), I, 85, 120, 309, 318; II, 437, 470, 502, 511
Bion, ancient Greek poet, I, 205, 279
Biron, Ernst Johann (1690-1772), favorite of Empress Anne, III, 731, 743
Birukov, Alexander Stepanovich (1772-1844), censor, I, 109, 110, 111, 128, 142, 143, 159, 160, 182, 208, 224, 227, 286; II, 377; III, 705, 777
Bludov, Dmitry Nikolaevich (1785-1864), I, 218, 284; II, 382, 456, 475, 500, 510, 566, 567
Boboly, Andrey, I, 262, 295

Bobrinskaya, Anna Vladimirovna (1769-1846), II, 559, 586; III, 662, 686
Bobrinskaya, Sofia Alexandrovna (1799-1866), wife of A. A., III, 700, 735
Bobrinsky, Alexey Alexeevich (1800-1868), III, 605, 625, 735
  Letter to, III, 700-1
Bobrinsky, Alexey Grigorievich (1762-1813), II, 586
Bobrov, Semen Sergeevich (d. 1810), minor poet, I, 121, 146
  Tavrida, I, 87, 90, 121, 146
Boccacio, Giovanni (1313-1375), Italian writer,
  Decameron, The, II, 529
Bogdanovich, Ippolit Fedorovich (1743-1803), poet, I, 222, 276
  Dushenka (Dušen'ka), I, 197, 276
Bogolyubov, Varfolomey Filippovich (ca. 1785-1842), III, 751, 786
Boiardo, Matteo Maria (1434-1494), Italian poet, I, 287
  Orlando Inamorato, I, 227, 287
Boileau-Despréaux, Nicolas (1636-1711), French poet and critic, I, 59, 67, 164
Boldyrev, Alexey Vasilievich (1780-1842), censor, III, 796, 797
Boltin, unidentified, I, 309, 318
Boltin, Ilia Alexandrovich, III, 736, 770, 793
Borchard, N., II, 391
Bordeaux, Duke of (1820-1883), Bourbon claimant to the throne of France, II, 425, 467
Borg, Karl Friedrich von der, writer,
  Poetic Production of the Russians, I, 273
Borisova, Maria Vasilievna, II, 359, 393
Borkh, Iosif Mikhaylovich, III, 821
Borozdin, Konstantin Matveevich (1781-1848), censor, II, 399
  Letter to, II, 377
Borrow, George (1803-1881), English man of letters,
  Targum, or a Metrical Translation from Thirty Languages, III, 757, 788
  Letter to, III, 757
Boshnyak, Aleksandr Karlovich (1786-1831), I, 51
Bossuet, Jacques Bénigne (1627-1704), French pulpit orator, II, 481, 504

INDEX 835

Bova Korolevich (*Bova Korolevič*), I, 60, 68
Bowles, William (1762–1850), English poet, I, 209, 281; III, 825
Bowring, John (1792–1872), English linguist, diplomat, and author, I, 201
Specimens of the Russian Poets, I, 277
Brantôme, Pierre de Bourdeille, Seigneur de (1527–1614), III, 619, 629
La Vie des dames galantes, III, 619, 629
Brillat-Savarin, Anthelme (1755–1826), French gastronome,
Physiology of Taste, The, III, 645, 682
Briskorn, Olga Konstantinova, house owner, II, 533, 549
Bronevsky, Semen Mikhailovich (1764–1830), I, 76, 117
Brueys, David-Augustin de (1640–1723), French author, I, 291
Glib Lawyer (*L'Avocat patelin*), I, 240, 291
Brutus, Marcus Junius, I, 148, 199; III, 737
Bryansky, Yakov Grigorievich (1760–1853), actor, I, 95, 125
Bryullov, Alexander Pavlovich (1798–1877), architect and portrait painter, II, 495, 508, 538; III, 690
Bryullov, Karl Pavlovich (1799–1852), painter, III, 761–62, 765–66, 767, 768, 790, 792
"Last Day of Pompeii, The" (*Poslednij den' Pompei*), III, 765, 792
"Taking of Rome by Genseric, The" (*Našestvie Genzerixa na Rim*), III, 765, 792
Bulgakov, Alexander Yakovlevich (1781–1863), Moscow post director, III, 604, 606, 624–25, 681, 785
Bulgakova, Ekaterina Alexandrovna (b. 1811), daughter of A. Y., III, 604, 606, 625
Bulgakova, Natalia Vasilievna (1785–1841), wife of A. Y., III, 604, 606, 625
Bulgarin, Faddey Venediktovich (1798–1859), writer and journalist, I, 46, 130, 151, 152, 154, 155, 159, 162, 163, 188, 201, 205, 206, 208, 209, 222, 226, 253, 263, 273, 279, 280, 293, 310, 319; II, 344, 351, 352, 354, 363, 374, 381, 382, 389, 390, 391, 394, 401, 410, 411, 413, 430, 434, 436, 446, 450, 453, 457, 462, 469, 472, 476, 484, 490, 502, 506, 520, 525, 542, 553, 554, 555, 571, 573, 577, 578, 580, 583; III, 638, 679, 680, 682, 754, 768, 791, 823
Dimitry the Pretender (*Dimitrij samozvanec*), II, 398, 401
Ivan Vyzhigin (*Ivan Vyžigin*), II, 398, 462, 505, 537, 578, 580
"Meeting with Karamzin, A." (*Vstreča s Karamzinym*), II, 344, 388
Peter Ivanovich Vyzhigin (*Petr Ivanovič Vyžigin*), II, 484, 490, 505
"Second Letter from Karlovo to Kameny Ostrov, The" (*Vtoroe pis'mo iz Karlova na Kammenyj Otrov*), II, 469, 536, 578
Letters to, I, 149; II, 347
Bułharyn, Tadeusz. *See* Bulgarin, Faddey Venediktovich
Bulwer-Lytton, Edward (1803–1873), English novelist,
Last Days of Pompeii, The, III, 792
Buntova (d. after 1848), III, 613, 627
Buovo d'Antona, medieval Italian tale, I, 227, 287
Burat de Gurgy, Edmond (1809–1840), French author,
Prima Donna and the Butcher Boy, The, II, 537, 578
Bürger, Gottfried August (1747–1794), German poet, II, 505. *See* Zhukovsky, V. A.
Butera di Ridali, Giorgio (d. 1841), Neapolitan diplomat, III, 741
Butera de Ridali, Varvara Petrovna (1796–1870), by first marriage Polier, II, 421, 423, 465; III, 726, 741
Butler, Samuel (1612–1680), English poet, *Hudibras*, I, 197, 276
Butterfly, The (*Babočka*), journal, II, 362, 394
Buturlin, Mikhail Petrovich (1786–1860), governor of Nizhny Novgorod, III, 607, 625
Buturlina, Anna Petrovna (1793–1861), wife of M. P., III, 607, 625
Byron, Anne Isabella Milbanke, Lady (1792–1860), wife of the poet, I, 268

Byron, George Gordon Noel, Lord (1788–1824), English poet, I, 32, 49, 82, 102, 120, 161, 163, 170, 171, 176, 177, 182, 192, 202, 209–10, 213, 219, 222, 224, 226, 229, 231, 237, 238, 239, 263–64, 267, 268, 271, 281, 282, 283, 284, 288, 290, 296, 297; II, 385, 504; III, 736
  Beppo, I, 32, 307, 318
  Bride of Abydos, The, I, 213, 275
  Cain, I, 161, 290
  Childe Harold, I, 119, 161, 176
  Conversations de Byron. *See* Medwin, Thomas
  Corsair, The, I, 268, 297
  Don Juan, I, 32, 141, 161, 170, 174, 209–10, 215, 263, 281; II, 576; III, 680
  Giaour, The, I, 146, 161, 213, 268, 275, 297
  Lara, I, 139, 169; III, 706
  Manfred, I, 290
  Parisina, I, 150, 173, 287
  Prisoner of Chillon, The. *See* Zhukovksy, V. A.
  Two Foscari, The, I, 238, 290

Calderon de la Barca, Pedro (1600–1681), Spanish dramatist, I, 237
Calendar for the Muses (*Kalendar' muz*), II, 389
Canning, George (1770–1827), British statesman, II, 458, 476
Catherine II, the Great (1729–1796), Empress (Tsaritsa) of Russia (1762–1796), I, 38, 48, 77, 117, 222, 286, 297; II, 416, 463, 552, 582, 586, 588; III, 625, 628, 677, 780, 782, 785, 798, 799
Catherine II, statue of, owned by A. N. Goncharov, II, 416, 418, 422, 423, 432, 433, 463, 464, 466, 469, 479, 504, 552, 563, 583, 587; III, 817, 826
Cato the Censor, ancient Roman statesman, I, 113, 130; II, 458, 476
Catullus, Gaius Valerius, Roman poet, "Epithalamium" (Poem LXI), I, 304, 317
Cervantes, Miguel de (1547–1616), Spanish novelist,

Don Quixote, I, 226
Chaadaev, Peter Yakovlevich (1794–1856), writer and thinker, I, 36, 39, 41, 88, 89, 109–10, 111, 122, 147, 172, 188, 196, 276, 294; II, 465, 473, 510, 515, 517, 521, 538, 557, 571, 572; III, 604, 738, 762, 765, 796, 798, 824
  Philosophical Letters (*Lettres philosophiques*), I, 122; II, 420, 465, 500–1, 510, 515, 517, 521, 570, 572; III, 779–81, 796–98
  Letters to, II, 449, 500–1; III, 779–81
Chamfort, Sébastien (1741–1794), French writer, I, 213, 282
Chapelle, Claude-Emmanuel Lhuillier (1626–1686), French poet, I, 59, 62, 67, 68
Charles X (1757–1836), King of France (1824–1830), II, 466, 467, 468, 475, 490, 507
Charles XII (1682–1718), King of Sweden (1697–1718), I, 278
Charlotta, Princess. *See* Elena Pavlovna, Grand Duchess
Chateaubriand, René de (1768–1848), French author and statesman, II, 425, 467
  Atala, I, 139, 169
  René, II, 459, 476
Chebotarev, Andrey Kharitonovich (1784–1833), I, 145, 171
Chénier, André (1762–1794), French poet, I, 128, 164, 177, 208, 263, 296, 310
  "Ode XI: The Young Captive Girl," I, 151, 174
Chernyshev, Alexander Ivanovich (1786–1857), Minister of War, II, 588
  Letter to, II, 565
Chernysheva, Nadezhda Grigorievna (1813–1853), III, 603, 624, 658, 685, 716, 739
Chertkov, Alexander Dmitrievich (1789–1858), historian and archaeologist, III, 765, 766–67, 791
  Recollections of Sicily (*Vospominanija o Sicilii*), III, 765, 791
Chertkova, Elizaveta Grigorievna, nee Chernysheva, wife of A. D., III, 765, 766

Chicherin, Alexander Petrovich (b. ca. 1809), officer, son of P. A., II, 450, 473
Chicherin, Peter Alexandrovich (1778–1848), general, II, 473
Chicherina, Ekaterina Petrovna (d. 1874), III, 661, 686
Chicherina, Varvara Vasilievna (ca. 1742–1825), great-aunt of ASP, I, 224, 246, 286, 287, 292
Child's Library, A (*Detskaja biblioteka*), III, 814, 825
Chlodwig (Clovis I, or Chlodowech, 466?–511), Merovingian ruler of the Franks (481–511), I, 81, 119
Circourt, Adolphe de (1801–1879), French publicist, III, 710, 738
Circourt, Anastasia Semenovna, nee Khlyustina, III, 738
Cloots, Anacharsis (1755–1794), French revolutionary, I, 147, 172, 220
Collection of New Russian Poems, Appearing from 1821 to 1823 (Part I), and ... *from 1823 to 1825* (Part II) (*Sobranie novyx russkix stixotvorenij, vyšedšix v svet s 1821 po 1823; ... s 1823 po 1825*), I, 206, 280
Collections of Memoirs Regarding the French Revolution (*Collections des Mémoires relatifs à la Révolution française*), II, 493, 508
Commercial Gazette, The (*Kommerčeskaja gazeta*), II, 523, 572
Complete Collected Laws of the Russian Empire from 1649 [to 1825] (*Polnoe sobranie zakonov Rossijskoj imperii s 1649 goda [po 1825 god]*), II, 549, 582; III, 614, 627, 665
Constant de Rebecque, Benjamin (1767–1830), French writer,
Adolphe, II, 376, 399. *See also* Vyazemsky, P. A.
Constantine, Grand Duke, brother of Alexander I and Nicholas I (1779–1831), I, 265, 297; II, 468, 494, 497, 508, 509, 519, 586
Constantine I, the Great, Roman emperor, I, 80, 119
Contemporary, The. See Pushkin, Alexander S.

Conversation (*Razgovor*), pamphlet, II, 499, 510
Conversation Society of Lovers of the Russian Word (*Beseda ljubitelej russkogo slova*), literary society, I, 32, 60, 67, 176, 183, 271
Corneille, Pierre (1606–1684), French dramatist, I, 95, 237
Cid, The, I, 95, 237; II, 367. *See also* Katenin, P. A.
Cornwall, Barry. *See* Procter, Bryan Waller
Corregio, Antonio Allegri da (1494–1534), Italian painter, I, 78, 118
Court Calendar, The (*Pridvornyj kalendar'*), I, 196, 276
Crabbe, George (1754-1832), English poet, II, 482

Dal, Vladimir Ivanovich (1801–1872), writer, lexicographer, and physician, III, 707, 737, 827
Dictionary of the Living Great-Russian Language (*Tolkovyj slovar' živogo velikorusskogo jazyka*), III, 737
Dante, Alighieri (1265–1321), Italian poet, I, 221, 226
Inferno, II, 481, 504
D'Anthès-Heeckeren, Georges Charles (1812–1895), adoptive son of Louis van Heeckeren, mortally wounded ASP in duel over ASP's wife, I, 29–30, 55, 56; III, 680, 786, 804–5, 805–7, 807–8, 815, 817–18, 820, 821, 822, 823, 825, 826, 827
Danzas, Konstantin Karlovich (1801–1871), ASP's second at fatal duel, III, 827
D'Archiac, Auguste, French diplomat, opponent's second at ASP'S fatal duel, III, 803, 823, 827
Letter to, III, 819–20
Dashkov, Dmitry Vasilievich (1788–1839), diplomat, I, 88, 121; III, 764, 791
David, Psalmist, II, 500, 542, 580; III, 645. *See also* Bible

Davydov, Alexander Lvovich (1773-1833), I, 78, 118, 123, 139, 169, 205; II, 395

Davydov, Denis Vasilievich (1784-1839), partisan warrior and poet, I, 67, 213, 229, 288; II, 450, 538, 559; III, 789, 793

"I Remember—Deeply . . ." (*Ja pomnju—gluboko* . . .), III, 770, 793

"Occupation of Dresden, The, . . ." (*Zanjatie Drezdena* . . .), III, 761, 769, 790, 793

"Of Partisan Warfare" (*O partizanskoj vojne*), III, 777, 795

"To Zaytsevsky, Poet and Sailor" (*Zajcevskomu, poètu-morjaku*), II, 377, 399

Letters to, III, 769-70, 777

Davydov, Dmitry Alexandrovich (1786-1851), II, 451, 474

Davydov, Ivan Ivanovich (1794-1863), professor, II, 559, 586

Davydov, V., suitor of Natalia N. Goncharova, II, 441, 471, 541, 558, 559, 580, 585, 586

Davydov, Vasily Lvovich (1792-1855), I, 78, 118, 139, 169; II, 395, 398

Letters to, I, 79-81, 166, 167

Davydova, Aglaya Antonovna (1787-1847), wife of A. L., I, 123

Dawn (*Dennica*) *for 1831*, II, 473

for 1834, III, 640, 680

Deguilly, French ex-officer in Kishinev, I, 121

Letter to, I, 86

Deguilly, Mme., I, 86, 121

Delaryu, Mikhail Danilovich (1811-1868), writer, II, 485, 505

Delavigne, Casimir (1793-1843), French poet, I, 164, 177, 226, 287; II, 446, 447, 472

La Parisienne, II, 425, 466, 467

Delille, Jacques (1738-1813), French abbé, poet, and translator, I, 45, 196, 276

Delvig, brothers of A. A. Delvig the Younger, II, 458, 460, 476, 501, 525

Delvig, Anton Antonovich (ca. 1772-1828), general, father of the poet, II, 448, 472

Delvig, Anton Antonovich (1798-1831), poet, close friend of ASP, I, 30, 31, 33, 40, 44, 51, 77, 79, 85, 88, 90, 96, 99, 100, 102, 106, 108, 113, 115, 117, 119, 120, 126, 148, 151, 152, 160, 173, 176, 183, 190, 193, 195, 197, 198, 205, 206, 207, 212, 214, 215-16, 217, 219, 220, 230, 232, 235, 258, 273, 275, 280, 283, 284, 288, 289, 295, 305, 308, 317; II, 338, 340-41, 347, 348, 349, 374, 384, 386, 387, 388, 389, 393, 398, 401, 410, 412, 430, 434, 437, 446, 448,449, 450, 451, 453, 454, 455, 456, 457, 458, 460, 470, 472, 473, 474, 475, 476, 479, 482, 484, 501, 502, 503, 505, 511, 516, 522, 533, 534, 535, 536, 542, 571, 577, 578, 580

Letters to, I, 82-83, 142-43, 224-25, 232-33, 262, 268-70, 301, 303-4, 304-5; II, 339-40, 344, 360-61, 361, 436

Delvig, Lyubov Matveevna (d. 1859), mother of poet, II, 448, 472

Delvig, Sofia Mikhaylovna, nee Saltykova (1806-1888), wife of the poet, I, 232, 262, 289, 296, 305; II, 344, 348, 359, 361, 388, 393, 456, 457, 458, 460, 475, 476, 479, 484, 503, 511, 525

Dembiński, Henryk (1791-1864), Polish general, II, 523, 572

Denisevich, Major, I, 253, 293

Derzhavin, Gavriil Romanovich (1743-1816), poet, I, 48, 99, 126, 212, 213, 222, 223, 224-25, 282, 285; II, 457, 484; III, 749

"Felitsa" (*Felica*), I, 222, 285

"God" (*Bog*), I, 222, 285

"Harp, The" (*Arfa*), I, 111, 129

"Morning" (*Utro*), I, 107, 128

"Noble Lord, The" (*Vel'moža*), I, 222, 285; III, 749, 785

"On the Birth of Tsaritsa Gremislava: To Lev Alexandrovich Naryshkin" (*Na roždenie caricy Gremislavy* . . .), III, 760, 789

"On the Death of Prince Meshchersky" (*Na smert' knjazja Meščerskogo*), I, 222, 285

"On the Return of Count Zubov from Persia" (*Na vozvraščenie grafa Zubova iz Persii*), I, 222, 223, 285, 286

Diakov, Alexey Nikolaevich (1790–1837), III, 762, 790
Diakova, Elizaveta Alexeevna, nee Okulova (1806–1886), II, 559, 585; III, 762, 790
Dibich. *See* Dibich-Zabalkansky
Dibich-Zabalkansky, Ivan Ivanovich (1785–1831), field marshal, I, 314, 319; II, 468, 489, 491, 492, 494, 506, 507
Didelot, Charles Louis (1767–1837), ballet choreographer, I, 107, 128; II, 554
Diderot, Denis (1713–1784), French encyclopedist,
Mémoires, II, 559, 586
Dimitry I, False (d. 1606), ruler of Russia (1605–1606), I, 219, 230, 284, 288; II, 365–66, 395, 396; III, 797. *See also* ASP: *Boris Godunov*
Dimitry Donskoy (1350–1389), Great Prince of Moscow (1359–1389), I, 204, 279
Dimitry Ivanovich (1581–1591), Tsarevich, I, 284, 294; III, 797
Dmitriev, Ivan Ivanovich (1760–1837), poet, I, 48, 65, 70, 94, 109, 124, 152, 154, 155, 159, 174, 222, 228, 284, 285, 287; II, 333, 379, 382, 384, 400, 485, 490, 538, 582; III, 736, 762, 794
"Fashionable Wife, The" (*Modnaja žena*), I, 208, 281
Horace, *Odes*, Book I, 3, tr. of, II, 437, 470
"Passer-By, Halt!" (*Proxožij stoj! . . .*), I, 225, 286
Poems (*Stixotvorenija*), I, 174
"Sparrow and the Finch, The" (*Vorobej i zjablica*), I, 219, 285; II, 520, 571
"To Masha" (*K Maše*), I, 311, 319
"To My Friends" (*K druz'jam moim*), I, 145, 171
Letters to, II, 547; III, 704–5, 706–7, 772
Dmitriev, Mikhail Alexandrovich (1796–1866), minor author, I, 162, 163, 175, 177, 219, 284
Doganovsky, V. S. *See* Ogon-Doganovsky, V. S.
Dolgorukov, Dmitry Ivanovich (1797–1867), I, 88, 121

Dolgorukov, Pavel Ivanovich (1787–1845), I, 98, 125
Dolgorukov, Peter Mikhaylovich (1784–1833), III, 604, 625
Dolgorukov, Vasily Andreevich (1804–1868), II, 374, 398
Dolgorukova, Ekaterina Alexeevna, nee Vasilieva (1781–1870), II, 446, 472; III, 655, 684
Dolgorukova, Olga Alexandrovna, nee Bulgakova (1814–1865), III, 604, 606, 625
Dondukov-Korsakov, Mikhail Alexandrovich (1794–1869), chairman of censorship committee, II, 532, 576; III, 707, 712, 728, 738, 742, 755, 788, 790, 795, 812, 823–24
Letters to, III, 755, 758, 761
Donskoy, Dimitry. *See* Dimitry Donskoy
Dorat, Claude Joseph (1734–1780), French poet and dramatist, I, 109, 129
Dorokhov, Rufin Ivanovich (d. 1852), II, 519, 571
Doroshenko, Peter Dorofeevich (1627–1698), hetman of the Ukraine, III, 603, 624
Dostoevsky, Fedor Mikhaylovich (1821–1881), novelist, I, 34; III, 793
Idiot, The (*Idiot*), II, 511
Dubrux, Augustin-Paul (ca. 1774–1835), archaeologist, I, 76, 117
Ducange, Victor (1783–1833), French author,
Thirty Years, or the Life of a Gambler, II, 427, 467
Dumas, *père*, Alexandre (1803–1870), French novelist and dramatist,
Stockholm, Fontainebleau, et Rome, II, 446, 472
Dumé, restaurateur, III, 641, 649, 657, 661, 673, 675, 705
Dunduk. *See* Dondukov-Korsakov, M. A.
Durier, III, 768, 792
Durov, Vasily Andreevich (b. 1799), brother of Nadezhda A., III, 739, 788
Letters to, III, 715, 756–57
Durova, Nadezhda Andreevna, married name Chernova (1783–1866), woman soldier, III, 739, 757, 785, 788, 793, 794

Durova, Nadezhda Andreevna, contd.
  Memoirs (*Zapiski*), III, 715, 747, 748, 756–57, 764, 771–72, 773–74, 785, 788, 793, 794
  Letters to, III, 747–48, 771–72, 773–74
Dushin, Semen Fedorovich (1792–1842), II, 533, 576; III, 603, 624

Edinburgh Review, The, I, 203, 279, 304; II, 572
Eikhfeldt, Maria Egorovna, II, 335, 385, 448, 473
Elena Pavlovna, Grand Duchess (1807–1873), wife of Grand Duke Michael, I, 146, 171, 318; II, 557, 585; III, 655, 661, 670, 684, 686, 689
Elena Timofeevna, unidentified, II, 526
Elizabeth I (1533–1603), Queen of England (1558–1603), I, 223
Emelian, servant, III, 697, 734
Encyclopedic Lexicon, The (*Enciklopedičeskij leksikon*), III, 656, 678, 679, 799
Engelgardt, Vasily Vasilievich (1785–1837), I, 193, 197, 275; III, 645, 705, 736
Ephraim the Syrian, Saint (d. 373), Lenten prayer, I, 82, 119
Eristov, Dmitry Alexeevich (1797–1858), minor poet and lexicographer, I, 262, 295; III, 622
  Historical Dictionary of the Saints (*Slovar' istoričeskij o svjatyx . . .*), III, 805, 822
Ermak Timofeevich (d. 1584), I, 204, 279
Ermolov, Alexey Petrovich (1777–1861), general, I, 75, 99, 116, 124, 282; II, 341, 364–65, 387, 395, 589; III, 601
  Letter to, II, 567
Ermolova, Josephine Charlotte, nee Comtesse de Lasalle, III, 670, 688
Esaulov, Andrey Petrovich (ca. 1800–1850's), composer, II, 495, 508, 519; III, 637
  Summer Night (*Letnjaja noč'*), II, 587
Essen, Peter Kirillovich (1772–1844), governor-general of Petersburg, II, 451, 474, 482
European, The (*Evropeec*), journal, II, 531, 534, 545, 546, 547, 553, 576, 577, 581, 582, 583; III, 738
Ezhova, Ekaterina Ivanovna (1787–1837), actress, I, 101, 126

Farikov, bookseller, III, 766, 792
Fauvel, French diplomat, I, 161, 176
Fedor Ivanovich (1557–1598), Tsar of Russia (1584–1598), III, 797
Fedorov, Boris Mikhaylovich (1794–1875), writer, I, 253, 267, 294, 297; II, 355, 360, 393; III, 706, 736
  "Byron" (*Bajron*), I, 267, 297
  "Prince Kurbsky" (*Knjaz' Kurbskij*), I, 267, 297
Feofan Prokopovich (1681–1736), church official and poet, III, 780, 797
Ficquelmont, Daria Fedorovna (1804–1863), wife of K. L., daughter of Elizaveta M. Khitrovo, II, 410, 414, 425, 448, 461, 462, 463, 467, 506, 538, 545, 581; III, 614, 627, 650, 653, 669
  Letter to, II, 409
Ficquelmont, Karl Ludwig (1777–1857), Austrian ambassador to Russia, II, 461, 508; III, 614, 627, 657, 737
Fielding, Henry (1707–1754), English novelist, I, 238
Fieschi, Giuseppi (1790–1836), Corsican conspirator, III, 754, 788
Filaret (Vasily Mikhaylovich Drozdov, 1783–1867), Metropolitan of Moscow, II, 372, 398; III, 798
  "Not in Vain, Not by Chance" (*Ne naprasno, ne slučajno*), II, 372, 398
Filimonov, Vladimir Sergeevich (1787–1858), author, I, 199, 277, 294; II, 362, 394
  Art of Living, The (*Iskusstvo žit'*), I, 277
Firska, confederate of Pugachev, III, 694, 733
Florian, Jean Pierre Claris de (1755–1794), French author, I, 94, 124
Flowers. See: *Northern Flowers*
Fomin, Nikolay Iliich (d. before 1848), poet, II, 540, 579
Fominsky, Fedor, writer, II, 539, 579
  Teodor and Rozalia (*Nevedomye Teodor i Rozalija*), II, 539, 579

INDEX

Fon-Fok, Maxim Yakovlevich (1777–1831), secret police official, II, 413, 462, 527
Fonvizin, Denis Ivanovich (1745–1792), dramatist, I, 188, 273; II, 438, 453, 470, 474, 484
Adolescent, The (*Nedorosl'*), I, 198, 203, 277, 279; III, 603, 624, 661, 686
Foscolo, Ugo (1778–1827), Italian writer, I, 221, 285
Fouché, Joseph, Duc d'Otrante (1759–1820), French statesman, I, 215, 227, 278
Memoirs, I, 202, 206, 278
Fournier, Victor André, I, 138, 169
Frebelius, Ivan, carriage maker, II, 558, 585
Frederick II, the Great (1712–1786), King of Prussia (1740–1786), I, 215, 223, 283
Frederick William IV (1795–1861), King of Prussia (1840–1861), III, 651, 659, 683, 685
Fréron, Elie Catherine (1719–1776), French author, I, 65, 70
Frolov, Stepan Stepanovich, I, 69
Letter to, I, 63
Frolova-Bagreeva, Elizaveta Mikhaylovna (1799–1857), daughter of M. M. Speransky, II, 423, 466
Fuchs, Alexandra Andreevna (d. 1853), wife of Karl, authoress, III, 609–10, 626, 734, 787
Poems of Alexandra Fuchs, The (*Stixotvorenija Aleksandry Fuks*), III, 698, 734
Letters to, III, 608, 698, 719–20, 753
Fuchs, Karl (1776–1846), historian, III, 610, 626, 698, 719, 753

Gaevsky, Pavel Ivanovich, censor, III, 789, 790
Gagarin, Fedor Fedorovich (1786–1863), II, 451, 474; III, 620, 622, 765, 769
Gagarin, Sergey Sergeevich (1795–1852), II, 379, 400
Galatea (*Galateja*), journal, II, 375, 399, 462
Galiani, Tver restaurateur, II, 331, 383

Galiani, Ferdinand (1728–1787), abbé, I, 313, 319; II, 331, 383; III, 674
Gannibal, Abram (*or* Ibragim) Petrovich (1697–1781), ASP's maternal great-grandfather, I, 48, 120, 203, 278, 291; II, 536, 578
Gannibal, Peter Abramovich (1742–ca. 1825), great uncle of ASP, I, 241, 291
Gavrila, ASP's servant, III, 611, 620, 627
Genlis, Comtesse de (1746–1830), French writer, I, 219; II, 425, 467
Memoirs, I, 285
George, Saint (d. ca. 303), Christian martyr, I, 220
George, Mme. *See* Wemmer, Marguerite Joséphine
Gerstner, František (1793–1840), engineer, III, 813, 824
Gesling, Nikolay Nikolaevich (1806–1853), II, 501, 510, 516
Gladkova, Ekaterina Ivanovna (b. 1805), daughter of I. I. Vulf, II, 368, 396
Glinka, Fedor Nikolaevich (1786–1880), poet, I, 87, 106–7, 109, 121, 128, 161, 177, 199, 228, 276, 288; II, 451–52, 474, 577–78
"Incomprehensible Thing, An" (*Neponjatnaja vešč'*), II, 451–52, 474
"Poverty and Consolation" (*Bednost' i utešenie*), II, 452, 474
Letter to, II, 535
Glinka, Mikhail Ivanovich (1804–1857), composer, II, 357, 392
Ivan Susanin (*A Life for the Tsar*) (*Žizn' za carja*), II, 577
Glinka, Sergey Nikolaevich (1775–1847), journalist, I, 244, 291; II, 379, 400
Glinka, Yustina Karlovna, nee Kyukhelbeker, sister of V. K., III, 732, 743
Globe, Le, II, 438
Glukharev, Alexander, actor, I, 99, 126
Gnedich, Nikolay Ivanovich (1784–1833), poet and translator, I, 82, 88, 90, 107–8, 109, 118, 122, 123, 127, 128, 130, 135, 148, 151, 162, 168, 177, 183, 189, 193, 208, 219, 222, 279, 280, 286, 306; II, 356, 361, 363, 393, 394, 451, 457, 474, 476, 480, 571; III, 757, 792
Andromaque, by Racine, tr. of, I, 78, 118
"Fishermen, The" (*Rybaki*), I, 91, 123

Gnedich, Nikolay Ivanovich, contd.
Folk Songs of the Modern Greeks (*Prostonarodnye pesni nyneśnyx grekov*), I, 204, 207, 279, 280
Iliad, The, by Homer, tr. of, I, 88, 113, 118, 120, 122, 128, 168, 204, 222, 286, 306; II, 361, 371, 393, 394, 397
"On the Death of Baron A. A. Delvig" (*Na smert' barona A. A. Del'viga*), II, 457
Tancrède, by Voltaire, tr. of, II, 356, 392
"Tarantine Maid" (*Tarentinskaja deva*), I, 108, 128
"To P. A. Pletnev: Answer to His Epistle" (*K P. A. Pletnevu: Otvet na ego poslanie*), II, 451, 474
Letters to, I, 78–79, 83–85, 91, 93–94, 101–2, 112–13, 203–4; II, 371
Godunov, Boris Fedorovich (1551?–1605), Tsar of Russia (1598–1605), I, 48, 254, 255, 261, 284, 292, 294; II, 366, 396; III, 797. *See also* ASP: *Boris Godunov*
Godunova, Ksenia Borisovna (d. 1622), daughter of Boris. *See* ASP: *Boris Godunov*
Goethe, Johann Wolfgang von (1749–1832), German poet, I, 100, 156, 163, 177, 226, 276, 290; II, 354, 355, 391
Faust, II, 368, 376, 391, 396, 399
Reineke-Fuchs, I, 197, 276
Gogol, Nikolay Vasilievich (1809–1852), writer, II, 485, 505, 524, 573; III, 618, 625, 627, 628, 683, 728, 763, 764, 789, 791, 792
"Calash, The" (*Koljaska*), III, 728, 742
Evenings on a Farm Near Dikanka (*Večera na xutore bliz Dikan'ki*), II, 505, 525, 531, 573, 576, 58ʀ
Inspector General (*Revizor*), II, 585; III, 625, 627, 763, 791
"Morning of a Man of Business: Petersburg Scenes" (*Utro delovogo čeloveka: Peterburkskie sceny*), III, 758, 789
"Nevsky Prospect, The" (*Nevskij prospekt*), III, 699, 734
"Nose, The" (*Nos*), III, 791

Vladimir, Third Class (*Vladimir 3-j stepeni*), III, 618, 628, 728, 742
Letters to, II, 524–25; III, 651, 699
Golenishchev-Kutuzov, Mikhail Ilarionovich (1745–1813), II, 388, 446–47, 472, 508, 529, 575; III, 614, 796
Golikov, Ivan Ivanovich (1735–1801), I, 264, 296
Acts of Peter the Great (*Dejanija Petra Velikogo*), I, 296
Golitsyn, Alexander Nikolaevich (1773–1844), I, 64, 69, 165, 178
Golitsyn, Dmitry Vladimirovich (1771–1844), governor-general of Moscow, II, 362, 394, 400, 421, 425, 444, 465, 466, 508; III, 682
Golitsyn, Nikolay Borisovich (1794–1866),
Fountain of Bakhchisaray, The, by Pushkin, tr. into French, III, 821
"To the Caluminators of Russia," by Pushkin, tr. into French, III, 821
Letter to, III, 804
Golitsyn, Sergey Grigorievich (1806–1868), II, 357, 392
Golitsyna, Princess, unidentified, II, 441, 442, 445, 471
Golitsyna, Anna Vasilievna, nee Lanskaya (1793–1868), II, 537, 578
Golitsyna, Evdokia Ivanovna (1780–1850), I, 85, 120, 146, 165, 212, 282
Golitsyna, Maria Arkadievna, nee Suvorova-Rymnikskaya (1802–1870), I, 212, 282
Golitsyna, Natalia Petrovna (1741–1837), II, 362, 394
Golitsyna, Tatiana Vasilievna (1782–1841), wife of D. V., III, 646, 647, 682
Goncharov, Afanasy Nikolaevich (ca. 1760–1832), grandfather of ASP's wife, II, 395, 407, 412, 415, 416, 422, 423, 424, 428, 432, 433, 462, 463, 464, 466, 467, 468, 469, 483, 488, 494, 495, 505, 506, 508, 526, 533, 540, 552, 574, 577, 579–580, 587; III, 643, 726
Letters to, II, 412, 418–19, 419–20, 424–25, 426, 428–29, 479, 486

Goncharov, Dmitry Nikolaevich (1808–1859), brother of ASP's wife, II, 395, 423, 466, 479, 538, 561–62, 579, 587; III, 603, 624, 643, 654, 658, 660, 662, 716, 765, 768, 792

Goncharov, Ivan Alexandrovich (1812–1891), novelist, III, 792

Goncharov, Ivan Nikolaevich (1810–1881), brother of ASP's wife, II, 382, 395, 401, 422, 423, 545, 581; III, 609, 650, 655, 664, 677, 684, 693, 754, 765

Goncharov, Nikolay Afanasievich (1788–1861), father of ASP's wife, II, 395, 422, 466, 562, 587; III, 603, 624, 643, 645, 681, 682

Goncharov, Sergey Nikolaevich (1815–1865), brother of ASP's wife, II, 395, 432, 445, 469; III, 609, 610, 655, 663, 664, 673, 677, 693–94, 733

Goncharova, Alexandra Nikolaevna (1811–end of 1870's), sister of ASP's wife, I, 54; II, 395, 422, 423, 428, 432, 435, 465, 486, 488, 494, 505, 506, 508, 566, 574; III, 637, 641, 643, 645, 647, 658, 659, 660, 662, 673, 679, 685, 700, 717, 722, 724, 725, 735, 739, 740, 741, 762, 763, 791, 792, 793, 815

Goncharova, Ekaterina Nikolaevna (1809–1843), sister of ASP's wife, I, 54, 55; II, 395, 422, 423, 428, 432, 435, 465, 486, 494, 505, 566; III, 616, 637, 641, 643, 645, 647, 658, 659, 660, 662, 673, 679, 685, 700, 717, 722, 724, 725, 735, 739, 740, 741, 742, 762, 763, 791, 792, 805, 808, 815, 822, 825, 826

Goncharova, Natalia Ivanovna, nee Zagryazhskaya (d. 1848), mother of ASP's wife, II, 395, 406, 407, 412, 415, 421, 422, 423, 426, 427, 428, 430–31, 432, 433, 435, 436, 440, 441, 444, 459, 461, 463, 467, 473, 476, 483, 488, 494, 506, 508, 509, 526, 533, 539, 562, 576, 589; III, 601, 602–3, 623, 637, 641, 645, 647, 651, 652, 658, 679, 696, 727, 768, 792
Letters to II, 364, 405–6, 495–96; III, 693–94, 710, 716–17

Goncharova, Natalia Nikolaevna. *See* Pushkina, Natalia Nikolaevna

Goncharovs, family of ASP's wife, II, 395, 420, 424, 433, 444, 461, 463, 464, 465, 579; III, 608, 624, 630, 658, 671, 680, 683, 726

Gorchakov, Alexander Mikhaylovich (1798–1883), I, 255, 258, 294

Gorchakov, Dmitry Petrovich (1758–1824), minor poet, II, 357, 392

Gorchakov, Vladimir Petrovich (1800–1867), I, 127; II, 487, 488, 489, 495, 516, 517, 519, 538
Letter to, I, 105

Gorgoli, Staff-Captain, III, 791

Gotovtsova, Anna Ivanovna, poetess, II, 360, 361, 393

Gourgaud, Gaspard (1783–1852), French general,
Memoirs, I, 278

Grabbe, Pavel Khristoforovich (1789–1875), army officer, I, 201, 278

Gray, Thomas (1716–1771), English poet, "Elegy in a Country Churchyard." *See* Zhukovsky, V. A.

Grech, Nikolay Ivanovich (1787–1867), journalist, I, 76, 90, 92, 94, 114, 117, 122, 124, 125, 155, 172, 175, 188, 206, 222, 279, 319; II, 411, 446, 457, 476, 527, 554, 580; III, 635, 678, 679, 796
"Attempt at a Short History of Russian Literature, An" (*Opyt kratkoj istorii russkoj literatury*), I, 104, 123, 127
Letters to, I, 88–89; III, 778

Green Lamp (*Zelenaja lampa*), society, I, 49, 65, 70, 87, 121, 126, 272, 275, 295

Gresset, Jean Baptiste Louis (1709–1777), French playwright,
Naughty One, The (Le Mechant), I, 124, 277
Vert-Vert, I, 197, 276

Gribko, Otton Nikolaevich, I, 145, 171

Griboedov, Alexander Sergeevich (1795–1829), dramatist and diplomat, I, 99, 126, 147, 158, 170, 199, 200, 201, 208, 220, 264, 280, 285, 296; II, 367
Woe from Wit (Gore ot uma), I, 126, 172, 199, 200–1, 202, 277; II, 453, 475, 485, 505; III, 638, 680

Grigoriev, Alexander, ASP's servant, II, 526, 574

Grigoriev, Ivan, ASP's servant, II, 526, 574

Grigory Fedorovich, dwarf, III, 622, 630
Grimm, Friedrich Melchior von (1723–1807), French author, III, 641, 681
Correspondence littéraire, III, 681
Grinvald, Rodion Grigorievich (1797–1877), III, 763, 791
Gubanov, Stepan Savelievich, III, 764, 791
Gubanova, widow of S. S., III, 764, 791
Guichard, Jean François (1731–1811), minor French poet, I, 155, 174
Guizot, François Pierre Guillaume (1787–1874), French historian and statesman, I, 202, 278; III, 788
Gurieva, Countess, I, 184, 195, 272
Gut, unidentified person, III, 771, 793

Hafiz, Persian poet, I, 213, 282
Hannibal (*surname*). *See* Gannibal
Hanskaya, Evva (Evalina) Adamovna (1803–1882), wife of Vatslav, and, later, of French novelist Balzac, I, 139, 169
Hansky, Vatslav (d. 1841), I, 139, 169
Hebel, Johann Peter (1760–1826), German author,
"Red Carbuncle." *See* Zhukovsky, V. A.
Heeckeren, George. *See* d'Anthès-Heeckeren, Georges Charles
Heeckeren, Louis van (1791–1884), Dutch diplomat, I, 42, 55; III, 680, 807, 808, 815, 821, 822, 826
Letters to, III, 805–7, 817–18
Heine, Heinrich (1797–1856), German poet, III, 707, 737
Works, III, 707, 737
Henry IV (1553–1610), King of France (1589–1610), II, 366, 396
Henry V (1387–1422), King of England (1413–1422), I, 265, 297
Herod, I, 106, 255
Herzen, Alexander Ivanovich (1812–1870), author, III, 796
Homer, ancient Greek poet, I, 65, 84, 88, 94, 99, 108, 204; II, 500, 527
Iliad, The, I, 68, 124; II, 500; III, 706, 736. *See also* Gnedich, N. I., and Zhukovsky, V. A.

Odyssey, The, I, 68, 124. *See also* Zhukovsky, V. A.
Horace, Roman poet, I, 97, 221, 285, 286; II, 470, 583
Art of Poetry, The, I, 95, 125
Epode II, I, 85, 120
Odes, I, 252, 293; II, 437, 470
Housewarming, The (Novosel'e), III, 760
Hugo, Victor (1802–1885), French author, II, 409, 414, 556
Cromwell, II, 452, 474
Hernani, II, 414, 463
Last Day of a Condemned Man, The, II, 409, 461
Notre Dame de Paris, II, 488, 490–91, 506
Hume, David (1711–1776), Scots philosopher and historian, I, 164
History of England, I, 177
Hutchinson, Dr. William, I, 156, 175

Ignaty, I, 246
Igor (d. 945), Prince of Kiev (912–945), III, 798
Iliinskaya, house owner, II, 536, 538
Invalide. See: *Russian Invalide*
Inzov, Ivan Nikitich (1768–1845), general, ASP's chief in Kishinev, I, 49, 75, 79, 87, 116, 135, 164, 165, 178; II, 448, 452, 474
Letter to, I, 153
Iokhim, carriage maker, II, 558, 585
Iordaki. *See* Olympios, Yorghakis
Ippolit, ASP's servant, II, 559, 585; III, 611, 627
Irina Kuzminichna, ASP's servant, II, 557, 585
Ishimova, Alexandra Osipovna (1806–1881), writer, III, 825, 827
History of Russia in Tales for Children (Istorija Rossii v rasskazax dlja detej), III, 820, 827
Letters to, III, 817, 820
Istomina, Evdokia Ilinichna (1799–1848), dancer, I, 107, 128, 296
Ivan III, the Great (1440?–1505), ruler of Russia (1462–1505), I, 127–28, 221; II, 443, 471; III, 780, 797

Ivan IV, the Terrible (1530–1584), ruler of Russia (1533–1584), I, 48, 131, 286; II, 332, 384, 398; III, 780, 795, 797
Ivanchin-Pisarev, Nikolay Dmitrievich (1790–1849), author, I, 199, 277
Ivelich, Ekaterina Markovna (1795–1838), I, 190, 274; II, 580
Izmaylov, Alexander Efimovich (1779–1831), man of letters, I, 142, 170, 174, 319; II, 389; III, 617, 628
"Black Tomcat, The" (*Černyj kot*), I, 205, 279
"Forbidden Beer, The" (*Zavetnoe pivo*), III, 617, 628
"Liar, The" (*Lgun*), II, 375, 399

Janin, Jules (1804–1874), French author, *Barnave*, II, 537, 578
Dead Ass and the Guillotined Woman, The, II, 409, 461
Jesus Christ, I, 64, 88, 91, 96, 99, 102, 106, 109, 128, 137, 141, 146, 147, 152, 195, 197, 203, 209, 214; II, 332, 355, 498, 501, 502, 539, 556, 561, 562; III, 606, 613, 617, 618, 643, 644, 650, 651, 655, 670, 672, 675, 697, 766, 779–80
Jobard, Alphonse (1793—after 1845), III, 788
"On the Convalescence of Lucullus," by ASP, tr. into French, III, 755–56, 788
Letter to, III, 755–56
Journal de Francfort, III, 680
Julia, exiled granddaughter of Augustus Caesar, I, 83, 120
Julius Caesar, Roman general and ruler, III, 771
Juvenal, Roman poet-satirist, I, 62

Kachenovsky, Mikhail Trofimovich (1775–1842), journalist and professor of history, I, 89, 91, 97, 108, 122, 129, 159, 162, 177, 187, 206, 219, 222, 280, 284; II, 375, 394, 399, 427, 560, 586; III, 736
Kalashnikov, Ivan Timofeevich (1797–1863), minor author, II, 589
Daughter of the Merchant Zholobov, The (*Doč' kupca Žolobova*), II, 568, 589
Kamchatka Girl, The (*Kamčadalka*), II, 567, 568, 589
Letter to, II, 567–68
Kalashnikov, Mikhail Ivanovich (ca. 1768–1858), Pushkins' serf, I, 43, 187, 188, 189, 192, 272, 275, 318; III, 621, 629, 670–71, 689, 773, 794
Kalashnikov, Vasily Mikhaylovich, ASP's servant, son of M. I., II, 526, 539, 540, 574, 579; III, 773, 794
Kalashnikova, Malania, nee Semenova (b. ca. 1812), wife of V. M., II, 540, 579
Kalashnikova, Olga Mikhaylovna, daughter of M. I., I, 308–9, 310, 318; III, 773, 794
Kalaydovich, Konstantin Fedorovich (1792–1832), journalist, II, 348, 389
Kalmuck, servant of N. V. Vsevolozhsky, I, 87, 101, 121, 126
Kankrin, Egor Frantsevich (1774–1845), Minister of Finance, II, 410, 419–20, 424, 430, 462, 464, 466; III, 722, 726, 740, 821, 823
Letters to, III, 721–22, 728–29, 803–4, 808
Kankrina, Ekaterina Zakharovna (1796–1879), wife of E. F., III, 722, 740
Kantakuzen, Georgy Matveevich (d. 1857), I, 80, 119
Karamzin, Alexander Nikolaevich (1815–1888), son of N. M., III, 763, 791
Karamzin, Andrey Nikolaevich (1814–1854), son of N. M., III, 704, 705
Karamzin, Nikolay Mikhaylovich (1766–1826), author and historian, I, 38, 44, 45, 48, 67, 85, 106, 109, 146, 154, 171, 188, 193, 196, 218, 225, 254, 259, 264, 285, 286, 294, 303, 306, 313, 319; II, 333, 344, 345, 388, 434, 455, 484, 509; III, 704, 763, 824
History of the Russian State, The (*Istorija Gosudarstva Rossijskogo*), I, 33, 85, 120, 192–93, 225, 247, 255, 262, 275, 286, 292, 294, 295, 313; II, 365, 382, 395, 398, 400, 484, 505

Karamzin, Nikolay Mikhaylovich, contd.
Family of, I, 64, 70, 85, 96, 182, 191, 196, 240, 311; II, 434; III, 613, 615, 650, 654, 727
Karamzin, Nikolay Nikolaevich (1818-1833), son of N. M., III, 623
Karamzina, Ekaterina Andreevna (1780-1851), wife of N. M., I, 85, 146, 165, 171, 196, 314; II, 379, 411, 492, 527, 574; III, 617, 623, 627, 629, 644, 645, 655, 827
Karamzina, Ekaterina Nikolaevna. *See* Meshcherskaya, Ekaterina Nikolaevna
Karamzina, Elizaveta Nikolaevna (1821-1891), daughter of N. M., II, 469
Karamzina, Sofia Nikolaevna (1802-1856), daugher of N. M., II, 434, 469, 492, 507; III, 613-14, 618, 647, 650, 655, 725
Karatygin, Vasily Andreevich (1802-1853), actor, I, 265, 297; III, 676, 690
Karatygina, Alexandra Mikhaylovna, nee Kolosova (1802-1880), actress, I, 190, 274, 304, 317; III, 676, 690
Karniolin-Pinsky, Matvey Mikhaylovich (1796-1866), I, 253, 294; II, 519
Karr, Alphonse (1808-1890), French author, II, 563
Under the Lindens, II, 563, 588
Kartsova, Sofia Vasilievna, II, 378, 400
Kassassi, Ivan Antonovich (d. 1837), II, 564, 588
Katenin, Pavel Alexandrovich (1792-1853), writer, I, 65, 70, 86, 94, 96, 101, 102, 111, 123, 124, 125, 129, 159, 210, 280, 281, 293, 296, 310, 317; II, 429, 452, 474; III, 736
Andromaque, by Racine, tr. of, I, 125, 253, 265, 266, 293, 296, 304
"Caucasus Mountains" (*Kavkazskie gory*), III, 705, 736
Cid, The, by Corneille, tr. of, I, 95, 124-25
Esther, by Racine, tr. of, I, 125
Gossip (*Spletni*), I, 95, 124
Letters to, I, 92, 94-95, 252-53, 265-66, 304; III, 705
Kavelin, Dmitry Alexandrovich (1788-1851), I, 63, 64, 69

Kaverin, Peter Pavlovich (1794-1855), I, 293
Letter to, II, 339
Kazantsev, Evgeny (1778-1871), bishop of Pskov, I, 262, 295
Kazarsky, Alexander Ivanovich (1797-1833), naval officer, II, 377, 399-400
Kaznacheev, Alexander Ivanovich (1788-1881), I, 144, 171, 242, 291
Letters to, 156-57, 157-58
Kaznacheeva, Varvara Dmitrievna (1793-1859), wife of A. I., I, 242, 291
Kern, Anna Petrovna, nee Poltoratskaya (1800-1879), wife of E. F., one of ASP's loves, I, 27, 42, 51, 194, 230, 231-32, 250-51, 260, 274, 275, 288, 289, 291, 292, 295, 297, 309, 318; II, 348, 351, 359, 389, 393; III, 601, 624, 683, 726, 741, 799
André, by George Sand, tr. of, III, 726, 741
Memoirs, III, 799
Letters to, I, 233-34, 242-43, 247-48, 248-50, 256-58, 268; II, 346; III, 782, 783
Kern, Ermolay Fedorovich (ca. 1770-1841), general, I, 233, 239, 240, 243, 247, 248, 249, 250, 260, 268, 289, 290, 292, 295, 309, 318
Khemnitser, Ivan Ivanovich (1754-1784), poet,
"Metaphysician, The" (*Metafizik*), II, 340, 386
Kheraskov, Mikhail Matveevich (1733-1807), poet, I, 155, 222
Rossiada, The, I, 60, 67
Khitrovo, Anastasia Nikolaevna (1764-1840), II, 459, 476, 482
Khitrovo, Elizaveta Mikhaylovna (1783-1839), friend of ASP, I, 31; II, 382, 388, 390, 401, 409, 438, 450, 460, 461, 463, 471, 482, 499, 504, 506, 508, 523, 538, 551-52, 572-73, 575, 576, 578, 581, 583, 584; III, 614, 627, 666, 686, 726, 782, 783, 799, 821
Letters to, II, 343, 350-51, 358, 372, 414, 414-15, 425, 446-47, 447-48, 455-56, 457-58, 481, 486-87, 488, 490-91, 492-93, 493, 529-30, 530, 537, 545, 563

Khlopusha. *See* Sokolov, A. T.
Khlyustin, Semen Semenovich (1810–1844), III, 662, 686, 738, 785, 786
Letters to, III, 710, 750–51
Khmelnitsky, Alexander Ivanovich, journalist, III, 776–77, 795
Khmelnitsky, Bogdan (ca. 1595–1657), Ukrainian hetman, I, 100
Khmelnitsky, Nikolay Ivanovich (1789–1845), dramatist, I, 101, 113, 126, 220, 285; II, 504
Irresolute One, The (*Nerešitel'nyj, ili sem' pjatnic na nedele*), I, 113, 130
Letter to, II, 480
Khomyakov, Alexey Stepanovich (1804–1860), poet, historian, and later Slavophile, II, 534, 577; III, 626, 762, 765, 767
Dimitry the Pretender (*Dimitrij samozvanec*), II, 534, 577
Ermak, II, 534, 577
Khomyakova, Ekaterina Mikhaylovna, nee Yazykova (1817–1852), wife of A. S., III, 762, 767, 790, 792
Khrapovitsky, Matvey Evgrafovich (1784–1847), II, 491, 492, 507
Khudobashev, Artemy Makarievich, II, 448, 473
Khvostov, Dmitry Ivanovich (1757–1835), poetaster, I, 100, 126, 142, 154, 174, 175, 199, 227, 251, 261; II, 360, 517, 522, 534, 570, 572, 584; III, 704, 736
"Epistle to N. N. on the Inundation of Petropolis . . ." (*Poslanie k N. N. o navodnenii Petropolja . . .*), I, 199, 277
"Nightingale in the Tavrida Garden, A," (*Solovej v Tavričeskom sadu*), II, 555, 584
"To A. A. Pushkin . . ." (*A. S. Puškinu . . .*), II, 534, 535, 555, 577, 584
"To Ivan Ivanovich Dmitriev" (*K Ivanu Ivanoviču Dmitrievu*), I, 142–43, 170
"Two Pigeons" (*Dva golubja*), I, 261, 295
Letter to, II, 555
Khvostova, Alexandra Petrovna (1765–1853), authoress, I, 227, 287

"Hearth and the Brooklet, The" (*Kamin i ručeek*), I, 227, 287
Kiprensky, Orest Adamovich (1783–1836), portrait artist, I, 145, 171
"Letter from Rome" (*Pis'mo iz Rima*), I, 145, 171
Pushkin, portait of, II, 460, 475, 476
Kireev, hussar, III, 768, 792
Kireevsky, Ivan Vasilievich (1806–1856), writer, II, 450, 474, 531, 534, 547, 576, 582, 583; III, 604, 626
"Survey of Russian Literature for 1831" (*Obozrenie russkoj literatury za 1831 g.*), II, 546, 581
Letters to, II, 545–46, 553–54
Kireevsky, Peter Vasilievich (1808–1856), collector of folk songs, II, 553, 583; III, 790
Kirillov, Ivan Kirillovich (1689–1737), historian, II, 509
All-Russian State's Flourishing Condition, Into Which Peter the Great. . . Initiated, Led, and Left It, The (*Cvetuščee sostojanie Vserosijskogo gosudarstva, v kakovoe načal, privel i ostavil neizrečennymi trudami Petr Velikij*), II, 497, 509, 519
Kiselev, Nikolay Dmitrievich (1802–1869), diplomat, II, 356, 357, 379, 392
Kiselev, Pavel Dmitrievich (1788–1872), general, I, 98, 125, 170; II, 336
Kiselev, Sergey Dmitrievich (d. 1851), II, 397
Letter to, II, 370
Kiseleva, Sofia Stanislavovna, wife of P. D., I, 141, 170, 172; II, 336
Kister, Vasily Ivanovich, II, 582
Letter to, II, 549–50
Kitaeva, Anna, house owner, II, 487
Klinder, Alexander Julius, painter, III, 790
Klyucharev, Pavel Stepanovich, I, 318
Knorring, Karl von,
Boris Godunov, by ASP, tr. into German, II, 452, 474
Knörzer, Heinrich Adam (Russ.: Andrey Khristianovich, 1789–1853), historian, II, 581; III, 749
Knyazhnin, Yakov Borisovich (1742–1791), dramatist, I, 222, 285

Knyazhnina, Varvara Alexandrovna (1774–1842), III, 730, 742
Kochetova, Ekaterina Nikolaevna (d. 1867), II, 538, 578
Kochubey, Maria Vasilievna (1779–1844), wife of V. P., III, 658, 676–77, 685, 690
Kochubey, Viktor Pavlovich (1768–1834), statesman, III, 643, 657, 658, 659, 676, 681, 685
Kolosova, Alexandra Mikhaylovna. See Karatygina, Alexandra M.
Koltsov, Alexey Vasilievich (1809–1842), poet, III, 764, 791
"Harvest, The" (*Urožaj*), III, 791
Konissky, Georgy (1717–1795), Belorussian archbishop,
Collected Works (*Sobranie sočinenij*), III, 760, 789
Konshin, Nikolay Mikhaylovich (1793–1859), minor poet, I, 202, 247, 278; II, 571; III, 823
Letters to, II, 518–19; III, 811
Konversations-Lexikon, III, 635, 656, 678, 679
Kopp, restaurateur, II, 379, 400
Koran, The, I, 162, 167, 187, 191, 274, 282. *See also* ASP: "Imitations of the Koran"
Korf, Modest Alexandrovich (1800–1876), Lyceum classmate of ASP, I, 87, 121; II, 590; III, 679, 720, 796
Letters to, II, 569, 778–79
Kornilovich, Alexander Osipovich (ca. 1795–1834), journalist and historian, I, 150, 151, 173, 174, 275, 317
Korotky, Dmitry Vasilievich, II, 519, 563, 571, 587
Korsakov, Peter Alexandrovich (1790–1844), censor, III, 795, 799
Letters to, III, 777–78, 782
Kosichkin, Feofilakt. *See* Pushkin, Alexander Sergeevich
Kotzebue, August Friedrich Ferdinand von (1761–1819), German playwright, I, 265, 296
Death of Rolla, The, I, 99, 126
Kozlov, Ivan Ivanovich (1779–1840), poet and translator, I, 193, 219, 230, 275, 284, 288

Monk, The (*Černec*), I, 219, 226, 284, 287
"To My Friend V. A. Zhukovsky" (*K drugu V. A. Žukovskomu*), I, 219, 284
"Venetian Night" (*Venecianskaja noč'*), I, 230, 231, 289
Kozlov, Nikita Timofeevich, servant of ASP, II, 421, 465, 541, 542, 580
Kozlov, Vasily Ivanovich (1792–1825), writer, I, 96, 125, 136, 149, 150
Kozlovsky, Peter Borisovich (1783–1840), writer and diplomat, III, 754, 781, 787
"Review of the Paris Mathematical Annual for 1836" (*Razbor Parižskogo Matematičeskogo ežegodnika na 1836 g.*), III, 754, 787
Kraevskaya, unidentified, III, 614, 627
Kraevsky, Andrey Alexandrovich (1810–1889), journalist, III, 739, 793, 824
Letters to, III, 715, 771
Krasovsky, Alexander Ivanovich (1780–1857), censor, I, 129, 160, 182, 198, 217, 227; II, 377; III, 655, 705, 777
Kridner, painter, III, 761
Krivtsov, Nikolay Ivanovich (1791–1843), diplomat, I, 70, 147, 171; II, 476
Letters to, I, 64, 144; II, 458–59
Kruglikova, Sofia Grigorievna, nee Chernysheva (1799–1847), III, 603, 624
Krukowiecki, Jan (1770–1850), Polish general, II, 572
Krupenskaya, Ekaterina Khristoforovna, wife of M. E., I, 182
Krupensky, Matvey Egorovich, I, 182, 271
Krylov, Alexander Lukich (1798–1853), censor, III, 758, 763, 788
Letter to, III, 755
Krylov, Ivan Andreevich (1768–1844), fabulist, I, 152, 174, 197, 222, 225, 261, 262, 286, 295; II, 355, 567
"Council of Mice, The" (*Sovet myšej*), I, 261, 295
"Demians' Fish Chowder" (*Dem'janova uxa*), I, 79, 91, 118, 123, 225, 286
"Eagle and the Bee, The" (*Orel i pčela*), II, 438, 470

Krylov, Ivan Andreevich, contd.
  Fables, I, 295
  "Frogs Seeking a King" (*Ljaguški, prosjaštie carja*, from La Fontaine), II, 447, 472
  "Little Raven, The" (*Voronenok*), I, 141, 170, 267, 297
  "Miller, The" (*Mel'nik*), I, 225, 286
Krylova, Maria Mikhaylovna, dancer, I, 64, 65, 70
Kukolnik, Nestor Vasilievich (1809–1868), poet, III, 647, 682
Kusovnikov, Aleksey Mikhaylovich (d. 1853), colonel, II, 368, 396
Kutuzov. *See* Golenishchev-Kutuzov, M. I.
Kyukhelbeker, Vilgelm Karlovich (1797–1846), poet, critic, Decembrist, I, 33, 62, 68, 77, 79, 82, 94, 96, 99, 108, 113, 118, 119, 120, 124, 128, 143, 147, 151, 152, 155, 161, 165, 172, 173, 178, 190, 192, 198, 213, 219, 220, 240, 247, 265, 274, 282, 285, 290, 292, 297, 305, 317; II, 551, 583; III, 653, 684, 732, 743, 790
  Archilochus (*Arxilox*), II, 503, 511
  Argives, The (*Arigvjane*), II, 503, 511
  "Epistle to Ermolov" (*Poslanie k Ermolovu*), I, 99, 213, 282
  "God's Voice Was to Me . . ." (*Glagol Gospoden' byl ko mne*), I, 99, 126
  Izhorsky (*Ižorskij*), II, 503, 511
  Shakespeare's Spirits (*Sekspirovy duxi*), I, 265, 266, 267, 296, 297
  "To Pushkin" (*K Puškinu*), I, 113, 130
  Letters to, I, 156, 266–67
Kyukhelbeker, Yulia Karlovna, sister of V. K., II, 551, 583
Kyukhlya. *See* Kyukhelbeker, V. K.

Laclos, Choderlos de (1741–1803), French author,
  Les Liaisons dangereuses, II, 359, 393
Ladies' Journal, The (*Damskij žurnal*), I, 219; II, 462
Lafayette, Marie Joseph, Marquis de (1757–1834), French statesman and officer, II, 425, 467
La Fontaine, Jean de (1621–1695), French fabulist, I, 197, 222

"Frogs Seeking a King." *See* Krylov, Ivan A.
"Old Man and the Three Young Men, The," I, 192, 274
Lagrené, Théodore-Marie de (1800–1862), French diplomat, II, 359, 392
La Harpe, Jean François (1739–1803), French poet,
  Philoctète, I, 237, 290, 367
Lamartine, Alphonse Marie Louis de (1790–1869), French poet and politician, I, 149, 164, 265, 288; II, 556
  Dernier chant du pèlerinage d'Harold, Le, I, 219, 285
  L'Homme, I, 229, 288
  Napoléon, I, 164
  Nouvelles méditations poétiques, I, 177
  Poèt mourant, Le, I, 149, 164, 173
Lambert, Karl Osipovich (1772–1843), general, II, 527, 574
Lambert, Uliana Mikhaylovna (b. 1791), wife of K. O., II, 527, 529, 574, 575
Lamennais, Félicité de (1782–1854), French publicist and theologian, II, 450, 473, 481, 504
Langer, Valerian Platonovich, artist, III, 728, 742
Langeron, Andrault de (Alexander Fedorovich) (1763–1831), French general in Russian service, I, 138, 169; II, 415
Lanskoy, Peter Petrovich (1799–1877), second husband of Natalia Nikolaevna Pushkina, III, 826
"Large Pointed Cap," a *jurodivyj*, I, 247, 254, 292
Laval, Alexandra Grigorievna,
  "To the Calumniators of Russia," by ASP, tr. of, III, 821
Lay of the Host of Igor, The (*Slovo o polku Igoreve*), II, 586; III, 736
Lazhechnikov, Ivan Ivanovich (1792–1869), novelist, III, 680, 743, 811, 823
  House of Ice, The (*Ledjanoj dom*), III, 640, 680, 693, 731, 733, 743
  Last Novik, The (*Poslednij novik*), III, 640, 680, 693, 731, 733
  Letters to, III, 639–40, 693, 730–31
Lebedev, Fedor Fedotovich, priest, III, 633–34, 678

Le Brun, Ponce Denis (1729–1807), French poet, I, 187, 272; II, 455, 475
Legouvé (or Le Gouvé), Gabriel Marie (1764–1812), French author, I, 94, 124
Lelewel, Joachim (1786–1861), Polish historian and politician, III, 639, 680
Lémontey, Pierre Edouard (1762–1826), French historian, I, 164, 177, 263
  Essai sur l'Etablissement monarchique de Louis XIV . . ., I, 164, 177
Lenclos, Ninon de (1620–1705), French courtesan, II, 562, 587; III, 617, 619
Leonidas the Spartan, I, 80, 119, 167
Lerch, II, 377, 400
Lermontov, Mikhail Yurevich (1814–1841), poet, III, 792
Letters to Unidentified Women, I, 115, 144–45
Library for Reading, A (*Biblioteka dlja čtenija*), I, 173; II, 590; III, 621, 628, 629, 679, 709, 736, 748
Life of Emelka Pugachev, The (*Ložnyj Petr III, ili žizn', xarakter i zlodejanija buntovščika Emel'ki Pugačeva*), I, 187, 272
Liprandi, Ivan Petrovich (1790–1880), army officer, I, 89, 122, 123, 140; II, 335, 385, 448
Literary Gazette (*Literaturnaja gazeta*), periodical, I, 44; II, 371, 372, 374, 377, 382, 397, 398, 399, 410, 434, 436, 446, 447–48, 453, 462, 468, 472, 473, 476, 482, 489, 508, 520, 522, 571; III, 814
Literary Leaves (*Literaturnye listki*), journal, I, 130, 154, 172, 173, 201, 277
Literary News (*Novosti literatury*), I, 174, 267, 279, 282, 297
Litta, Yuly Pompeevich (1763–1839), Head Chamberlain, II, 537, 578; III, 640, 662, 681
Liza, Naked. *See* Khitrovo, Elizaveta Mikhaylovna
Ljubomudry (Lovers of Wisdom), literary group, I, 33; II, 386
Lobanov, Mikhail Evstafievich (1787–1846), writer, I, 150, 173; III, 706, 736
  Phèdre, by Racine, tr. of, I, 150, 173

Lobanov-Rostovsky, Alexander Yakovlevich (1788–1866), Russian statesman and bibliophile, I, 100, 102, 126
Lobanova-Rostovskaya, Elizaveta Petrovna (d. 1854), II, 332, 384
Lomonosov, Mikhail Vasilievich (1711–1765), scientist and man of letters, I, 154, 159, 163, 174, 177, 222, 285; II, 382, 567; III, 657, 685
  "Ode IX: Taken from Job" (*Oda 9-aja: Vybrannaja iz Iova*), I, 163, 177
Lomonosov, Sergey Grigorievich (1799–1857), I, 61, 63, 68
Louis XIV (1638–1715), King of France (1643–1715), I, 223, 286
Louis XVIII (1755–1824), King of France (1814–15, 1815–24), III, 724
Louis Philippe (1773–1850), King of France (1830–1848), I, 38; II, 425, 431, 447, 456, 467, 468, 472, 475, 476; III, 619, 788
Lovelace. *See* Richardson, S.: *Clarissa*
Lubomirska, Mme., II, 366, 395
Luchich, Filipp Lukianovich, I, 241, 291
Lucretius, Roman poet, I, 221
Lützerode, Karl Theodore, Saxony Ambassador, III, 698, 734
Lvov, Alexey Ivanovich, III, 811, 823
Lvov, Vladimir Vladimirovich (1804–1856), III, 814, 825
Lyrical Album for 1829 (*Liričeskij al'bom na 1829 g.*), II, 393
Lyutsenko, Efim Petrovich (1776–1854), writer, III, 740
  Pervonte oder die Wünsche, by Wieland, tr. as *Vastola ili želanija* . . ., III, 720, 740, 785, 786
  Letter to, III, 720

Macpherson, James (1736–1796), Scots author,
  Fingal, I, 128
Maecenas, I, 159, 286
Magenis, Arthur (1801–1867), English diplomat, III, 827
Magnitsky, Mikhail Leontievich (1778–1855), I, 227, 287
Maiguine, Mme., I, 140, 169
  Letter to, I, 144–45

Maison, Joseph (1771-1840), French diplomat, III, 674, 689-90
Maistre, Joseph de (1754-1821), French writer,
Du pape, III, 700, 735
Makary (1482-1563), Metropolitan of Moscow (1542-1563), I, 292
Maksutov, Prince, II, 368, 397
Malinovskaya, Anna Petrovna (1770-1847), wife of A. F., II, 421, 465, 559, 585
Malinovskaya, Ekaterina Alexeevna (1811-1872), II, 421, 465, 559, 585
Malinovsky, Alexey Fedorovich (1762-1840), government official, II, 559, 585; III, 720, 740, 765, 791
Malinovsky, Ivan Vasilievich (1795-1873), I, 197, 276
Mansur (d. 1794), Circassian warrior, I, 70
Mansurov, Pavel Borisovich (1795-1880's), I, 70, 87, 101
Letter to, I, 64-65
Manzoni, Alessandro (1785-1873), Italian author, II, 537, 578
Betrothed, The (*I Promessi sposi*), II, 578
Marcus Aurelius, II, 500
Maria Fedorovna, Empress (1759-1828), wife of Paul I, I, 182, 271
Maria Ivanova, ASP's Moscow housekeeper, II, 487, 488, 506
Marlinsky. See Bestuzhev, A. A.
Martynov, Ivan Ivanovich (1771-1833), educational official, I, 67
Letter to, I, 59
Masons, I, 302, 316
Matrena Sergeevna, gypsy, II, 495
Matthisson, Freidrich von (1761-1831), German poet, I, 94, 124
Maturin, Charles Robert (1782-1824), Irish writer,
Melmoth the Wanderer, I, 139, 169
Matyushkin, Fedor Fedorovich (1799-1872), I, 155, 174, 197
Maximovich, Mikhail Alexandrovich (1804-1873), II, 450, 453, 473, 475; III, 640
Maykov, Vasily Ivanovich (1728-1778), poet, I, 114, 130; II, 453
Agriopa, II, 453, 474

Elisey, or Angry Bacchus (*Elisej, ili razdražennyj Vakx*), I, 114, 130
Medwin, Thomas (1788-1869), English author,
Conversations of Lord Byron, I, 188, 202, 206, 273
Mefody, bishop of Pskov, III, 724
Memoirs of the Fatherland (*Otečestvennye zapiski*), III, 739, 787
Menologion, The (*Čet'i Minei*), I, 247, 292; II, 485
Menshikov, Alexander Sergeevich (1787-1849), naval officer, III, 777, 795
Merder, Karl Karlovich (1788-1834), tutor of future Alexander II, III, 644, 681
Merzlyakov, Alexey Fedorovich (1778-1830), poet, critic, professor, I, 60, 67, 68, 222; II, 349, 483
Meshcherskaya, Ekaterina Nikolaevna (1806-1867), wife of P. I., daughter of N. M. Karamzin, II, 382, 401, 434, 469, 538, 578, 579; III, 613, 615, 618, 651, 683, 725, 727
Meshchersky, Alexander Alexeevich (b. 1807), II, 375, 399
Meshchersky, Peter Ivanovich (1802-1876), II, 538, 578, 579; III, 613, 683, 725, 727
Meshchersky, Platon Alexeevich (1805-1889), II, 375, 399
Meshchersky, Platon Stepanovich (1713-1799), III, 628
Meshcherskys. See Meshcherskaya, Ekaterina N., and Meshchersky, P. I.
Messalla, I, 286
Messenger, The (*Vestnik*), Lyceum journal, I, 126
Messenger, The Russian. See: *Russian Messenger, The*
Messenger of Europe, The (*Vestnik Evropy*), journal, I, 48, 122, 138, 155, 159, 163, 168, 219, 222, 280; II, 399, 464
Michael I (1596-1645), Tsar of Russia (1613-1645), II, 366, 396; III, 797
Michael (Mikhail Pavlovich), Grand Duke (1798-1840), I, 36, 171, 305; II, 585; III, 684, 798
Mickiewicz, Adam (1798-1855), Polish poet, II, 447, 456, 472

Mieris, Franz van (1635-1681), Dutch painter, II, 546, 581
Mignet, François Auguste (1796-1884), French historian, II, 493
  History of the French Revolution from 1789 to 1814, II, 493, 508
Mikhelson, Ivan Ivanovich (1740-1807), general, III, 819, 827
Miller, unidentified man, II, 368
Miller, Gerard Friedrich (1705-1783), historian, II, 382, 401
Miller, Pavel Ivanovich (1813-1885), II, 573
  Letters to, II, 523, 528
Milman, Henry Hart (1791-1868), English author, III, 825
Milonov, Mikhail Vasilievich (1792-1821), poet, I, 121, 159, 258, 295; II, 357, 392
  Creation of the World, The (Sotvorenie mira), I, 85, 121
Miloradovich, Mikhail Andreevich (1771-1825), I, 311, 319
Miltiades, Athenian general, I, 161
Milton, John (1608-1674), English poet, I, 221, 276
Minin, Kuzma (d. 1616), II, 366, 396
Mirabeau, Honoré Gabriel Riqueti, Comte de (1749-1791), French liberal, I, 63, 69, 223, 286
Mirabeau, Victor Riqueti, Marquis de (1715-1789), French soldier and economist, I, 63, 69
Mithradates VI Eupator, the Great, King of Pontus and Bosporus, I, 76, 117, 268
Mnemosyne (Mnemozina), almanac, I, 65, 147, 172, 178, 274
Mniszek, Marina (d. 1614). *See* ASP: *Boris Godunov*
Mohammed (570-632), I, 213, 282
Molchanov, Alexander Petrovich (1811-1828), son of P. S., I, 77, 117
Molchanov, Nikolay Nikolaevich (b. 1802), I, 77, 117
Molchanov, Peter Stepanovich (1770-1831), II, 502, 510, 516
Molière, *pseud.* of Jean Baptiste Poquelin (1622-1673), French dramatist, I, 150, 223, 286

  Amphytrion, III, 772, 794
  Bourgeois gentilhomme, Le, II, 536, 578; III, 640, 681
  Tartuffe, I, 223, 286
Montaigne, Michel de (1533-1592), French writer,
  Essays, III, 724, 741
Montholon, Charles Tristan de (1783-1853), French general, I, 202
  Memoirs, I, 278
Moore, Thomas (1779-1852), Irish poet, I, 89, 122, 124, 213, 221, 263, 296; II, 368
  Lalla Rookh, I, 89, 122, 124, 169, 263. *See also* Zhukovsky, V. A.
Mordvinov, Alexander Nikolaevich (1782-1869), subordinate of Benkendorf, III, 623, 699, 768, 790
  Letters to, III, 599-600, 653, 749-50, 760
Mordvinov, Nikolay Semenovich (1754-1845), admiral and statesman, I, 155, 174
Moreau de Brasey, Jean, brigadier,
  Memoirs, III, 588
Mornay, "traveler," II, 523, 575
Mortemart, Casimir Louis de Rouchechouart, Duc de (1787-1875), II, 458, 476
Moschus, ancient Greek poet, I, 205, 279
Moscow Messenger, The (Moskovskij vestnik), journal, II, 332, 333, 338, 340, 344, 345, 346, 351, 354, 355, 384, 385, 386, 388, 389, 390, 391, 399, 464; III, 737-8
Moscow Observer, The (Mosvkoskij nabljudatel'), III, 709, 728, 737, 739, 755, 762, 789, 790, 793
Moscow Record, The (Moskovskie vedomosti), II, 437, 470, 471; III, 679, 794
Moscow Telegraph, The (Moskovskij telegraf), journal, I, 198, 199, 203, 212, 225, 227, 228, 238, 277, 279, 280, 282, 287, 288, 290, 292, 295, 296, 319; II, 338, 345, 346, 355, 363, 384, 389, 391, 399, 401, 449, 450, 473, 556, 580, 584, 589; III, 651, 683-84
Moscow University Society of Lovers of Russian Literature, II, 381, 401; III, 638, 679
Moses, I, 139; II, 500, 527. *See also* Bible

Mourouzi, Prince, I, 144, 171
Moyer, Ivan Filippovich (1786–1858), surgeon, I, 236, 241, 252, 254, 259, 260, 289, 290, 293
 Letter to, I, 235
Mstislav (d. 1036), founder of principality of Tmutarakan, I, 204, 279
Mukhanov, Alexander Alexeevich (1800–1834), I, 255, 294
Mukhanov, Peter Alexandrovich (1799–1854), I, 203, 205, 278, 294
Mukhanov, Vladimir Alexeevich (1805–1876), II, 560, 586
Muraviev, Andrey Nikolaevich (1806–1874), writer, III, 603, 624
Muraviev, Nikolay Nazarievich (1775–1845), II, 374, 398
 Certain of the Amusements of Relaxation, Since 1805 (Nekotorye iz zabav otdoxnovenija, s 1805), II, 399
Muraviev-Apostol, Ivan Matveevich (1768–1851), I, 147, 170, 268, 269, 270; II, 505
 Journey over the Tavrida (Putešestvie po Tavride), I, 141, 147, 170, 187, 268, 269, 298
Musin-Pushkin, Fedor Matveevich, II, 559, 560, 586
Musin-Pushkin, Vladimir Alexeevich (1798–1854), II, 561, 586
Musina-Pushkina, Emilia Karlovna, nee Shernval (1810–1846), wife of V. A., II, 561, 586; III, 722, 740
Musin-Pushkin-Bryus, Vasily Valentinovich (1773–1836), I, 101, 126
Myasoedov, Pavel Nikolaevich (1799–1868), III, 779, 796

Nadezhdin, Nikolay Ivanovich (1804–1856), journalist and critic (*pseud.* Nikodim Nadoumko), II, 399, 417, 418, 451, 464, 465, 470, 474, 525, 553, 554–55, 573, 584; III, 759, 796, 797
Nakhimov, Akim Nikolaevich (1783–1815), poetaster, I, 151, 173
Napoleon I Bonaparte (1769–1821), Emperor of the French (1805–1815), I, 75, 116, 117, 146, 171, 202, 227, 229, 278, 288, 291; II, 456, 470, 508, 567, 575; III, 739, 770, 785, 793, 796, 798, 827
Naryshkin, Alexander Lvovich (1760–1826), diplomat, I, 82, 119
Naryshkin, Dmitry Lvovich (1764–1838), III, 646, 652, 682, 821
Naryshkin, Kirill Alexandrovich (1786–1838), III, 640, 647, 681, 683
Naryshin, Lev Alexandrovich (1785–1846), I, 153, 174
Nashchokin, Pavel Pavlovich, son of P. V., II, 531, 563, 576, 587; III, 622, 630
Nashchokin, Pavel Voinovich (1800–1854), friend of ASP, 1, 31, 187, 272; II, 326, 452, 455, 459, 463, 473, 506, 508, 526, 537, 538, 539, 540, 541, 557, 558, 559, 561, 570, 571, 574, 576, 578, 580, 581, 584, 585, 586, 587, 588; III, 603, 604, 605, 606, 607, 610, 614, 629, 630, 679, 735, 761, 765, 767, 768, 785, 786, 790, 793
 Memoirs, III, 769, 793
 Letters to, II, 449, 487, 488–89, 491, 493–94, 494–95, 515–16, 517, 519–20, 525–26, 530–31, 533, 543–44, 562–63, 565–66; III, 600, 620–21, 622, 636–37, 701–2, 702, 748–49, 769
Nashchokin, Vasily Voinovich (b. 1796), brother of P. V., II, 543, 581; III, 636, 679,
Nashchokina, Ekaterina Pavlovna, III, 701, 735
Nashchokina, Vera Alexandrovna, nee Narskaya (d. 1900), wife of P. V., III, 629, 630, 636, 679, 701, 702, 735, 761, 769
Natalia, Grand Duchess (Natalia Alexeevna), I, 293
 Comedy About St. Catherine (Komedija o sv. Ekaterine), I, 253, 293
Nazimov, Gavriill Petrovich (1794–1850), I, 312, 319
Nebolsin, Nikolay Andreevich (1785–1846), civil governor of Moscow, II, 562, 587
Nechaev, Stepan Dmitrievich (1792–1860), III, 678
 Letter to, III, 633–34

Neelov, Sergey Alexeevich (1778–1852), minor poet, I, 226, 287
Nesselrode, Karl Vasilievich (1780–1862), statesman, I, 104, 127
Neva Almanac, The (*Nevskij almanax*), for *1825*, I, 205, 213, 279, 282
Neva Spectator, The (*Nevskij zritel'*), journal, I, 71, 118
Nicene Creed, I, 192, 226, 287; II, 564, 588
Nicholas I (1796–1855), Emperor (Tsar) of Russia (1825–1855), I, 29, 30, 33, 35, 36, 37, 38, 46, 47, 51, 52, 53, 54, 55, 118, 130, 267, 271, 276, 297, 301, 302, 303, 305, 307, 313, 316, 317, 320; II, 329, 333, 334, 337, 338, 341, 345, 347, 349, 353, 355, 356, 362, 369, 378, 379, 380, 383, 384, 385, 386, 387, 389, 391, 394, 397, 400, 406–7, 411–12, 413, 414, 415, 418, 419–20, 422, 429, 438, 441, 446, 447, 454, 456, 458, 461, 462, 463, 466, 470, 471, 480, 490, 494, 497, 499, 509, 510, 515, 517, 518, 520, 522, 526, 532, 533, 538, 543, 544, 546, 548, 549, 551, 553, 554, 557, 566, 570, 573, 576, 578, 579, 581, 582, 583, 584, 589; III, 599, 615, 621, 623, 624, 625, 629, 634, 637, 640, 642, 643, 651, 660, 666, 667, 668, 670, 672, 678, 683, 684, 685, 686, 687, 688, 689, 695, 699, 700, 703, 711, 712, 713, 714, 716, 717, 718, 719, 720, 721, 724, 729, 732, 735, 738, 739, 740, 742, 747, 763, 774, 780, 785, 788, 791, 794, 798, 803, 809, 815, 821, 822, 823, 825
  Letter to, I, 312–13
Nicholas, Grand Duke (1831–1891), son of Nicholas I, II, 511, 517
Nicole, Abbé, II, 432, 469
Nikita, Delvig's servant, I, 224, 232, 286
Nikitenko, Alexander Vasilievich (1805–1877), censor, III, 728, 742
Nordin, Gustav (1799–1867), Swedish diplomat, III, 737
  Letter to, III, 707
Norov, Avraam Sergeevich (1795–1869), minor poet, III, 767, 792
Northern Archive, The (*Severnyj arxiv*), journal, I, 149, 172
Northern Bee, The (*Severnaja pčela*), I, 172, 204, 206, 228, 264, 279, 288, 290, 296; II, 351, 355, 390, 391, 394, 411, 413, 450, 457, 469, 473, 476, 542, 556, 578; III, 679, 711, 712, 823
Northern Flowers (*Severnye cvety*), almanac, for *1825*, I, 160, 173, 176, 189, 197, 198, 202, 273, 274, 275, 276, 278, 279
  for *1826*, I, 217, 295, 298, 305, 318
  for *1827*, II, 340, 387
  for *1828*, II, 344, 349, 388
  for *1829*, II, 360, 363, 393, 394
  for *1830*, II, 398
  for *1831*, II, 450, 451–52, 470, 473, 474
  for *1832*, II, 456, 473, 475, 482, 501, 503, 504, 521, 525, 531, 533, 534, 535, 542, 545, 546, 548, 577, 578, 581, 582
  for *1833* (proposed), III, 601, 624
Northern Mercury, The (*Severnyj Merkurij*), journal, II, 522, 572
Northern Observer, The (*Severnyj nabljudatel'*), III, 795
Novikov, Nikolay Ivanovich (1744–1818), man of letters, III, 736
Novomlensky, student, III, 647, 683
Novosiltsev, Peter Petrovich (1797–1869), II, 493, 508

Ober, Lavrenty Nikolaevich (1802–1884), II, 557, 585
"Observers." Contributors to *Moscow Observer, The*, q.v.
Ochkin, Amply Nikolaevich (1791–1865), III, 814, 825
Odoevsky, Vladimir Fedorovich (1803–1869), writer and associate of ASP, I, 172, 178; II, 389; III, 628, 649, 678, 679, 764, 768, 787, 789, 824, 825
  "Conversation of the Discontented Ones" (*Razgovor nedovol'nyx*), III, 758, 789
  "Crossing, The," Indian tale, tr. of, II, 345, 389
  "How Novels Are Written Among Us" (*Kak pišutsja u nas romany*), III, 757, 789
  "Of Enmity Toward Enlightment, as Observed in Most Recent Literature" (*O vražde k prosveščeniju, zamečaemoj v novejšej literature*), III, 757, 789

INDEX 855

Odoevsky, Vladimir Fedorovich, contd.
"Princess Zizi" (*Knjaginja Zizi*), III, 757, 787, 813
"Segeliel" (*Segeliel*), III, 757, 789
"Sylphide, The" (*Sil'fida*), III, 813
Letters to, III, 618, 635, 711, 754, 757–58, 782, 808–9, 812, 813, 813–14, 814
Ogarev, Nikolay Alexandrovich (1811–1867), III, 615, 628
Ogon-Doganovsky, Vasily Semenovich (1776–1838), nobleman and gambler, II, 465, 494, 508, 516, 517, 525, 530, 533, 538, 574, 576, 579, 580
Letter to, II, 420–21
Okhotnikov, Konstantin Alexeevich I, 111, 129
Okulov, Matvey Alexeevich (1793–1853), brother-in-law of P. V. Nashchokin, III, 764, 791
Okulova, Elizaveta Alexeevna. See Diakova, Elizaveta Alexeevna, nee Okulova
Okulova, Varvara Alexeevna (1802–1879), sister-in-law of P. V. Nashchokin, II, 599, 585; III, 762, 790
Oldekop, Evstafy Ivanovich (d. 1845), book pirate, I, 166, 178, 181, 191, 198, 214, 215, 271, 283; II, 343, 347, 349; III, 823
Oleg (d. ca. 912), Prince of Kiev (882–ca. 912), I, 106, 221, 278; III, 780, 798
Olenin, Alexey Alexeevich (1798–1855), son of A. N., II, 357, 392
Olenin, Alexey Nikolaevich (1763–1843), president of Academy of Arts, I, 84, 118, 120, 233, 289; II, 392
Olga Andreevna, gypsy, II, 487, 488, 491, 495, 506, 508, 531, 544, 557, 566, 570, 576, 584, 587; III, 620, 621, 629, 630, 679, 701, 735, 785
Olivio (Oliv'e), Alexander Karlovich, III, 626, 663, 664, 673, 687, 689
Olympios, Yorghakis (1772–1821), Greek revolutionary, I, 111, 129
Opochinin, Konstantin Fedorovich (1808–1848), II, 530, 576
Orlov, Alexander Anfimovich (ca. 1790–1840), man of letters, II, 534, 573, 577, 580
Letter to, II, 542–43

Orlov, Alexey Fedorovich (1786–1861), I, 63, 69; II, 520
Orlov, Grigory Grigorievich (1734–1783), favorite of Catherine II, II, 586
Orlov, Grigory Vladimirovich (1777–1826), I, 262, 295, 296
Orlov, Mikhail Fedorovich (1788–1842), general, member of Arzamas, I, 77, 83, 85, 90, 104, 106, 112, 116, 117, 122, 129, 135, 271, 302, 316; II, 398; III, 605, 762, 765, 781
Orlova, Ekaterina Nikolaevna (1797–1885), wife of M. F., daughter of General N. N. Raevsky, I, 77, 85, 116, 120, 172, 254, 261, 294
Orlova-Chesmenskaya, Anna Alexeevna (1785–1848), II, 329, 383
Orlovsky, Alexander Osipovich (1777–1832), artist, I, 78, 118
Osipov, Nikolay Petrovich (1751–1799), writer, I, 114, 130
Osipova, Alexandra Ivanovna. See Bekleshova, Alexandra Ivanovna
Osipova, Ekaterina Ivanovna (1823–1908), daughter of Praskovia A., I, 184, 240, 272, 291
Osipova, Maria Ivanovna (1820–1895), daughter of Praskovia A., I, 184, 272; III, 601, 624, 723, 741
Osipova, Praskovia Alexandrovna (1781–1859), Vulf by earlier marriage, close friend of ASP, I, 31, 51, 184, 186, 189, 192, 193, 195, 232, 237, 242, 248, 249, 250, 256, 257, 259, 271, 272, 275, 280, 289, 290, 292, 295, 305; II, 360, 383, 384, 389, 390, 392, 396, 445, 471, 571, 575, 580, 582, 589; III, 601, 624, 689, 722, 724, 740, 743, 775
Letters to, I, 234, 236, 239, 240–41, 250–51, 305–6, 314–15; II, 329, 342, 349–50, 352, 359–60, 438–39, 496–97, 517–18, 528–29, 541–42, 550–51, 568; III, 670–71, 729–30, 731–32, 811–12
Osipova(-Vulf) family, 1, 184, 194, 196, 271, 275; II, 352, 396, 529, 551; III, 741
Otrepiev, Grigory. See Dimitry, False
Ovid, Roman poet, I, 83, 99, 120, 123, 127, 221. See also ASP: "To Ovid"
Tristia, I, 91, 123

Ovoshnikova, Evdokia Mikhaylovna, ballet dancer, I, 87, 121, 184, 272
Ozerov, Sergey Petrovich (1809-1884), III, 659, 681, 685
Ozerov, Vladislav Alexandrovich (1769-1816), dramatist, I, 108-9, 128
Fingal, I, 109, 128
Ozerova, Natalia Andreevna, nee Obolenskaya (1812-1901), wife of S. P., III, 643, 659, 681, 685

Pakatsky, Gavriil Abramovich (d. 1830), priest and translator, I, 205, 279
Palaprat, Jean, Sieur de Bigot (1650-1721) French author, I, 291
Glib Lawyer (*L'Avocat patelin*), I, 240, 291
Paleologue, Sophia (d. 1503), wife of Ivan III, III, 797
Panaev, Vladimir Ivanovich (1792-1859), poetaster, I, 107, 128, 193
Pancake (*Blin*), projected almanac, II, 450, 473
Panin, Alexander Nikitich (1791-1850), education official, II, 382, 401
Panin, Peter Ivanovich (1721-1789), general, III, 656, 683, 684
Panin, Valerian Alexandrovich (1803-1880), II, 337, 385
Parasha, servant of ASP, III, 605
Parny, Evariste Désiré Desforges (1753-1814), French poet, I, 89, 122, 205, 207, 279, 280
Déguisements de Vénus, Les, I, 279
Pashkov, Sergey Ivanovich (1801-1883), III, 606, 625
Pashkova, Nadezhda Sergeevna (1811-1880), wife of S. I., III, 606, 625
Paskevich-Erivansky, Ivan Fedorovich (1782-1856), general, II, 365, 395, 397, 483, 489, 491, 494, 502, 505, 506, 507, 523; III, 773, 794
Paul I (1754-1801), Emperor (Tsar) of Russia (1796-1801), I, 271, 286; II, 443, 471; III, 643, 681
Pauli, a Greek, I, 80
Pavlishchev, Lev Nikolaevich, son of N. I. and Olga S., III, 776, 781, 795

Pavlishchev, Nikolay Ivanovich (1802-1879), ASP's brother-in-law, I, 117; II, 360, 361, 393; III, 683, 705, 708, 736, 737, 770, 771, 781, 793, 795, 811-12, 823
Letters to, III, 648-49, 708-9, 714, 775, 776, 816
Pavlishcheva, Olga Sergeevna, nee Pushkina (1797-1868), wife of N. I., sister of ASP, I, 117, 121, 183, 186, 187, 188, 189, 190, 212, 213, 214, 216, 217, 243-44, 258, 272, 273, 275, 291, 310, 318; II, 341, 360, 393, 518, 531, 570-71; III, 637, 648, 649, 650, 658, 671, 683, 708, 709, 714, 737, 742, 770, 775, 776, 781, 793, 795, 811, 815
Letters to, I, 86-87, 95-96, 192-93, 243-44; III, 411-12
Pavlov, III, 768, 792
Pavlov, Nikolay Filippovich (1805-1864), actor and dramatist, II, 443, 471, 491, 515, 546, 570
Pavsky, Gerasim Petrovich (1787-1863), tutor to later Alexander II, III, 798
Pelagea Ivanovna, unidentified, III, 697
Penkovsky, Iosif Matveevich (d. 1885 or 1886), manager of Boldino, I, 43; III, 637, 670-71, 679, 680, 708, 734
Letters to, III, 639, 699, 708, 772-73
Perfiliev, Stepan Vasilievich (1796-1878), governor of Ryazan, III, 764, 791
Pericles, Athenian statesman, I, 161
Perovsky, Alexey Alexeevich (*pseud.* Pogorelsky) (1787-1836), writer, I, 79, 118, 211, 281, 292; II, 372, 398; III, 761-62, 765-66, 790
"Lafertovsky Poppy-Cakes Woman, The" (*Lafertovskaja makovnica*), I, 211, 281
Perovsky, Vasily Alexeevich (1795-1857), brother of A. A., I, 247, 292; III, 610, 625, 626
Letter to, III, 707
Pertsov, Erast Petrovich, III, 698, 734
Perugino, Il (1446-1523), Italian painter, II, 423, 466
Peshchurov, Alexey Nikitich (1779-1849), I, 185, 240, 247, 272, 291, 294; III, 815, 825

INDEX 857

Peter I, the Great (1672-1725), ruler (Tsar and then Emperor) of Russia (1682-1725), I, 38, 48, 53, 120, 203, 278; II, 379, 400, 498, 520, 526, 536, 566, 570, 575, 578, 582, 588, 589; III, 680, 684, 685, 738, 747, 780, 790, 796, 798, 814
Peter III (1728-1762), Emperor (Tsar) of Russia (1762), II, 570, 588
Peter, ASP's cook, II, 557, 558, 585
Petrarch (1304-1374), Italian poet, I, 136, 221
Petrov, Ignaty, serf, II, 527, 574
Pictorial Review of Memorable Objects from the Sciences, Fine Arts, Trade, and Society (*Živopisnoe obozrenie dostopamjatnyx predmetov iz nauk, iskusstv, xudožestv, promyšlennosti i obščežitija . . .*), III, 709, 737
Pindar, Greek poet, I, 99
Pisarev, Alexander Alexandrovich (1780-1848), II, 381, 401
Pisarev, Alexander Ivanovich (1803-1828), writer, I, 163, 175
Pisarev, Dmitry Ivanovich (1805-after 1865), II, 368, 397
Pizani, Andrey Nikolaevich, diplomat, I, 79, 80, 119
Platov, Matvey Ivanovich (1756-1818), I, 265, 296
Pleshcheev, Alexander Pavlovich, III, 706, 736, 770, 793
Pleshcheev, Alexey Romanovich (d. 1607), II, 366, 396
Pletnev, Peter Alexandrovich (1792-1865), man of letters, associate of ASP, I, 47, 92, 99-100, 104, 110, 123, 126, 150, 189, 193, 197, 198, 199, 202, 205, 212, 214, 216, 219, 224, 232, 234, 235, 276, 281, 282, 284, 289, 296, 304, 317; II, 340, 345, 355, 378, 387, 412, 436, 462, 466, 474, 475, 476, 499, 502, 503, 504, 509, 510, 511, 516, 524, 525, 558, 570; III, 610, 614, 622, 635, 660, 664, 670, 673, 722, 726, 727, 763, 782, 799, 817
"B[atyushkov] from Rome" (*B. iz Rima*), I, 100, 106, 126, 127
"I Am Not Angry at Your Caustic Reproach" (*Ja ne seržus' na edkij tvoj uprek*), I, 104, 127
"Native Land" (*Rodina*), I, 151
"Necrology" (*Nekrologija*), of Delvig, II, 460, 476
"To Gnedich" (*K Gnediču*), II, 451, 474
Letters to, I, 105-6, 183, 208-9, 230, 267, 301, 306, 307-8; II, 413, 427-28, 429-30, 430-31, 433-34, 445-46, 451-52, 453-54, 455, 456-57, 459-60, 479-80, 482-83, 484, 484-85, 598, 501-2, 502, 516-17, 521-22, 524; III, 723, 728
Pletneva, Olga Petrovna (1830-1851), daughter of P. A., II, 431, 479, 504, 516, 570; III, 670, 589
Pletneva, Stepanida Alexandrovna (ca. 1795-1839), wife of P. A., II, 413, 431, 462, 479, 504, 516, 570
Plyushar, Adolf Alexandrovich (1806-1865), bookseller, II, 509; III, 656, 678, 679, 799, 824
Letter to, III, 812
Podolinsky, Andrey Ivanovich (1806-1886), minor poet, II, 349, 389, 485, 532
Pogodin, Mikhail Petrovich (1800-1875), historian, author, friend of ASP, I, 282; II, 332, 337, 338, 339, 344, 348, 374, 382, 384, 386, 388, 389, 390, 399, 462, 464, 465, 470, 483, 509, 534, 584, 589; III, 604, 625, 679, 680, 737, 789
Boris Godunov, II, 556, 584
Historical Aphorisms (*Istoričeskie aforizmy*), III, 759, 789
Marfa, the Novgorod Burgomaster's Wife (*Marfa posadnica*), II, 414, 417, 437, 443-44, 451, 463, 464, 470, 471, 482, 498, 509, 554, 571, 576, 583
Peter I, II, 498, 509, 554
Letters to, II, 333, 342, 345-46, 348-49, 351, 354-55, 367, 414, 415, 417, 417-18, 418, 419, 420, 437, 443-44, 451, 497-98, 519, 554-55, 556, 566-67; III, 638, 709, 759
Pogodina, Elizaveta Vasilievna, nee Vagner (1804-1844), wife of M. P., III, 604, 625
Pogorelsky. *See* Perovsky, A. A.

Pokatilov, Vasily Osipovich (d. 1838), III, 612, 627, 707
"Poland Has Not Perished Yet" (*Jeszcze Polska nie zginela*), Polish national anthem, II, 489, 506
Polar. See: *Polar Star, The*
Polar Star, The (*Poljarnaja zvezda*), almanac, I, 283, 524
  for *1823*, I, 96, 104, 107, 109, 113, 123, 127, 128, 129, 130, 286
  for *1824*, I, 114, 130, 142, 147, 149, 151, 162, 172, 173
  for *1825*, I, 170, 178, 190, 196, 197, 210, 214, 217, 277, 281, 283, 285, 286
Polenov, Vasily Alexeevich (1776–1851), archivist, III, 740
  Letter to, III, 720
Poletika, Idalia Grigorievna (d. 1889), friend of ASP's wife, I, 55; II, 560, 586; III, 618, 763, 791, 826
Polevoy, Ksenofont Alexeevich (1802–1867), brother and collaborator of N. A., II, 355, 378, 391; III, 694, 733, 792
  Mikhail Vasilievich Lomonosov (*Mixail Vasil'evič Lomonosov*), III, 766, 792
  Letter to, III, 766
Polevoy, Nikolay Alexeevich (1796–1846), journalist and writer, I, 213, 226, 227, 228, 240, 253, 255, 258, 263, 277, 287, 290, 310, 319; II, 332, 349, 355, 375, 378, 379, 384, 391, 400, 401, 436, 437, 450, 502, 525, 527, 543, 553; 554, 555, 566, 568, 573, 580, 581, 584; III, 679, 683, 684, 706, 733, 736, 754, 768, 791, 814, 824
  "Elegy" (*Elegija*), I, 213, 282
  History of the Russian People (*Istorija russkogo naroda*), II, 374, 398, 399, 400, 437, 470, 473, 554, 568, 580, 584, 589; III, 733, 736
  Oath at the Lord's Tomb (*Kljatva pri grobe Gospodnem*), II, 589
  Letters to, I, 238; II, 381, 449
Polier (*Russ*. Pol'e), Varvara Petrovna. See Butera di Ridali, Varvara P.
Polignac, Auguste Jules de (1780–1846), French statesman, II, 431, 433, 438, 450, 468, 469, 471, 473
Polivanov, Alexander Yurievich (b. 1795), suitor of Alexandra N. Goncharova, II, 487, 488, 494, 495, 506, 526, 574
Polonsky, Vasily Ivanovich, III, 775, 795
Poltoratskaya, Ekaterina Pavlovna, nee Bakunina (d. 1869), III, 647, 683
Poltoratskaya, Elizaveta Petrovna, daughter of P. M., II, 359, 393
Poltoratsky, Alexander Alexandrovich (1792–1855), III, 683
Poltoratsky, Alexey Pavlovich (1802–1863), I, 110, 129, 140, 169; II, 356, 392
Poltoratsky, Mikhail Alexandrovich, I 110, 129, 140, 169; II, 356, 392
Poltoratsky, Peter Markovich (ca. 1775–after 1851), father of Anna Petrovna Kern, II, 360, 393; III, 799
Poltoratsky, Sergey Dmitrievich (1803–1884), II, 343, 388, 389
Polychroni, Calypso, Greek girl "whom Byron kissed," I, 111, 129; II, 335, 385
Popandopulo, Konstantin Anastasievich (1787–1867), physician, I, 89, 122
Pope, Alexander (1688–1744), English poet, I, 221
Potemkin, Grigory Alexandrovich (1739–1791), favorite of Catherine II, II, 463; III, 749
Potemkin, Sergey Pavlovich (1787–1858), II, 378, 400
Potemkina, Elizaveta Petrovna, wife of S. P., II, 378, 400
Potocki, Artur (1787–1832), Polish officer and author, II, 484, 505
Pototskaya, Maria Alexandrovna (d. 1845), III, 754, 788
Pototskaya, Sofia Konstantinovna, I, 147, 172
Pozharskaya, Daria Evdokimovna, Torzhok innkeeper, III, 602, 624
Pozharsky, Torzhok innkeeper, II, 331, 383
Pozharsky, Dmitry Mikhaylovich (1578–ca. 1642), I, 204, 279
Pradt, Dominique (1759–1837), French prelate and diplomat, I, 98, 125, 202
Primary Chronicle, The (*Povest' vremennyx let*), I, 221, 277–78, 285; II, 589

Procter, Bryan Waller (*pseud.* Berry Cornwall) (1787–1874), English author, III, 817, 825, 827
  Amelia Wentworth, III, 827
  Falcon, The, III, 827
  Love Cured by Kindness, III, 827
  Ludovico Sforza, III, 827
  Way to Conquer, The, III, 827
Propertius, I, 286
Pugachev, Emelian Ivanovich (ca. 1742–1775), Cossack leader of rebellion, I, 38, 53, 55, 187; II, 565, 588, 589; III, 605, 608, 613, 614, 626, 627, 639, 647, 656, 674, 680, 683, 689, 690, 693, 694, 702, 703, 704, 706, 719, 720, 730, 733, 735, 736, 737, 739, 753, 782
Pushchin, Ivan Ivanovich (1798–1859), close friend of ASP, I, 51, 142, 170, 197, 199, 200, 201, 211, 214, 276, 277, 282, 305, 317
Pushchin, Pavel Sergeevich (1785–1865), general, I, 302, 316; II, 335, 385
Pushkin, Alexander Alexandrovich (1833–1914), son of ASP, II, 587, 590; III, 601, 605, 606, 610, 611, 613, 615, 616, 618, 620, 622, 623, 624, 625, 626, 640, 641, 642, 643, 644, 646, 647, 652, 653, 657, 659, 660, 664, 670, 672, 673, 674, 675, 680, 696, 697, 717, 724, 726, 727, 732, 740, 762, 763, 767, 769, 773, 776, 781
Pushkin, Alexander Sergeevich (1799–1837), poet,
  "Accursed City Kishinev!" (*Prokljatyj gorod Kišinev*), I, 139–40, 169
  "Again I Visited" (*Vnov' ja posetil*), III, 741
  "Amiable Vyazemsky, Poet and Chamberlain" (*Ljubeznyj Vjazemskij, poèt i kamerger*), II, 522
  "Anchar" (*Ančar*), I, 52; II, 546, 548–49, 581, 582
  "André Chénier," I, 52, 229, 262, 267, 288, 307
  Angelo (*Andželo*), I, 54, 175; III, 628, 742
  "Anniversary of Borodino, The" (*Borodinskaja godovščina*), II, 529, 530, 575
  "Answer to Katenin" (*Otvet Kateninu*), II, 360, 393

  "Are You Still Burning, Our Icon-Lamp" (*Goriš' li ty, lampada naša*), I, 100
  "Assembly of the Insects" (*Sobranie nasekomyx*), II, 577–78
  "Autumn" (*Osen'*), II, 386
  Avaricious Knight, The (*Skupoj rycar'*), I, 53; II, 446
  Bandit Brothers, The (*Brat'ja razbojniki*), I, 50, 114, 130, 138, 142, 147, 160, 163, 165, 169, 170, 176, 178, 220, 285
  "Before the Sacred Tomb" (*Pered grobniceju svjatoj*), II, 493, 508, 529, 575; III, 796
  Blackamoor of Peter the Great, The (*Arap Petra Velikogo*), I, 53, 120; II, 344, 388; III, 684, 799
  "Black Shawl, The" (*Černaja šal'*), I, 87, 121, 247, 291
  "Blessed Is He Who Admist the City Noise" (*Blažen, kto v šume gorodskom*), I, 60, 67
  "Blessed Is He Who in a Far-Off Spot" (*Blažen, kto v otdalennoj seni*), I, 196, 276
  Boris Godunov, I, 33, 34, 35, 41, 47, 51, 52, 175, 218, 229, 237, 254–55, 258, 259, 261, 265, 267, 284, 286, 288, 290, 292, 294, 295, 296, 297, 306, 308, 318; II, 333, 334, 338, 344, 365–67, 371, 384, 385, 386, 395, 396, 397, 398, 408, 412, 413, 430, 434, 446, 449, 450, 451, 452, 453, 454, 458, 461, 462, 463, 468, 469, 472, 473, 474, 475, 476, 497, 499, 509, 510, 511, 516, 534, 546, 554, 576, 577, 581, 582, 587
  "Both Mistrustfully and Greedily" (*I nedoverčivo i žadno*), II, 393
  "Bova," I, 60, 68
  Bronze Horseman, The (*Mednyj vsadnik*), I, 35, 54, 273; II, 472; III, 622, 623, 628, 629, 637, 638, 684
  "Budrys and His Sons" (*Budrys i ego synov'ja*), III, 628
  "But on Gloomy Days" (*A v pasmurnye dni*), II, 356, 392
  Captain's Daughter, The (*Kapitanskaja dočka*), I, 33, 55; II, 588; III, 599–600, 623, 629, 778, 782, 795, 799

ASP, contd.
"Cart of Life, The" (*Telega žizni*), I, 198, 203, 274, 277, 279
"Cloud, The" (*Tuča*), III, 715, 739
"Collected Works of Georgy Konissky, The" (*Sobranie sočinenij Georgija Konisskogo*), article, III, 760, 789
"Coming Up to Izhory" (*Pod"ezžaja pod Ižory*), II, 368, 396
"Confession" (*Priznanie*), III, 723, 741
Contemporary, The (*Sovremennik*), ASP's journal, I, 33, 55, 176, 279; III, 629, 734, 738, 742, 748, 753, 754, 756, 757, 758, 759, 760, 762, 763, 765, 766, 768, 769, 770, 771, 772, 774, 781, 785, 787, 788, 789, 790, 791, 792, 793, 794, 795, 796, 813, 815, 817, 822, 824, 825, 827
"Conversation of a Bookseller and a Poet, A" (*Razgovor knigoprodavca s poètom*), I, 189, 192, 203, 226, 273, 274, 287
Count Nulin (*Graf Nulin*), I, 51, 175, 307, 318
"Cut Me" (*Rež' menja*), I, 258, 295
"Dagger, The" (*Kinžal*), I, 218, 284
"Demon" (*Demon*), I, 192, 274, 399
"Devils, The" (*Besy*), I, 53
Diary, projected journal, II, 551, 553, 554, 556, 560, 561, 583, 584, 586, 587; III, 711, 726, 738
Diary (personal), I, 47; II, 570; III, 679, 681, 682, 683, 684, 688, 689, 738, 798. See also ASP: *Memoirs*
"Don Juan list," II, 461
Dubrovsky (*Dubrovskij*), II, 561, 562–63, 586, 587; III, 623
"Elegy on the Death of Anna Lvovna" (*Elegija na smert' Anny L'vovny*), by ASP and Delvig, I, 217, 258
"Epistle to Delvig" (*Poslanie Del'vigu*), II, 344, 388
"Epistle to the Censor" (*Poslanie censoru*), I, 109, 128
"Epistle to V., Composer of a Satire on Gamblers" (*Poslanie k V., sočinitelju Satiry na igrokov*), II, 391
Evgeny Onegin, I, 32, 34, 35, 44, 50, 51, 53, 127, 129, 141, 143, 146, 151, 155, 156, 159, 160, 162, 163, 165, 166, 170, 174, 175, 177, 183, 184, 187, 188, 189, 190, 191–92, 193, 195, 196, 197, 198, 202, 203, 204, 205, 209, 210, 212, 214, 216, 220, 223, 224, 225, 227, 229, 253, 262, 265, 271, 272, 273, 274, 275, 276, 278, 279, 280, 281, 282, 283, 285, 286, 288, 295–96, 306, 311, 319; II, 336, 339, 344, 348, 349, 350, 351, 352, 353, 361, 385, 386, 387, 388, 389, 390, 393, 413, 446, 462, 472, 545, 554–55, 558, 562, 581, 582, 583, 585; III, 628, 723, 741, 804
Ex ungue leonem, I, 228, 288
"Fairy Tales: A Noel" (*Skazki: Noël*), I, 107, 128, 276, 316
"Farewell" (*Proščanie*), II, 508
"Farewell, Ukrainian Sage" (*Prosti, ukrainskij mudrec*), I, 194
Feast in the Time of the Plague (*Pir vo vremja čumy*), I, 53; II, 446, 534, 577; III, 826
"Few Words About Mr. Bulgarin's Little Finger, and Other Things, A" (*Neskol'ko slov o mizince g. Bulgarina i o pročem*), II, 413, 462, 571, 580
"Flying Bank of Clouds Is Thinning Out, The" (*Redeet oblakov letučaja grjada*), I, 148, 149, 172, 173
Fountain of Bakhchisaray, The (*Baxčisarajskij fontan*), I, 50, 112, 129, 136, 138, 141, 143, 146, 147, 149, 150, 151, 152, 153, 154, 155, 160, 162, 170, 171, 172, 173, 174, 175, 176, 177, 211, 213, 214, 215, 219, 282, 283, 297, 298; II, 411, 462; III, 804, 821
"Freedom" (*Vol'nost'*), I, 49
"Friend Delvig, My Parnassian Brother" (*Drug Del'vig, moj Parnasskij brat*), I, 82
"Friendship" (*Družba*), I, 212, 282
Gavriiliada, The, I, 27, 50, 52, 85, 98, 120, 125, 130; II, 357, 391, 392, 470, 587
"Great Leader" (*Polkovodec*), III, 778, 796
"Greetings, Vulf, My Friend!" (*Zdravstvuj, Vul'f, prijatel' moj!*), I, 181
Gypsies, The (*Cygany*), I, 50, 51, 174, 182, 194, 197, 198, 200, 201, 203, 204, 219, 235, 258, 265, 275, 276, 277, 278, 289,

ASP, contd.
  295, 307; II, 340, 343, 387, 431, 468
"Half-Hero, Half-Ignoramus" (*Polugeroj, polunevežda*), I, 182, 271
"Hero" (*Geroj*), II, 437, 470
"He Said with Woe" (*Govoril on s gorem*), I, 262
History of Pugachev, The (*Istorija Pugačeva*), I, 54; II, 588; III, 613, 621, 622, 623, 627, 628, 629, 633, 634, 637, 638, 648, 662, 664, 665, 667, 669, 671, 673, 674, 675, 677, 678, 680, 686, 687, 688, 689, 690, 694, 695, 698, 699, 700, 702, 703, 704, 706, 707, 718, 730, 733, 735, 736, 738, 739, 740, 753
"How Wide, How Deep" (*Kak široko, kak gluboko*), I, 260
"Hussar, The" (*Gusar*), III, 628
"Imitations of the Koran" (*Podražanija Koranu*), I, 191, 272, 274
"Incantation, The" (*Zaklinanie*), II, 484, 505
"In Hours of Amusement or Idle Boredom" (*V časy zabav il' prazdnoj skuki*), II, 398
"In the Academy of Sciences Sits Prince Dunduk" (*V Akademii nauk zasedaet knjaz' Dunduk*), III, 812, 823–24
"In the Country Where, Crowned by Julia" (*V strane, gde Julij venčannyj*), I, 83
"In the Wilds, Worn Out by a Life of Fasting" (*V gluši, izmučas' zizn'ju postnoj*), I, 261
"John Tanner" (*Džon Tenner*), III, 781, 797
Journey to Erzurum, A (*Putešestvie v Arzrum*), II, 395, 396, 589; III, 627, 728, 742, 754, 787, 794
Kirdzhali (*Kirdžali*), I, 129
Kosičkin, Feofilakt, *pseud.* of ASP, II, 462, 525, 528, 531, 534, 542, 556, 571, 573, 577
"Lamp of Day Has Gone Out, The" (*Pogaslo dnevnoe svetilo*), I, 76, 85, 100, 117, 120
"Land and Sea" (*Zemlja i more*), I, 205, 279
"Lay of Oleg the Seer, The" (*Pesn' o veščem Olege*), I, 201, 277
"Little Bird, A" (*Ptička*), I, 113, 130, 212
Little House in Kolomna, The (*Domik v Kolomne*), I, 53; II, 446, 472, 545, 581
"Long Ago Recollection of Her . . ." (*Davno o nej vospominan'e*), I, 212, 282
Long Poems and Verse Tales of Alexander Pushkin, The (*Poèmy i povesti Aleksandra Puškina*), III, 699, 734
"Losing Tongue and Mind Simultaneously" (*Jazyk i um terjaja razom*), II, 370, 397, 528, 574–75
"Madonna," II, 466, 560, 586
Memoirs (personal), I, 190, 203, 253, 264, 296. See also ASP: Diary (personal)
"Memoirs of Brigadier Moreau de Brasey, The" (*Zapiski brigadira Morode-Braze*), III, 747, 785
"Monument" (*Pamjatnik*), III, 684
Mozart and Salieri (*Mocart i Sal'eri*), I, 53; II, 446, 501, 582
"My Genealogy" (*Moja rodoslovnaja*), II, 453, 475, 536, 578
"Napoleon," I, 146, 171, 220, 285
"Nereid, The" (*Nereida*), I, 149, 173
"Occasion Has Arisen . . ., The" (*S toboj mne vnov' sčitat'sja dovelos'*), I, 311–12
"October 19" (*19 oktjabrja*), II, 341, 387; III, 779, 796
"Of Mme. Staël and Mr. A. M-v" (*O g-že Stal' i o g. A. M-ve*), I, 229, 288
"Of Mr. Lémontey's Preface to the Translation of the Fables of Krylov" (*O predislovii g-na Lemonte k perevodu basen I. A. Krylova*), I, 295
"Of Popular Education" (*O narodnom vospitanii*), II, 336, 385
"Of Prose" (*O proze*), I, 286
"Of the Causes Delaying the Advance of Our Literature" (*O pričinax, zamedlivšix xod našej slovesnosti*), I, 174
"Of the Memoirs of Vidocq" (*O zapiskax Vidoka*), II, 413, 462
"Of the Nullity of Russian Literature" (*O ničtožestve literatury russkoj*), III, 797

ASP, contd.
"Oleg the Seer" (*Oleg veščij*), I, 151, 173
"Oleg's Shield" (*Olegov ščit*), I, 127
"Once a Tsar Was Told" (*Skazali raz tsarju . . .*"), I, 198, 277
"One Raven Flies to Another" (*Voron k voronu letit*), a version of Scott's "Twa Corbies," II, 360, 393
"Onegin's Journey" (*Putešestvie Onegina*), II, 339, 386, 472; III, 741
"One Had My Aglaya" (*Inoj imel moju Aglaju*), I, 91
"On the Convalescence of Lucullus" (*Na vyzdorovlenija Lukulla*), I, 52; III, 738, 742, 749–50, 755, 785, 786, 788
Ostrovsky. *See* ASP: *Dubrovsky*
Peter I—ASP's researches on, III, 638, 654, 660, 680
Poems of Alexander Pushkin (*Stixotvorenija Aleksandra Puškina*), I, 114, 208–9, 211, 212, 220, 224, 234, 262, 280, 282, 283, 285, 289, 296, 301, 305, 307, 316, 317, 318
Poltava, I, 278, 287; II, 554
"Portents" (*Primety*), III, 740
Prisoner of the Caucasus, The (*Kavkazskij plennik*), I, 49–50, 79, 83, 84, 88, 89, 90, 91, 93, 96, 101, 102, 104, 105, 107, 109, 110, 113, 118, 120, 123, 124, 126, 127, 128, 135, 137–38, 159, 160, 162, 166, 168, 170, 176, 177, 178, 188, 192, 193, 264, 271, 275, 283, 296; II, 343, 353, 391, 435, 470; III, 800, 823
"Proserpine" (*Prozerpina*), I, 279
"Queen of Spades, The" (*Pikovaja dama*), I, 54; II, 392, 394; III, 628, 684
"Reared to the Beat of a Drum" (*Vospitannyj pod barabanom*), I, 316
"Recollections in Tsarkoe Selo" (*Vospominanija v Carskom sele*), I, 48, 212, 220
"Refutation of Béranger, A" (*Refutacija Beranžera*), II, 433, 469
"Richard Is Himself Again" (*Živ, živ kurilka*), I, 219, 284
Rusalka, III, 678
Ruslan and Lyudmila (*Ruslan i Ljudmila*), I, 32, 49, 66, 70, 79, 82, 84, 89, 94, 96, 104, 105, 107, 112, 118, 119, 120, 123, 124, 129, 130, 135, 137, 264, 305; II, 353, 391; III, 789
"Satirist and Poet of Love" (*Satirik i poèt ljubovnyj*), I, 258
"Scene from Faust, A" (*Scena iz Fausta*), II, 345, 388
"Second Epistle to the Censor" (*Vtoroe poslanie censoru*), I, 198
"Smirdin Has Plunged Me into Misfortune" (*Smirdin menja v bedu poverg*), III, 783–84, 799–800
"Songs About Stenka Razin" (*Pesni o Sten'ke Razine*), II, 346
"Sonnet" (*Sonet*), II, 504
"So the Sea, the Ancient Killer of Men" (*Tak more, drevnij dušegubec*), I, 314; III, 816, 825
"Sower of Freedom in the Desert, The" (*Svobody sejatel' pustynnyj*), I, 146, 171
"Stanzas" (*Stansy*), II, 346, 348, 389
Stone Guest, The (*Kamennyi gost'*), I, 53; II, 446, 472
"Table Talk" [ASP's English], III, 739
"Talentless Slanderer . . ." (*Klevetnik bez darovan'ja*), I, 91
Tale of the Dead Tsarevna and of the Seven Heroes, The (*Skazka o mertvoj carevne i o semi bogatyrjax*), III, 602, 624, 628
Tale of the Fisherman and the Fish, The (*Skazka o rybake i rybke*), III, 628
Tale of the Golden Cockerel, The (*Skazka o zolotom petuške*), I, 55
Tale of the Priest and His Workman Balda, The (*Skazka o pope i o rabotnike ego Balde*), I, 53; II, 527, 574
Tale of the Tsar Saltan, The (*Skazka o care Saltane*), I, 64; II, 527, 542, 574, 580
Tales of Belkin, The (*Povesti Belkina*), I, 53; II, 388, 446, 460, 472, 476, 498, 501, 509, 510, 516, 522, 524, 526, 531, 533, 570, 572, 573, 574; III, 618, 628, 684, 709, 737
"Shot, The" (*Vystrel*), II, 524
"Snowstorm, The" (*Metel'*), II, 388
"Station Master, The" (*Stancionnyj smotritel'*), II, 524
"Undertaker, The" (*Grobovščik*), II, 470

ASP, contd.
 Tales Published by Alexander Pushkin (*Povesti, izdanny Aleksandrom Puškinym*), III, 684
 "There Was on Earth a Poor Knight" (*Byl na svete rycar' bednyj*), II, 503, 511
 "There Where Ancient Kochegovsky" (*Tam, gde drevnij Kočegovskij*), II, 394
 "To a Kalmuck Girl" (*Kalmyčke*), III, 627
 "To Alexander" (*Aleksandru*), I, 59, 67
 "To Alexeev" (*Alekseevu*), II, 448, 473
 "To Chaadaev (In the Land Where I Have Forgotten the Alarms of Former Years)" (*Čaadaevu* [*V strane, gde ja zabyl trevogi prežnyx let*]), I, 88, 89, 94, 96, 97, 124, 125, 213, 216, 269, 282, 283, 298
 "To F. N. Glinka" (*F. N. Glinke*), I, 106-7, 128
 "To Friends" (*Prijateljam*), I, 199, 277, 288
 "To Orlov" (*Orlovu*), I, 63, 69
 "To Ovid" (*K Ovidiju*), I, 92, 96, 99, 104, 107, 120, 123, 127, 128, 212
 "To Pletnev (You Advise Me, Dear Pletnev)" (*Pletnevu* [*Ty mne sovetueš', Pletnev ljubeznyj*]), III, 741
 "To the Calumniators of Russia" (*Klevetnikam Rossii*), II, 506, 529, 530, 532, 575; III, 804, 821
 "To the Sea" (*K morju*), I, 161, 176, 182, 192, 198, 212, 271, 274, 277
 "To Yazykov (From Ancient Times the Sweet Union)" (*Jazykovu* [*Izdrevle sladostnyj sojuz*]), II, 333, 384
 "To Yazykov (Yazykov, Who Inspired You)" (*Jazykovu* [*Jazykov, kto tebe vnušil*]), II, 333, 384
 "Triumph of Friendship, or A. A. Orlov Justified, The" (*Toržestvo družby ili opravdannyj Aleksandr Anfimovich Orlov*), II, 525, 527, 528, 573, 575, 577, 580
 "Tsar, Knitting His Brows, The" (*Brovi car' naxmurja*), I, 262
 "Tsar Nikita and His Forty Daughters" (*Car' Nikita i sorok ego dočerej*), I, 209, 249, 281, 292, 335, 385
 "Under the Blue Sky of Her Native Land" (*Pod nebom golubym strany svoej rodnoj*), II, 344, 388
 "Vain Gift, Chance Gift" (*Dar naprasnyj, dar slučajnyj*), II, 372, 398
 "Village, The" (*Derevnja*), I, 49
 "Voevoda, The" (*Voevoda*), III, 628
 "Voltaire" (article), III, 781
 "War" (*Vojna*), I, 107, 128
 "Who Will Send Me Her Portrait?" (*Kto mne prišlet ee portret*), I, 304, 317
 "Yesterday Was a Day of Noisy Parting" (*Včera byl den' razluki šumnoj*), I, 212
 "You Published My Uncle" (*Ty izdal djadju moego*), I, 183
Pushkin, Alexey Mikhaylovich (d. 1825), minor writer, I, 121, 228, 287
Pushkin, Andrey Nikiforovich (d. 1831), minor writer, I, 121
Pushkin, Gavrila Grigorievich (d. after 1643), ancestor of ASP, II, 366, 395
Pushkin, Grigory Alexandrovich (1835-1905), son of ASP, III, 710, 716, 717, 724, 727, 738, 739, 762, 763, 766, 767, 773, 776, 781, 792
Pushkin, Lev Alexandrovich (1723-1790), grandfather of ASP, II, 432, 469
Pushkin, Lev Sergeevich (1805-1852), brother of ASP, I, 54, 83, 88, 106, 117, 125, 126, 135, 143, 181, 182, 183, 186, 198, 200, 210, 217, 218, 221, 224, 226, 227, 232, 263, 271, 272, 277, 278, 279, 280, 281, 283, 284, 285, 286, 289; II, 340, 369, 387, 395, 421, 422, 435, 437, 438, 441, 442, 452, 469, 481, 487, 504, 505, 515, 530, 542, 570, 575, 580; III, 619, 620, 621, 628, 629, 636, 637, 642, 645, 648, 649, 650, 655, 658, 662, 664, 671, 673, 674, 683, 689, 708, 709, 714, 736, 737, 775, 781, 793, 794, 795, 799, 811, 812, 815, 825
 Letters to, I, 75-77, 86-87, 90-91, 95-96, 98-100, 102-4, 104, 106-7, 107-8, 135-36, 149-51, 153-54, 160, 187, 188-89, 189-90, 192-93, 195-96, 197, 201-3, 204-5, 206, 206-7, 207, 208-9, 211-12, 214-15, 215-16, 216, 219-20, 225-27, 234-35; II, 341, 483; III, 705-6, 708, 770-71

Pushkin, Peter Lvovich (d. 1825), uncle of ASP, I, 224, 286, 287
Pushkin, Sergey Lvovich (1770–1848), father of ASP, I, 48, 50, 52, 54, 96, 98, 100, 117, 121, 126, 136, 154, 168, 173, 174, 181, 183–84, 185–86, 188, 190, 215, 227, 230, 271, 274, 279, 282, 284, 308; II, 341, 343, 348, 383, 387, 410, 422, 428, 435, 436, 439, 440, 447, 461, 467, 476, 483, 518, 527, 570–71, 574; III, 614, 620, 621, 627, 629, 637, 639, 645, 648–49, 650, 655, 657, 658, 659, 662, 671, 680, 683, 684, 685, 686, 687, 699, 705, 706, 708, 709, 712, 714, 724, 726, 730, 732, 733, 734, 736, 737, 742, 770, 771, 772, 773, 775, 776, 793, 794, 821
  Family of, I, 28, 50, 77, 117, 183; II, 433; III, 717
  Letters to, II, 406–7, 411–12; III, 781, 815
Pushkin, Vasily Lvovich (1767–1830), uncle of ASP, poet, I, 48, 61, 68, 69, 89, 109, 121, 129, 141, 155, 158, 159, 183, 192, 199, 217, 227–28, 246, 258, 271, 274, 282, 284, 287, 295, 311; II, 349, 382, 389, 411, 412, 425, 426, 429, 468, 471, 475, 525, 573, 574; III, 614, 619, 622, 627, 630, 714, 733, 738, 739, 827
  Dangerous Neighbor, The (*Opasnyj sosed*), I, 61, 68, 89, 108, 122, 128, 183, 228; II, 362, 394, 558, 585
  Poems (*Stixotvorenija*), I, 271
  "To Her" (*K nej*), I, 274, 283
  "To P. N. Priklonsky" (*K P. N. Priklonskomu*), II, 572
  "To the Hearth" (*K kaminu*), I, 287
  Letters to, I, 61–62, 63
Pushkina, Anna Lvovna (d. 1824), maiden aunt of ASP, I, 146, 172, 189, 193, 217, 246, 258, 273, 275, 283–84, 287; II, 330, 383
Pushkina, Maria Alexandrovna (1832–1919), daughter of ASP, II, 552, 557, 558, 559, 560, 561, 562, 568, 583, 585, 589; III, 601, 602, 605, 606, 608, 610, 611, 613, 615, 616, 618, 620, 623, 624, 626, 640, 641, 642, 643, 644, 645, 646, 647, 652, 653, 655, 657, 659, 660, 664, 670, 672, 673, 674, 675, 680, 696, 697, 717, 724, 726, 727, 732, 740, 762, 763, 767, 773, 776, 781
Pushkina, Nadezhda Osipovna, nee Gannibal (1775–1836), mother of ASP, I, 56, 69, 117, 175, 188, 189, 232, 233, 243–44, 279, 284, 291; II, 341, 387, 518, 570–71; III, 645, 655, 657, 658, 659, 671, 684, 685, 706, 708, 709, 730, 731, 740, 742, 748, 789, 793, 794
  Letters to, II, 406–7, 411–12
Pushkina, Natalia Alexandrovna (1836–1913), daughter of ASP, III, 769, 773, 776, 781
Pushkina, Natalia Nikolaevna, nee Goncharova (1812–1863), wife of ASP, I, 28, 40, 41, 46, 52, 53–56; II, 364, 375, 378, 382, 395, 396, 397, 399, 405–6, 407, 410, 411, 412, 413, 414, 416, 418, 419, 427, 430, 433, 434, 437–38, 459, 461, 462, 464, 465, 466, 467, 468, 469, 471, 474, 479, 483, 486, 487, 489, 491, 494, 495, 496, 498, 505, 506, 509, 516, 518, 519, 523, 525, 526, 528, 533, 543–44, 552, 563, 566, 568, 571, 573, 575, 576, 578, 579, 580, 581, 584, 585, 586, 589; III, 620, 623, 624, 625, 626, 628, 636, 637, 679, 680, 682, 683, 685, 686, 688, 689, 690, 693, 694, 697, 700, 702, 710, 712, 716, 717, 730, 732, 733, 735, 741, 749, 752, 769, 781, 786, 791, 792, 805–6, 807, 808, 812, 815, 818, 821, 822, 825, 826
  Letters to, II, 417, 421–22, 422–23, 423–24, 426, 428, 431–32, 432–33, 434–35, 435–36, 439–41, 441–42, 444, 444–45, 537, 537–39, 539, 539–40, 540–41, 556–57, 557–59, 559–60, 560–61, 561–62; III, 600–1, 601–2, 602–4, 604–5, 605–6, 606–8, 609–10, 610–11, 611–12, 612–13, 613–14, 614–15, 615–16, 616–18, 619–20, 640–41, 641–42, 642–44, 644, 644–45, 646, 646–47, 649–50, 650–51, 651–52, 652–53, 653–54, 654–56, 656–57, 658–60, 660, 661–62, 662–63, 664–65, 669–70, 671–72, 672–73, 674, 675, 675–77, 695–96, 696–97, 722, 723–24, 724–25, 725–27, 727, 761–62, 762–63, 764, 764–66, 766–67, 767–68

INDEX 865

Pushkina, Olga Sergeevna. *See* Pavlishcheva, Olga S.
Pushkina, Sofia Fedorovna (1806–1862), II, 332, 336, 337, 383, 384, 385, 386
Pushkins, historical figures, I, 225, 286
Putyata, Nikolay Vasilievich (1802–1877), II, 392
Letter to, II, 358

Quarterly Review, The, II, 572
Quinet, Edgar (1803–1875), French poet, *Napoléon*, III, 793

Rabaut de Saint Etienne, Jean Paul (1743–1793), French revolutionary and historian, I, 164, 177
Rabelais, François (1490?–1553), French writer, II, 439, 471
Racine, Jean Baptiste (1639–1699), French dramatist, I, 150, 164, 173
  Andromaque, II, 374, 398
  Britannicus, I, 112, 129
  Phèdre, I, 150, 173
  Translations from. *See* Gnedich, N. I., Katenin, P. A., and Lobanov, M. E.
Radishchev, Alexander Nikolaevich (1749–1802), writer, I, 114, 130
  Journey from Petersburg to Moscow, A (*Putešestvie iz Peterburga v Moskvu*), I, 130; II, 383
Raevskaya, Ekaterina Nikolaevna. *See* Orlova, Ekaterina Nikolaevna
Raevskaya, Ekaterina Petrovna, nee Kindyakova (1812–1839), wife of A. N., III, 765, 791
Raevskaya, Elena Nikolaevna (1803–1852), daughter of General N. N., I, 116; II, 373, 398
Raevskaya, Maria Nikolaevna. *See* Volkonskaya, Maria Nikolaevna
Raevskaya, Sofia Alexeevna (1769–1844), wife of General N. N., I, 116; II, 373, 398
Raevskaya, Sofia Nikolaevna (1806–1881), daugher of General N. N., I, 75, 116; II, 373, 398
Raevsky, Brigadier, III, 604, 625
Raevsky, Alexander Nikolaevich (1795–1868), son of General N. N., I, 77, 116, 236, 274, 290, 301, 302, 316; II, 357, 392, 398; III, 604, 625, 762, 765, 781
  Letter to, I, 138–39
Raevsky, Illarion Evdokimovich, priest, I, 213, 215, 282, 283
Raevsky, Nikolay Nikolaevich (1771–1829), general, I, 49, 75–77, 78, 98, 116, 117, 118, 125, 255, 270, 298; II, 373, 398, 450, 474
  Family of, I, 27, 49, 75–77, 116, 296, 298; II, 373; III, 821
Raevsky, Nikolay Nikolaevich (1801–1843), son of General N. N., and close friend of ASP, I, 75, 114, 116, 130, 149, 151, 173, 247, 263, 290, 292, 296, 302, 316; II, 341, 369, 381, 387, 395, 401; III, 604, 605–6
  Letters to, I, 236–38; II, 365–67
Raevsky, Vladimir Fedoseevich (1795–1872), poet and army officer, I, 302, 316
Raich, Semen Egorovich (1792–1855), educator and journalist, I, 136, 137, 168; II, 399, 410, 546
Raukh, Egor Ivanovich (1789–1864), physician, III, 730, 742
Razin, Stepan (Stenka, Senka) Timofeevich (d. 1671), Cossack hetman and rebel, I, 189, 273; III, 694, 733
Razumovsky, Alexey Kirillovich (1748–1822), I, 59, 60, 67
Record of the Condition of the City Moscow, The (*Vedomost' o sostojanii goroda Moskvy*), II, 470
Reichman, Karl (d. 1835), manager of Mme. Osipova's estate Malinniki, III, 601, 624, 664, 670, 671, 687, 689
Reiff, Philipp (1792–1872),
  Russo-French Dictionary . . . or Etymological Dictionary of the Russian Language (*Russko-francuzskij slovar' . . . ili Etimologičeskij leksikon russkogo jazyka*) III, 783, 799
Reineke-Fuchs. *See* Goethe, J. W.
Remer, Nikolay Fedorovich (1806–1889), III, 640, 681
Renkevicheva, house owner, II, 338

Repnin-Volkonsky, Nikolay Grigorievich (1778–1845), III, 786, 787
  Letters, to III, 751–52, 752
Revue de Paris, II, 543
Rhigas, Constantine (1760–1798), founder of the Greek Hetairia society, I, 119
Ricci, Count, Italian singer in Russia, II, 363, 394
Richardson, Samuel (1689–1761), English novelist, I, 262, 274
  Clarissa, I, 139, 169, 190, 274; II, 359, 368, 392, 396, 397; III, 760, 789
  Pamela, I, 274
  Sir Charles Grandison, I, 274
Rimskaya-Korsakova, Alexandra Alexandrovna (1803–1860), I, 112, 129; II, 341, 387
Rimskaya-Korsakova, Maria Ivanovna (d. 1832), I, 112, 129; II, 341
Ringel, steward at Mikhaylovskoe, III, 775, 795
Riznich, Amalia (d. 1825), II, 388
Robertson, William (1721–1793), Scots historian, I, 164, 177
  History of the Reign of the Emperor Charles V, I, 164
Rodzyanko, Arkady Gavrilovich (1793–1846), minor poet, I, 115, 130, 131, 136, 151, 275
  "To My Dear One" (*K miloj*), I, 151, 173
  Ukrainian Girl, The (*Čupka*), I, 194, 275
  Letter to, I, 194
Rodzyanko, Porfiry Gavrilovich, brother of A. G., I, 194, 275
Rojas Zorilla, Francisco de (1607–1648), Spanish author, I, 293
Rokhmanov, Alexey Fedorovich (1799–1862), II, 491, 494, 507, 543, 544, 565, 581; III, 701, 735
Rokotov, Ivan Matveevich (1782–1840's), I, 189, 195, 236, 250, 274, 292
Romanovs, Russian ruling house, I, 225, 286; III, 797
Rosset, Alexandra Osipovna. *See* Smirnova, Alexandra Osipovna
Rosset, Klementy Osipovich (1811–1866), II, 527, 564, 574; III, 797
Rossi, Count, III, 682
Rossini, Gioacchino Antonio (1792–1868), Italian opera composer, I, 141, 143, 170, 184, 246
  Barber of Seville, The, I, 170
Rostopchin, Fedor Vasilievich (1763–1826), governor of Moscow in 1812, II, 332, 384; III, 605, 625
Rotrou, Jean de (1609–1650), French playwright, I, 253, 293
  Venceslas, I, 293
Rouget de Lisle, Claude Joseph (1760–1836),
  La Marseillaise, II, 425, 466, 467
Rousseau, Jean Baptiste (1671–1741), French poet, I, 198, 222, 277
Rousseau, Jean Jacques (1712–1778), French philosopher and author, I, 111, 263, 296
  Confessions, I, 263, 296
Roza Grigorievna, housekeeper, I, 204–5, 279
Rozen, Egor Fedorovich (1800–1860), writer, II, 497, 509, 577, 581
  Ivan Susanin (*A Life for the Tsar*) (*Žizn' za carja*), II, 577
  Letter to, II, 534
Rozen, Grigory Vladimirovich (1782–1841), general, III, 815, 825
Rudykovskij, Evstafy Petrovich (1784–1851), physician, I, 75, 116
Ruehland, Heinrich Christian Matthew (1784–1837), surgeon, I, 259, 295
Rumyantsev, Nikolay Petrovich (1754–1826), II, 332, 384
Rumyantsov-Zadunaysky, Peter Alexandrovich (1725–1796), field marshal, II, 418, 464
Russian Academy, I, 60, 67, 306, 317; II, 355, 391; III, 617, 628, 664, 687, 704, 705, 706–7, 736, 812, 823–24
  Dictionary of the Russian Language, I, 67, 88, 122, 160; II, 569, 589; III, 704, 736, 799
Russian Antiquity (*Russkaja starina*), I, 193, 205, 206, 219, 275, 285
Russian Invalide, The (*Russkij invalid*), newspaper, I, 193, 198, 199, 205, 275, 277; II, 580; III, 742, 794
Russian Messenger (*Russkij vestnik*), I, 291

Russian Spectator, The (*Russkij zritel'*), II, 389
Russian Thalia for 1825, The (*Russkaja Talija na 1825*), I, 188, 205, 206, 219, 273, 276, 285, 293
Rybushkin, Mikhail Samsonovich (1792–1849), professor, III, 719, 739
Brief History of the City of Kazan, A (*Kratkaja istorija g. Kazani*), III, 719, 739
Rychkov, Peter Ivanovich (1712–1777), III, 639, 680, 690, 731, 733
Ryleev, Kondraty Fedorovich (1795–1826), poet and Decembrist, I, 33, 93, 106, 107, 110, 118, 126, 150, 152, 170, 190, 196, 200, 202, 203, 207, 209, 224, 226, 265, 274, 276, 277, 278, 281, 283, 285, 287, 290, 293, 317, 319
"Ah, Where Are the Islands . . ." (*Ax, gde te ostrova . . .*), with A. A. Bestuzhev, I, 149, 173
Dumy, I, 148, 172, 209, 214, 219, 220–21, 226, 284, 285, 287
"Bogdan Khmelnitsky," I, 100, 126
"Boris Godunov," I, 107, 128
"Ivan Susanin," I, 115, 130, 220, 285
"Oleg the Seer" (*Oleg veščij*), I, 106, 127, 220–21, 285
"Peter the Great in Ostrogozhsk" (*Petr Velikij v Ostrogožske*), I, 220, 285
Nalivayko (*Nalivajko*), I, 216, 221, 283, 285
Paley (*Palej*), I, 202, 278
Voynarovsky (*Vojnarovskij*), I, 150–51, 197, 203, 209, 214, 219, 220, 224, 226, 240, 276, 278, 285, 287, 290
Letters to, I, 197, 220–21, 251–52
Ryurik (d. 879), reputed founder of Russia, and ruling house, III, 797, 798

Saadi, Persian poet, I, 169, 213, 282
Saburov, Yakov Ivanovich, I, 187, 190, 205, 216, 272
Sainte-Beuve, Charles Augustin (1804–1869), French poet and critic, II, 414
Consolations, II, 415, 463
La Vie, les poésies et les pensées de J. Delorme, II, 463, 484, 505

St. Florent, Petersburg bookseller, I, 187, 206, 215, 272; II, 457
St. Petersburg Record (*S.-Peterburgskij vestnik*), II, 499
Salaev, Ivan Grigorievich (d. 1858), Moscow bookseller and publisher, II, 453, 475
Salnikov, Ivan Savelievich, professional fool, II, 351, 390
Saltykov, Mikhail Alexandrovich (1767–1851), father of poet Delvig's wife, I, 232, 262, 289, 296; II, 454, 455, 460, 476, 565
Saltykova, Sofia Mikhaylovna. *See* Delvig, Sofia Mikhaylovna
Samoylov, Nikolay Alexandrovich (d. 1841), II, 337, 386
Sand, George, *pseud.* of Amantine Dudevant (1804–1876), French novelist, III, 726
André, III, 726, 741
Sankovsky, Pavel Stepanovich (1798–1832), newspaper editor, II, 588
Letter to, II, 564
Saveliev, Peter Yakolevich (1801–after 1838), III, 763, 790–91
Savelov, Avtonom Petrovich, I, 199, 241, 263, 277
Schelling, Friedrich Wilhelm von, German philosopher (1775–1854), II, 384
Schiller, Friedrich von (1759–1805), German poet, I, 70; II, 505
Dramatic Works, I, 215
Translations from. *See* Zhukovsky, V. A.
Schlegel, August Wilhelm von (1767–1845), German man of letters, I, 215; II, 452
Of Dramatic Art and Literature, I, 206, 280
Schlözer, August Ludwig von (1735–1809), German historian of Russia, II, 567, 589
Nestor, III, 736
Scott, Sir Walter (1771–1832), Scots poet and novelist, I, 148, 172, 188, 215, 221, 263, 273; II, 386, 450, 452, 504, 527; III, 696, 724, 725
Antiquary, The, III, 700, 735
"Eve of Saint John." *See* Zhukovsky, V. A.

Scott, Sir Walter, contd.
"Grey Brother, The." *See* Zhukovsky, V. A.: "Remorse"
Marmion, II, 531, 576
"Twa Corbies, The" (from *Minstrelsy of the Scottish Border*), II, 393
Waverly, Novels, I, 33, 35
Woodstock, III, 797
Scribe, Augustin Eugène (1791-1861), French playwright, II, 554, 584
Sejanus, favorite of Tiberius, I, 161, 176
Selivanovsky, Semen Ioannikievich, bookseller, I, 214, 282
Semen, August, bookseller and publisher, III, 709, 737
Semenova, Ekaterina Semenovna (1786-1849), actress, I, 99, 101, 126, 129
Semenova, Nimfodora Semenovna (1789-1876), opera singer, I, 101, 126
Senkovsky, Osip Ivanovich (Polish: Jósef Sękowski, 1800-1858), journalist, I, 151, 173; III, 728, 737, 742, 748, 750, 751, 785, 786, 791
"Tale Lost to the World, A" (*Poterjannaja dlja sveta povest'*), III, 709, 728, 737, 742
Warrior of the Dun Steed, The (*Vitjaz' bulanogo konja*), I, 151, 173
Senyavin, Ivan Grigorievich (1801-1851), I, 154, 174
Serbinovich, Konstantin Stepanovich (1796-1874), censor, II, 377, 399
Severin, Dmitry Petrovich (1791-1865), I, 138, 169, 196
Severina, Anna Grigorievna, I, 155
Shakespeare, William (1564-1616), English poet and dramatist, I, 32-33, 156, 175, 202, 221, 223, 237, 238, 266, 290, 304; II, 365, 444, 462, 482, 504
Henry IV, I, 297
Henry V, I, 297
Measure for Measure, I, 175; III, 628, 742
Rape of Lucrece, The, I, 175
Richard III, II, 492, 507
Tempest, The, I, 296, 297
Shakhovskoy, Alexander Alexandrovich (1777-1846), playwright, I, 60, 62, 65, 68, 97, 101, 104, 117, 125, 138, 169, 253, 293

Lesson to Coquettes, or the Lipetsk Waters, A (*Urok koketkam, ili Lipeckie vody*), I, 77, 117
Negligent Landlords (*Pustodomy*), I, 65, 70
New Sterne, The (*Novyj Stern*), I, 68
Sorceress, The (*Vorožeja*), I, 220, 285
Shalikov, Prince Peter Ivanovich (1765-1852), writer and journalist, I, 60, 68, 136, 151, 193, 203, 226, 275, 287; II, 410, 440, 470, 471, 527; III, 604, 638, 679
"To A. S. Pushkin (On His Swearing Off Singing of Women)" (*K A. S. Puškinu* [*Na ego otrečenie pet' ženščin*]), I, 226, 287
"To Vasily Lvovich Pushkin: On the Passing Away of His Sister, Anna Lvovna Pushkina" (*K Vasiliju L'voviču Puškinu: na končinu sestry ego, Anny L'vovny Puškinoj*), I, 193, 275
Shambo, Ivan Pavlovich (1783-1848), II, 519, 571
Shcheglov, Nikolay Prokofievich (1794-1831), professor and censor, II, 377, 399, 430, 499, 510; III, 814
Shchepin, Artemy Mardarievich, brother of P. M., II, 421, 465
Shchepin, Pavel Madarievich (d. ca. 1853), opera singer and producer, II, 421, 465
Shchepkin, Mikhail Semenovich (1788-1863), actor, III, 763, 791
Shcherbatov, Peter Alexandrovich (b. 1811), II, 562, 587
Shcherbatova, Sofia Nikolaevna, nee Gorstkina (d. 1858), II, 562, 587
Sheremetev, Dmitry Nikolaevich (1803-1871), rich landowner, III, 615, 628, 783, 799
Sheremetev, Vasily Vasilievich (d. 1817), I, 264, 296
Shernval, Avrora Karlovna (1813-1902), II, 561, 586
Shevyrev, Stepan Petrovich (1806-1864), poet and critic, II, 351, 354, 355, 390, 391, 462, 483; III, 604, 737
"Survey of Russian Literature for 1827" (*Obozrenie russkoj slovesnosti za 1827 god*), II, 390

Shevyrev, Stepan Petrovich, contd.
"Thought, A" (*Mysl'*), II, 355, 391
Letter to, II, 410
Shikhmatov. *See* Shirinsky-Shikhmatov, S. A.
Shilling, Sergey Romanovich, II, 582
Shirinsky-Shikhmatov, Sergey Alexandrovich (1783–1837), writer, I, 60, 68, 240, 266, 290; II, 383
Peter the Great, I, 290
Shiryaev, Alexander Sergeevich (d. 1841), bookseller, II, 339, 386, 453, 564
Shishkov, Alexander Ardalionovich (1799–1832), minor poet, I, 170; II, 555, 583
Selected German Theater (*Izbrannyj nemeckij teatr*), tr., II, 583, 584
Letter to, I, 143–144
Shishkov, Alexander Semenovich (1754–1843), vice admiral, literary conservative, minister of public education (1824–1828), I, 32, 44, 62, 67, 88, 122, 160, 161, 162, 163, 176, 177, 178, 196, 198, 203, 224, 244, 276, 281, 286, 291; II, 355, 383, 391, 664, 687
Letter to, I, 215
Shishkova, Elaterina Vasilievna, III, 664, 687
Shishkova, Praskovia Dmitrievna, daughter of Ekaterina V., III, 664, 687
Shneyder, Fedor Danilovich, Moscow physician, II, 495, 508, 562, 565
Shulgin, Dmitry Ivanovich (1785–1854), Moscow Chief of Police, II, 378, 400
Shumkov, F. I., III, 787
Shuvalov, Ivan Ivanovich (1727–1797), II, 549, 582
Shuysky, Vasily Ivanovich (1552–1612), Tsar of Russia (1606–1610), II, 366, 396. *See also* ASP: *Boris Godunov*
Shvarts, Dmitry Maximovich (1797–1839), I, 140, 169
Letter to, I, 195
Siberian Messenger, The (*Siberskij vestnik*), journal, I, 215, 283
Sibilev, Evgraf Ivanovich (ca. 1759–1839), II, 378, 379, 400
Sichler, Mme., II, 538, 579; III, 605, 702, 768, 792

Sieyès, Emmanuel Joseph (1748–1836), leader in French revolution, I, 223, 286
Sirach. *See* Bible: Ecclesiasticus
Sismondi, Simonde de (1773–1842), Swiss author,
Of the Literature of the South of Europe, I, 206, 280
Skaryatin, Fedor Yakovlevich (b. 1806), II, 481, 504
Skobeltsyn, Fedor Afanasievich (b. 1781), III, 825
Letter to, III, 816
Skrzynecki, Jan (1787–1860), Polish general, II, 489, 506, 523, 572
Slav, The (*Slavjanin*), II, 355, 391; III, 824
Slenin, Ivan Vasilievich (1789–1836), bookseller, I, 94, 96, 100, 102, 104, 122, 155, 185, 188, 193, 215
Slepushkin, Fedor Nikiforovich (1783–1848), peasant poet, I, 305, 306, 308
"Carnival in the Country" (*Sel'skaja masljanica*), I, 305, 317
"Christmas Fortune Telling" (*Svjatočyne gadan'ja*), I, 305, 317
"Wooden House" (*Izba*), I, 305, 317
Smirdin, Alexander Filippovich (1795–1857), bookseller, II, 351, 390, 413, 462, 474, 492, 498, 501, 507, 516, 524, 554, 562, 569, 583, 587, 590; III, 605, 615, 621, 622, 628, 629, 656, 699, 701, 705, 720, 726, 740, 748, 783, 800
Smirnov, Nikolay Mikhaylovich (1807–1870), II, 572, 574; III, 661
Smirnova, Alexandra Osipovna, nee Rosset (1809–1882), wife of N. M., II, 423, 466, 482, 501, 504, 510, 517, 521, 522, 527, 531, 574, 575; III, 614, 627, 645, 650, 655, 661, 673, 674, 676, 683, 686, 689
Letter to, II, 529
Smirnova, Ekaterina Evgrafovna (1812–after 1888), II, 368, 397
Snegirev, Ivan Mikhaylovich (1793–1868), censor, II, 345, 388, 394
Letter to, II, 363
Sobanskaya, Karolina Adamovna (1794–1885), one of ASP's loves, I, 138, 139, 169; II, 399
Letters to, II, 375, 375–77

Sobolevsky, Sergey Alexandrovich (1803–1870), close friend of ASP, I, 31, 45, 64, 69, 118; II, 332, 339, 342, 355, 383, 386, 387, 388, 389, 390, 391; III, 600–1, 604, 614, 616, 621, 623, 636, 637, 641, 642, 645, 647, 655–56, 658, 669, 673, 685, 701, 733, 751, 786
"Herons" (*Capli*), II, 331, 383
Letters to, II, 330–31, 337–38, 342–43, 348, 349, 351–52, 355; III, 694
Socrates, I, 115, 130
Sofia Ostafievna, Petersburg "madam," II, 360, 393, 544, 581; III, 641, 681
Sokolov, Afanasy Timofeevich, nicknamed Khlopusha, military leader under Pugachev, III, 674, 689
Sokolov, Peter Ivanovich (1764–1835), secretary of Russian Academy, II, 589; III, 704, 706, 707, 736
Letter to, II, 569
Soldaen, Vera Yakovlevna (1790–1856), II, 540, 541, 580
Sollogub, Nadezhda Lvovna (d. 1903), II, 561, 586; III, 615, 649, 650, 651, 653, 655, 661, 669
Sollogub, Sofia Ivanovana (1791–1854), mother of V. A., II, 561, 586; III, 655
Sollogub, Vladimir Alexandrovich (1814–1882), writer, II, 586; III, 786, 787, 822, 827
Letters to, III, 752, 804–5
Solntsev, Matvey Mikhaylovich (1779–1847), uncle of ASP by marriage, I, 217, 284; II, 379, 400, 411, 412; III, 762, 765, 790, 791, 815, 825
Solntseva, Elizaveta Lvovna, nee Pushkina (1776–1848), ASP's aunt, I, 217, 284; II, 379, 400–1, 412; III, 762, 765, 790, 791, 815, 825
Solntseva, Olga Matveevna (d. 1880), daughter of M. M., II, 379, 401
Solovkina, Elena Fedorovna, II, 335, 385
Somov, Orest Mikhaylovich (1793–1833), journalist, I, 142, 170; II, 344, 374, 398, 456, 475, 482, 484, 520, 521, 543, 571, 580, 581
Son. See: Son of the Fatherland
Son of the Fatherland, The (*Syn otečestva*), journal, I, 71, 78, 87, 88, 91, 98, 100, 113, 117, 123, 125, 128, 145, 148, 206, 280, 319; II, 583; III, 704
Sontag, Henriette Gertrude Walpurgis (1806–1854), singer, III, 646, 682
Sophia (Sofia Alexeevna, 1657–1704), Tsarevna, regent (1682–1689), I, 253, 293
Sophianos, Rodoes, Greek girl, I, 182, 190, 274
Sorokhtin, II, 558, 585; III, 647, 683
Sosnitskaya, Elena Yakovlevna (1800–1855), actress, wife of I. I., I, 65, 70, 101, 126
Sosnitsky, Ivan Ivanovich (1794–1871), actor, I, 101, 126
Southey, Robert (1774–1843), English poet, I, 124, 221; II, 482, 505
Roderick, I, 94
Translations from. *See* Zhukovsky, V. A.
Spassky, Grigory Ivanovich (1784–1864), I, 283
Spassky, Ivan Timofeevich (1795–1861), physician, II, 557, 585; III, 641, 650, 651, 660, 681, 686, 730, 742, 827
Speransky, Mikhail Mikhaylovich (1772–1839), statesman, II, 423, 466; III, 633, 654, 664, 700, 735
Staël, Mme. de (1766–1817), French writer, I, 229, 255, 288, 294, 311, 319
Ten Years of Exile, I, 319; III, 809, 823
Stamo, Ekaterina Zakharovna (or Zemfirovna), II, 448, 473
Stendhal, *pseud.* of Marie Henri Beyle (1783–1842), French novelist,
Red and the Black, The, II, 488, 491, 506
Stepan, servant, III, 641, 681
Stepanov, Alexander Petrovich (1781–1837), writer,
Inn, The (*Postojalyj dvor*), III, 757, 789
Sterne, Laurence (1713–1768), English writer,
Sentimental Journey, A, I, 68
Tristram Shandy, I, 62, 69, 89
Stolypin, Pavel Grigorievich (1806–1836), III, 768, 792
Stroev, Pavel Mikhaylovich (1796–1876), historian, II, 382, 401
Stroganov, Grigory Alexandrovich (1770–1857), III, 680
Letter to, III, 639

Stroganova, Yulia Pavlovna (d. 1864), wife of G. A., III, 639, 680

Struysky, Dmitry Yurievich (1806–1856), poet,
"Kutuzov's Tomb" (*Grobnica Kutuzova*), II, 493, 508

Sturdza, Alexander Skarlatovich (1791–1854), writer, I, 138, 169
La Grèce en 1821–22, I, 138, 169

Sudienko, Alexander Mikhailovich (1832–1882), son of M. O., III, 606, 625

Sudienko, Iosif Mikhaylovich (1830–1892), son of M. O., III, 606, 625

Sudienko, Mikhail Osipovich (1802–1874), friend of ASP, II, 398, 400; III, 604, 606, 625
Letters to, II, 374, 377–78, 544–45

Sudienko, Nadezhda Mikhaylovna, nee Miklashevskaya (d. 1876), wife of M.O., III, 606, 625

Sue, Eugène (1804–1857), French novelist,
Plock et Plick, II, 488, 506

Sukhorukov, Vasily Dmitrievich (1795–1841), officer and writer, III, 787
Letter to, III, 753–54

Sukhorukova, Olga Vasilievna, nee Shvetsova, wife of V. D., III, 753, 787

Sumarokov, Alexander Petrovich (1718–1777), dramatist and theatrical director, II, 382, 401

Sushkov, Nikolay Vasilievich (1796–1871), writer, II, 332, 336, 384

Sutzu, Michael (ca. 1784–1864), hospodar of Moldavia, I, 79, 80, 119

Suvorov, Alexander Vasilievich (1729–1800), field marshal, I, 99, 126, 213, 225, 265, 297; II, 565, 576, 588

Sviniin, Pavel Petrovich (1788–1839), author, I, 290; II, 399; III, 679

Svistunov, Alexey Nikolaevich (1808–1872), cavalry officer, II, 492, 507

Svyatoslav (d. 972 or 973), ruler of Kiev (ca. 945–972 or 973), I, 214, 279; III, 780, 798

Tacitus, Roman historian, I, 233
Annals, The, I, 233, 289

Talleyrand-Périgord, Charles Maurice de (1754–1838), French statesman, II, 425, 467

Tanner, John, III, 781, 797

Tarasenko-Otreshkov, Narkiz Ivanovich (1805–1873), II, 561, 587; III, 614, 627, 813, 824

Tardif de Mello, Achille, French man of letters, III, 800
Prisoner of the Caucasus, The, by ASP, tr. of, III, 784, 800
Letter to, III, 784

Tarquin, III, 771

Tasso, Torquato (1544–1595), Italian poet, I, 97, 221, 223
Jerusalem Delivered, I, 124

Tatiana Demianovna (b. 1810), gypsy singer, II, 450, 474, 495

Telegraph, The. See: *Moscow Telegraph, The*

Telescope, The (*Teleskop*), journal, II, 450, 451, 453, 462, 465, 470, 527, 531, 554, 556, 571, 573, 584; III, 759, 796

Temps, Le, French newspaper, II, 425, 438, 467

Thalia. See: *Russian Thalia, The*

Themistocles, Athenian statesman and general, I, 80, 119, 128, 161, 167

Thierry, Augustin (1795–1856), French historian,
History of the Conquest of England by the Normans, The, III, 695, 734

Thiers, Louis Adolphe (1797–1877), French statesman and historian, III, 788
History of the French Revolution, The, II, 493, 508

Three Poems on the Taking of Warsaw (*Na vzjatie Varšavy, Tri stixotvorenija*), poems by ASP and Zhukovsky, II, 575

Tiberius, Roman emperor, I, 161, 176, 233; III, 771

Tibullus, Roman poet, I, 221

Tieck, Ludwig (1773–1853), German author,
Fortunat, II, 555, 584

Tiflis Record, The (*Tiflisskie vedomosti* newspaper, II, 564, 588

Timasheva, Ekaterina Alexandrovna (1798–1881), II, 332, 384

Timiryazev, Ivan Semenovich (1790–1867), general, III, 682
Timiryazeva, Sofia Fedorovna (b. 1799), wife of I. S., III, 644, 682
Timkovsky, Ivan Osipovich (1776–1857), censor, I, 82, 119
Tizengauzen, Ekaterina Fedorovna (1803–1888), daughter of Mme. Khitrovo, II, 390, 397, 414, 425, 448, 463, 467, 506
Letter to, II, 370–71
Tocqueville, Alexis de (1805–1859), French writer,
Démocratie en Amérique, De la, I, 39; III, 798
Tol, Karl Fedorovich (1777–1842), general, II, 492, 507; III, 826, 827
Letter to, III, 819–20
Tolchenov, Pavel Ivanovich (d. 1840's), actor, I, 95, 125
Tolmachev, Feodosy Sidorovich, II, 499, 509
Tolstaya, Sarra Fedorovna (1820–1838), daughter of F. I., III, 762, 790
Tolstoy the American, *See* Tolstoy, F. I.
Tolstoy, Fedor Ivanovich (1782–1846), *nickname:* the American, I, 88, 89, 97, 104, 122, 124, 125, 169, 216, 282, 283; II, 365, 391, 395, 452–53; III, 686, 762
Letter to, II, 364–65
Tolstoy, Fedor Petrovich (1783–1873), painter and illustrator, I, 208, 281
Tolstoy, Lev Nikolaevich (1828–1910), novelist and thinker, I, 5; II, 583
Anna Karenina, II, 583
Two Hussars (*Dva gusara*), III, 627, 629
War and Peace (*Vojna i mir*), III, 625
Tolstoy, Yakov Nikolaevich (1791–1867), chairman of Green Lamp society, I, 65, 70, 112, 148, 172
My Idle Time (*Moe prazdnoe vremja*), I, 101, 126
Letter to, I, 100–1
Town Talk (*Molva*), II, 542
Trediakovsky, Vasily Kirillovich (1703–1769), poet, II, 351; III, 731, 743
"Little Song" (*Pesenka*), II, 351, 390
Trubetskoy, unidentified man, II, 348

Trubetskoy, Peter Petrovich (1793–1840), I, 160, 176
Tsertelev, Nikolay Andreevich (1790–1869), minor critic, I, 127, 266
Glance at Russian Fairy Tales and Songs . . . , A (*Vzgljad na russkie skazki i pesni . . .*), I, 104, 127
Of the Works of Ancient Russian Poetry (*O proizvednijax drevnej russkoj poèzii*), I, 104, 127
Tsitsianov, Fedor Ivanovich (1801–1832), I, 308, 318
Tumansky, Vasily Ivanovich (1800–1860), poet, I, 136, 148, 168, 202, 278; II, 348, 386, 457
"Blue Eyes" (*Golubye glaza*), II, 348, 389
"Elegy" (*Elegija*), I, 202, 278
"Little Song" (*Pesenka*), II, 389
"Maid to a Poet in Love, A" (*Devuška vlublennomy poètu*), I, 202, 241–42, 278, 291
Letters to, I, 241–42; II, 339
Turgenev. *See* Turgenev, Alexander Ivanovich
Turgenev, Alexander Ivanovich (1784–1845), government official, Arzamas member, friend of ASP and Puskhin family, I, 64, 65, 69, 70, 87–88, 106, 120, 121, 150, 151, 171, 173, 178, 196, 227; II, 492, 493, 499, 507, 521, 538, 571; III, 735, 738, 754, 825, 826
"Letters from Paris" (*Pis'ma iz Pariža*), III, 754, 755, 765, 787, 788, 791
Letters to, I, 63–64, 85–86, 145–46, 164–65; III, 694, 700, 816, 819
Turgenev, Ivan Sergeevich (1818–1883), man of letters, I, 69; III, 792
Turgenev, Nikolay Ivanovich (1789–1872), brother of A. I., I, 63, 64, 69, 70, 85, 87–88, 120, 121, 146, 171, 178, 314, 319; III, 825
Turgenev, Sergey Ivanovich (1790–1827), brother of A. I., I, 63, 64, 69, 70, 121, 146, 171
Letter to, I, 87–88

Ubri, Sergey Pavlovich, III, 662, 686
Uhland, Johann Ludwig (1787–1862), German poet, II, 505

Uhland, Johann Ludwig, contd.
Translations from. *See* Zhukovsky, V. A.
Uncle. *See* Pushkin, Vasily Lvovich
Urania (Uranija), almanac, I, 282; II, 345, 346, 388
Urusov, Nikolay Alexandrovich (1808–1843), II, 562, 587
Urusova, Anastasia Nikolaevna, nee Borozdina (1809–1877), wife of N. A., singer, II, 562, 587
Urusova, Natalia Alexandrovna (1812–1882), II, 561, 586
Ushakov, Nikolay Ivanovich (1802–1861), general, military historian, III, 794
  History of the Military Activities in Asiatic Turkey in 1828 and 1829 (Istorija voennyx dejstvij v Aziatskoj Turcii v 1828 i 1829 godax), III, 773, 794
  Letter to, III, 773
Ushakov, Vasily Apollonovich (1795–1838), writer, II, 382, 401
Ushakova, Ekaterina Nikolaevna (1809–1872), II, 370, 375, 379, 397, 399
Ushakova, Elizaveta Nikolaevna (1810–1872), II, 370, 379, 397, 461
Ustryalov, Nikolay Gerasimovich (1805–1870), historian, III, 814, 824
  "Of the System of Pragmatic Russian History" (*O sisteme pragmatičeskoj russkoj istorii*), III, 824
Utkin, Nikolay Ivanovich (1780–1863), engraver, I, 208, 281
Utkina, midwife, II, 558, 585
Uvarov, Sergey Semenovich (1786–1855), Minister of Public Education, II, 560, 576; III, 651, 683, 707, 712, 738, 742, 756, 785, 786, 788, 796, 811, 814, 823, 824
  Aux détracteurs de la Russie: Imitation libre de Pouchkine, II, 532; III, 821
  Letter to, II, 532–33

V., alchemist, III, 749, 785
Valmont. *See* Laclos, Choderlos de: *Les Liaisons dangereuses*
Valuev, Peter Alexandrovich (1815–1880), III, 790

Valueva, Maria Petrovna (1813–1849), wife of P. A., daughter of P. A. Vyazemsky, II, 558, 562, 585, 587; III, 618, 643–44, 676, 681, 762, 790
Varfolomey, Egor Kirillovich, I, 139, 169, II, 335, 385
Varfolomey, Pulkheria Egorovna (ca. 1800–1863), daughter of E. K., I, 140, 169; II, 448, 473
Vasily, serf, I, 205, 279
Vasily Lvovich. *See* Pushkin, Vasily Lvovich
Vasily the Blessed, sixteenth century holy fool, I, 247, 292
Vattemare, Alexandre, French ventriloquist, III, 653, 669, 684, 688
Vega, Lope de (1562–1635), Spanish dramatist, I, 237
Veliasheva, Ekaterina Vasilievna (1813–after 1860), II, 368, 396; III, 601
Velikopolsky, Ivan Ermolaevich (1797–1868), poet, I, 318; II, 349, 390–91
  "I Recognized You at Once by Your Manner" (*Uznal ja totčas po zamaške*), II, 352, 391
  "To Erast (A Satire on Gamblers)" (*Erastu [Satira na igrokov]*), II, 391
  Letters to, I, 308, 311–12; II, 352–53
Veltman, Alexander Fomich (1800–1870), novelist, II, 489, 505, 563, 587
  Pilgrim, The (Strannik), II, 486, 506
  Summer Night, A (Letnjaja noč'), II, 587
Venevitinov, Alexey Vladimirovich (1806–1872), brother of D. V., II, 498, 509; III, 815, 825
Venevitinov, Dmitry Vladimirovich (1805–1827), poet, II, 339, 386, 522; III, 825
Vergil, Roman poet, I, 221, 276
  Aeneid, The, I, 130, 135, 168, 456, 475
  Fourth Georgic, I, 76, 117
Verses About Alexey, Man of God (Stixi ob Alexee, božiem čeloveke), III, 760, 789–90
Verstovsky, Alexey Nikolaevich (1799–1862), composer, I, 155, 170, 258; II, 401; III, 680
  Letter to, II, 442–43
Vibius Serenus, I, 233

Vidocq, François Eugène (1775–1857), French police officer and adventurer, II, 413; III, 638, 679, 682
Memoirs, II, 462
Vielgorskaya, Luiza Karlovna (1791–1853), wife of M. Y., III, 657, 660, 685
Vielgorsky, Mikhail Yurievich (1788–1856), composer, I, 258, 295; III, 616, 652, 654, 657, 660
Vigel, Filipp Filippovich (1786–1856), government official, I, 138, 169; III, 615–16, 628, 797, 823
Letter to, I, 139–40
Vigny, Alfred de (1797–1863), French author, II, 556
Cinq-Mars, II, 584
Stello, II, 584
Vitali, Ivan Petrovich (1794–1855), sculptor, III, 790, 792
Vitgensteyn, Peter Khristianovich (1768–1843), general, I, 167, 178
Vladimir (d. 1015), ruler of Kiev (980–1015), I, 81, 119, 204, 279
Vladimirescu, Tudor (d. 1821), Rumanian revolutionary leader, I, 79, 81, 118–19
Vlasov, Alexander Sergeevich (1777–1825), II, 539, 579
Voeykov, Alexander Fedorovich (1778–1839), journalist, I, 78, 87, 108, 118, 148, 150, 154, 159, 173, 205, 212, 267, 273, 279, 280, 282, 297; II, 349, 391, 543, 580; III, 814, 824
Voeykova, Alexandra Andreevna (1795–1829), wife of A. F., I, 187, 232, 273
Volkhovsky, Vladimir Dmitrievich (1798–1841), general, III, 739
Letter to, III, 718
Volkonskaya, Alexandra Petrovna (1804–1859), I, 165, 178
Volkonskaya, Maria Nikolaevna (1805–1863), wife of S. G., daughter of General N. N. Raevsky, I, 75, 116, 168
Volkonskaya, Sofia Grigorievna (1786–1868), I, 165, 178; III, 781, 786
Volkonskaya, Zinaida Alexandrovna (1792–1862), II, 363, 394
Volkonsky, Sergey Grigorievich (1788–1865), general, Decembrist, I, 116, 153, 174; II, 398; III, 786

Volkov, Alexander Alexandrovich, general of gendarmes, II, 378, 400
Volkov, Matvey Stepanovich (1802–1878), III, 813–14, 824
Voltaire (1694–1778), French author, I, 65, 68, 70, 97, 125, 164, 215, 223, 226, 283; II, 433, 549, 582; III, 677, 690
"Epistle to Mme. de Saint-Julien," II, 361, 393
History of the Russian Empire Under Peter the Great, The, II, 549, 582
History of the Travels of Scarmentado, The, I, 83, 120
Letters, II, 433, 469
Maid of Orleans, The (La Pucelle), I, 62, 68, 197, 276, 286
Poem on the Natural Law, I, 286
Tancrède. See Gnedich, N. I.
Taureau blanc, Le, I, 142, 170
Zadig, I, 62, 68
Volynsky, Artemy Petrovich (1689–1740), statesman and diplomat, III, 731, 743
Vorontsov, Mikhail Semenovich (1782–1856), ASP's chief in Odessa, I, 50, 135, 136, 154, 156–57, 158, 159, 160, 161, 164, 165, 168, 169, 171, 174, 175, 176, 182, 190–91, 195, 196, 203, 223, 271, 275, 276, 306; II, 392
Vorontsova, Elizaveta Ksaverievna (1792–1880), wife of M. S., I, 46, 50, 171, 175, 273, 281; II, 357, 392; III, 678
Letter to, III, 635
Vorontsov-Dashkov, Ivan Illarionovich (1790–1854), III, 647, 683
Vorontsova-Dashkova, Alexandra Kirillovna, nee Naryshkina (1817–1856), wife of V. I., III, 647, 683
Vorozheykina, Anna Nikolaevna, common-law wife of V. L. Pushkin, III, 622, 630
Voss, Johann Heinrich (1751–1826), German writer, I, 226, 287
Vrevskaya, Evpraxia Nikolaevna, nee Vulf (1810–1883), wife of B. A., daughter of Praskovia A. Osipova, I, 184, 188, 189, 193, 214, 272, 273, 275, 283; II, 350, 352, 368, 390, 496, 509, 542, 550, 582; III, 601, 624, 723, 724, 725, 741, 759, 789, 812, 823

Vrevsky, Alexander Borisovich (1832–1833), son of B. A., II, 550, 582
Vrevsky, Boris Alexandrovich (1805–1888), II, 509, 570; III, 724, 741, 821
Vsevolodov, Vsevolod Ivanovich (1790–1863), veterinarian, I, 228, 229, 246, 259, 288, 292, 312, 319
Vsevolozhskaya, Pelageya Nikolaevna, II, 357, 392
Vsevolozhsky, admirer of Natalia N. Goncharova, II, 421
Vsevolozhsky, Alexander Vsevolodovich, I, 101, 126
Vsevolozhsky, Nikita Vsevolodovich (1799–1862), friend of ASP, I, 64–65, 70, 87, 98, 100, 101, 121, 126, 163, 177, 190, 191, 206, 207, 272, 280, 289; III, 606
  Letter to, 184–85
Vsevolozhsky, Vsevolod Nikitich, son of N. V., I, 185
Vulf, Alexey Nikolaevich (1805–1881), son of Praskovia A. Osipova, friend of ASP, I, 195, 231, 233, 243, 247–48, 250, 257, 271, 272, 276, 289, 292, 293, 294, 295, 318; II, 333, 338, 388, 389, 391, 392, 393, 396, 397; III, 759–60, 789
  Letters to, I, 181, 252, 260, 309; II, 359, 368–69
Vulf, Anna Ivanovna (d. 1835), daughter of I. I., I, 207, 214, 242, 249, 250, 251, 280, 283, 291, 292, 293, 306, 317; II, 329, 368, 369, 383, 396; III, 601, 624
Vulf, Anna Nikolaevna (1799–1857), daughter of Praskovia A. Osipova, in love with ASP, I, 87, 121, 181, 184, 187, 188, 189, 193, 206, 214, 215, 216, 234, 240, 243, 248, 257, 272, 273, 275, 280, 283, 289, 291, 292, 306, 309, 317; II, 329, 346, 368, 383, 389, 392, 568, 589; III, 601, 624, 726
  Letters to, I, 221, 230–32
Vulf, Evpraxia Nikolaevna. *See* Vrevskaya, Evpraxia Nikolaevna
Vulf, Frederika Ivanovna (d. 1848), wife of Pavel I., II, 368, 396
Vulf, Ivan Ivanovich (1776–1860), uncle of A. N., II, 368–69, 396, 397; III, 624
Vulf, Mikhail Nikolaevich (1808–1832), son of Praskovia A. Osipova, I, 272
Vulf, Pavel Ivanovich (1775–1858), uncle of A. N. Vulf, II, 368, 396; III, 601, 624
Vulf, Peter Ivanovich (1768–1832), uncle of A. N., II, 393
Vulf, Valerian Nikolaevich (1812–1845), son of Praskovia A. Osipova, I, 272
Vulf-Osipova family. *See* Osipova(-Vulf) family
Vulfert, Alexander Evstafievich, I, 143, 170, 178
Vyazemskaya, Alexandra Alexandrovna, nee Rimskaya-Korsakova, II, 538, 579
Vyazemskaya, Maria Petrovna. *See* Valueva, Maria Petrovna
Vyazemskaya, Praskovia Petrovna (1817–1835), daughter of P. A., II, 558, 585; III, 617, 618, 628, 674, 676, 689, 690
Vyazemskaya, Vera Fedorovna (1790–1886), wife of P. A., friend of ASP, I, 31, 158, 160, 161, 165, 175, 176, 181, 190, 192, 198, 199, 202, 203, 229, 241, 258, 271, 272, 277, 281, 289; II, 332, 333, 336, 357, 378, 379, 382, 383, 384, 391, 400, 453, 466, 490, 492, 522, 538, 541, 557, 558, 559, 560–61, 562, 572, 585; III, 615–16, 618, 649, 651, 674, 827
  Letters to, I, 183–84, 210–11; II, 330, 354, 409–10, 424, 427, 551–52
Vyazemsky, Alexander Nikolaevich (b. 1804), II, 538, 579
Vyazemsky, Nikolay Petrovich (1818–1825), son of P. A., I, 281
Vyazemsky, Pavel Petrovich (1820–1888), son of P. A., II, 354, 357, 375, 391, 399
Vyazemsky, Peter Andreevich (1792–1878), poet, man of letters, close friend of ASP, I, 31, 43, 48, 62, 67, 68, 69, 70, 113, 121, 122, 125, 128, 129, 136, 143, 153, 160, 163, 169, 170, 171, 172, 174, 175, 176, 177, 184, 191, 198, 210, 211, 212, 216, 218, 219, 220, 227, 234, 238, 264, 271, 272, 276, 281, 283, 284, 288, 290, 291, 294, 295, 318, 319; II, 330, 338, 346, 361, 383, 384,

Vyazemsky, Peter Andreevich, contd.
385, 389, 391, 392, 393, 394, 398, 399, 400, 405, 424, 427, 459, 461, 462, 466, 470, 471, 474, 484, 487, 489, 495, 506, 510, 520–21, 533, 538, 540, 553, 560, 562, 571, 572, 574, 576, 585, 587; III, 601, 604, 615, 624, 637, 654, 655, 674, 675, 679, 687, 701, 760, 770, 797, 824, 825, 827
Adolphe, by Constant, tr. of, II, 454, 475, 499, 509
"Bare-Headed One, The," (*Prostovolosaja golovka*), II, 357, 392
"Conversation" (*Razgovor*), as Introduction to ASP's *Fountain of Bakhchisaray*, I, 154, 155, 174
"Despondency" (*Unynie*), I, 66, 70
"Epistle to M. T. Kachenovsky" (*Poslanie k M. T. Kachenovskomu*), I, 89, 122
"Feature of the Locality" (*Čerta mestnosti*), I, 198
"Figljarin—Here Is an Exemplary Pole" (*Figljarin, vot poljak primernyj*), II, 490, 506
"First Snow" (*Pervyj sneg*), I, 66, 70, 110
Fonvizin, I, 203, 279; II, 438, 470, 484, 499, 510
"Forbidden Rose" (*Zapretnaja roza*), II, 332, 384
"Information on the Life and Poems of I. I. Dmitriev" (*Izvestie o žizni i stixotvorenijax I. I. Dmitrieva*), I, 152, 154, 174
"Madrigal (To Two Beauties—Mother and Daughter)" (*Madrigal [K dvum krasavicam—materi i dočeri]*), I, 147, 172
"Maiden's Dream, The" (*Devičij son*), II, 449, 450, 473
"Napoleon and Julius Caesar" (*Napoleon i Julij Cezar'*), III, 771, 793
"Narva Waterfall" (*Narvskij vodopad*), I, 121, 244–45, 254, 291
"New Poem by E. Quinet, The" (*Novaja poèma E. Kine*), III, 793
"Newstead Abbey: From the Works of Lord Byron" (*N'ju-Stidskoe abbatsvo—Iz sočinenij Lorda Bajrona*), I, 263, 296

"Of the Analysis Written by Denis Davydov, of Three Articles Placed in the Memoirs of Napoleon" (*O razbore trex statej, poměščennyx v Zapiskax Napoleona, napisannom Denisom Davydovym*), I, 229, 288
"Ride in the Steppe, A" (*Progulka v stepi*), II, 507
"Rose and the Cypress, The" (*Roza i kiparis*), III, 754, 788
"Sea, The" (*More*), I, 314, 319
Seven Fridays in a Week (*Sem' pjatnic na nedele*), I, 310, 318
"Simple-Hearted Answer, A" (*Prostoserdečnyj otvet*), I, 198
"To an Imaginary Happy Woman" (*K mnimoj sčastlivice*), I, 310, 318
"To a Partisan-Poet" (*K partizanu-poètu*), I, 60, 67
"To Journal Twins" (*K žurnal'nym bliznecam*), I, 158, 175
"To Olga Sergeevna Pushkina" (*O. S. Puškinoj*), I, 310, 318
"To Them" (*K nim*), II, 375, 399
"To Tolstoy" (*Tolstomu*), I, 138, 169
"To V. A. Zhukovsky" (*K V. A. Žukovskomu*), I, 102, 127, 225, 287
"To Yazykov." (*K Jazykovu*), III, 760, 789
"What's the Use? Says Prudent Sviniin" (*Čto pol'zy,—govorit rasčetlivj Svin'in*), I, 239, 290
Who Is the Brother? Who Is the Sister? Or Deceit After Deceit (*Kto brat? Kto sestra? ili obman za obmanom*), with A. S. Griboedov, I, 141, 170
"Winter Caricatures" (*Zimnie karikatury*): "Bumpy Roads, Wagon Train" (*Uxaby, oboz*), II, 449–50, 453, 473
"Zhukovsky: Pushkin: Of the New Poetics of Fables" (*Žukovskij: Puškin: O novoj piitike basen*), I, 225, 240, 261, 287, 290
Letters to, I, 59–61, 63, 65–66, 89–90, 97–98, 108–110, 110–11, 111–112, 135, 137–38, 141, 142, 146–47, 147, 152–53, 154–55, 158–59, 160–62, 164, 165–66, 181–82, 191–92, 198–99, 199, 201, 203, 212–13, 213–14, 216–17, 225–27, 227–28, 229–30, 239–40, 244–

Vyazemsky, Peter Andreevich, contd.
46, 253–55, 258, 261–62, 263–64, 308–9, 309–10, 310–11, 313–14, 314; II, 331–33, 336, 356–57, 361, 362–63, 374–75, 378–79, 379–80, 382, 410–11, 437–38, 449–51, 452–53, 454, 489–90, 491–92, 499, 520–21, 522–23, 525, 526–28, 531; III, 754, 764, 783, 814

Wallenstein (or Waldstein), Albrecht von (1583–1634), German soldier and statesman, III, 707, 737
Walpole, Horace (1717–1797), English man of letters, I, 25
Wellington, Arthur Wellesley, First Duke of (1769–1852), British general and statesman, II, 453, 475
Well-Intentioned, The (*Blagonamerennyj*), journal, I, 121, 153, 155, 170, 174, 222, 228, 279, 310, 319; II, 346, 357, 389, 391, 392
Wemmer, Marguerite Joséphine (1787–1867), French actress, III, 602, 624, 676
Weyer, Nicette (1786–1841), merchant, II, 565, 576
Wieland, Christoph Martin (1733–1813), German author,
Wünsche oder Pervonte, Die. See Lyutsenko, E. P.
William I, the Conqueror (ca. 1027–1087), King of England (1066–1087), III, 798
William I (1772–1843), King of the Netherlands (1815–1840), II, 523, 572
Wilson, John (1785–1854), Scots author, II, 534, 577, 825
City of the Plague, The, II, 534, 577; III, 826
Wintzengerode, Ferdinand von (1770–1818), German-born marshal and diplomat in Russian service, III, 770, 793
Wordsworth, William (1770–1850), English poet, II, 482
"Scorn Not the Sonnet, Critic," II, 504

Yakov, Zhukovsky's valet, I, 106
Yakovlev, Alexey Ivanovich, II, 363
Yakovlev, Ivan Alekseevich (1804–1882), friend of ASP, II, 374, 395, 544, 581; III, 795
Letters to, II, 363–64, 775
Yakovlev, Mikhail Lukianovich (1798–1868), Lyceum classmate and friend of ASP, II, 511, 521; III, 662, 669, 673, 675, 676, 686, 687, 690, 734, 796
Historical Dictionary of the Saints . . . (Slovar' istoričeskij o svjatyx . . .), III, 805, 822
Letters to, II, 502–3; III, 665, 667, 677, 698, 779, 783–84, 805
Yakovlev, Pavel Lukianovich (1796–1835), II, 449, 450, 473
Yakubovich, Alexander Ivanovich (1792–1845), I, 264, 296
Yaroslav the Wise (978–1054), Prince of Kiev (1019–50), II, 530
Yazykov, Alexander Mikhaylovich (1799–1874), brother of N. M., III, 612, 627, 696, 697, 734
Yazykov, Dmitry, II, 471
Yazykov, Dmitry Ivanovich (1773–1845), III, 706–7, 736
Nestor, by Schlözer, tr. of, III, 707, 736
Yazykov, Nikolay Mikhaylovich (1803–1846), poet, I, 127, 142, 151, 181, 252, 260, 271, 293, 309, 318; II, 384, 388, 444, 531, 545, 546, 553, 576, 581; III, 609, 610, 612, 734, 762, 770, 789
"Dramatic Tale About Ivan Tsarevich . . ., A" (*Dramatičeskaja skazka ob Ivane Careviče . . .*), III, 789
"Epistle to Davydov" (*Poslanie k Davydovu*), III, 760, 789
"Go Away" (*Podite proč'*), I, 252, 293, 295
"To A. N. Vulf (Don't Call Me Poet)" (*A. N. Vul'fu* [*Ne nazyvaj menja poètom*]), II, 391
"To P. A. Vyazemsky" (*K P. A. Vjazemskomu*), III, 760, 789
"Trigorskoe," II, 333, 338, 384, 386; III, 759, 789
"We Love Noisy Feasts" (*My ljubim šumnye piry*), I, 104, 127
Letters to, II, 333, 338; 534–35, III, 697, 759–60

Yazykov, Peter Mikhaylovich (1798–1851), brother of N. M., III, 610, 612, 626, 627, 734
Young, Edward (1683–1765), English poet, II, 556, 584
Night Thoughts, II, 584
Ypsilanti, Alexander (1792–1828), Greek revolutionary, son of Constantine, I, 49, 80–81, 118–19, 204
Ypsilanti, Constantine (1760–1816), Greek revolutionary, I, 79, 118
Ypsilanti, Georgios (1795–1829), son of Constantine, I, 80, 119
Ypsilanti, Nicholas (b. 1796), son of Constantine, I, 80, 119
Yurgenev, Alexander Tikhonovich (ca. 1785–1867), II, 368, 396
Yuriev, Fedor Filippovich (1796–1860), member of Green Lamp society, I, 65, 70, 87
Yuriev, Vasily Gavrilovich, officer, III, 603, 624, 664, 687, 722, 740, 817, 826
Yusupov, Nikolay Borisovich (1750–1831), statesman, II, 453, 474, 515, 517, 570

Zabalkansky. *See* Dibich-Zabalkansky, I. I.
Zabela, Count, III, 718, 739
Zagorsky, Mikhail Pavlovich (1804–1824), author, I, 267, 297
Ilia Muromets (*Il'ja Muromec*), I, 267, 297
Zagoskin, Mikhail Nikolaevich (1789–1852), novelist, II, 465, 556, 574; III, 688
Askold's Tomb (*Askol'dova mogila*), III, 669, 688
Yury Miloslavsky (*Jurij Miloslavskij*), II, 372, 374, 398
Letters to, II, 372, 421; III, 668–69
Zagryazhskaya, Ekaterina Ivanova (1779–1842), aunt of ASP's wife, II, 421, 423, 465, 488, 559, 560, 562; III, 601, 602, 604, 605, 606, 610, 611, 612, 614, 615, 616, 618, 620, 625, 642, 644, 645, 649, 650, 651, 654, 655, 657, 658, 659, 660, 662, 670, 673, 677, 697, 724, 725, 727, 762, 763, 767, 791
Zagryazhskaya, Karolina Osipovna, wife of A. M., III, 618, 628
Zagryazhskaya, Natalia Kirillovna (1747–1837), great-aunt of ASP's wife, II, 421, 422, 465; III, 655, 657, 658, 659, 676, 685
Zagryazhsky, Alexander Mikhaylovich (1796–1878), governor of Simbirsk, III, 609, 618, 626, 628
Zaikin, Alexey Ivanovich (1793–1831), bookseller, I, 235, 289, 307
Zaikin, Ivan Ivanovich (d. 1834), bookseller, I, 235, 289, 307
Zakrevskaya, Agrafena Fedorovna (1799–1879), wife of A. A., I, 280; II, 357, 392
Zakrevsky, Arseny Andreevich (1783–1865), general, I, 207, 280; II, 442, 471
Zavadovsky, Vasily Petrovich (1798–1855), officer, I, 101, 126
Zavalievsky, Nikita Stepanovich (d. 1864), I, 140, 169; II, 332
Zaytsevsky, Efim Petrovich (d. ca. 1860), minor poet, II, 377, 399
Zhandr, Andrey Andreevich (1789–1873), author, I, 253, 293, 317; III, 795
Venceslas, by Rotrou, tr. of, I, 253, 293
Letter to, III, 776–77
Zhemchuzhnikov, Luka Ilich (1783–1856), II, 530, 533, 537, 576, 579, 580
Zhikarev, Stepan Petrovich (1788–1860), II, 379, 400
Zhikhareva, Feodosia Dimitrievna (1795–1850), II, 484, 505
Zhukovsky, Vasily Andreevich (1783–1852), poet and translator, close friend of ASP, I, 30, 48, 51, 66, 68, 70, 79, 89, 94, 96, 99, 102, 104, 106, 118, 124, 127, 128, 137, 142, 146, 152, 155, 160, 171, 172, 183, 187, 188, 189, 196, 197, 208, 209, 212, 220, 222, 225–26, 235, 236, 240, 254, 261, 266, 267, 271, 272, 280, 284, 285, 286, 287, 289, 290, 297, 301, 305, 307, 308, 309, 316, 318; II, 362, 371, 372, 374, 375, 394, 399, 411, 430, 434, 457, 474, 480, 482, 485, 490, 492, 497–98, 499, 501, 507, 509, 516, 519, 522, 523, 525, 527, 531, 534, 545, 551, 553, 572, 573, 574, 575, 580; III, 613, 616, 618, 627, 640, 652, 654, 672, 682, 683, 686, 687, 688, 738, 811, 822, 823, 827

Zhukovsky, Vasily Andreevich, contd.
"Alonzo," by Uhland, tr. of, II, 485, 490, 492, 507
Ballads and Tales (*Ballady i povesti*), II, 507
"Battle with a Serpent, A" (*Sraženie s zmeem*), II, 501, 510
"Butterfly and the Flowers, The" (*Motylek i cvety*), I, 208, 281
"Castle by the Sea, The" (*Zamok na beregu morja*), by Uhland, tr. of, II, 485, 490, 492, 507
"Choir of Maids of Catherine's Institute, The" (*Xor devic Ekaterininskogo instituta*), I, 303, 316
"Coming of Spring, The" (*Pojavlenie vesny*), by Uhland, tr. of, II, 485, 490, 492, 507
"Count of Habsburg, The" (*Graf Gapsburgskij*), by Schiller, tr. of, II, 457, 476
"Donica" (*Donika*), by Southey, tr. of, II, 485, 490, 492, 507
"Dream, The" (*Mečta*), I, 218, 284
"Elegy in a Country Churchyard (*Sel'skoe kladbišče*), by Gray, tr. of, I, 213, 282
"Glove, The" (*Perčatka*), by Schiller, tr. of, II, 485, 490, 492, 507
"Goblet, The" (*Kubok*), by Schiller, tr. of, I, 219, 284
"God's Judgment on a Wicked Bishop" (*Sud božij nad episkopom*), by Southey, tr. of, II, 485, 490, 492, 507
"Gromoboy" (*Gromoboj*), I, 94, 124, 202, 278
Iliad, The, by Homer, tr. from, II, 363, 394
"I Used to Meet the Young Muse . . ." (*Ja muzu junuju, byvalo, vstrečal . . .*), I, 226, 287; II, 485, 505
"Lament of Ceres, The" (*Žaloba Cerery*), by Schiller, tr. of, II, 485, 490, 492, 507
Lenore, by Bürger, tr. of, II, 485, 505
Lyudmila (*Ljudmila*), I, 102
Maid of Orleans, The (*Orleanskaja deva*), by Schiller, tr. of, I, 99, 125
Odyssey, The, by Homer, tr. of, I, 124
"Of a Priest" (*O pope*), I, 309
"Old Song to a New Tune, An" (*Staraja pesnja na novyj lad*), II, 530, 575
Peri and the Angel, The (*Peri i angel*), tr. from Thomas Moore's *Lalla Rookh*, I, 94, 122, 124
Poems (*Stixotvorenija*), I, 218, 284
"Polycrates' Ring" (*Polikratov persten'*), by Schiller, tr. of, II, 485, 490, 492, 507
Prisoner of Chillon, The (*Šil'onskij uznik*), by Byron, tr. of, I, 94, 98, 99, 101, 102, 124, 125, 126, 135-36, 142, 168, 170, 171
"Queen Orraca and the Five Martyrs of Morocco" (*Koroleva Uraka i pjat' mučinikov*), by Southey, tr. of, II, 485, 492, 507
"Red Carbuncle, The" (*Krasnyj karbunkul*), by Hebel, tr. of, II, 492, 507
"Remorse" (*Pokajanie*), tr. of W. Scott's "Grey Brother," I, 485, 490, 492, 507
"Sea, The" (*More*), II, 363, 394
"Sleeping Tsarevna, The" (*Spjaščaja carevna*), II, 545, 546, 581
"'Smayho'me Castle" (*Zamok Smal'gol'm*), tr. from W. Scott, "Eve of Saint John," I, 168
"Song to the Russian Tsar from His Warriors" (*Pesn' russkomu tsarju ot ego voinov*), I, 223, 286
"Subterranean Trial, The" (*Sud v podzemel'e*), tr. from W. Scott's *Marmion*, II, 531, 576
Svetlana, I, 102
"There Were Two Women and Another" (*Dve byli i ešče odna*), II, 492, 507
"To a Genie Acquaintance Who Has Flown Past" (*K mimoproletevšemu geniju*), I, 218-19, 284
"To a Portrait of Goethe" (*K portretu Gëte*), I, 218, 284
"To Bludov, Upon His Departure to the Turkish Army" (*K Bludovu, pri ot"ezde ego v Tureckuju armiju*), I, 218, 284

Zhukovsky, Vasily Andreevich, contd.
"Traveler, The" (*Putešestvennik*), II, 357, 392
"Twelve Sleeping Virgins, The" (*Dvenadcat' spjaščix dev*), I, 102; II, 335, 385
"Voice from the Other World, A" (*Golos s togo sveta*), adapted from Schiller's "Thekla: A Spirit Voice," I, 66, 70
"War of the Mice and the Frogs, The" (*Vojna myšej i ljagušek*), II, 545, 546, 581
Letters to, I, 62, 182, 185–86, 190–91, 218–19, 228–29, 246–47, 259–60, 302–3, 306–7; III, 666, 667

Zolotov, Grigory Kuzmich, II, 419, 465

Zontag, Anna Petrovna (1785–1864), I, 147, 172

Zubarev, Dmitry Eliseevich (1802–1850), writer, II, 351, 390

Zubkov, Vasily Petrovich (1799–1862), II, 338, 339, 355, 382, 383, 385, 386, 515, 570
Letters to, II, 329–30, 336–37

Zykov, Dmitry Petrovich (d. 1827), I, 79, 118